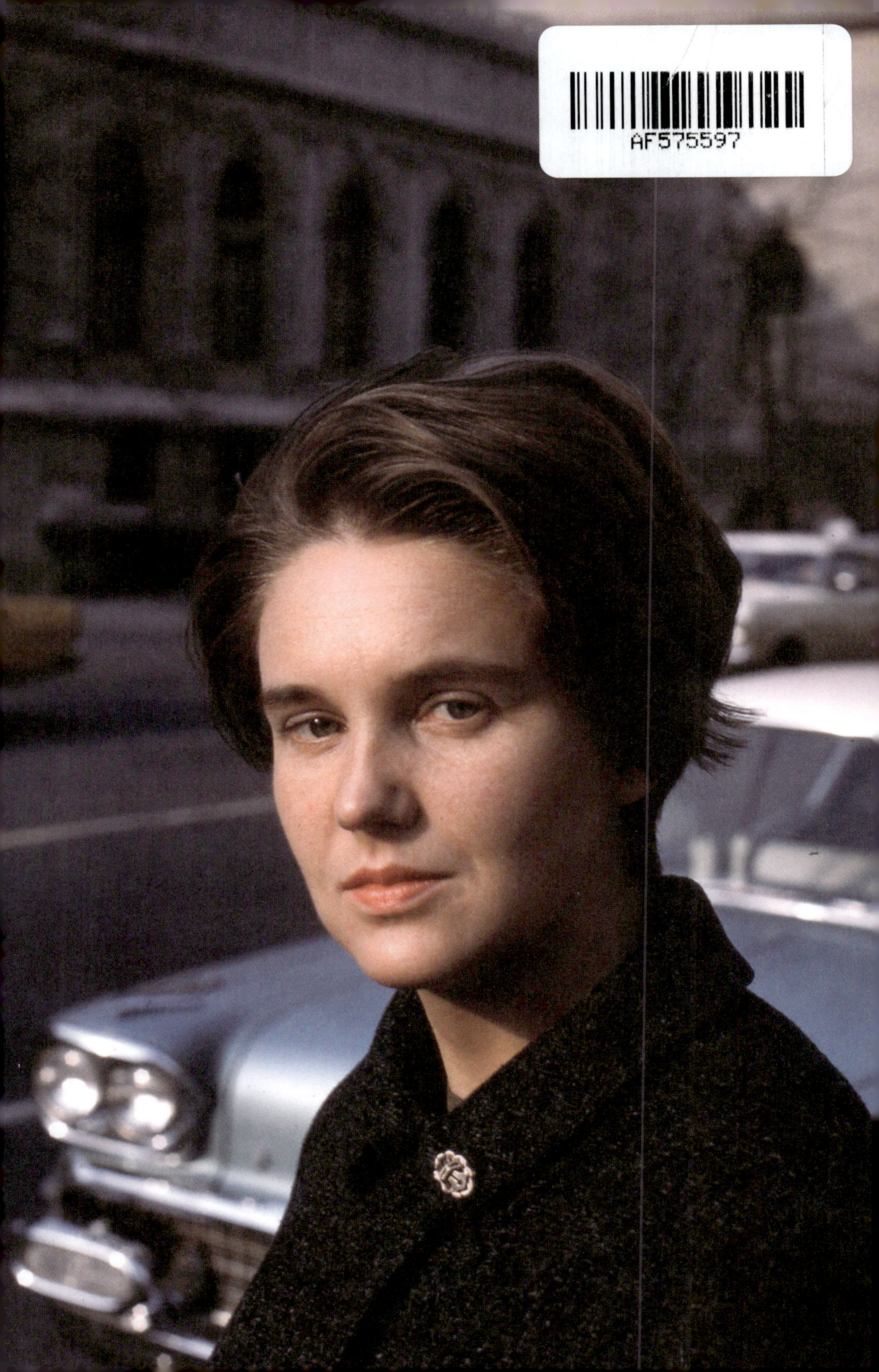

Giving and Receiving

Giving and Receiving

Memoirs of an Immigrant Curator and Philanthropist

MARICA VILCEK WITH JUSTIN SPRING

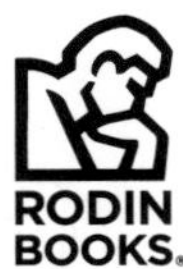

Hardcover ISBN 978-1-957588-38-4
eBook ISBN 978-1-957588-39-1

PUBLISHED BY RODIN BOOKS INC
666 Old Country Road
Suite 510
Garden City, New York 11530

www.rodinbooks.com

Cover design by Abbott Miller, Daniel Varillas, Pentagram
Book design by Barbara Aronica

Printed in Canada

To my mother, who shaped my character, values, and work ethic

CONTENTS

Giving and Receiving

1

Czechoslovakian Beginnings

Many people have asked me over the years why my husband and I risked our lives to flee Czechoslovakia in 1964. The truth is, I simply insisted to him that we leave, and he recognized the wisdom in our taking such a chance. Under the Communists, life held little promise for us and a great deal of danger.

If you were to visit Bratislava today, you might wonder why we ever left, for this handsome city on the Danube is both orderly and tranquil. While perhaps provincial by comparison to those two major European capitals, Vienna and Budapest, just up and down the Danube, Bratislava is nonetheless prosperous and well maintained. Just forty miles east of Vienna and close to the Austrian border, it has cobblestone streets, a medieval old town, and a massive castle on a promontory overlooking the river. The surrounding countryside is a mixture of woods, pastures, and farms.

In the years before World War II, my family was living relatively comfortably, for my father, Dezider Gerháth, came from a long-established family of farmer-landowners. Our farm lay in a fertile area sixty miles northwest of Bratislava and was by far the largest landholding in the area, upon which we raised sugar beets, potatoes, barley, and wheat. In my childhood the farm was run by my father's older brother, Emil, who hadn't taken an interest in education or big cities, preferring the more traditional ways of country life. My father was the opposite: he got a university education and used his small inheritance to make his way in the world. Leaving home was traditional for younger sons and daughters in farm families; it was a way of keeping the farm intact from one generation to the next.

Since my father had no interest in farming, he was happy enough to lease the bit of land he had inherited (as were his two sisters), but in later years he quarreled with his brother over the ownership of some cattle, and as a result the two became estranged. I visited the farm only once in my life, when I was eight years old. The Communists seized it four years later.

During the early 1920s, my father moved to Bratislava, where he made a career in education—first, briefly, as a teacher, and subsequently as an administrator within the national school system. To facilitate his career, he changed his name to a Hungarian version—the family name, Gerhardt, being too suggestive of our family's German ancestry, left him at a professional disadvantage, for the Czechoslovakian civil service had many Hungarian bureaucrats back then, particularly in Slovakia, which borders on Hungary and has many Hungarian-speaking residents. So Gerháth seemed preferable to Gerhardt. Though not Hungarian, my father spoke perfect Hungarian, and would ultimately rise in the Ministry of Education to oversee all the Hungarian-language schools of southern Slovakia.

The relationship between Slovakians and Hungarians is a complicated one. Hungarians ruled Slovakia from the Middle Ages onward, and during an invasion of lower Hungary by the Ottoman Turks, Bratislava had even briefly become the Hungarian capital. Even so, Slovakia had always retained an identity separate and apart from Hungary, largely because the Slovak language is far closer to Czech in vocabulary and syntax. (Both Czech and Slovak are West Slavic languages; Hungarian, more difficult to learn, descends from Finno-Ugric.) While in the early years of the twentieth century one was far more likely to hear German and Hungarian spoken in Bratislava (thanks to its having been part of the Austro-Hungarian Empire), after the creation of Czechoslovakia, Czech and Slovak became the nation's official languages when it was formed after World War I.

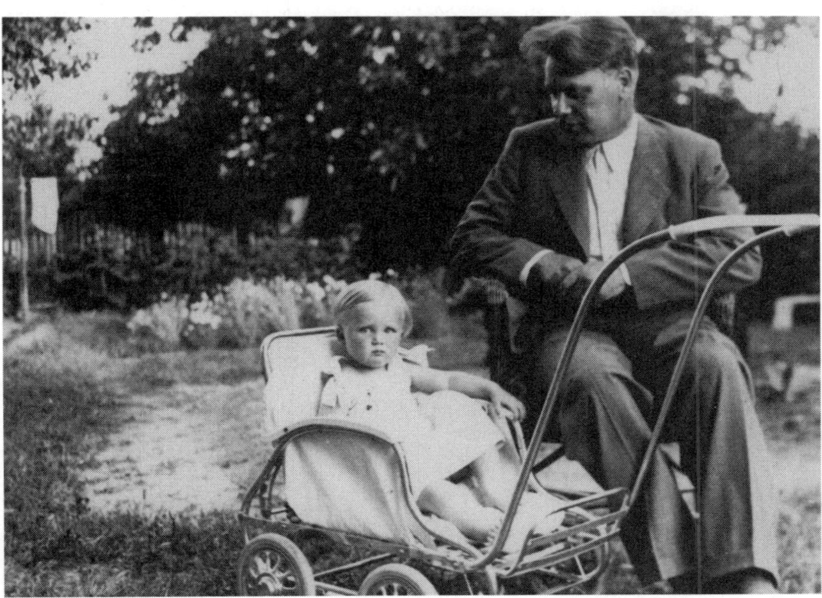

With my father in the garden of our home in Ivanka pri Dunaji

My father was in many ways a gentleman of the Austro-Hungarian Empire. An officer in the Austrian army in World War I, he had a lifelong fondness for the pageantry and spectacle of the dual monarchy through which Austria and Hungary (including Slovakia) had been united in 1867. In the few photographs of him that remain with me, my father is ruggedly handsome. His hair is cut short in the military style, and he has a solid, compact build. In my memories, as in the photos, he is always well dressed—even when relaxing in his back garden with his daughter on his knee.

Unfortunately for my father, the Austro-Hungarian Empire came to an end with its defeat in the war. During that time of transition, Slovakia separated itself from Hungary, and instead became part of the newly formed First Czechoslovak Republic. My father didn't like that new development; often he would remark upon how much better off everyone had been in the years before the war, saying things like "If we still had the Austro-Hungarian monarchy, we would still have access to the ocean. We would have this, we would have that." But his affection for Austro-Hungary was more than backward-looking nostalgia: the Austrians had been far more cosmopolitan in outlook than the Hungarians, and far more considerate of the Slovaks (and other ethnic minorities, including Germans). I mention all this only as a way of explaining that the home I grew up in did not have a specifically Slovakian identity; nor did we have a Czechoslovakian, German, or Hungarian one. And in fact, everyone in our family could speak all four languages—Czech, Slovak, Hungarian, and German—though of course with different degrees of fluency.

In the mid-1920s my father met and married my mother. Mária Hámošová was a schoolteacher, and just as good-looking as my father, albeit in a different way: dark haired, which was unusual in her family (and unusual in Slovakia), with bright green eyes. A photo of Mária as a young woman shows her to be nicely plump and very well dressed, with her long wavy hair pulled back in a low bun. In all the photos I have of her, she has an intensely focused expression—particularly in the photos that were taken of her behind her office desk at the school, where she rose quickly from teacher to headmistress.

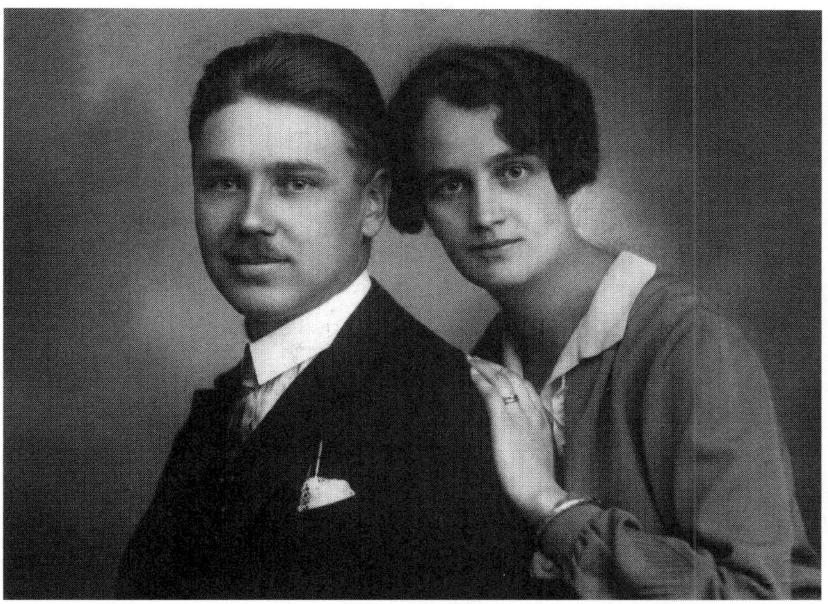

My father and mother

Their first child, my brother Ivan, was born in 1928. I followed eight and a half years later, in 1936. I was christened Mária after my mother, but I quickly became known instead as Marica, a name that had recently been popularized by the operetta *Gräfin Mariza* by Emmerich Kálmán. (Mariza is the Hungarian spelling, Marica the Slovak.) The nickname came naturally enough, for ours was a family of music lovers—though that's hardly extraordinary in Central Europe. I grew up playing the piano and continued to practice well into adulthood.

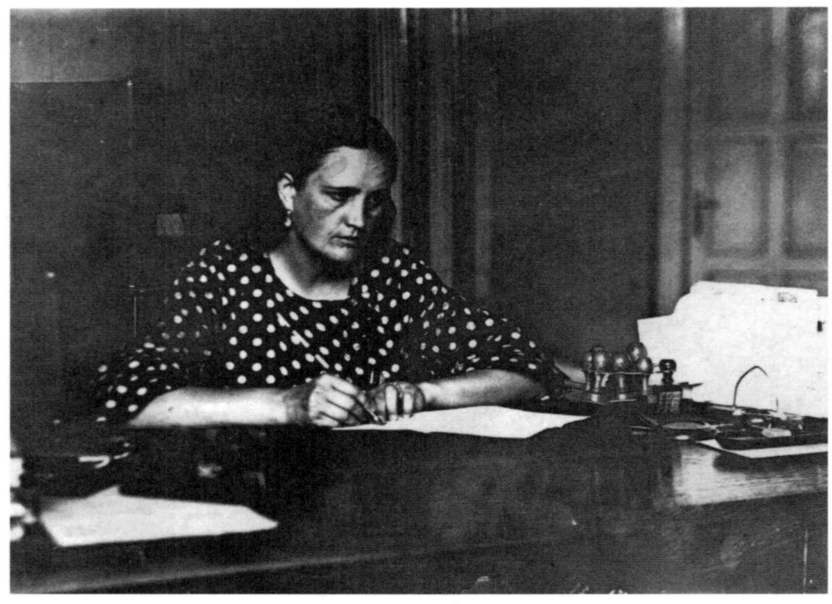

My mother as school headmistress

In contrast to my well-born father, my mother came from a poor family. But what the Hámoš family lacked in material riches they made up for in brains, determination, and strength of character. My maternal grandmother, Mária (or, within the family, Marčika) Herchl, born in 1881, was a beauty who attended school in the medieval town of Banská Štiavnica, where she perfected her German and Hungarian. At the age of twenty she married Jozef Nemček, a Czech who subsequently took the Hungarian name of Hámoš. Together they moved to the remote hamlet of Čierny Balog, where he worked in forest management. But just as they began their lives together, he died of Spanish influenza, leaving Mária with four young girls, aged between six and one. As a result, my mother and her three sisters had few memories of him. Because their mother was still young and beautiful, several other men in the village immediately wanted to marry her, but (according to my mother) each man wanted only Mária, not her daughters, and stipulated that all four girls must be sent away permanently (to become servants) before any marriage could take place. My grandmother was unwilling to abandon them in this way, and so she declined all these marriage offers, instead finding a job in the village general store.

Of my three maternal aunts, my mother's youngest sister, Alžbeta (or rather Eržika, the Hungarian diminutive of her name), was the most accomplished: after studying at Charles University in Prague and spending two years in France, she married Antonín Filip, a professor of Latin. She herself became a teacher of French, and both then worked at a *gymnázium* (a high school for accomplished students) in the university town of Banská Bystrica. Eržika loved literature and languages. Apart from her teaching, she translated Proust into Slovak and wrote regularly for *Family and School*, a Slovak educational journal.

My mother's eldest sister, Pavlína (whom I knew as Palka), became the village postmistress, then later married and moved to Bratislava. My aunt Ilona (whom I knew as Ilonka) attended an institution known as the Family School, where young ladies were taught the domestic arts, and she, too, later married and moved to Bratislava, where she worked as an administrative assistant. By the time I was a teenager all three—Eržika, Palka, and Ilonka—were frequent Sunday visitors to our home. I think that of all my aunts, I loved Ilonka best, for she was always so generous and thoughtful. A fine needlewoman, she often gave me clothes that she had made with her own hands: a beautiful blouse, or a skirt, or a dress.

Having seen all her daughters into adulthood and employment, my grandmother married again, at the age of thirty-four, and had two more children. As a result, my mother had a much younger half brother, Gustáv, and half sister, Eleonóra (whom I knew as Leonka). When I was a little girl, Leonka came to stay with us for several years to attend a good school, and she became very close to my brother Ivan during that time—for though she was his aunt, they were approximately the same age.

Like Aunt Eržika, my mother became a schoolteacher. Shortly after receiving her accreditation, she found work at a state school in Ivanka pri Dunaji, a village ten miles east of Bratislava. She was, I am told, a very inspiring teacher. Her firm belief in the power of education led her to exhort her best students to continue to university, and many did. While she later became the school's chief administrator and headmistress, she never gave up teaching, since it was the aspect of her job she loved best.

At the time of my birth in 1936, my parents were living in Ivanka pri Dunaji, but within three years they had purchased a home in the medieval Old Town of Bratislava on a narrow, steep, and winding street just below Bratislava Castle, for in doing so Ivan became eligible to attend the city's best school. By this time my father was working in Bratislava, so it made good sense for our family to be there: now it was only my mother who needed to commute. Because four other women who lived on our street were schoolteachers, my parents felt right at home in our new neighborhood.

Our home on Krátka Ulica (literally, "Short Street") was a fine two-family house in pebbled stucco, and our half of it had three bedrooms, a dining room, a living room, a kitchen, a maid's room, and a partially finished basement (the unfinished part was for the storage of coal, firewood, and root vegetables; the finished part was a tiny one-bedroom apartment). There was also a small, low-ceilinged attic that we used for drying laundry in winter. A long, narrow balcony ran the width of the garden side, with a wall separating our balcony from our neighbors'. While the rooms of our house were not large, the garden made our home feel expansive. During the summer we had a table and chairs out there to enjoy the fresh air and sunshine. I remember doing my homework there. And thanks to the garden, my bedroom had a beautiful view of Bratislava Castle. Devastated by fire and subsequently bombarded during the Napoleonic invasions, the ruined castle was a romantic and haunting sight, particularly by the light of a full moon. The ghost of St. Lucy was said to haunt it, and to abduct and enslave all bad children. "Don't misbehave," the mothers on our street would tell the little ones. "If you do, St. Lucy will take you to the castle!"

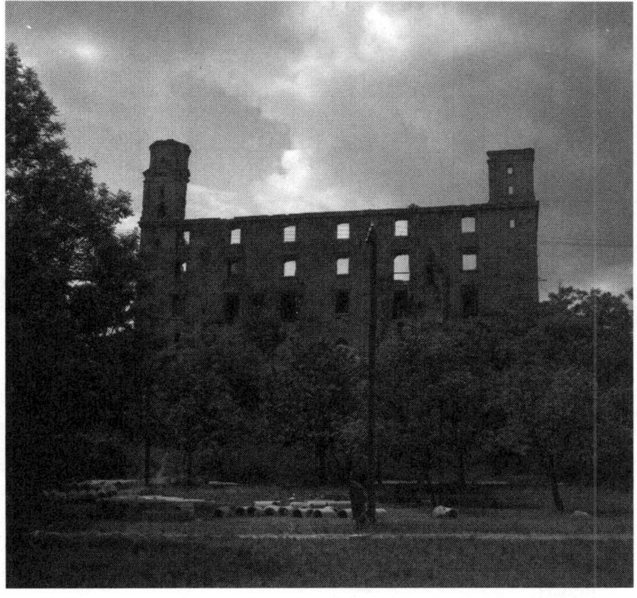

The ruins of Bratislava Castle

In September 1939, just after we moved into our home, Germany invaded Poland. Ethnic tensions had existed throughout Central Europe for centuries, and nowhere more so than in Czechoslovakia—for when Slovakia had been separated from Hungary and incorporated into the First Czechoslovak Republic in the aftermath of World War I, this new nation was made up not only of Czechs and Slovaks, but also of Germans, Hungarians, Jews, and Romani. It was also an uneasy consolidation of four culturally distinct regions: Bohemia, Moravia-Silesia, Slovakia, and Carpathian Ruthenia. There was little unity or coherence in this young and artificial nation; nor was there a common language. The ethnic, religious, and cultural tensions within Czechoslovakia became most visible to the outside world with the signing of the Munich Agreement of 1938, in which Czechoslovakia was compelled to cede its Sudetenland to Germany, ostensibly on behalf of Czechoslovakia's resident population of aggrieved ethnic Germans.

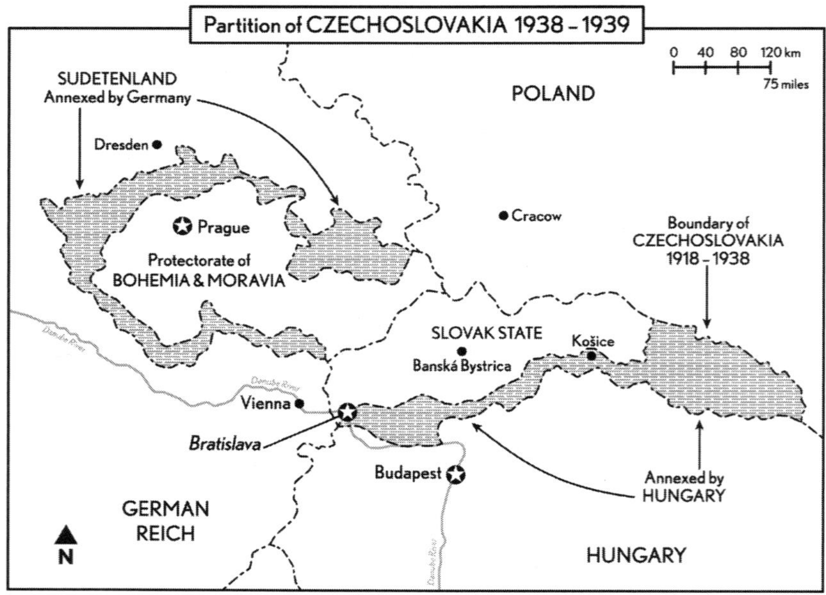

The Partition of Czechoslovakia in 1938–1939, showing lands ceded in October 1938 to Germany (via the Munich Agreement) and November 1938 to Hungary (via the First Vienna Award). Upon Hitler's partial annexation of the Protectorate of Bohemia and Moravia in March 1939, the Slovak State became the Slovak Republic, a client state of Nazi Germany.

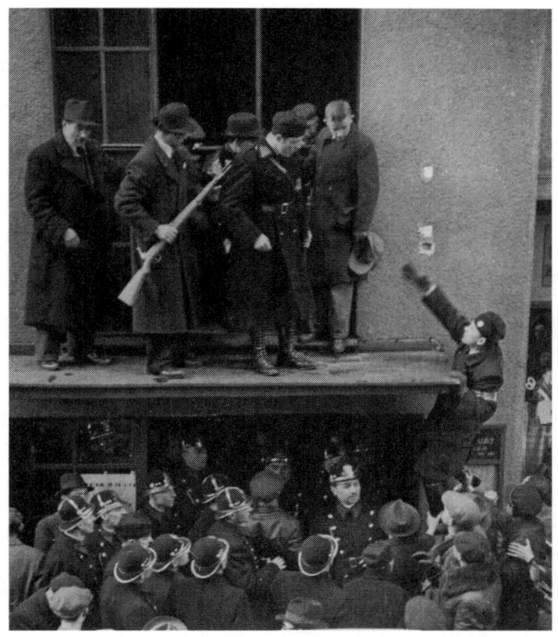

March 1939 rioting in Bratislava

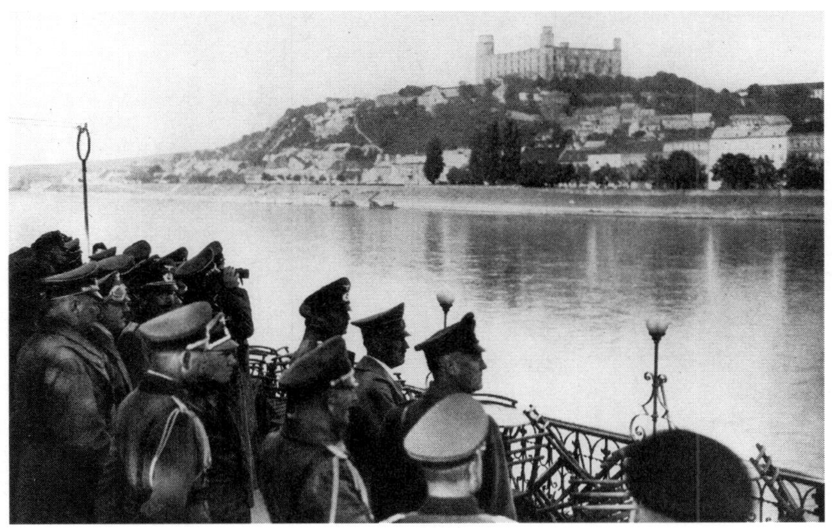

Hitler visits Bratislava in October 1938, shortly after the Munich Agreement

Paradoxically, though, even as Nazi Germany worked to dismantle Czechoslovakia (not only through the Munich Agreement, but also through a second international treaty of 1938, the First Vienna Award, which compelled Czechoslovakia to cede a significant portion of southern Slovakia to Hungary), right-wing Slovak nationalists were forging an alliance with the Nazis that would ultimately lead to the dissolution of Czechoslovakia. These Slovak nationalists wanted to purge Slovakia of all non-Slovaks—not only Jews, but also Hungarians, Czechs, and Romani. Because both my parents came from ethnically German or Czech families that had Hungarianized their names, they were potential targets of this xenophobic Slovak nationalist movement—even though we had always considered ourselves Slovaks.

In 1942 the Slovak nationalists seized control of Slovakia and quickly came to an agreement with Germany about Slovakia's Jews: by its terms, they paid the Nazis to deport all Slovakian Jews to camps in Occupied Poland. Of the eighty-nine thousand Jews who had lived in Slovakia before the outbreak of the war, sixty-nine thousand—78 percent—died in the camps. The news of the deal horrified my parents. The agreement had been orchestrated by Jozef Tiso, a Catholic priest who had become president of the newly declared Slovak Republic. Under his dictatorial leadership, the Slovak People's Party would continue to promote a toxic combination of Catholic fundamentalism, authoritarianism, and xenophobia throughout the war—and in doing so, bind Slovakia ever more tightly to the Nazis.

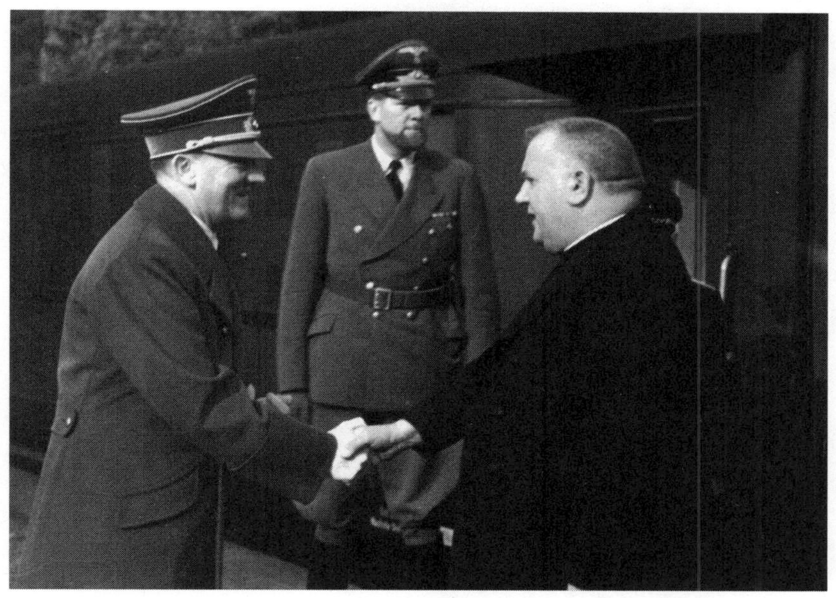

Jozef Tiso, president of the Slovak Republic, meets with Hitler in Germany in 1941

2

Wartime

During the opening years of the war, our life in Bratislava remained relatively unchanged. But the city was clearly a strategic target, because it was a center for oil refining and a regional transit hub. Railroad lines from the north, south, east, and west all converged at Bratislava, and its significant port facilities made it a center for Danube shipping. As a result, my parents lived with a growing expectation that the city would soon be bombed, besieged, or destroyed. Our home was particularly vulnerable, for it lay just below the city's largest and most visible landmark—Bratislava Castle—and just above all the vital roads and railway lines that ran along the Danube.

No wonder, then, that by 1943 our life was being disrupted almost daily by air raid sirens and evacuation drills. The army and the police were everywhere, and no one knew what was going to happen. My schooling suffered accordingly. I had an excellent teacher in first and second grade—I loved her, she had a great influence on me—but then one day she simply disappeared. Because she was Jewish, she was taken away and murdered. You never knew what happened to people—they just vanished. Changes and disruptions of this sort were everywhere, and we had no choice but to accept them.

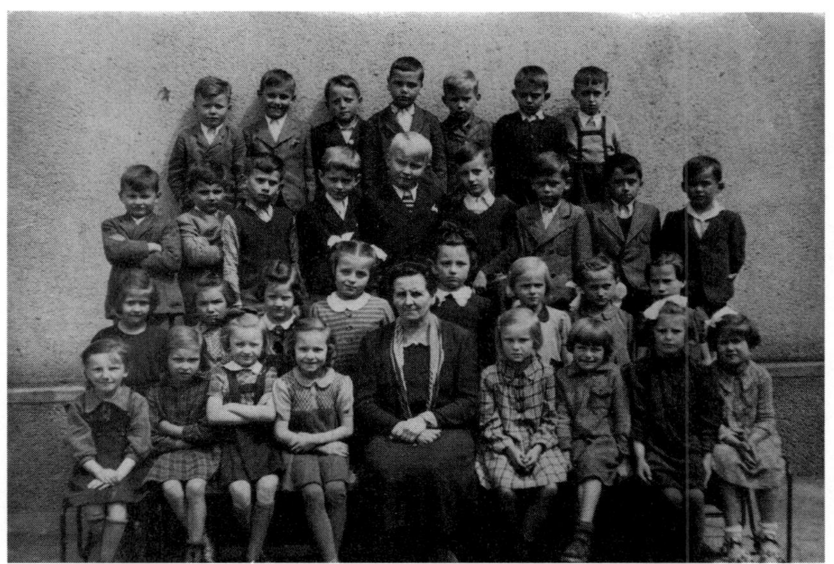

My first-grade class photograph. I am seated to the right of my teacher, a place reserved for the best student.

I think my deepest sense-memory of the war years was of being achingly lonely. My friends kept disappearing as their families evacuated for safety. In the summers of 1941, 1942, and 1943, I was sent to live at the home of my maternal grandmother, who had recently relocated to Banská Bystrica, the picturesque university town, which was surrounded by forests and mountains. Some of my cousins had taken refuge with her as well, but they were so much older than me—around twelve or thirteen—that they never included me in their games and never allowed me to come swimming with them. Separated from my parents and with no one my age for company, I was terribly bored. I had no toys or books, so instead I did chores and housework for my grandmother—weeding the garden, dusting, drying the dishes. But without a single friend, I often cried myself to sleep.

During the final summer of the war, in June 1944, the U.S. Fifteenth Air Force began a strategic campaign to help the Allies reach Germany from the south, and they bombed Bratislava. Their aim was to cut off German supply lines and to destroy the city's Jupiter oil refinery. The part of the city near the oil refineries was flattened, with many of its residents killed; other parts of the city, including our own, were very badly damaged. Several weeks after the air raid we learned that the Russian army was advancing on Bratislava. No one knew what the Russians would do when they arrived—but they had a reputation for brutality and, since the Tiso government had bound Slovakia so closely to the Nazis, everyone expected the worst.

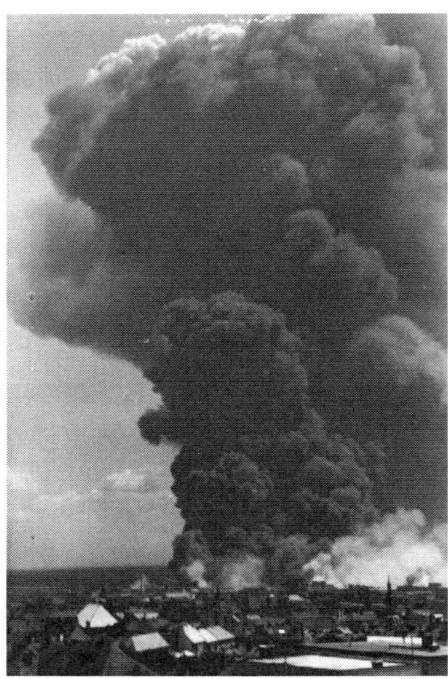

The Allied bombing of Bratislava, June 1944

I have only a few memories of that terrifying time—most strongly, of running into a tunnel as people screamed and bombs fell and exploded. When we emerged, the buildings and streets were destroyed. There was broken glass everywhere. I dimly remember also that my mother was pregnant and unwell, and that daily life was terribly difficult. My parents wanted me to evacuate, but my grandmother's home was no longer safe, because Banská Bystrica had become the center of a partisan uprising against the pro-Nazi Slovak government. So my father sent me instead to a rural village to live with one of his cousins, the director of a grammar school. He and his wife had no children and didn't know what to do with me. I spent most of those six weeks alone in an empty classroom, fearful and anxious, reading and doodling on scrap paper.

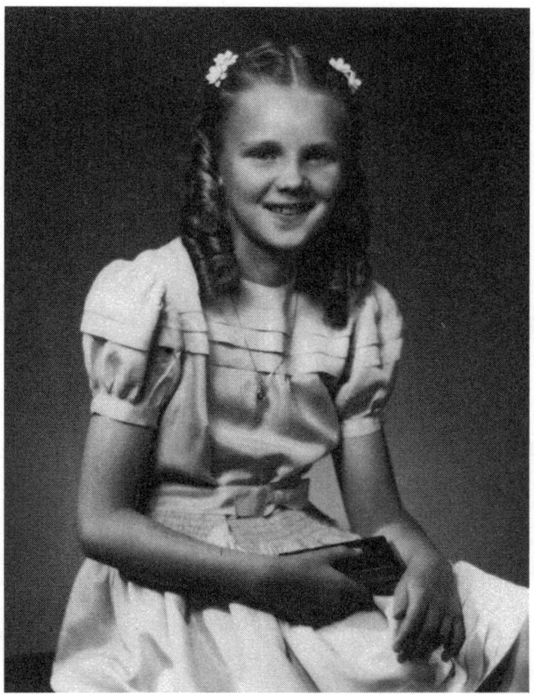

My first communion, 1944

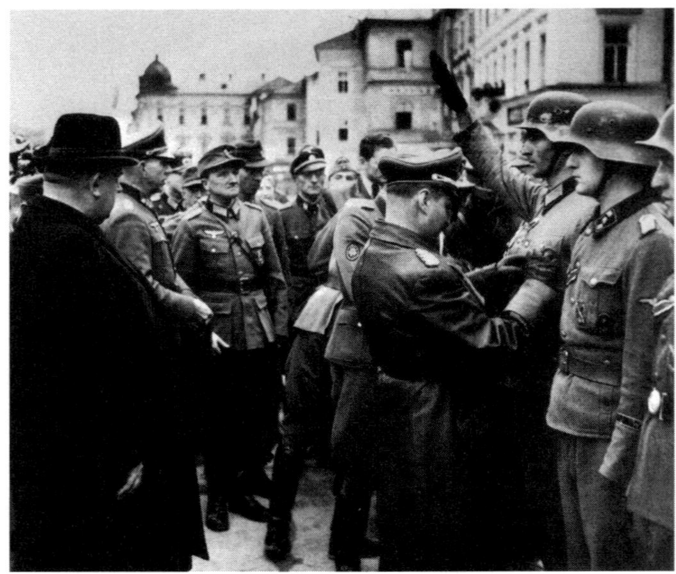

Jozef Tiso (left, in black) and General Hermann Höfle, the commander in chief of the German troops, decorate German soldiers in Banská Bystrica, following their suppression of the Slovak National Uprising, October 1944.

Due to the ever-increasing danger, my father came up with another plan for me in the fall, sending me to some people who had a farm near my father's family's farm. It would have been better if I had been sent to my father's relatives, but that wasn't possible because my father had never resolved his differences with his brother. I didn't know these farm people; I think my parents must have paid them to put me up there, for many farms in the area were at that point sheltering Bratislavan refugees for money. The farm was in a place called Chrabrany, two miles outside the hamlet of Ludanice, and on the outskirts of the small town of Topoľčany, which lies about seventy miles northeast of Bratislava. My father put me on the train alone on a very cold, dark afternoon in late October, telling the conductor to let me off at the Topoľčany train station, where someone would be waiting for me. I don't have memories of the trip, or of who picked me up—I only remember being very frightened.

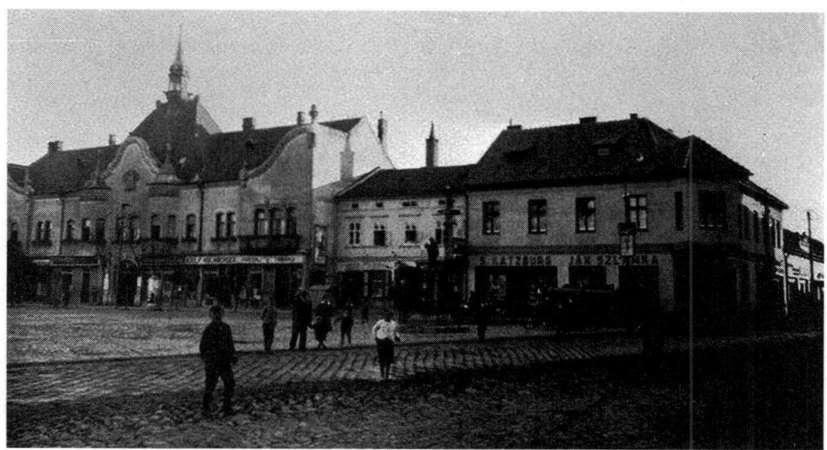

Topoľčany

The people at the farm were not friendly, and the animals scared me too. I had never been around farm animals before. Apart from cows and horses, there were pigs, ducks, chickens, and geese. Most of the smaller animals were kept in pens and were waiting to be slaughtered; every week a new batch were killed and dressed for sale at the local regional market. Seeing and hearing the slaughter was nightmarish. Rough country women did the butchering.

My mother arrived in Ludanice several weeks later, heavily pregnant. Ivan, who was sixteen, had come along with her, partly to look after her, and partly to attend the high school in Topoľčany, which was a fifteen-minute train ride away (school had been canceled in Bratislava). My father, meanwhile, remained behind, because our house had been damaged by bombs and could not be secured. Two of my older cousins were staying with him to protect it from looters.

Looking back, I realize that my mother, who was nearly forty, must have been terribly frightened at having to deliver a child alone, in the middle of a war, so far from her husband and relatives. She gave birth on January 10, 1945, in a hospital filled with badly wounded soldiers. I had expected I would spend more time with my mother once she delivered the baby, but it did not work out that way. Little Pavol developed a painful, full-body skin rash for which there was no medicine available. My mother was convinced the disease came from the dirty wounded soldiers in the hospital. For all of January and February she was terrified he would develop sepsis. I needed her love and reassurance, but instead of being comforted, I was either left alone at the farm or else brought in to hold and comfort the baby, since my mother was completely exhausted. I did as best I could—but I was only eight, and he cried incessantly, his little face so angry and ugly and red.

Ivan, meanwhile, didn't do much on my behalf. He was so much older than me—eight and a half years—and we had little in common. But apart from that, he made a point of avoiding anything stressful, including our home life. Instead he simply focused on himself. It was his way of coping, I suppose. He cared very little for me, or for Pavol, or even for my mother. Other people's feelings simply did not interest him. He had a mean streak, as well: very early in my childhood, for example, he had told me that unless I did *exactly* as he ordered, he was going to trade me away to the gypsies for a truckload of chocolate. To Ivan, this was a great big joke; but to me, it was terrifying—I suppose because I had a very strong sense that my parents would hardly have minded.

More baffling to me was the favor my parents showed him. All my life I have wondered why my parents gave him so much love, and me so little. Perhaps it was because they had had him at a very different moment in their lives, when their own relationship was strong and loving. Also he was undeniably handsome, a top student, and a fine athlete. I, by contrast, was born at a time when their marriage was less happy, and their circumstances increasingly difficult. Plus, I was rather plain looking: clearly I did not charm or dazzle them. I got top grades, but I was just a girl. So perhaps it is natural that they had less love for me.

Whatever the reason, during our time in Ludanice my mother paid me little attention. She was exhausted and depressed, needed help with the baby, and apart from that she was tremendously worried about money and food and the war. Ivan passed most of his days playing sports with his new friends in Topoľčany, returning home only to eat and sleep. I had wanted to attend school too, but I was only eight, so it simply wasn't possible.

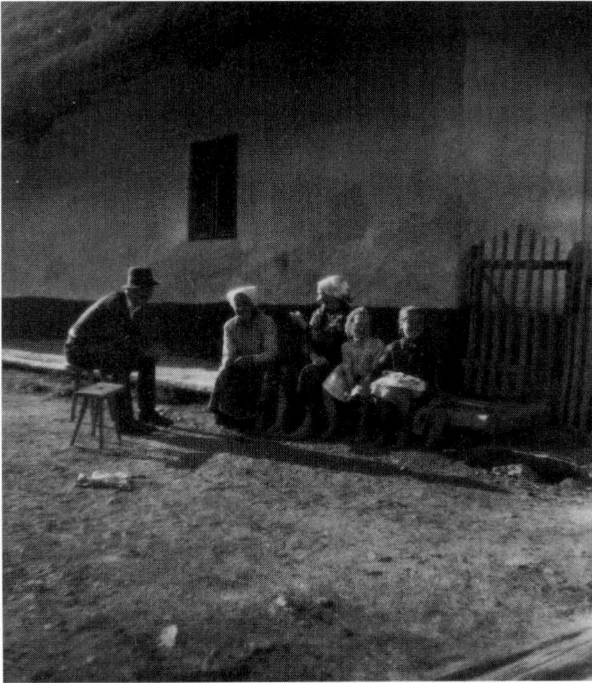

Farm life in rural Slovakia

I would have made myself useful at the farm, but the family who owned the place took little interest in my well-being and had nothing for me to do. Also the slaughter of the animals bound for the market continually upset me; I simply could not get used to the squeals and squawks of terror coming from the slaughterhouse, and the heavy odors of the barnyard and slaughterhouse left me constantly nauseated.

One day when I was alone in the farmhouse one of the workers grabbed me and assaulted me. There was no one around to see her or stop her. The terror, confusion, and shame I felt at the violation was compounded by the fact that I didn't understand what she was doing. It was all so horrible. I had no one to protect me, no one to stop it from happening. When she had finished with me I retreated to my room and hid myself under the covers of my bed and cried. I never told anyone about having been attacked in this way, not even my mother. I was so profoundly ashamed and felt that it was all my fault. Even today, seventy-five years later, the trauma of it haunts me.

In the weeks that followed I was so afraid of being assaulted again that I left the farmhouse early every morning and stayed away all day. It was wintertime, and very cold, so I hid in the outbuildings, in a room where the field hands gathered. Having no work during the coldest months of winter, they were instead holed up inside, drinking beer, smoking, and playing cards.

At first the men ignored me as I watched them play. After a few days, though, one asked if I knew how to write and add. When I told him I could do both, he handed me a pencil and told me to keep score. I did so and became a sort of mascot to them. Eventually they invited me to play cards too. I played cards with the field hands all day long, every single day, for weeks. I wasn't learning anything, but I felt safer with them than in the farmhouse. But then the snow melted, and the workers were called back to the fields, and I was once again alone.

Being so young, I had no understanding of what was going on in the world beyond the farm. But Slovaks across the country had rebelled against the occupying Nazis and Tiso's Slovak nationalists. Although the uprising was crushed within two months, partisan fighting would continue against the Nazis and Slovak nationalists until the Russians arrived. In response, the German forces and the Slovak nationalist militia engaged in an ongoing campaign of terror and retaliation, ultimately burning down ninety-three Slovakian villages and murdering thousands of Slovaks, many of whom were unarmed agricultural laborers.

That spring of 1945, Ludanice was occupied by these Germans and nationalists, as was the farm. All women and girls were instructed to keep out of sight. Everyone feared for their lives. But then, just as suddenly as they arrived, the Germans departed. We soon learned why: the Russian army was advancing on the town.

Nobody knew what to expect of the Russians, but they quickly made a name for themselves by seizing all the liquor they could find and drinking it. The war officially came to an end in early May, but the Russians stayed on in Ludanice for all of May, June, and July. Finally my mother felt it was more dangerous for us in Ludanice than Bratislava. Though unable to reach my father, she had enough money to get us all on a train. So we packed our bags and left, not knowing what might await.

Like Ludanice, Bratislava was now under Russian occupation. It had sustained very heavy damage in the last months of the war, and with no materials to make repairs, it remained mostly in ruins. The other half of our two-family home had been hit by a bomb, as were several other houses on our street. Roughly a quarter of our roof had been taken off by the bomb, and every window had been shattered by the blast, but the structure was still habitable. Houses in those days had double sets of windows to keep out the cold—one on the outside of the house, the second on the inside—so there was broken glass everywhere, and no way of repairing or replacing the windowpanes. My father and his cousins had used paper or salvaged boards to seal the window openings shut. Everyone was making piecemeal repairs with whatever they could find, worried about the impending winter.

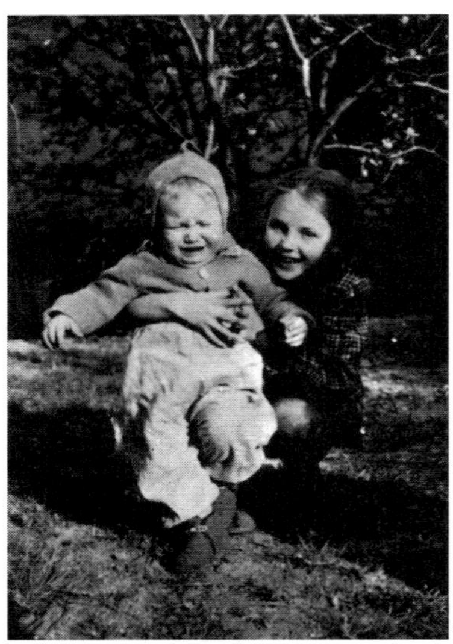

(right) With baby Pavol shortly after the war

(below) Bomb damage in Bratislava

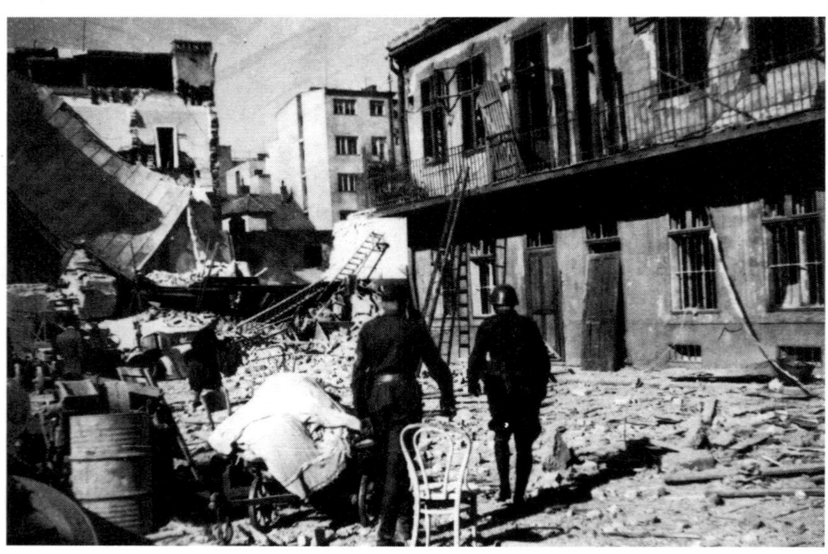

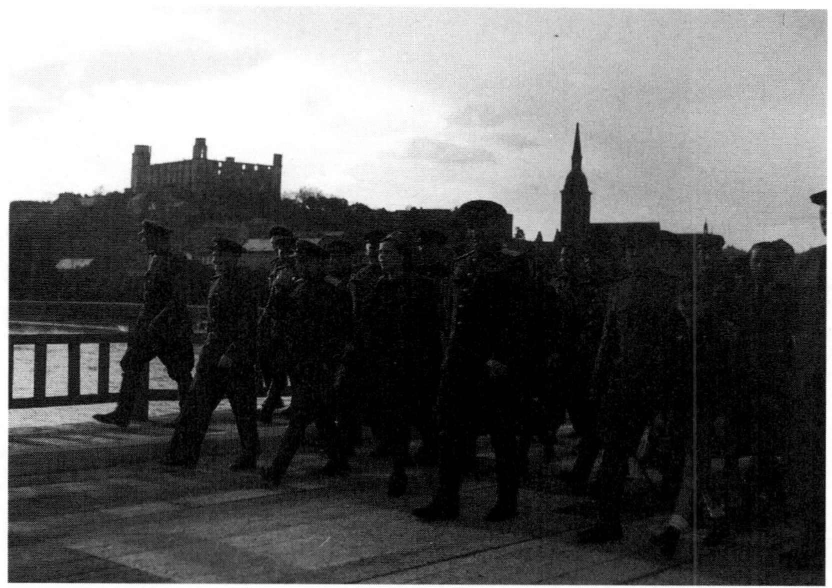

Russians in April 1945 crossing the bridge constructed across the Danube, with Bratislava Castle in the background

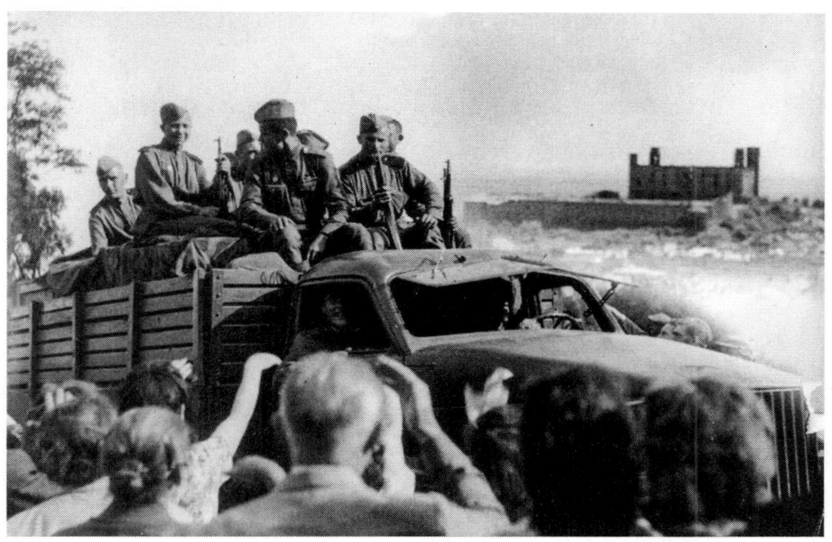

The Red Army in Bratislava in 1945, with distant view of Bratislava Castle

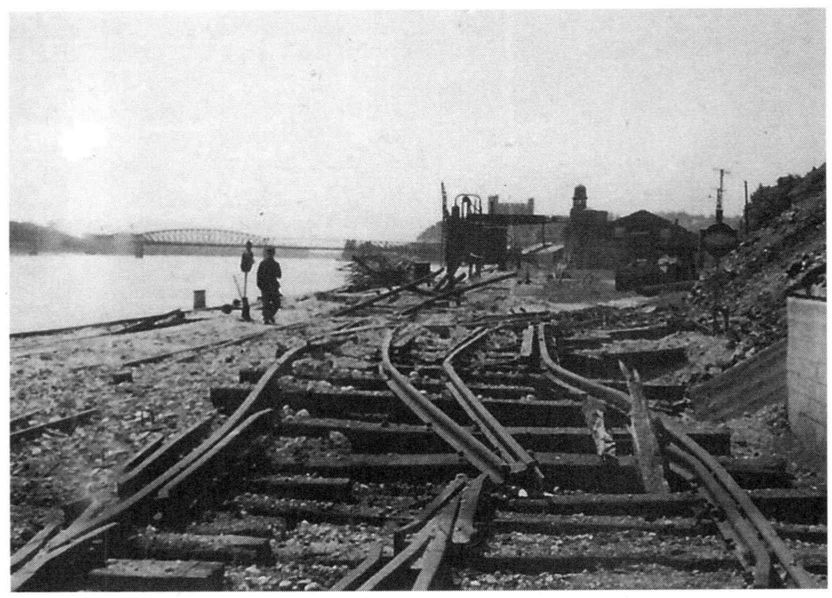

Bomb damage along the Danube, just below our home

Despite the lack of food, the destruction, and the political confusion, my parents were nonetheless hopeful that life would soon return to normal. I remember how relieved I was when school started that September. Never had I been so happy. I saw many old friends again, and many of my favorite teachers too. Even better, I discovered that I hadn't been left back. I would be able to continue my studies with my classmates and my friends.

One reason I was especially happy to be back to school was that our life at home remained very difficult. The stresses of the war, the forced evacuation to the countryside, and Pavol's health problems—all these things hit my mother very hard. While she had always been a rather dark and critical presence in my life, she was now so depressed, so bitter, and so angry—so quick to criticize, scold, and blame me for things that really were not my fault—that I often dreamt of running away. Pavol, too, ought to have been a source of joy to her, but by the time we returned to Bratislava, we all sensed he was a deeply troubled infant. His skin infection had cleared up, but even so he cried incessantly, which was exhausting and stressful for everyone in the family. On top of that, neither of my parents seemed to feel much warmth toward each other or their children. It was so confusing. I expected that when the war ended our family might be happy, but it was simply not to be.

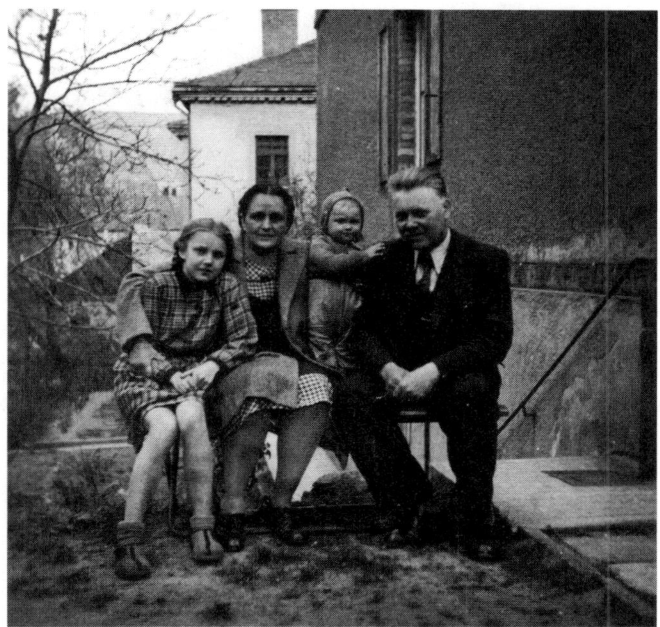

With my mother, father, and baby Pavol in the backyard of our home in Bratislava

Ivan remained my parents' great hope. In 1945, upon turning seventeen, he announced to my parents that he was going to become a doctor. His good looks, top grades, and demonstrated ability at sports made him widely admired by all who knew him. Small wonder, then, that my parents did everything they could on his behalf.

I, on the other hand, was a girl. There were few professions then open to women in Bratislava apart from teacher, librarian, or secretary—and all these jobs were badly paid, with no career security. So perhaps my parents were right to care less about me than they did about Ivan. Quite apart from that, however, my mother seemed chronically dissatisfied with me, for reasons I could never understand. She constantly compared me to Ivan, asking why I couldn't be more like him. Ivan had been such a perfect, happy baby, she would say: he always fell asleep quickly and never woke in the middle of the night. I, by comparison, had always been fretful, needy, sickly, and disruptive. My father had fewer words of criticism, I suppose because he had grown up in a time and place when children were looked after by their mothers, their nurses, and their nannies, and girl children were simply less valued than boys. Even so, his nearly complete indifference to me made me feel equally awful.

In retrospect, I recognize that there was another family dynamic affecting our home. To put it simply: my parents were deeply unhappy, and had grown steadily apart since their marriage. The stresses of the war had worsened that estrangement. Feeling trapped and resentful, each was nonetheless compelled to remain in the marriage, for Slovakia was deeply Catholic, divorce was extremely rare, and even if they had wanted to flout convention, they didn't have enough money to separate. Like it or not they were bound together for life, and that was that.

Trapped in their unhappy marriage, my parents fought. After their fights my mother would remain extremely agitated, often for hours. Needing to blame someone, she would frequently turn to us and say, "All of this happened because of *you!*" And since Ivan was her darling and Pavol was her baby, I was usually the scapegoat. On some level I knew that I wasn't *really* the cause of their fighting, but her accusations affected me: I developed a sense that everything was my responsibility, that I had failed, that I was to blame. For a very young person, that's a heavy burden. But with it came something else: a determination not to be crushed. And I think, looking back, that it was that same determination that led me, ultimately, to leave home, to leave Bratislava, to leave Czechoslovakia, and, ultimately, to leave Europe.

3

Postwar Life

In the bleak years following the war I did exceptionally well in school, in large part because I loved the encouragement and recognition given to me by my teachers, who made me feel special and gifted. Of course, I worked tremendously hard at my schoolwork. At home, my mother insisted upon it—she recognized my potential and pushed me endlessly to do better. The pressure she put on me was, I think, an extension of the pressure she had always put upon herself, since she had grown up at a time when any girl hoping to have a career needed to excel in all ways. And doubtless my maternal grandmother, who had raised all four of her daughters as a widow, had been equally driven and demanding, both of herself and her daughters.

At times though, my mother's perfectionism could border on mania, her anger toward me becoming irrational, even violent. For example, my mother's sisters would come to our house every Sunday for tea, and as part of the visit my mother would always show them around the house, taking pride in my perfectly tidy bedroom and my perfectly organized closet. But if my closet was even a tiny bit out of order, after my aunts left my mother would turn on me in a rage, shouting, "You have embarrassed and humiliated me!" More shouting, scolding, and physical punishment inevitably followed.

To give another example: every Saturday afternoon it was my job to help clean the kitchen. Kitchen work was woman's work, so the boys were never called upon to do it. And the kitchen had to be perfectly clean. No matter how hard I worked, however, and no matter how well I cleaned, my mother would always find something wrong. I had neglected to scour out a corner, for example. At that point the shouting and scolding would begin. I was a disappointment, an embarrassment! Why couldn't I follow instructions! Why didn't I understand about cleanliness! The shouting always brought me to tears, because I could not understand the intensity of her rage. Worse yet, there was no one to protect me from the beating that followed, always with a heavy wooden spoon.

This same spirit of perfectionism extended to my grades in school. If I got an A– rather than an A, my mother told me I was a tremendous disappointment. And if I got an A, my mother would say, "But how could you get an A? Your handwriting is terrible!" There was no escape from this torrent of criticism. If my mother attempted to scold Ivan, by comparison, he was gone in a second, out of the house—and because he was a boy, it was somehow all right. But I could not leave. Girls were not allowed to wander the streets unaccompanied—and besides, where would I go? My place was at home, doing housework and chores. I had no alternative but to remain and submit.

Even my body was at fault. As I approached adolescence, my mother began insisting I was too tall and too skinny. She made a mark on the wall in our corridor, and every week when my aunts came for their Sunday visit, she would stand me there to be measured in front of them, and then humiliate me by saying, "What a pity that you are so thin and tall and unattractive." If I had grown, my aunts would say, "Oh, we are praying for you to stop growing!" They all felt certain that no tall, skinny girl would ever find a husband.

Naturally, I wasn't perfect. No one is. Occasionally I would do something wrong at school—something minor, like whispering in class—and I would have to stay afterward for detention, to write on the blackboard a hundred times, "I must not talk in class." One day when this had happened, my mother saw my friend Magda and asked where I was. Magda, not wanting to lie, told her I'd been put in detention. That night I was punished very soundly, beaten yet again with the wooden spoon.

No doubt about it: with age and the ill health that followed Pavol's birth, my mother had become an increasingly angry and embittered person. Throughout the war and now in its aftermath, she had been frustrated, depressed, and enraged by our diminished life circumstances, but the postwar years were, if anything, even more difficult for her. There was destruction all around, nobody had any money, and, most traumatic of all, she lost her job. As a woman who had worked all her life, she was used to earning a salary, doing good in the community, and commanding the respect, admiration, and deference of others. Her new, lonely existence at home must have felt empty and desperate by comparison. Without her salary we could barely keep food on the table, and our house, having sustained so much bomb damage, was cold, grimy, and shabby. No matter how hard she and I worked to keep it in order, it was looking worse all the time.

In 1946 the government requisitioned our basement, giving its little apartment to a local war widow and her daughter. Having these strangers downstairs was terribly awkward, but we had no choice in the matter. I suppose the one good thing about our house being damaged, dilapidated, and subdivided by the state was that it was no longer attractive enough to be appropriated by the government officials. Our neighbors with prettier homes were not so lucky: they were simply evicted. Their homes were requisitioned, they were thrown out, and upper-level politicians moved in, taking possession of everything in the house.

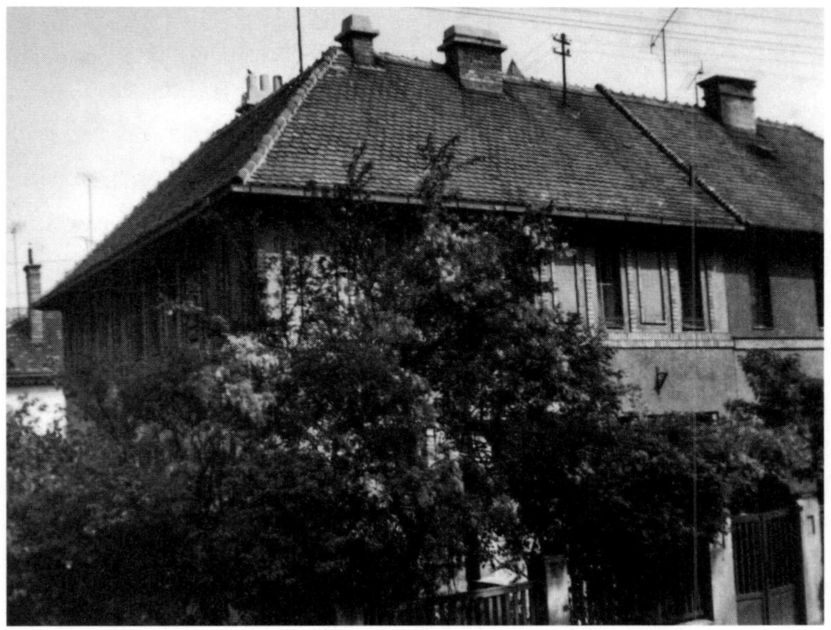

Our home

In October 1945, my father had managed through the Ministry of Education to get Ivan a fellowship to a French *lycée*. My father pushed this educational strategy because he felt life would be far more secure for Ivan in France than Czechoslovakia: upon attaining a *baccalauréat* degree, he would even be given the option of living and working there permanently. As a result he left us, spending his first year at a *lycée* in Dijon. He subsequently transferred to one in Nîmes, where he spent another three years earning his degree and gaining acceptance to a French medical school. My mother missed him terribly, but at this point we all sensed an invasion by Stalin was imminent.

Food and fuel were scarce in the first two postwar winters, and the winter of 1946–1947 was one of the coldest on record. Because of wartime damage to railways and other transport systems, nearly all the European supply chains had been disrupted, and many populations were threatened with starvation. There were food riots in the streets of Vienna. In Bratislava, too, we were short of everything—food, fuel, and medicine—and we battled against cold and disease. I was thin and malnourished, and prone to sinus, throat, and ear infections. That winter of 1946–1947, my exhaustion and coughing fits led my parents to suspect I had contracted tuberculosis, for my father's younger sister was living with an advanced case of it, and her daughter, my cousin, had recently died of it. For several months I was convinced that I was going to be sent away to a sanitarium to die alone. But in the end, the doctor found no evidence of the disease in my X-rays, so I was allowed to remain with the family.

A few months later, however, I came down with scarlet fever. Before antibiotics came into widespread use, scarlet fever was a leading cause of child mortality, and there was a major outbreak of it in Bratislava in 1947. For me it began with a deeply painful streptococcal infection of the throat, followed by a high fever and a bright red rash that spread over most of my body—the horrible scarlet rash that gives the disease its name. The fever persisted for weeks. I vomited constantly and had the most excruciating abdominal pain. Many of my school friends became ill with it too, and some died.

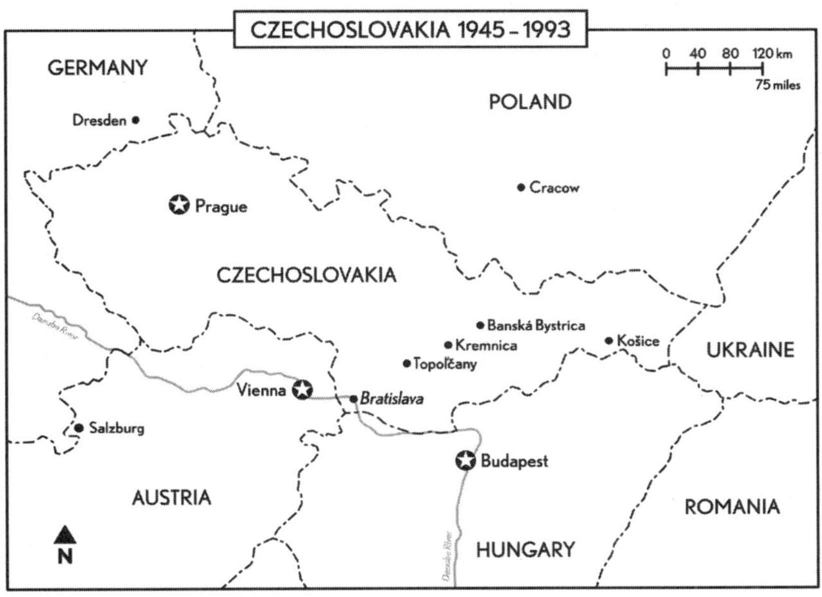

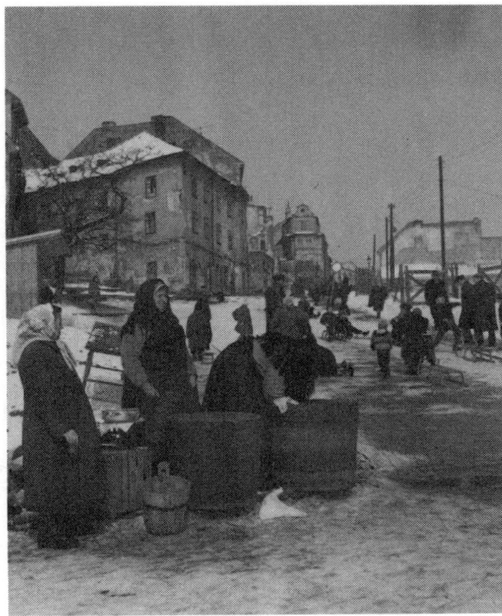

(above) Czechoslovakia as it was reestablished after the war.

(left) Farm women selling cabbages on the streets of Bratislava

Penicillin, the drug most effective at treating streptococcal infections, had come into use during the war, and it might well have saved many of the children who died in Bratislava that winter. However, doctors in Czechoslovakia had no access to it in 1947. Instead, they had only sulfonamide, a broad-spectrum antibacterial drug that worked far less well. At first my parents kept me at home, in my room, disinfecting the house daily in their attempt to keep the illness from spreading to others. When my condition worsened and it seemed likely I might die, they took me to the hospital.

Once admitted, I was put into an isolation ward filled with other sick and dying children. The nurses on the ward were few and terribly overworked. While my parents could visit the hospital, they were not allowed to enter the ward, so I endured the worst of my illness with minimal care. There was little anyone could have done for me in any case. When at last my condition stabilized, the doctors told my parents to take me home—not because I was cured, but because there were so many other children so much closer to death, and they needed my hospital bed. My parents were afraid I would infect Pavol, and therefore decided not to bring me home, but rather to leave me with my aunt Ilonka.

When I was told where I was going, I simply couldn't understand it: how could my parents abandon me when I was so sick? It brought back to me the horrors I had experienced in Ludanice. I begged my mother, but she didn't seem to care; she just gave Ilonka my suitcase and told her I could come home again when I was no longer infectious.

During those weeks with her, Ilonka seemed to understand how traumatized I was by my parents' seeming indifference. I found another ally in my aunt Eržika, who came to visit me. Before the war, Eržika had lived and worked in Banská Bystrica with her husband, the Latin professor. Because he was Czech, however, the Slovak nationalists deported both of them in 1939, and they relocated to Prague. During the war she had taken a museum job there, and also given birth to a son. She even did a modest bit of art collecting. But then, toward the end of the war, her husband died, and she had no choice but to pack up and return to Bratislava.

Eržika felt a special tenderness toward me. She would talk to me about things that I rarely heard about: art, books, museums. She had a small collection of silver, porcelain, furniture, and paintings, and every so often she would give me some small thing of beauty, like a teacup or a plate, to keep for myself. At the same time she taught me that while it was good to cherish beautiful things, one need not own something to enjoy its beauty: to look at furniture, porcelain, or fine clothing was always a treat for the eyes, she said, even if they were not one's own. She encouraged me to go to museums and read books. Eržika had excellent taste, but like all of us she lived very simply.

I don't have many photos of myself from childhood. In one that has survived, from around 1947, I see a thin, pale girl with a pretty profile and ash blond hair. Back then I had no sense of my own looks, apart from knowing that I was too tall and too skinny. It never occurred to me that I might be pretty. I had only the most basic clothing and shoes, all of it secondhand. Everyone was given ration points intended for clothing in the postwar years, but the points didn't add up to much—and besides, even if one had cash to buy things, it was impossible to get good clothing or new shoes. My haircuts, too, were the simplest possible: my mother gave them to me with a kitchen scissors. Every summer she would cut my hair so short that my head looked like it had been shaved—done (she said) so that it would grow back stronger and thicker. Because of these haircuts, the other children teased me, dubbing me Moritz (a boy's name) instead of Marica. I spent much of my childhood feeling embarrassed and ugly.

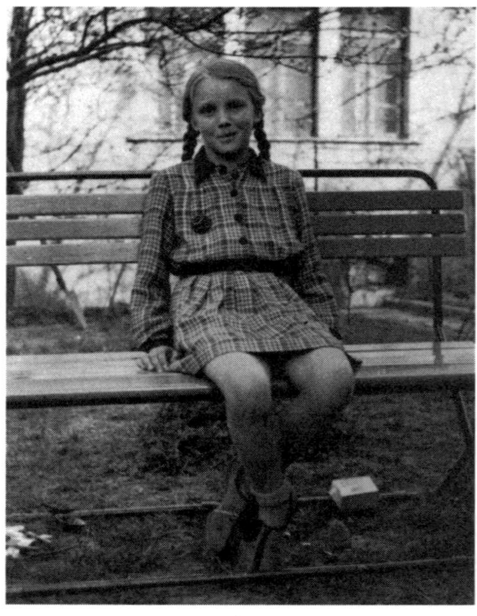

Me in the garden of our home, 1947

There was one person who did help me with my looks, though: my father's sister Philomena Latkóczy. She and her family lived in Topoľčany, where her husband, a very successful tailor and dressmaker, had accrued a small fortune by tailoring high-end military uniforms and luxury religious garments. Philomena had four daughters—the youngest of them, Eva, would grow up to become a well-known actress on the Bratislava stage. Philomena and my mother were not friendly, but my father went out to visit her several times a year to discuss family-related business, and since he and Philomena had always been very close, she took an interest in helping him, most notably by having her husband make my father a fine new suit of clothes every year. She was equally good about sending me her daughters' hand-me-downs—which for years were the nicest clothes I owned.

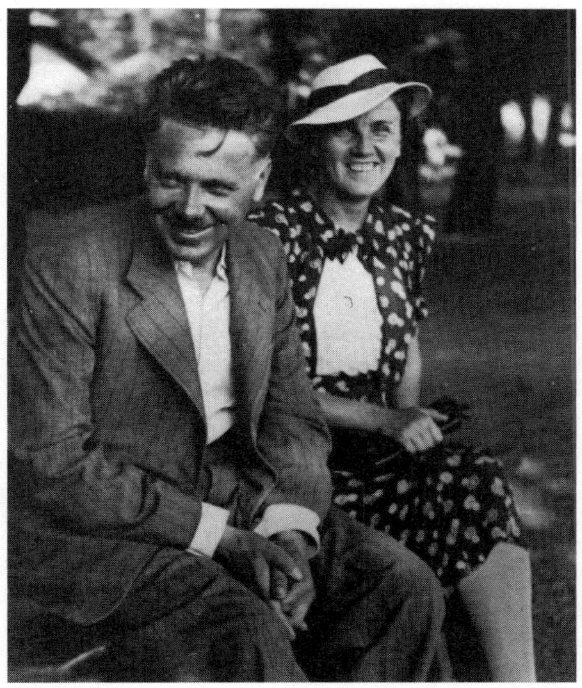

My father with his sister Philomena Latkóczy, sometime in the 1930s

The one thing that sustained our family in the postwar period was the expectation that our lives would return to normal. With Germany's unconditional surrender, Slovakia had become part of a reconstituted Czechoslovak Republic, and with farming and industry starting up again, it seemed only a matter of time before food and material goods returned to Bratislava, along with the prosperity of the prewar years.

Unfortunately, ethnic tensions remained strong. In retaliation for the war, the new Czechoslovakian government decided to expel all ethnic Germans from the country. Likewise, many of Czechoslovakia's ethnic Hungarians were ordered back to Hungary. Families were uprooted, communities were fractured, and lives were thrown into chaos.

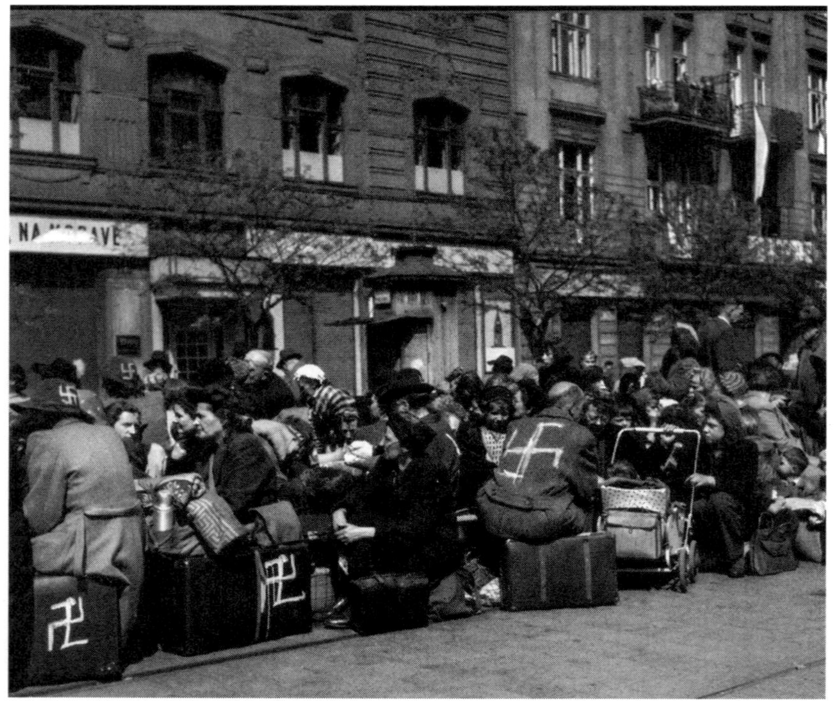

Ethnically German Czechoslovakians being rounded up for deportation from Czechoslovakia in the postwar period

In Bratislava, the Slovaks now openly denounced all the ethnic Hungarians remaining in their midst, insisting that the Hungarians had driven the Slovaks to side with the Nazis. My family was neither Hungarian nor German, but we did have German ancestors, and my father had changed his name to the Hungarian-sounding Gerháth as a young man. Moreover his job overseeing Slovakia's Hungarian-language school system required him not only to speak perfect Hungarian but to interact with ethnic Hungarians daily. Because of this, our family became potential targets for Hungarian-hating Slovakians.

I remember one day my mother and I went out with our longtime housekeeper, Katka, to go food shopping. We were speaking Hungarian because Katka could not speak Slovak. (Unlike my parents, I never learned the language formally, but I had picked up conversational Hungarian from Katka, who spoke to me in Hungarian from my earliest infancy.) A group of young men overheard us, started following us, and then surrounded us. These men had been told by police that if you saw somebody speaking Hungarian you must let them have it, and that's just what they did—they started shouting at us and roughing us up. We were lucky to escape only bruised and terrified. If my mother hadn't shouted back at them quite angrily in Slovak, they might have seriously injured us. That evening, after a long conversation, my parents decided that our immediate family would speak only Slovak in future. No more Hungarian—the risks of speaking Hungarian in public were simply too great.

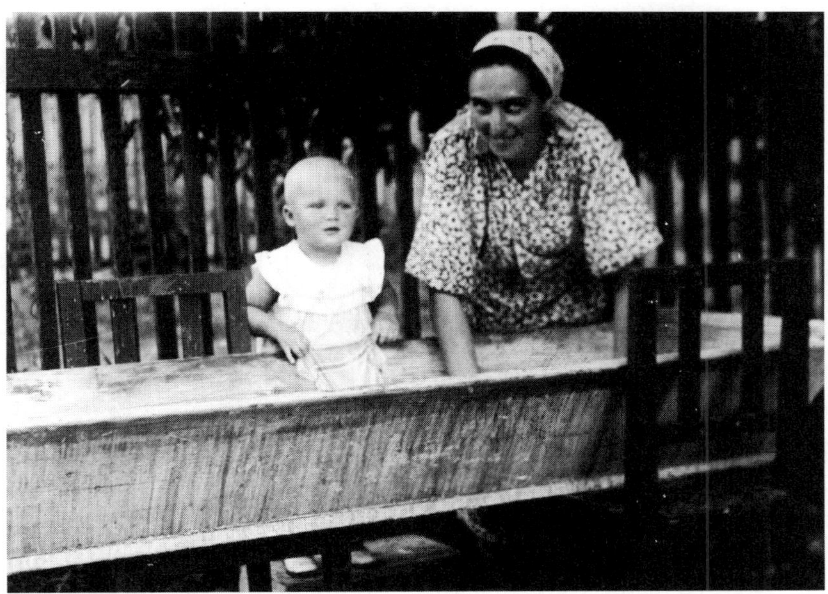

Me as a baby, doing the washing with our beloved Hungarian housekeeper, Katka

Far worse than these random threats to our safety on the streets of Bratislava was the great upheaval that took place in Prague in February 1948, when a group of Communist politicians backed by the Soviet Union seized control of the nation. Within a few weeks the Communists had identified my father's family as prominent landowners and (by extension) denounced us as enemies of the State. In short order all the Gerháths and Gerhardts—my father, his brother Emil, their two sisters—were forcibly compelled to sign away our landholdings. While my father's share of the farm had been relatively modest compared to that of his brother, he nonetheless felt the loss. I had visited the family farm only once (and very briefly) before it was seized, but the small rental income generated by my father's portion of the land had helped finance the purchase of our home and paid many of our bills over the years. More important, the farm had kept us supplied with a modest amount of flour, potatoes, and pork, both during the war and after, when such staples were almost impossible to locate and buy. Now, though, everything was gone.

The Communist takeover also resulted in the complete reorganization of all government offices, including the Ministry of Education, where my father worked. With this takeover, all the administrators in the ministry were summarily fired, including my father, and none would receive their pensions or other retirement benefits. Thus in 1949 my father went from being a relatively comfortable senior government official to being unemployed, blacklisted, and broke. Even so, he was lucky not to have been shipped away to a factory. He had been spared, he was told, only because he was too old and weak to be of any use in factory work.

After his dismissal, my father could not find employment of any sort: everyone in Bratislava was afraid to hire him because he had been blacklisted. I remember how he searched for work every day, and how profoundly depressed and humiliated he was by rejection after rejection. Several times he threatened to shoot himself. He was around fifty, and he could no longer contribute to the support of our family. It was only after many months of searching that he finally managed to obtain work—a menial and degrading job shelving books at our local library. It paid very little, and with my mother unemployed, that small wage was all we had to live on.

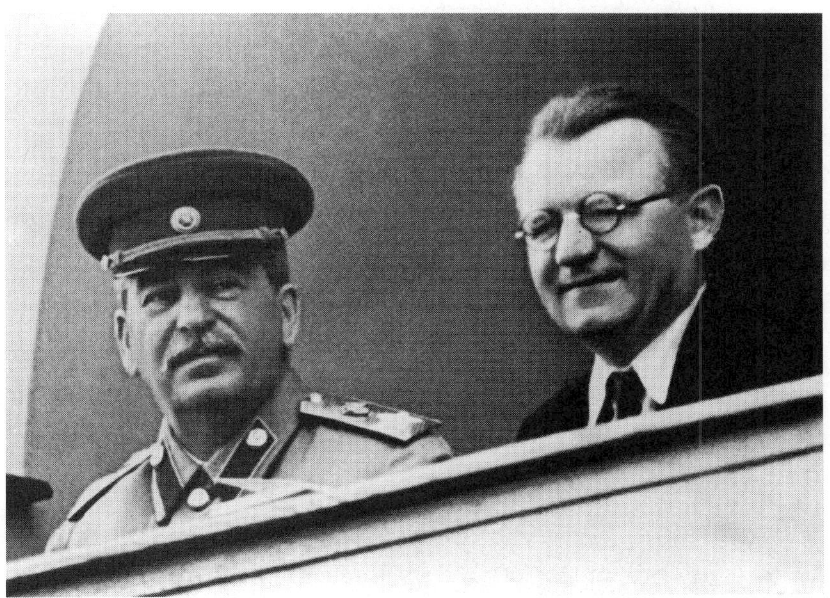

A 1946 photograph of Joseph Stalin and Communist politician Klement Gottwald, taken in Moscow shortly after Gottwald was elected prime minister of Czechoslovakia. Two years later, in the wake of the 1948 Soviet-backed coup d'état, Gottwald became president and imposed a Stalinist Soviet model of government on Czechoslovakia.

We were not alone in the challenges we faced. Converting a formerly capitalist society to a Communist one involved the widespread confiscation of personal property, the shutting down of businesses, the reorganization of government, and, in essence, a complete reshuffling of the social order. Long-established systems and networks were upended, replaced by a single-party government that quickly took on the feel of a criminal enterprise. Our new Communist ruling class, many of them not much more than thugs, now dictated how people were to live, where they were to work, what they could say, and what they could believe.

Following the Communist Party in the USSR, the Communist Party in Czechoslovakia embraced state atheism and actively discouraged the practice of religion. Despite the fact that Slovakia was deeply Catholic, roughly half the country's priests, nuns, monks, and lay brethren were sent to prisons or forced-labor camps. Parents who gave their children religious instruction were fired, demoted, or denounced to the secret police. Neither of my parents had ever been particularly religious, but we had always attended church, and we could not comprehend why the government felt it had the right to intrude on our personal lives and beliefs in this way. We had no alternative, though: to challenge or oppose the Communists was to risk death.

Our quality of life suffered too. Just as Bratislava had seemed poised to recover from the war, food once again disappeared from the markets. Building materials were scarce or nonexistent, and shops offered few dry goods. Products from Western Europe became impossibly expensive. Few restaurants could function, given all the food shortages, and those that did were beyond the reach of the average Bratislavan. Cafés had no coffee, only locally grown herbal tea. Medicine, clothing, and fuel were only sporadically available, and the food supply was so limited that we could rarely offer a meal to anyone outside our immediate family.

The Communist takeover was shocking in other ways. During the war one had always been careful never to express a political opinion, but now, under the new regime, people were actively bullied into silence. Expressing even a mild point of view was enough to get one arrested, beaten, or killed. A powerful new secret police force, the ŠtB (short for Štátna Bezpečnosť, or State Security), was trained by the Soviets to terrorize, abduct, interrogate, torture, and blackmail anyone they decided might be a threat to the State. As a result, average citizens were subject to wiretaps, street surveillance, and middle-of-the-night raids on private homes, as well as to brutal, hours-long interrogations. The disappearance of friends and neighbors became a common occurrence. Because the powers of the ŠtB were unlimited, literally anyone could be jailed or "disappeared" at any time, for no apparent reason. We had already been blacklisted due to my father's family being landowners, and my father's connections to the previous government and to the Hungarian-speaking community made us even more suspect. As a result, many people we knew began avoiding our home—because, simply by being friendly with us, they too would be in danger of being interrogated, beaten, or murdered.

While our home was never raided by the ŠtB, our neighbors in the two-family home were not so lucky. The husband, who had held a high government position before the Communist takeover, was simply handcuffed and led away one afternoon. His wife then called to us over the garden-side balcony we shared, telling us they were being evicted. She tearfully begged my mother to hide her best possessions in our attic until she could come back and claim them, because the ŠtB was allowing her and her children to take away only one suitcase. We did so, reaching over the wall between our balconies to take her things and put them in our attic. The next day she and her children were escorted from their home. We never saw them again.

A few days later, two ŠtB secret policemen and their families moved in. The men were very rough looking, and so were their wives. In the weeks that followed, these women began asking my mother questions about how things worked in the city—how to put their children into school, where to find doctors, that sort of thing. My mother did her best to help, even as she feared and resented them. I remember we were surprised when the two women told us they had brought three piglets with them from the country and were raising them in their bathtub. The piglets were never released into their garden, so I suspect that they were eaten soon after arrival.

The year before the Communist takeover, I had been selected to attend the Cvičné Gymnázium, the best high school in Bratislava. Being admitted was an honor that put me on track for early admission to university. I should explain that in Czechoslovakia, as in much of Central Europe, high schools were divided into three different types. *Gymnázium* was the most advanced of these schools, the training ground for gifted students as they rose to become professionals and academics. Then there was *priemyslovka*, a four-year technical school for students who wanted to become workers, nurses, typists, salespeople, and secretaries. Finally there was *meštianka,* a basic school for laborers and factory workers. The Cvičné Gymnázium was at that time divided into two sections, one for science and technology, and the other for the study of classics. Since my friends and I were all hoping to go into medicine or engineering, we all joined the first section, and I felt I was destined, like my brother, for a career in medicine.

But in February 1949 the new Communist president, Klement Gottwald, abolished all the *gymnáziums*, *priemyslovkas,* and *meštiankas* in the nation, replacing them with an "Eleven Years" school in which *all* students, whatever their aptitude, were lumped together for all eleven years of elementary and secondary education. I attended the Cvičné Gymnázium for only one year before it became a far less distinguished Eleven Years school. The school system would change three more times before I graduated, as would the school's location. (My future husband, Jan, whom I would not meet for another decade, had a similar experience: three years older than me, he enjoyed three rigorous years at the Second State Gymnázium in Bratislava, but after the Communist takeover he was demoted to an Eleven Years school, where he learned very little.)

While the government made these changes in the name of educational equality for the new classless society, my own experience was essentially of being denied the accelerated learning that a gifted student needs, desires, and deserves. Moreover, as I was soon to discover, the new Communist schooling system was not about equality or opportunity at all, given that it was sexist: for example, the State awarded prizes to its top students, but only if they were boys. No girl, however accomplished, could win one. And while boys who excelled in mathematics were routinely given scholarships to study in Moscow, no girl ever received one. Girls were not allowed to study outside Czechoslovakia.

The Communist government also restricted its own citizens' ability to travel abroad. This new development was terrible for Ivan, who after receiving his *baccalauréat* in Nîmes had been admitted in the spring of 1950 to a French medical school, with plans of attending it in the fall. But then while home in Bratislava during the summer of 1950, he was told he could not return to France: the border had been closed. Forced to give up his place, he was instead compelled to apply to medical school in Bratislava, for Czechoslovakia—like Poland, East Germany, Bulgaria, Romania, and Albania—was now behind the Iron Curtain, and in the future, no Czechoslovak citizen would be allowed outside the Soviet sphere of influence.

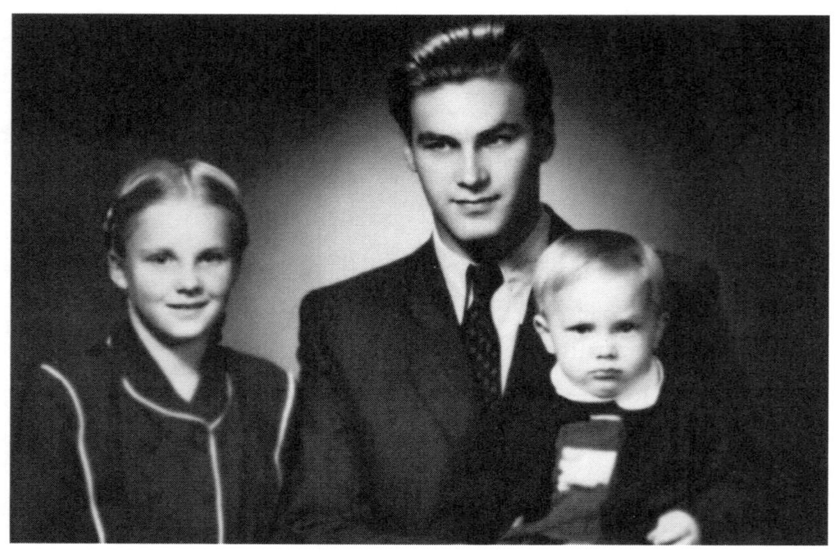

A 1948 studio photograph of me, Ivan, and Pavol

4

Adolescence

My life changed significantly with Ivan's return, but not altogether for the better. While my parents were disappointed that he hadn't been able to study medicine in France, they were tremendously pleased to have him home. Their joy and relief at having him back was augmented by the enormous pride they took in him, for Ivan had developed into a fine competitive figure skater and a discus thrower while studying in France, and his feats of athleticism (combined with his good looks, charm, and academic achievement) essentially dazzled my parents, blinding them to those darker aspects of his nature that he would periodically unleash on me. Essentially, they felt he could do no wrong.

While I was surely jealous of the attention he received from them, I was also quite frankly the recipient of his cruelty. Whenever we were alone he made endless disparaging comments about my looks, my size, and my personality. He also ordered me around a great deal, making clear as he did so that I was less a sister to him than a servant and scapegoat. It was not unusual for him to order me out of bed at six in the morning to make him some pancakes—because he had been up all night studying, he said. He also regularly forced me to clean his room, to make his bed, and to carry up the firewood from the basement (which was one of very few household chores my parents had specifically assigned to him). I was also told to build and light the fire, to clean out the ashes from the fireplace . . . the list went on and on.

While resentful of Ivan, I was equally angry at my parents for allowing him to treat me in such a way. They simply did not care. Perhaps they felt that young men were entitled to be waited upon—and because there were no longer any household servants under communism, I was the only viable alternative.

There were some very difficult situations that developed between us during these years, many of which developed out of his very active social life. While Ivan's medical studies at Comenius University kept him busy, he had girlfriends, went to parties, and enjoyed late nights out with his friends. He was twenty-two, and while living in France he had largely been unsupervised, spending many evenings out at cafés and *guinguettes*. He saw no reason to change his habits just because he had returned to Bratislava. My parents felt otherwise, however, insisting that he focus on his studies. Yet when my father set curfews, Ivan simply ignored them.

Eventually my father began locking Ivan out if he came home after ten p.m.: he would turn the key on the inside lock of the front door, leaving Ivan no alternative but to ring the doorbell, awaken the household, and face my father's wrath. But after several such confrontations, Ivan came up with a plan: he alternately cajoled and menaced me into removing the key from the locked door after my parents went to bed, essentially leaving the house's front door open to anyone who might try the doorknob. The arrangement worked well a few times, but then my parents figured out what was happening, and as a result, I was given a very severe beating—since I had basically left our home open to burglary.

After that, my father locked the door and took the key to bed with him. But Ivan then persuaded me to unlock the ground-floor bathroom window just before I went to bed, an arrangement that allowed him to crawl through it whenever he came home. I did so, and it worked—but only once or twice, after which my father realized what Ivan had done. Once again, I was punished, and the beating I received amused Ivan to no end.

After a certain point, Ivan's intimidation tactics no longer worked on me. I didn't want any more beatings. Ivan would threaten me, but his threats were so unreasonable that I refused to take them seriously. At this point he changed his approach and started making promises, saying things like "Bring up the firewood and I'll take you to the movies," or "Clean my room and I'll buy you some chocolate." But he never kept the promises, instead simply laughing at me for having believed him. So that was my experience of my older brother: a person who, for whatever reason, thought of me only as a fool to be manipulated and used.

Ivan's return to us in the summer of 1950 coincided with the departure of our last household helper. Katka had left us to marry in 1948, after which several live-out cleaning women had come and gone, none of them staying long. The Communists were now in control, and Communists did not believe in housekeepers. Women who had once been domestics were instead encouraged to take factory jobs, which the Communists insisted was far better and far more dignified work. Perhaps it was. At any rate, in the new, classless society, we were all to clean our own homes.

And yet of course men did not do such work, so it all fell instead to the women. Scrubbing floors, laundering, ironing, marketing, and cooking were all traditionally the duties of women, not men. Neither Ivan nor my father would ever have thought of helping with any of these tasks. Nor would they have looked after five-year-old Pavol, for men did not babysit. As a result, my days were suddenly very busy—not only with school, homework, German lessons, and piano practice, but also with cleaning, shopping, laundry, ironing, cooking, and (of course) tending Pavol.

Perhaps the most challenging chore I faced was the laundry, for in those days there were no washing machines. Today, thanks to such appliances—as well as clothes dryers, highly effective detergents, and so-called miracle fabrics—laundry isn't so difficult to do. But we had none of these things in Bratislava in the 1950s. Women needed to boil water and soap, add the clothes, and then scrub each item by hand. To facilitate this process, our basement was equipped with a huge copper bucket (it was built into the furnace) and three wooden troughs. I would first boil the water with the soap, then add the washing, then stir it vigorously with a paddle. After that I would retrieve each item individually, scrubbing it by hand in the first of the water-filled wooden troughs, using a washboard to aid in the scrubbing. I then used the next tub and washboard to rinse out the soap, and then gave it a final rinse in the third. Each piece then went through the hand-cranked mangle to squeeze out the excess water. When all the items had gone through the mangle, I would carry the basket of sodden laundry up to the attic or out to the garden, there to hang the clothes on a clothesline to dry. Hours later, of course, I would take it all down, fold it, and iron whatever required ironing.

In the years before communism, Katka would spend the day doing laundry, or else we would hire in a laundress to do this grueling work; but after 1949 all the laundresses disappeared. Instead, I did our family's laundry in this way every week from 1950 until just before I left Bratislava in 1964—at first, assisting my mother, but then, when she became too ill to help, doing it all myself. Ironically, 1964 was the year the city's first laundromat opened—but of course our family would never have taken our things there, for the new laundromat was far too expensive for the average household to afford.

I was challenged by the housecleaning too. All the major tasks needed to be done weekly. Dusting took a good deal of time, for we heated our home with wood, and so there was always wood ash in the air, as well as the soot that was endemic to city life in the days before coal was replaced by clean energy. But we were luckier than most, for we had an excellent vacuum cleaner that my father had purchased before the war, and we used it all the way through the 1950s into the 1960s. After vacuuming our carpets and floors, I would mop. Twice yearly my father and I would take all the carpets outside and beat them free of dirt; this was the one household chore in which he readily engaged. In the winter, he and I would lay them out on the snow for a few hours—the freezing temperatures killed off any carpet beetles or moths. Similarly, four times a year I would wash each window using a rag soaked in vinegar, then dry it using old newspaper. Of course our family's one bathroom needed to be scoured regularly. The kitchen was cleaned after every use and received its customary deep-cleaning (by me) every Saturday afternoon.

Shopping also took up many hours, for there were no supermarkets in Bratislava and everything was rationed, including food. Each family received a certain number of points, and the points were deducted from a booklet as one went around to the butcher, the greengrocer, the dairy, and so forth. (After 1953, that rationing system was abolished, but food, fuel, and clothing shortages persisted.) One needed to stand in line at each small shop to gain entry to it, not knowing what might be available within. The ration points were never sufficient for feeding the family, though, so one needed to purchase on the black market as well, even though doing so was illegal and expensive. There really was no alternative: either you bought from the black market or you starved. If we had maintained a connection to our family farm, we might have supplemented our meager portion with fresh eggs, chickens, rabbits, and produce. But our family land had been taken away, and our little garden in town was small, shady, and north facing—completely unsuitable, in other words, for growing vegetables. Keeping chickens or rabbits was illegal within the city limits, so we couldn't do that, either. However, we did have two cherry trees, an apricot tree, a pear tree, and a walnut tree, and we kept a few herbs in pots, which meant that during the warmer months we had a little variety in our diet.

Keeping food fresh was a great challenge, for few people I knew had a refrigerator. (I would purchase our first refrigerator only in 1963, soon after I married Jan, and I sold my beloved piano in order to do so.) Instead we used an unfinished area of our basement as a root cellar for the vegetables that made up the bulk of our diet: beets, onions, potatoes, and cabbage. With no refrigeration food spoils quickly, especially in the heat of the summer; as a result, all meals were made daily. Fresh fruits, vegetables, and salad greens were available only in season, and eggs, cheese, and dairy products were expensive and difficult to obtain, so we ate very simply. Coffee and tea were likewise only for special occasions.

I helped my mother with cooking all through my childhood and started taking charge of the kitchen at the age of fifteen, after she became too unwell to manage. The food I prepared was mostly dried beans and pulses, cabbage, onions, and sauerkraut. Pasta was not sold commercially, so I made noodles and dumplings from scratch. Pork was available intermittently; cured pork shoulder and pork sausages were the cuts most readily available. When we had money I would try to find a chicken or a duck for our Saturday dinner. Mostly, though, we ate soups. *Székely gulyás* (Hungarian sauerkraut goulash with cured pork) was a family favorite. *Töltött paprika* (Hungarian stuffed peppers) was another regular meal—and oddly enough, a dish that Jan and I enjoy to this day. *Palacinky*, crepes stuffed with jam or farmer cheese, were a special treat, as was *kaiserschmarn*, a scrambled pancake served with plum compote—these were meatless supper dishes traditionally served on Fridays. If today I am an able cook with proficiency (I'm not a good cook, only an able one), it is because I cooked such meals daily for years.

I was also Pavol's de facto babysitter, fetching him from school and keeping him entertained from then until bedtime. From the time he was born, in 1945, I had been expected to look after Pavol as if he were my own child, and because of that, I was increasingly cut off from my own afterschool playtime, athletic activities, and the company of friends. Instead I was expected to take Pavol for a walk—and with nothing to say to him, I didn't much enjoy it. As a teenager I acutely felt the injustice of being made his caretaker—especially when Pavol, who resented me equally, threw one of his many tantrums. I was invariably blamed for this bad behavior: in my parents' way of thinking, if I had been taking *proper* care of Pavol, he wouldn't have thrown the tantrum. Likewise, if Pavol broke something (which he did constantly), the fault was mine—I hadn't minded him properly, therefore I was to be punished. Such punishments and scoldings seemed to take place every few days. After one particularly harsh punishment, I began to fantasize about leaving Bratislava forever, to live on the moon—a fantasy that would evolve into an idée fixe as I passed from adolescent to young adult. I wanted so much to go somewhere—*anyplace*—where at long last my life would be my own.

I was under a lot of pressure as I entered my teen years, and I was often unhappy, but good things were happening too. Even though my mother and aunts had always despaired of my appearance—saying I was far too tall, skinny, and homely to find a husband—I now began to fill out and grow pretty. Boys began giving me looks. Even men in the street would sometimes whistle or make comments. I was tall for my years—approximately five feet eight inches—so I suppose I stood out. Looking back at the few photos I have, I see that I was tall, slender, and athletic, with a fine if pale complexion. My blue eyes and ash blond hair were nothing extraordinary, but my face had a classic (if melancholy) expression. Seeing that I was becoming almost beautiful, my aunts now began to give me little gifts: ribbons, a blouse, that sort of thing. And with their encouragement, I began to take an interest in fashion.

Dressing nicely and looking good was in fact a family tradition. Ivan, of course, was the best looking of all of us, and he knew it, and he always dressed as finely as possible. But my father, too, had always made a point of dressing well, first as a young military officer, and later as a civil servant. Even after the Communists deprived him of a job and an income, he had been able to keep up his appearance thanks to his sister Philomena. Although her husband had built up his business during the war by creating dashing uniforms for the Slovak nationalists and Nazis, he found an entirely new set of clients after 1948: top Communist officials and military men, all of them wanting the best possible uniforms, exquisitely tailored and made of the finest materials. Whether fascist or Communist, these top party members and officers all wanted to dress impeccably—and as a result, by the early 1950s Latkóczy's shop had grown so much that he employed about fifteen workers.

Philomena was my godmother, and with her husband's newfound affluence, she was able to increase her generosity toward me: along with her daughters' usual hand-me-downs she would now send home with my father a few new pairs of underwear or stockings. New clothes were a rarity in Bratislava, so I was delighted.

As my looks improved, my father and Ivan began treating me with a bit more respect—Ivan especially, for he tended to judge others on their looks. But not all the attention I received was flattering. Men on the streets routinely gave me rude whistles or catcalls or else whispered obscenities when I walked by. Whenever I was on a crowded bus or tram, some man would invariably pinch me or rub up against me—this sort of low-grade physical harassment was something women had to endure back then, in a way no woman would ever tolerate now.

The first man to attempt to force himself on me was my piano instructor. The day it happened neither of my parents was home, and while I played a piano exercise for the teacher, he slipped his hand under my skirt. I jumped up and told him to leave. I later found out from my friends that he had made similar attempts on them.

A man on our street, meanwhile, repeatedly attempted to lure me into his automobile. I knew it would be useless to tell either of my parents about him: my mother would only have blamed me; my father wouldn't have cared. So I simply avoided the man and his auto, detouring home daily through a back alley. I had to take this detour for several years.

Around the fall of 1952 my mother began to feel extremely unwell. I knew that she had not been well for some time, since she had been struggling with housework and other chores that in the days before the war had been easy for her. But in those days one didn't go to a hospital or see a doctor unless something was very wrong, because hospitals were considered places of death and doctors were expensive. So she consulted a doctor only when the pain became unbearable. She saw him on the day before Christmas Eve, and the next day he diagnosed her as being in an advanced stage of illness—but at that point he would not name the illness, for in those days (at least in Czechoslovakia) people were not immediately told such things, particularly if the illness was grave. On some level, we all intuited that she was very sick, and probably dying. But because we were not told the diagnosis, we were unable to discuss it openly, and we all just told her we hoped the pain would go away soon, even as we knew it would not.

That Christmas Eve of 1952 was the worst of my life. None of us felt at all like celebrating, but at the same time, we didn't want to disappoint or scare my mother by disrupting our usual routine. Although I was only sixteen, I did my best to decorate the house and prepare the Christmas dinner.

In Slovakia (as well as in some of its neighbors) Christmas dinner is a four-course meal beginning with a soup of sauerkraut flavored with smoked meats, sausages, and dried mushrooms. Then comes the Slovakian equivalent of potato gnocchi, sprinkled with poppy seeds and drizzled with honey—both of which are said to bring good fortune. The main dish, a Christmas specialty, is fried carp (which nobody much likes, because its flesh has a muddy taste and many little bones) accompanied by a big potato salad. The dessert, too, is traditional: wafers drizzled with honey for good luck. Other bonbons and Christmas cookies usually follow.

Needless to say a feast of this sort requires a good deal of shopping and cooking. The serving of the meal is also rather complicated. In previous years my mother and I had only just managed it by working together as a team. Now, however, all the duties fell to me.

It was a difficult evening. The meal was not a great success, but nobody seemed to taste it or care. When it ended, the family went and sat by the Christmas tree while I cleared away the dishes and began the washing up. When I rejoined the family for the giving of the gifts, I saw that Ivan had already been given his present, and Pavol too. I looked for mine but found nothing. My mother shook her head and said she hadn't bought me one. While I knew she was ill and depressed, I don't think I'd ever felt so unloved.

A month later, in late January, my mother went to the hospital for a double mastectomy accompanied by radiation. The radiation burned her terribly, and she was sent home in great pain with wounds that would not heal. All that winter we thought my mother had only a few weeks to live—but in fact she would last two and a half more years, becoming more and more helpless with each passing month. She also became less and less like the strong, capable person I'd always respected and feared. There was no good palliative medicine available for her, only drugs that made her groggy, and the only ongoing therapy she received was radiation, which had gruesome side effects. The cancer eventually spread into her joints and spine, making even the smallest movements tremendously painful for her. The only way to minimize the pain was for her to keep to her bed. The pain pills the doctor gave her made her groggy and incoherent, so she avoided taking them.

As her illness progressed, my mother began spending more and more time at the hospital—first a few days per month, and then for weeks per month. Those first months we looked forward to her return, for we knew she would be far more comfortable at home than on the cancer ward. But as her condition worsened, she needed round-the-clock care. At that time in Czechoslovakia there was no such thing as a home-health-care aide or private nurse; rather, such work fell to family—which is to say, to me, with help from my maternal aunts.

During these months, when my mother was in the hospital for

treatment, I would pick up Pavol after school and bring him to the hospital to visit her. Then I would go home and make dinner for my father and brothers, eat with them, wash the dishes, and put Pavol to bed. I tried to make sure my mother was being treated well, but the staff was overworked and largely indifferent to her needs.

Due to her illness, or perhaps because of the radiation treatments, my mother's appearance changed dramatically. Her skin became blotchy and dry, her face pale and bloated, and even her facial expression was altered by her pain. I tried not to distress her and did my best to hide my emotions, but her appearance was so shocking that I could barely conceal my distress. Apart from telling her about my day, I hadn't much to talk to her about, and I could do nothing to ease her pain. After saying good night I would go to my room and do my homework. It was around this time, I remember, that I first said to myself, "I'm leaving this place as soon as I can leave"—there was simply too much sadness, life felt unbearable.

Of course, everyone in our family was suffering. My father, never very talkative, became tremendously withdrawn. Ivan avoided coming home except for meals. But I think that Pavol suffered most. He was doing poorly in his third-grade class, and was so angry and disruptive that he was often punished. I was the only available family member to go to the school for the parent-teacher meetings about him. When his teachers threatened disciplinary action, I explained about our mother being so ill and promised to do what I could to get Pavol to behave.

Being young, I also tried to find some fun in life. Two or three afternoons a week my friends would get together to play basketball, and they begged me to join them. I loved playing basketball, and knew it would be such a relief to get away from my mother's sickroom and into the fresh air! But I could go to the playground only if I brought Pavol, and he soon got into mischief by shouting and distracting the players. After a few such incidents, the coach took me aside and told me that I must take him home—in other words, that I could not play, I had to leave. It was a very sad moment for me, but hardly surprising; looking after Pavol had taken up so much of my life already.

Around this time I became anorexic. In those days there was no psychiatry, no understanding of an eating disorder. My aunts simply admonished me to eat more. I couldn't explain to them that even *attempting* to swallow food made me feel terribly sick. Self-starvation, painful as it was, put me into a state of dizziness and disconnection that often seemed preferable to quotidian reality. My stomach hurt terribly—so badly I needed to lie down. And in fact that stomach trouble has remained with me all my life, reappearing in moments of great stress.

I had another great disappointment around this time. As a top science student, I had always expected I would go to medical school. My mother had encouraged me in this direction, and since I had a natural aptitude for math and a lifelong interest in science, it seemed only natural that I would succeed. But then one day I was informed that I would not be allowed to take the courses preparing students for medical studies. When I asked why, no one could give me a reason. At home my father surmised it was because our family had been blacklisted. Others, however, seemed to think that only one student per family was now allowed to study medicine at Comenius University—and since Ivan was already there, the family quota had been filled. Still others informed me that you needed to either pay a bribe or else have connections within the Communist Party to study medicine—and of course neither option was possible for us. Whatever the reason, I was denied access to the science program and instead placed into the history program—which was devastating to me, not only because it canceled all my future plans and took me away from my favorite studies, but also because it separated me from all my friends.

A few weeks into the history program I was told to pick a specialty, and for some reason I chose art history. It was not a very popular field of study—understandably so, for there were few career opportunities for art historians in Bratislava. (The great art treasures once housed in Bratislava Castle under Empress Maria Theresa had long since been removed to what is now Vienna's Albertina Museum, taken there by Albert Casimir, Duke of Teschen, in 1781.) Since the formation of the Czechoslovak Republic after World War I, Prague had been the nation's artistic and cultural capital; although Bratislava had a city museum, its holdings were mostly in archaeological excavations and objects relating to municipal history. The city's one art museum, the Slovak National Gallery, was founded only in 1948, and it held few works of artistic significance. In fact from 1949 onward its collecting focus had been specifically on Slovak national art by state-approved artists—in other words, locally produced Communist-themed visual propaganda.

Why, then, had I taken up art history? I suppose my decision came partly out of a love of history and culture, and partly out of the love of beauty that my aunt Eržika had awakened in me. Partly, too, it came out of a desire for an academic career, hopefully not in Bratislava. After all, scholarship ran in my family: both my parents had built careers in education, and so had Eržika and her late husband. I enjoyed learning, researching, and sharing knowledge with others. Since I had already been denied the life I wanted—a life in science and medicine—a teaching career in the field of art history seemed a reasonable second choice.

The first problem I encountered with my new specialty was my inability to draw, for in those days all would-be art scholars were expected to draw with proficiency. But no one in my family had ever considered drawing a worthwhile skill: we all preferred music to visual art. So I began drawing late, and I struggled with it. Today, in an age of instant photography, drawing proficiency is no longer necessary to the study of art history—but in those days, one was expected to take visual notes by way of sketches, and I simply couldn't do it. As I struggled to acquire these basic skills, I developed a new respect for all those artists through history who have drawn so beautifully and well.

Luckily for me, I *did* possess another, more essential talent for a would-be art historian—languages. Slovak was my first language, and Czech was close enough to Slovak that I had no problem with it. I could speak a bit of Polish too, since it is related to both Slovak and Czech. Thanks to our housekeeper, Katka, I had been speaking Hungarian from childhood, and I was acquainted with Latin from attending mass. Of course, I spoke Russian too: from 1949 it had been mandated in the schools, and all students had no choice but to study it intensively. French, meanwhile, had long been the traditional second language of Czechoslovakia (just as it had been in the Austrian and Russian Empires), so everyone in my immediate family knew and spoke French.

But for studying art history in Czechoslovakia, the most valuable of all languages was German—because, despite the nation's newfound "connection" to Russian language and culture, Czechoslovakia had relied on German as the lingua franca of its art history since the days of the Austrian (and later Austro-Hungarian) Empire. All official records of Czechoslovakian art holdings had been kept in German for hundreds of years. Luckily my parents had hired the aunt of my friend Líza Aichová to give me private German lessons for an hour every day after school since the end of the war. As a result, I spoke and wrote German with proficiency.

I did extremely well during my last years at school and passed my *matura* exams (the Slovakian equivalent of English A levels, the German *Abitur*, or the French *baccalauréat*) at the relatively young age of seventeen (most students did not even take them until age twenty). I was also one of very few students to be accepted at the Univerzita Karlova in Prague. Better known in the West as Charles University, Karlova was the most prestigious university in Czechoslovakia. Hardly anyone from our school was ever accepted there, and it was particularly unusual that I should have been, for I was a girl. I was the only student from my graduating class of five hundred—and in all of Bratislava—to be accepted there.

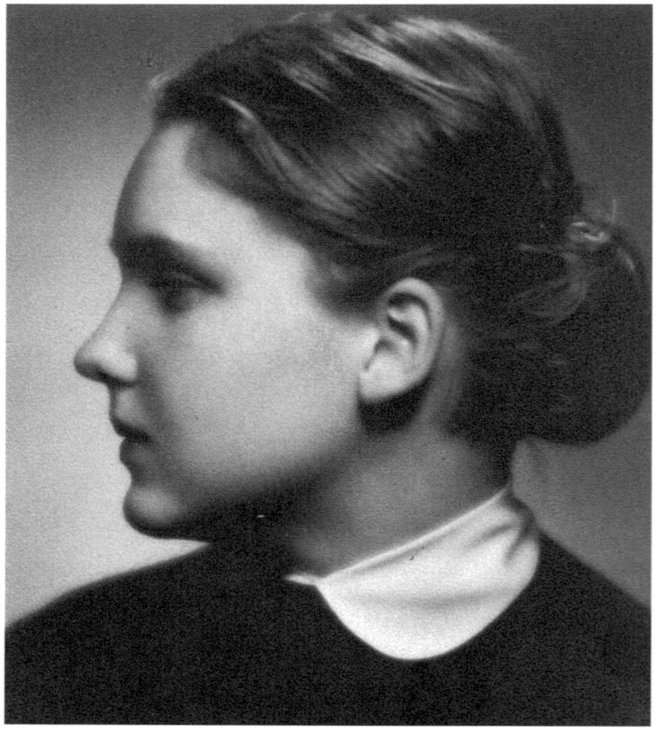

My high school graduation portrait

My acceptance at Univerzita Karlova was something that made my whole family very happy, and for that I will always be grateful. My mother was so ill, our family so distraught, that news of my acceptance gave us all a rare cause for celebration. To my mother it was a validation of all the hard work she had put into my education, and to my father it was a consolation to know that, however badly his own career might have ended, his children's lives promised to be better. Even Ivan seemed impressed.

Happy as I was with my acceptance at the university, I was even more gratified by the thought that in distinguishing myself as a young scholar I had bestowed a great honor upon my parents.

5

Higher Education and Family Obligations

When I matriculated at Charles University in the fall of 1954, I could not have been more excited, for going to Prague was itself an adventure. Even in those dark days of communism, the city was indescribably beautiful. I was now officially enrolled at one the most distinguished centers of learning in all Europe, and as a result I would *reside* in Prague's ancient center, attending a university dating back six hundred years. It made me tremendously happy. Taking my advanced degree in art history would require five years of study; within my first month I decided my specialty would be in late medieval art.

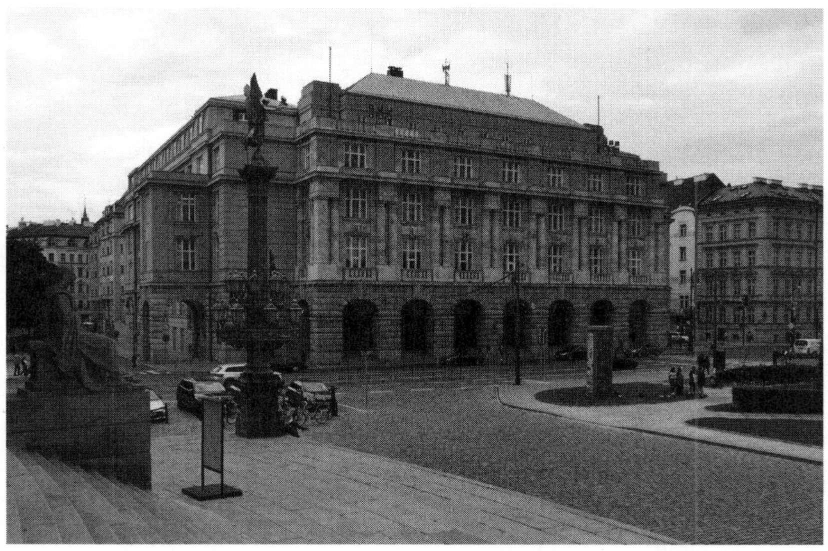

Charles University in Prague

Mostly, though, I loved my independence. For the first time in my life, I was completely free of my family and all domestic obligations: no cooking, no housework, no babysitting. My time was my own, and I was free to enjoy the company of new friends. My fellow students at Charles University were all so excited about learning: history, philosophy, psychology, and languages were all available for study. Despite being rather shy, I quickly found myself meeting many wonderful people my own age.

No sooner had I settled into my studies, however, than I began receiving letters from my father telling me to return. At first it seemed hardly possible, for we had discussed my educational plans at length before I left, and by mutual agreement, I was to remain in Prague until I received my degree. My father now wrote that while he had thought he would be able to manage on his own, he could not. He had no housekeeping skills, and neither did Ivan or Pavol, and there was no one to help with my mother, who needed assistance at home and in the hospital.

I resisted these entreaties for as long as I could, but during my second semester my father demanded I return immediately, and I had no choice but to withdraw at the end of the semester. I packed up all my belongings, said goodbye to my new friends, and arranged with the university's registrar to continue my studies at Comenius University in Bratislava. If all went well, I was told, I would be able to complete my university degree (the Czechoslovakian equivalent of a master of fine arts) in art history there.

The year 1956 was the most difficult one of my life. My academic future was entirely on hold as I took care of my dying mother. It was expected, in those days, that family members look after the sick, both at the hospital and at home; nurses were few and those who worked in the hospitals were concerned primarily with medical and administrative duties, not with giving sponge baths, disinfecting wounds, changing dressings, or emptying bedpans. Aunt Ilonka came and helped me, and to be honest she was a far better nurse than I, for she had previous experience in looking after the bedridden and terminally ill. I was emotionally unprepared for what I was doing, overwhelmed at the sight of my mother's near skeletal condition, and stricken by the awareness of her impending death.

I wish I had been more able to speak openly with my mother during those last months, for she had expressed so much anger toward me throughout my life, particularly during the difficult years following the war, that I would very much have liked to make peace with her, and to assure her of my love for her even as I sought reassurance of her love for me. But Ivan, who was by then doing his residency at the hospital, had been able to obtain opioid injections for her that she would not otherwise have been able to obtain, and he was even able to arrange that she get these strong injections at home. They were a godsend, of course; the lasting radiation burns on her chest and the spread of the cancer into her bones had left her in extraordinary pain. But as a side effect, she was rarely capable of lucid thought. All those important end-of-life discussions we might have had went unspoken, and our feelings toward each other, unexpressed and unresolved.

In the last days of June, the hospital sent my mother home for the last time. They could do no more on her behalf. My godmother, Aunt Philomena, came from Topoľčany to help us, since she knew from my father that Ilonka and I were worn out. She also wanted to look after her brother—for my father, despite his many quarrels with my mother, was completely undone by her dying.

In the early hours of July 19, 1956, I sat watch with my mother at her bedside. Her breathing slowed perceptibly, but thanks to the opiates her body did not struggle, and sometime near dawn she breathed her last.

We held a memorial service several days later, at which many of her former students and fellow teachers from the school came to pay their respects. All of them spoke so glowingly about my mother—not only about how important she had been to the running of the school, but also how she had encouraged them to believe in the power of education and how she had urged so many of them to go on to university. It was beautiful to discover all the good my mother had done, and how important she had been to so many. Suddenly I was proud of her and wanted to be like her.

In the days that followed, my mother's three sisters and half sister came to visit our home, bringing food and helping with the housekeeping, for the daily rituals of cleaning had been much neglected during those last, difficult months. By sharing our grief as well as our chores, we helped one another through the worst. Toward the end of their stay, my father and I divided up my mother's few possessions—her clothing, her shoes, some pieces of jewelry—giving most of it to her sisters. I was in a strange sort of daze: exhausted, numb, detached. I had no strong sense of what I would do next, apart from returning to my studies.

Six weeks later, in early September, Ivan left on a vacation to Egypt, having purchased a berth on a state-run tourist ship departing from Split, Yugoslavia, for a closely supervised guided tour of the ancient Egyptian sites. But sometime after boarding the ship he was discovered to be missing. The first we heard about his disappearance was from a neighbor who had been on the same tour. According to the neighbor, Ivan had vanished while the ship was at sea. Some thought he might have disembarked when it stopped in Italy to refuel, while others thought he had fallen or jumped overboard. Could it be suicide? Nobody knew.

Two or three weeks after his disappearance, an officer from the Štátna Bezpečnosť came to our door and ordered me to the police headquarters for an interview. I was placed in a room where several ŠtB policemen spoke with me in turn, each one asking very specific questions about my brother and the rest of our family. I had the very strong feeling that they were trying to catch me in a lie. They wanted to know everything I knew about Ivan, his travel plans, and his disappearance. They also wanted to know what I had heard from him since he disappeared. I told them I knew absolutely nothing—which was the truth, because Ivan had never told me about the Egypt vacation, and had never so much as hinted that he might someday attempt an escape to the West.

When pressed for more, I reminded the police that Ivan was eight years older than I, that he had gone to school in France for four years during my childhood, and that we had never been close. The policemen then asked for the names of my extended family. I explained I wasn't a social person, that I wasn't close to any of my relatives, and that most of my days were taken up with housework, attending university, and looking after my motherless little brother. The news that I was attending Comenius University aroused some suspicion in the officers, but only until I told them that I was studying art history. After two hours of intensive questioning, they dismissed me with a warning me not to leave my home.

The police summoned me to two more long interrogations in the weeks that followed, and each time several different officers questioned me. But they learned very little about Ivan from me, for the simple reason that I knew very little about him. I didn't know any of his friends, and I hadn't heard from him since his disappearance.

Still, the ŠtB was not about to let our family get away without penalty. While we had nothing of value that they could take from us, they menaced us. At the end of the first interrogation, the officer told me that our entire family was going to be closely watched. By the third interview, the police knew that I was working part-time at a menial job at the Bratislava City Museum. They instructed my employer to fire me. I was now out of a job and would not have another one anytime soon, because anyone applying for state employment in Bratislava first had to be approved by the ŠtB. Time and again for the next three years I would apply for a job, get the position, and then three weeks later I would be let go. In each instance the ŠtB had not approved my hiring.

Knowing that we were now under constant surveillance, my father and I decided it would be best to cease communication with our extended family. We didn't want to damage their lives in the way that ours had been damaged. Only Aunt Ilonka and her much younger half sister, Leonka, insisted on maintaining contact with us; the rest agreed to distance themselves. We quietly told our friends to keep their distance too. Knowing of our troubles and knowing the ŠtB would come after anyone who supported us, nearly everyone ceased communication with us. We were not invited out and we allowed no guests in our home.

In losing my mother and my older brother that summer of 1956, our family was already facing a major readjustment. We were struggling with grief, but we were also struggling with confusion about how to get on with our lives. My mother had always been our guiding force, and Ivan had always been the family's great hope: with his success as a doctor nearly assured, my father had assumed our money worries would lessen once Ivan was established in his medical practice. Now, though, my mother was dead and my brother had vanished. My father and I had minimal income, and having been blacklisted, we had no prospects for employment. I specifically remember that October, on my birthday, sitting alone in our house, thinking about Ivan and my mother, and suddenly realizing how very similar I was to my mother, and how it was clearly my duty to look after Pavol and my father, just as she had once done.

Without the possibility of a real job, I came to rely on freelance work, making a little money each week by typing term papers for university students, or cleaning house, or else babysitting. My father continued with his low-paying employment at the library despite being lost in depression; occasionally he would also help out at a pharmacy owned by a friend. Pavol, who was now eleven, began arguing a lot with my father. Unlike me, he had no emotional support from his schoolteachers, having alienated most of them through years of disruptive behavior. When I look back on my life during the period, I wonder how any of us managed. There was never much food, no money to spare, and nothing in our future. Even our ability to travel around

Bratislava was extremely limited—Pavol and I shared an old bicycle, and my father, who did not bicycle, simply walked.

Luckily the university was just a twenty-minute walk from my home. Though by no means as important or historic as Charles University, Comenius (which had been founded relatively recently, in 1919) was considered Slovakia's leading institution of higher education. While primarily a technical and scientific university, it did have a reputable college of humanities and social sciences. While I missed being in Prague, I could at least still work toward my degree. Even though our family had been blacklisted, I was still free to study and learn.

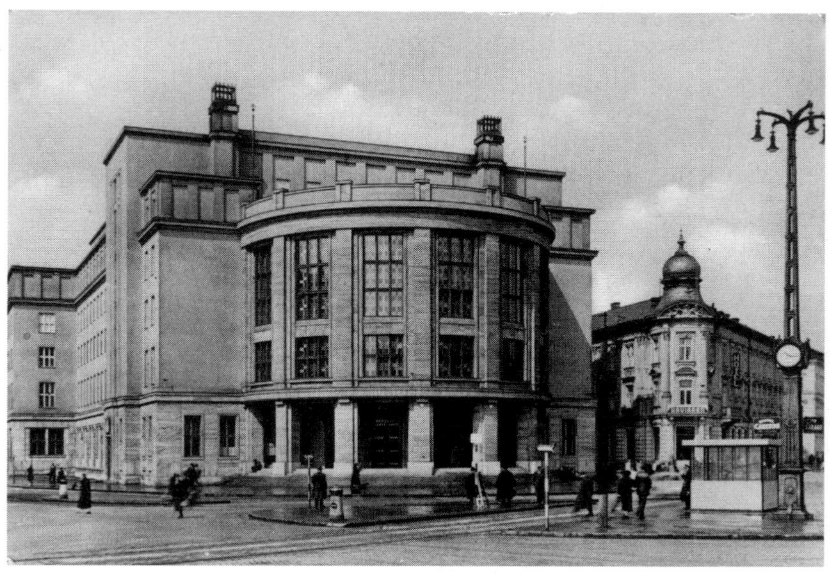

Comenius University in Bratislava

About a year after Ivan's disappearance, in late 1957, I received a letter with a French postmark. It was from Ivan. He apologized for his silence, then explained that after jumping ship in Bari, he had made his way from Italy to France; he was living in Paris while awaiting a visa to immigrate to the United States. Although he had been eligible to apply for French citizenship thanks to his French *baccalauréat* and his medical degree, he hadn't wanted to do so, because the French government would have immediately conscripted him for military service in Southeast Asia—and he was much more interested in launching a profitable medical practice than in tending wounded soldiers. Unfortunately, getting his U.S. visa was taking him longer than expected, because the Russians had marched into Hungary in 1956, with the result that the American immigration authorities were prioritizing Hungarians over Czechoslovakians for visas.

We were all glad to know that Ivan was alive, safe, in good health, and hopefully on his way to the United States. My secret hope was that, in time, he would be able to offer my father some kind of financial support, for our home was badly in need of it. In the months that followed, several more letters from Ivan arrived, and even a few small care packages—these were always sent to me, not to my father, to escape the notice of ŠtB.

My life was changing in other ways too. During the summer of 1956, I had been introduced to a young man who subsequently took an interest in me. Ladislav Mokrý had come to our home to meet my father when he arrived at Comenius University to study and teach musicology, for his father and mine had been childhood friends. Ladislav had grown up in Topoľčany. His father was now a prosperous physician there, and was making good money even under Communist rule. Apparently, they had a very nice home.

Four years my senior, Ladislav was relatively good-looking, and he was also both intelligent and ambitious. Most important to me, he was musical, for I had been studying piano for years and found joy in classical music. Discovering that we had some other interests in common,

I started dating Ladislav informally. I wasn't romantically inclined at first; I was still traumatized and grieving. But our seeing each other continued for about a year, and in the summer of 1957, he asked me to marry him.

My father never encouraged the match—I think he would have preferred that I remain his unmarried housekeeper—but since Ladislav came from a prosperous family, had good prospects at the university, and was the son of an old friend, he could hardly object. As for myself, I didn't know that I wanted Ladislav for a husband, only that I admired his talent. At this point my experience of men was very limited, and I was still so overwhelmed by the loss of my mother and the derailment of my educational plans that romance was the last thing on my mind. But in those days most people married young. Many of my high school friends were already raising children. Feeling that time was passing and that I needed a change, I decided to accept. My father then surprised me by saying since Ladislav was teaching at Comenius University, he would live with us. It was a convenient arrangement for my father, since it ensured that I would continue to cook and keep house for him, even as Ladislav and I started out our married life.

Looking back on those years, I have often wondered why I accepted Ladislav. I didn't love him. But being appreciated was something new to me. Certainly I desired more stability in my life, both financial and emotional. Also, to put it plainly, I was so tremendously lonely and sad. Had she been alive, my mother might have given me some good strong advice on whom to marry and why—but she was gone, and I had only my father to turn to, and he had nothing to say to me on the matter. My aunts, meanwhile, had always urged me to find myself a husband as soon as possible, assuring me that no woman would ever be secure socially without one. And I think Ladislav's love of music appealed to me too, because it suggested he had a sensitive and artistic side. Well educated, multilingual, and a fine musicologist, he did seem to have a promising future ahead of him.

We were married on October 19, 1957. Within three weeks, however, I realized I'd made a terrible mistake. Ladislav was not at all the romantic young artist I expected him to be. Rather, starting a few days after the wedding, he ceased treating me as a friend and intellectual equal, and regarded me instead as a combination of cook, laundress, housekeeper and personal secretary. To make matters worse, he seemed entirely focused upon making a career for himself in arts administration—and indeed, he would eventually rise to become the director of the entire Slovak Philharmonic, a position he held for twenty-four years, in large part because of his wholehearted and unquestioning embrace of Communist ideology. But, once I realized that his idea of a wife was someone who waited on him hand and foot, my response was not one of subservience. On the contrary, I was angry: having spent so many years being ordered about by my father and older brother, I wasn't going to be dominated by my husband. Instead I fought back, and in response Ladislav became bitter, vindictive, and temperamental. It was then that I knew, with all the bodily certainty of a person fleeing a burning building, that I needed to exit this marriage *immediately*. I did not want this man in my home and I certainly did not want him for a husband.

My father was an old-fashioned man whose own marriage had been far from perfect, and as I soon learned, he took no interest in my complaints. He didn't mind having Ladislav at the dinner table with us every evening, and he didn't want our household situation to change. Perhaps Ladislav was paying him rent—I don't really know; my father would never discuss money with me. At any rate, because of the way he had divided up our living quarters and the way he now spent his days, my father rarely saw Ladislav or me, except when I was serving him his dinner. So he expressed no support for my sudden change of heart, and declined to side with me over ending the marriage.

Although it was only our third week as man and wife, I told Ladislav I was filing for a divorce and that he needed to move out. To my surprise, Ladislav refused—he wasn't happy either, he said, but he needed a wife and a place to live. Our marriage, he said, entitled him to residence in our family's home: it was now his home too, and he was going to stay put.

With no way of ejecting him, and no place else for me to live—housing was extremely limited in Bratislava, and I had very little money and a graduate degree to complete—I realized I had no alternative but to stay. So I moved out of my childhood bedroom, the room Ladislav and I shared, and into the tiny maid's room down the hall. It was awkward, but not impossible: avoiding Ladislav was hardly difficult, since he spent most of his waking hours at the university. After I started the divorce proceedings, I rarely saw Ladislav at all, except at mealtimes.

Meanwhile I got on with my degree. My great mentor at Comenius was Dr. Alžbeta Güntherová-Mayerová, an extraordinary woman who is today hailed as the leading twentieth-century scholar of Slovakian art history.[1] Under her direction I wrote my candidate's paper (the equivalent of a master's thesis) on the development of pietàs in Central Europe and their relationship to Beautiful Madonnas in the first

1 In "Alžbeta Güntherová-Mayerová (1905–1973): A Life Dedicated to Monuments," Július Barczi writes: "To date, two exhibitions, several book publications, studies and articles have been dedicated to her life and work, and her contribution to Slovak culture is also commemorated by two plaques unveiled in 2005. Despite the fact that, when learning about the artistic history of Slovakia, it is almost impossible not to come into contact with the results of her research, so far there has not been a monograph dedicated to her, which would have been supported by comprehensive research in domestic and foreign archives, or a collective edition of the huge amount of texts she left behind. From time to time, however, there are attempts to partially process her contribution to the formation of [various branches of Slovakian] social science: primarily art history, [but also] museology, ethnography, and . . . monumentology": https://www.academia.edu/44329952/Al%C5%BEbeta_G%C3%BCntherov%C3%A1_Mayerov%C3%A1_1905_1973_%C5%BDivot_zasv%C3%A4ten%C3%BD_pamiatkam.

twenty years of the fifteenth century. ("Beautiful Madonnas" refers to Madonnas sculpted in the Beautiful Style, a style that had developed in Central Europe around 1375; it was characterized by elegance, delicate details, soft facial expressions, and smooth forms.)

Because Dr. Güntherová-Mayerová was so pleased with my candidate's paper, she gave me some confidential advice that had recently come down to her from the upper-level administrators of Comenius University: namely, that I should not attempt to write my final thesis on another religious subject, because doing so was going to get me into serious difficulties with Communist Party members within the university's faculty. Since I wanted to graduate from Comenius in the summer of 1959, I needed to settle quickly on a medieval thesis topic featuring a minimally religious subject—which would be no small feat, considering that nearly all medieval art is based upon Christian themes. Luckily Dr. Güntherová-Mayerová had a list of subjects that had already been preapproved by the Communist leaders at the university. One caught my eye: a study of the commercial nature of the medallions crafted during the Middle Ages and early Renaissance in Kremnica, a city in Slovakia famous for its gold and silver mines. Dr. Güntherová-Mayerová was delighted to think that I wanted to study and write about them.

Kremnica, I soon learned, had grown from a mining town to an internationally recognized center for coin production during the Middle Ages—first through its minting of florins (the coin first introduced in Florence, Italy, bearing the image of a lily flower, hence its name) and later through a coin called the Kremnica ducat, which eventually rivaled the florin throughout Central Europe. The silversmiths and goldsmiths of Kremnica also developed a large, coinlike medallion (or medal) to be worn as a bodily decoration, with the production regulated and authenticated in such a way that any such medal could be readily exchanged for money. Approximately two and a half inches in diameter, these medals often featured a loop so that they might be worn on a chain.

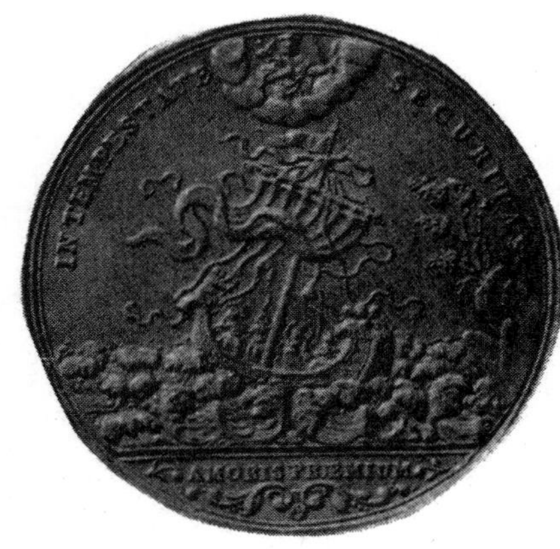

A Kremnica medallion

But much to my dismay, I now discovered that no Kremnica medals existed in Slovakian or Czech collections: with the dissolution of the Austro-Hungarian Empire, the Hungarians had seized all the medals kept in the museum in Kremnica, removing them to the Old Hungarian Collection of the Hungarian National Gallery in Budapest. All the other remaining Kremnica medals were apparently in various collections in Vienna and elsewhere in Austria—that was because the medals had been made primarily for Viennese clients. Since as a Czechoslovakian I could visit neither Hungary nor Austria—both countries were then closed to us—I was suddenly faced with the absurdity of writing my dissertation on an art form that I had never seen and might well *never* see. Instead I would need to rely on line illustrations, engravings, written descriptions, and photographic reproductions—some of which were very, very poor.

Little had yet been written about the medals, so my research would be based upon original documents. Most of those documents were in the State Archives at Kremnica Castle, with a few others in Kremnica's Museum of Coins and Metals. The question now became: How could I possibly do research there? Kremnica was 125 miles northeast of Bratislava, and the only way to get there was by a bus service that would take roughly six hours. After considering all the options, I saved up some money and in the summer of 1958, my fourth year of graduate work, I moved there for a month, renting a room within walking distance of the State Archives. Kremnica is a beautiful medieval city set in the mountains, and it was the perfect time of year to be there to enjoy the alpine climate, but I was so focused on my work that I barely noticed any of the historic old town or its idyllic, mountainous countryside.

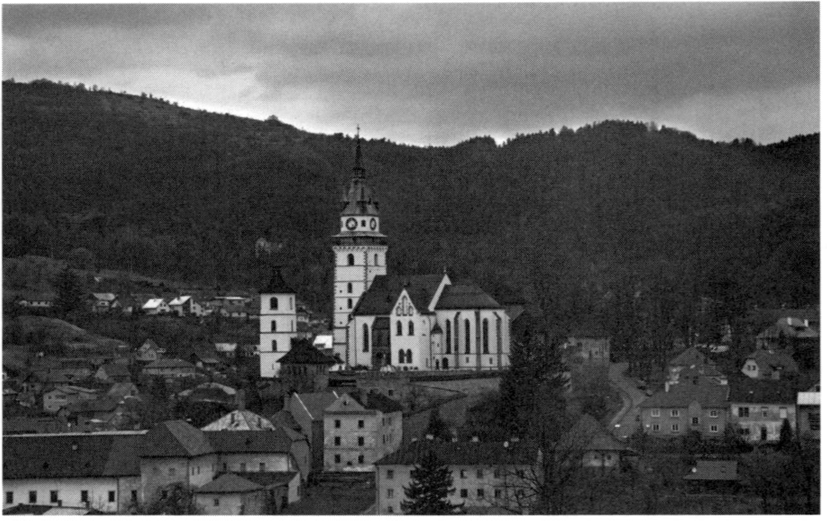

Kremnica

To write authoritatively about these medals, I needed to learn who the artisan producers were—and to my surprise, many of the best of them turned out to be the same artisans who designed coins for the mint:

> they produced these decorative medals in their free time. I also had to read through the official government correspondence regarding the medals, which mostly concerned the regulation of gold and silver usage in their manufacture. Apart from these documents, I investigated correspondence between the artisans and their clients, which consisted largely of the clients fretting about the medals' weight (that is, their monetary value), and the artisans reassuring them they would be getting their money's worth.

Reading through this correspondence (some of it four hundred years old) was unexpectedly complicated, for apart from being in German, there were various forms of German being employed—Old High German and Middle High German, as well as various dialects. I also had to contend with variant orthography, for the German alphabet was not standardized until the late nineteenth century. As it happened, most of the handwritten documents were in *Kurrent*, an old form of German-language handwriting based on late medieval cursive, and much of it in *Sütterlinschrift,* the last widely used form of *Kurrent*. But I also needed to read early printed documents composed in *Fraktur*, a typeface related to *Kurrent* and *Sütterlinschrift* but substantially different from both. And since the vocabulary and grammar of the sixteenth through eighteenth centuries was so different from contemporary German, I was constantly needing to refer to specialized dictionaries. To make matters worse, the handwriting and grammar of the artisans were often very poor.

Among the most interesting of my archival finds were a series of drawings of medals and coins dating from the sixteenth through eighteenth centuries. But again, because I was focusing upon the transactional nature of the enterprise rather than the artistic value of the medals, the bulk of the writing was focused upon history and commerce, rather than the innovative beauty of the art objects.

I received high marks for my thesis and the defense went well too. As a result, in May 1959 I was granted a graduate of art history degree from Comenius. Dr. Güntherová-Mayerová strongly encouraged me to develop the thesis into a doctoral dissertation, but warned me that before I could submit it, I would need to satisfy a three-year work requirement at a qualifying institution, after which I would also need to sit for an art history exam, a foreign-language exam, and an exam through which I demonstrated my full understanding of Marxism and Leninism. When I had passed all three, I would be free to submit the completed dissertation and (if it was approved) I would earn my candidate of sciences degree, the Czechoslovakian equivalent of a PhD.

The next few years were busy ones for me. While continuing work on my dissertation, I did various freelance jobs to make money. Simultaneously, I searched for some sort of museum work through which I might satisfy the candidate of sciences degree requirement, even though there were only a few museums in Bratislava, and all curatorial appointments were dependent upon clearance by the ŠtB and a connection of some sort to the Communist Party. On several occasions I managed to get an entry-level museum job, only to be let go within a month. No one would ever say why, but of course it was because I had been blacklisted. I tried not to become bitter or pessimistic about the situation. After all, I was young, and I had faith in myself and my abilities. I knew it was only a matter of time before I found my way to lasting employment.

After a year and a half of asking Ladislav to move out, I began to lose patience. I appealed to my father, but rather than taking my side, he surprised me by insisting quite firmly that I remain married and stop complaining. To divorce, he now said, would bring shame on the family. But as the child of an unhappy couple, I knew how toxic such unhappiness could be, and I was determined not to make the same mistakes he himself had made. I told him very firmly that divorce was no longer considered shameful or wrong: several of my friends had already divorced and had suffered no social stigmatization from it. And I reminded him that, being only twenty-two, I had no intention of throwing my life away on a man who didn't respect me or my wishes. My father refused to listen, and after the fight went on for months, he finally gave me an ultimatum: accept Ladislav as my husband or leave our home for good.

Shocked, I called my old friend Líza Aichová and told her I needed a place to stay. Líza was a musicologist and she hadn't much money, but she lived with her parents in a large apartment they had occupied since before the war. Líza's aunt had been my German tutor, and because I had known the family all my life, they very kindly invited me to come and stay with them for as long as I needed. A few hours later I packed my suitcase and left home.

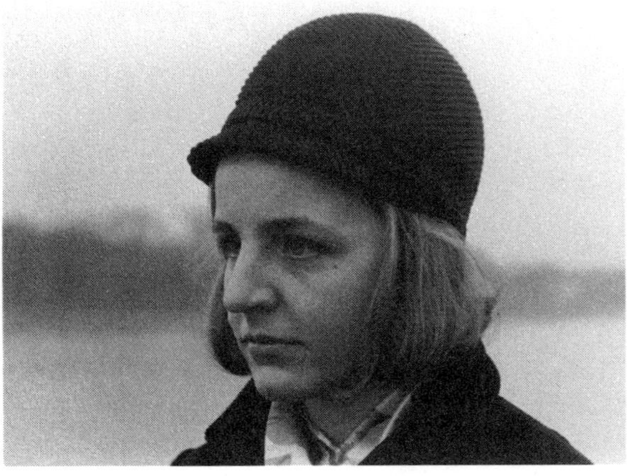

Liza Aichová

Líza and her parents would have let me stay with them indefinitely, but I did not want to inconvenience them. Líza's father was in fact very ill with late-stage tuberculosis, and possibly dying. I was there for only three or four weeks when I was given an extraordinary and unexpected opportunity: to keep house for my cousin Eva Latkóczy, who had just moved to Bratislava from Topoľčany.

6

Divorce, Museum Work, and Remarriage

Eva Latkóczy was the youngest child of my aunt Philomena and her husband, the highly successful tailor and dress designer. A year older than I, she had had recently moved to Bratislava to attend Comenius University. While perhaps a little spoiled by her doting parents, she was also extraordinarily accomplished, even brilliant: a student actress, she was earning straight As even while starring in one dramatic production after another. Popular, talented, and beautiful, she was already the talk of the town: young people all over Bratislava seemed to know her and have an opinion about her. Within months of starting at Comenius, she had become notorious for ending her wild nights out by dancing on the tables of popular cafés. Of course, as a born actress, she loved provoking attention. Whenever she went to a concert or the theater, for example, she would book a seat in the first few rows, a spot at which everyone could see her and her beautiful clothes (designed, of course, by her father) in the moments before the lights went down. Quite often she would leave dramatically at the end of the first intermission, which was similarly noticed and discussed. Having trained as a ballet dancer, she had a wonderfully expressive figure, and she carried herself beautifully.

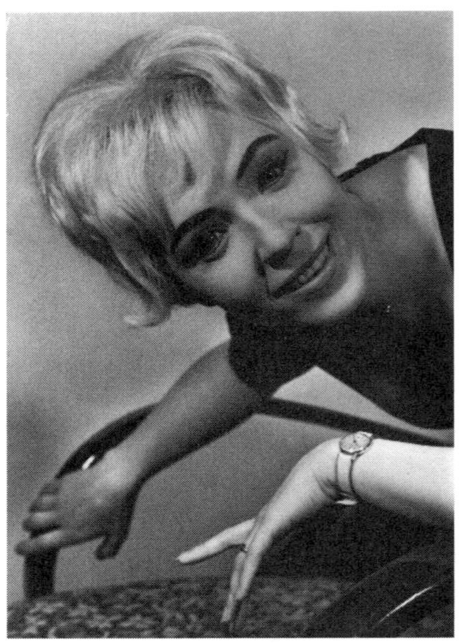

My cousin Eva Latkóczy

While most students at Comenius lived either in dormitories or at home, Eva had her own apartment—a gift from her parents, who had wanted to give her every possible advantage. Of course, as a would-be starlet, leading lady, and scholar, Eva had no time for cooking, laundry, or housekeeping—and, perhaps more important, she needed someone discreet to answer her phone, since she was having affairs or flirtations with any number of men, and did not want them running into one another. So along with my housekeeping duties, I needed to be a very diplomatic telephone answering service and social secretary for Eva, someone who could reassure each of these men that, however much my cousin would love to see him, Eva was studying, or rehearsing, or else simply "out."

Because Eva and I had known each other all our lives, we could laugh about her many adventures and intrigues, and also about the madcap life she was leading, so different from my own. We got along well; in some ways, she was the sister I never had. During all the time I lived with her, she generously shared with me her vast knowledge of all those things I knew relatively little about—clothing, hair, makeup, the theater, and (of course) men. Full of mischief, she was also forceful and ambitious, and (unlike me) she had a thorough understanding of the power of her own youth, beauty, and sexuality. Through her, I began to understand how a young woman could take charge of her destiny. And I also realized how much fun it could be simply to be young. I began to enjoy myself a little as a result, and to take questions of fashion, beauty, and romance more seriously than previously.

Of course, I spent most of my time working on my art history studies. Work on my dissertation came to a temporary halt, however, when Dr. Güntherová-Mayerová, my academic mentor, was denounced by the Communists and lost her position at Comenius University. I was now without a dissertation adviser and no other professor at Comenius was capable of advising me. Nonetheless, I was able to continue to work toward my candidate of sciences degree through a program at Charles University that granted special allowances for students working full-time and living outside of Prague. Since attending lectures there was basically impossible, my only requirement was to return to Prague periodically to take my exams.

While the examinations were not overly difficult, the only way for me to get to Prague was by train, which was expensive and took six hours. Since I needed to travel cheaply, I always took a third-class ticket on the night train, which meant sitting up all night on a bench seat and arriving in Prague exhausted. I would then walk to the university, take the exam, and immediately board another train back to Bratislava, since I couldn't afford a room in Prague for the night.

The last of my examinations were different, however: they needed to be administered orally. As a result, three distinguished art history professors traveled from Prague to Comenius University especially to give the tests. I passed all three of these viva voce exams (as mentioned earlier, the three subjects were foreign languages, Marxist-Leninist history, and art history), and was subsequently granted my candidate of sciences degree in June 1959, contingent (of course) upon the completion of my dissertation.

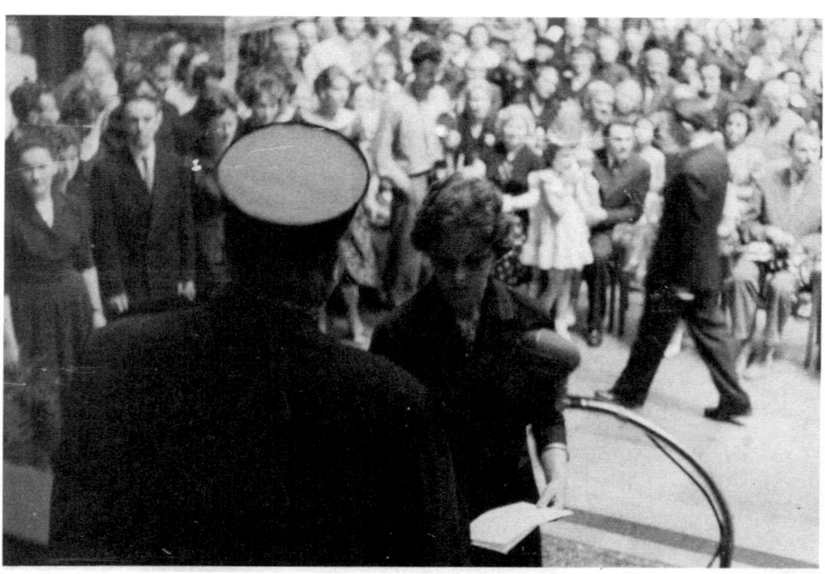

Receiving my Candidate of Sciences diploma

ČESKOSLOVENSKÁ REPUBLIKA

DIPLOM

číslo 10123

Mária MOKRÁ r. GERHÁTHOVÁ

narodený(á) 18. OKTÓBRA 1936 v IVÁNKE PRI DUNAJI

študoval(a) v rokoch 1954–1959 a ukončil(a) štátnou záverečnou skúškou na fakulte FILOZOFICKEJ

vysokej školy UNIVERZITY KOMENSKÉHO v BRATISLAVE

štúdium odboru (špecializácie) DEJINY UMENIA

Rozhodnutím štátnej skúšobnej komisie zo dňa 22. JÚNA 1959 nadobúda vysokoškolskú kvalifikáciu

PROMOVANÝ HISTORIK

dekan — rektor — predseda štátnej skúšobnej komisie

V BRATISLAVE dňa 26. JÚNA 1959 Evid. číslo: 4528/59

My diploma, granted under my married name of Mokrá

When the Communist government issued my divorce papers in April 1961, the process had taken more than three years. The official notification also made clear that Ladislav was no longer entitled to live with my father, so he moved out. After he had left, I went home and spoke to my father.

While not yet reconciled to my disobedience, he told me I was free to return home and live in my old room as long as I once again agreed to keep house, look after Pavol, and cook all our meals. I agreed, for I continued to feel a familial obligation to both of them, and anyway I had always considered my father's house my home.

But a very ugly surprise awaited me in my bedroom: I opened the door to find it had been stripped. Ladislav had taken every piece of furniture, every artwork, every book and keepsake—everything in the room was gone, including my bed. Only an old piece of carpet remained.

The things he had taken away couldn't have meant anything to Ladislav, but to me they were my whole life: things I had collected, things given to me by my mother, by my father, by my aunts, by my friends. Books, pictures, objects . . . all were gone. I was so shocked and devastated that I burst into tears.

In time, though, I came to realize that Ladislav's final act of malice was also a gift to me, in that it confirmed once and for all I had been right to divorce him. Anyone capable of doing something so hateful was surely someone one could gladly avoid for the rest of one's life—and so I did. I never saw Ladislav again. I recently learned that he died in 2000, eight years after retiring from his directorship of the Slovak Philharmonic.

With no one looking after our home, the interior had become terribly run-down. After living in Eva's elegant little apartment, I saw it with new eyes: the place was dirty, shabby, and in desperate need of painting and basic repairs. The work of bringing it back initially overwhelmed me, but in the days and weeks that followed my return, I made slow progress: I scoured the kitchen and bathroom, washed the windows, vacuumed, mopped, dusted. Eventually it once again began to resemble the home I remembered from my mother's time. While doing this work, I thought frequently of my mother, and realized how important it was that I should create for Pavol a clean, safe, and well-maintained home. Now sixteen, he had been miserable without me, and fought constantly with my father. With no one checking up on his schoolwork, his grades had suffered too.

Shortly after receiving my diploma, I had started working unofficially at an entry-level job at the Slovak National Gallery. Eva Šefčáková, my best friend, had been named the head of the museum's print department—in part due to her scholarly achievements, and in part due to her family's strong ties to the Communist Party. When

Eva was authorized to hire a part-time clerical helper to deal with an enormous backlog of cataloguing work, she immediately contacted me because she knew I was committed to making a career in the arts, and that I would work very hard. She then introduced me to Ľudmila Peterajová, the head of the paintings department, another very accomplished art historian with family ties to the Communists. Both women admitted that they were terribly overworked, for many of the Communist Party appointees to the museum were essentially no-shows, collecting paychecks but rarely reporting for work. I promised them that, should I be hired, I would work nonstop to clear their backlog. Taking me at my word, they advocated repeatedly on my behalf, and that was how I got my first lasting museum job—through sympathetic friends who were willing to take a risk on me, despite the fact that my family had been blacklisted.

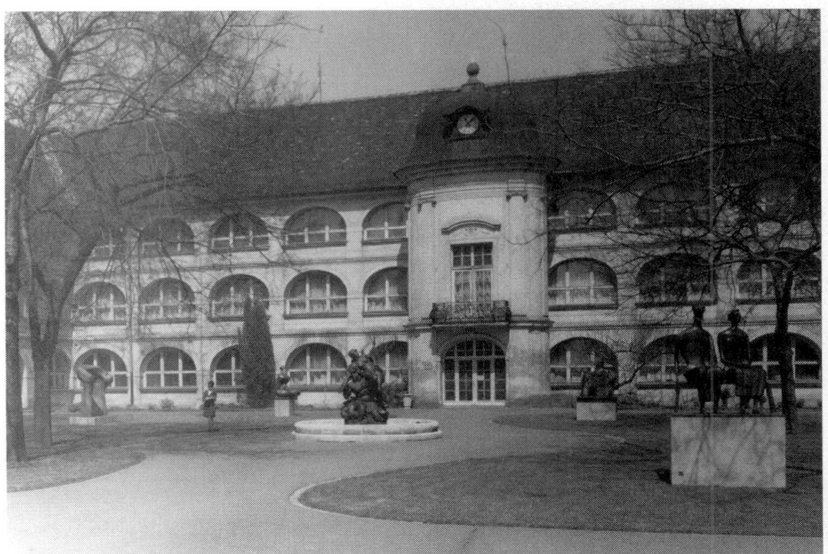

The Slovak National Gallery, Bratislava

As the months passed, I rose from entry-level clerk to curatorial assistant, spending most of my days cataloguing contemporary Slovak prints, photographs, and drawings under Eva's direction. Because of my family's history with the ŠtB, Eva and Ľudmila made sure that my family name was never submitted for review—something that was only possible because after many months of menial clerical work I was no longer considered an "outside" hire by the gallery. Nonetheless, I remained on guard, knowing that at any moment some Communist official might recognize my name and terminate my employment.

In due course I learned that only four Communist Party members were currently working within the museum—apart from Eva and Ľudmila, there was just a furniture restorer and a janitor. And because I was very careful around both, neither ever thought to denounce me. In this way, I eventually rose to the position of associate curator.

Contemporary Slovakian printmaking did not interest me much, but as a scholar and curator I did my best to keep an open mind about the art I was cataloguing. And I was soon caught up in the science of cataloguing, which involves documenting and organizing the many details pertaining to each museum acquisition. Cataloguing art objects was (and remains) a specialist activity—one related to library science, yet substantially different from it—and it appealed to my scientific interests, for it is essentially a taxonomic endeavor.

Because the museum was short staffed, I took on other curatorial activities as well: giving guided tours and lectures about the collections, writing journal articles, press releases, and wall texts, and ultimately curating "Slovak Contemporary Graphic Artists (1945–1960)," a print exhibition that ultimately traveled to Prague, where it was shown at the Hollar Gallery, the exhibition space of the Association of Czech Graphic Artists. It was an exciting time for me as a young professional.

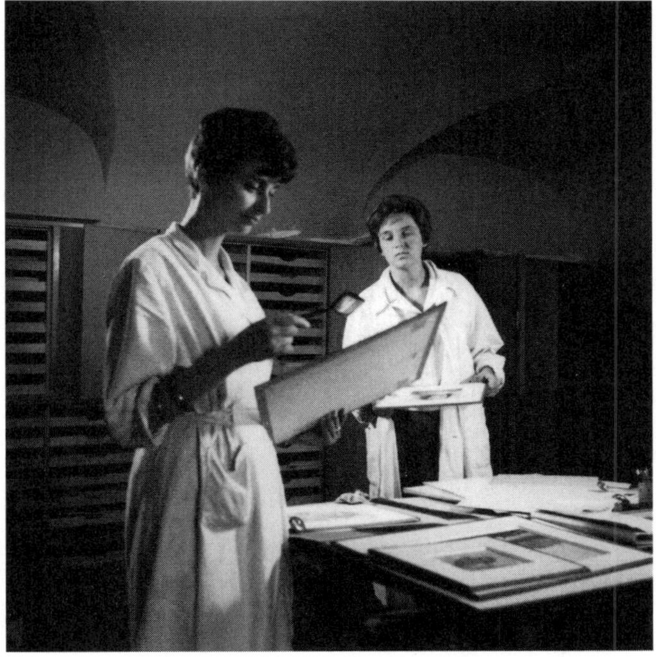

At work in the Slovak National Gallery with my friend and boss, Eva Šefčáková

An important new person entered my life the very same month that my divorce was finalized, when I was twenty-four. A friend from Comenius whom I had known since high school invited me to celebrate the Russian Orthodox Easter with dinner at her home on April 9, 1961. Nina Židovská was of Russian extraction, and she had recently married Alexander Vietor (better known by his nickname, Šaci), a Hungarian who had moved to Bratislava with his mother at the end of World War II. Šaci's best friend, Jan Vilcek, joined us that evening. I was immediately impressed by Jan—not so much because he was good-looking (though he was), or because he was highly accomplished. Rather, what struck me most was that he was so gentle and well mannered, and above all a fine conversationalist.

There were certainly many differences between us: Jan was a research scientist specializing in virology, and I was a museum curator. Jan's father was an executive in the coal business, his mother a well-established ophthalmologist, and their first language was Hungarian, whereas both my parents had held careers in education, and our primary language had always been Slovak. Also, Jan's family background was Jewish, while mine was Catholic. But we were both ambitious, well informed, multilingual, and hardworking. And (as I learned over the course of the dinner) our tastes in art, music, and even food were quite similar. Jan, who was three years older than me, shared my distaste for all Communist ideology and propaganda, and he disliked any sort of snobbery or pretense. Neither of us was the least bit interested in religion. I remember thinking as we sat enjoying Nina's delicious *pashka* that Jan Vilcek was someone I would like to meet again soon. However, doing so would not be possible, because he was just about to leave for Moscow on a scientific exchange program.

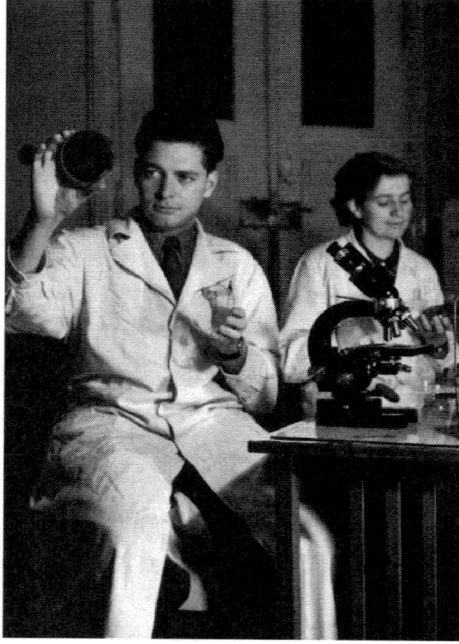

Jan Vilcek examining bacterial cultures, Comenius University School of Medicine,1955

Several months later I was helping to install a prints exhibition at the Slovak National Gallery when I heard a voice call my name. I turned to find Jan. Handsome and happy, he explained he had only just recently returned from Moscow, and had taken some time out of his workday to visit the museum—what a coincidence to run into me again! We fell easily into conversation, just as we had at Šaci and Nina's, but this time there was a certain twinkle in Jan's eye. I liked that Jan cared enough about art to visit the gallery, and I was glad he remembered me. After spending a very nice few minutes together, he asked me out on a date.

Looking back, I realize that while I was not specifically interested in marrying again—the experience with Ladislav had been too awful—I nonetheless enjoyed Jan's company and wanted to be with him. Every time we got together, I had a feeling of warmth and reassurance. I was always sorry to say goodbye, always looked forward to our next meeting. And even when he was not there, I found myself thinking of him.

Jan was charming and warm, and I have to admit I felt a strong attraction to him—he was handsome, with a great smile, and had remarkably thick, wavy, dark hair, which is unusual in Slovakia (most Slovaks are fair haired). His eyes were large and expressive too. And there was something so pleasant about his quiet, thoughtful, studious manner. He was always so courteous toward me, even when we were just having a cup of tea in a café. At one point he told me I was beautiful. It made my heart race.

But more important than physical attraction was my rapidly growing sense that I had found in Jan someone who *recognized* me. And even better, who recognized my *potential*. After so many years of being ignored, passed over, discounted, or underestimated (by not only my parents, but also my older brother, my would-be employers, and, most recently, Ladislav), I felt that in Jan I had finally found someone who saw me both for who I was—a person determined to make something of herself—and for the person I might someday become—a fully independent career woman. He listened to me and encouraged me to take pride in myself and my dreams. Years later, this memory of being recognized and encouraged by Jan would inspire me to do the same for others—both through mentoring my young interns at the Metropolitan Museum of Art, and, later, through my and Jan's work together in philanthropy.

As I got to know him, I realized that Jan was deeply immersed in his research. He was happiest when working. When not spending hours in the lab, he was earning money on the side by writing translations from Slovak to English. (He was, in fact, even more accomplished a linguist than I, for his mother was a Hungarian who had been educated in Austria and Switzerland, while his father was a Slovak; his nanny was German, and he had studied both English and Russian assiduously throughout high school and college.) While some women might have been put off by his single-minded focus on work—there were long periods when I did not hear from him because he was working—I completely encouraged it, since I also felt most alive when researching and writing. Moreover, Jan's work struck me as heroic: unlike my brother Ivan, who had always seen medicine as a way to prosperity, Jan had gone into biomedical research knowing that it promised few if any material rewards. The thrill for him was in the daily challenge of understanding and conquering disease—and the reward for him was in knowing that his research had the potential to eradicate human suffering. He was, at heart, an altruist and idealist.

Much to my surprise, my relationship with Jan progressed quickly—from acquaintance to friendship to romance, and from romance to a decision to marry, all within nine months. I was hardly expecting it, especially since Nina had told me that Jan had an eye for beautiful women, and that he had dated many over the years, but never once expressed a desire to marry, for he was primarily devoted to his research.

But, as Jan later explained, he had never before met someone with whom he wanted to spend his life—and he felt that way about me immediately. As for me, being hesitant to trust any man again, after Ladislav, I was in no hurry to remarry, because I wanted a museum career far more than I wanted children or a husband—and what Slovakian man would put up with an independent wife with a demanding full-time job?

To my astonishment, however, Jan accepted my desire to work; after all, he had grown up in a dual-career household, with his mother having a career in ophthalmology. He had no inhibitions about marrying a career woman. He knew firsthand the fulfillment that comes from meaningful employment, and within a few weeks of knowing me, he could see how much my work meant to me. If working made me happy, he said, he wanted me to work.

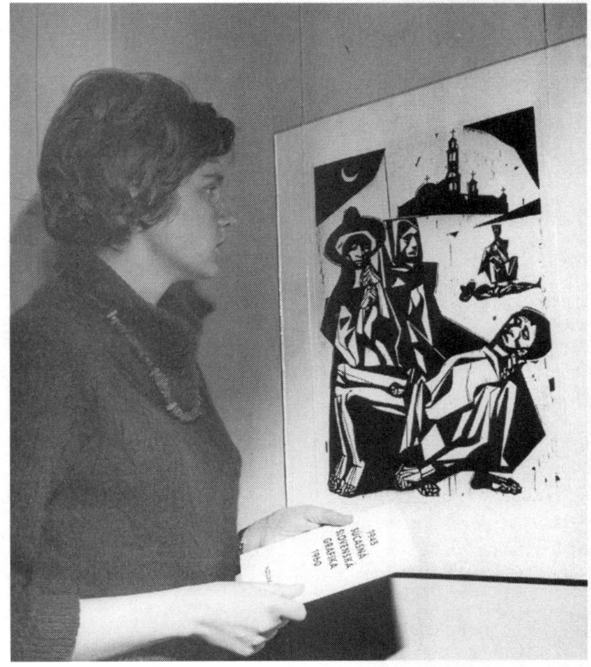

At the opening of my exhibition "Slovak Contemporary Graphic Artists (1945–1960), Hollara Gallery, Prague, March 1961

We also discovered we shared an interest in art. While the only objects he had ever actually collected were postage stamps, he had nonetheless decorated his room at home with works by Picasso that he had cut from the pages of a Polish magazine. As he later explained to me, he had done so because the Communists had banned abstract painting as "formalist bourgeois art," and he felt that by putting the images up on his walls, he was not just enjoying modernism, but engaging in a quiet form of protest. He had been raised, moreover, to appreciate culture. He enjoyed going to art exhibitions and art galleries whenever he could—in fact, he did so regularly.

Most important to me was my sense that Jan was a very good person. I knew this because he not only treated me well, but he also treated others well. He was generous and kind—thoughtful, fair, and considerate. Nearly everyone who worked with him liked him. Somehow, wary as I was of marriage, I found I trusted him absolutely, and with that trust came the sense that he and I were destined to share a life.

Of course, there was much we needed to discuss about our future. Our families, for example: Would Jan's parents accept me as their daughter-in-law, even though my family background was so different from theirs? And what about my father—being so tradition bound, would he mind if I married a non-Catholic? There was also the question of where we should make a life for ourselves, for I was entirely determined to leave Bratislava—and Czechoslovakia too, if possible.

As Jan and I got to know each other, I came to understand that he was exceptionally accomplished. The year before we met, he had published his first research (on a connection between interferon and tick-borne viral encephalitis) in the world's most prominent science journal, *Nature*. Through his groundbreaking research on interferon—a protein that somehow inhibits the replication of viruses—he had quickly established friendships with top scientists in the USSR and the West.

Because he had already done some traveling abroad, Jan was immediately receptive to the idea of moving to the West. He knew our nation was seriously troubled: like me, he resented the constant Soviet interference in Czechoslovakian affairs, and he readily agreed that the Czechoslovakian Communist Party was both intellectually backward and criminally corrupt. He hated state propaganda and doublespeak, and he particularly despised the brutality of the Czechoslovak secret police, the ŠtB. He had seen firsthand how the current regime persecuted the innocent and destroyed lives for no reason. Then again, he had already established a fine professional reputation for himself in Bratislava. Having recently defended the first-ever dissertation in the entire world about interferon, he was widely acknowledged as a rising star in Czechoslovakian biomedical research. If he stayed in Bratislava, he seemed destined for a future filled with top national honors and awards.

Even so, I told him I dreamt of leaving Bratislava—not because I had been unhappy here, but because of the many personal and professional setbacks: the denial of my studying science in high school; the postponement of college; being blacklisted; the assumption by both my father and my first husband that I should give up all my own hopes and dreams to be their housekeeper; my marginal existence at the Slovak National Gallery. Clearly Czechoslovakia was never going to be a place where we could thrive. There was no freedom here, no security, very little opportunity, and altogether too much corruption. Even now, despite my curatorial title, I lived in fear that I would be fired—not because of anything I had done, but merely because my brother had defected to the West.

In admitting all this to Jan, I half expected him to shrug and say, "Oh, lighten up, it's not so bad." But he didn't. My words interested him, and so did my certainty. I remember being amazed at this, and wondering that he should agree. (Only many months later would he confess his own horrific early-life experiences, when he and his parents had barely escaped extermination, and he had been hidden in a Catholic orphanage to avoid deportation to a Nazi death camp.)

As we talked about the various possibilities in our future, Jan seemed particularly interested in Ivan's experience of escaping to the West. My brother had finally managed to obtain a visa and moved from France to the United States in early 1959. Now a resident anesthesiologist at the NYU Medical Center in Manhattan, he was doing well financially and enjoying his new life: he wrote that he had many girlfriends and a nice apartment, and regularly took costly, exotic vacations. Through my conversations about Ivan, Jan and I began to hope that we too might ultimately be able to find a new home in America.

In the spring of 1962 Jan proposed. There was no engagement ring; we didn't have the money. He simply asked me to marry him. I accepted, and we began to discuss how and when we would have the ceremony. There weren't many options of course, for the Communists discouraged church weddings and recognized only civil ceremonies. That was hardly a problem for us: nobody in my family went to church these days, and Jan, though ethnically Jewish, had been raised entirely nonobservant.

The bigger question was of logistics. Since Jan lived with his parents, he and I would need to find our own place to live—no small challenge, because housing was in short supply, and neither of us had savings. Jan had by now visited my home several times, and he got along well enough with my father (Jan's exact words about the situation were "I have a feeling that your father does not dislike me"). So after some deliberation I suggested we ask my father if we might live there with him, sharing the expenses of the house.

The widow who had been living in our subdivided basement apartment had recently died and her daughter had moved out, so we had a little more space than previously. And since my father now preferred to sleep on the first floor, I suggested to Jan that we create a small apartment for ourselves on the second, converting the smallest bedroom there into a kitchenette. In this way, Jan and I might have an independent existence, even though I would continue to look after Pavol and my father. Jan then asked my father's permission. After my father agreed to the marriage, Jan and I discussed with him our thoughts about renovating the second floor of the house. My father agreed to that too, on the condition that none of it happen until we were officially married.

We wed on July 28, 1962, in a simple civil ceremony at a registry office in downtown Bratislava. It was a Saturday but also a workday, so Jan and I dressed simply: I wore a white skirt and green blouse with a flower design, and he wore a summer-weight suit and tie. We wrote and spoke our own vows. By mutual agreement we had chosen not to exchange wedding rings—they didn't seem necessary. Our witnesses were Ľudmila Peterajová, the curator of paintings at the Slovak National Gallery, and Břetislav Rada, a colleague of Jan's from the Bratislava Institute of Virology. The four of us had lunch afterward at the Hotel Devín, just across the street from the gallery, after which we all returned to our respective offices to work.

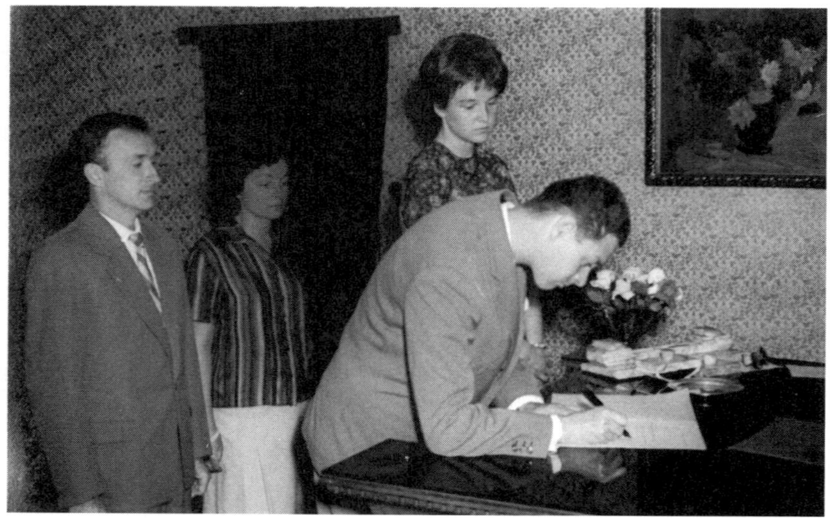

Our marriage in Bratsilava, with witnesses
Ľudmila Peterajová and Břetislav Rada

Our honeymoon was equally simple: a weeklong expedition by car. Jan's parents had recently sold a plot of family-owned land to buy a silver Škoda 440 "Spartak" sedan. For months Jan had been setting aside money for the gas, food, and lodging we would need to make our trip. (Gas was so expensive at the time that it seriously limited the use of the car, even though it had only a four-cylinder, forty-horsepower engine.) After filling up the tank, we set out on our road trip, intending to join Jan's parents, who were taking their yearly vacation three hundred miles away in the spa town of Mariánské Lázně (or, in German, Marienbad), which sits on the Czech-German border. Jan's mother was a member of the national bridge team; she vacationed at Mariánské Lázně yearly in order to participate in an important international bridge tournament there.

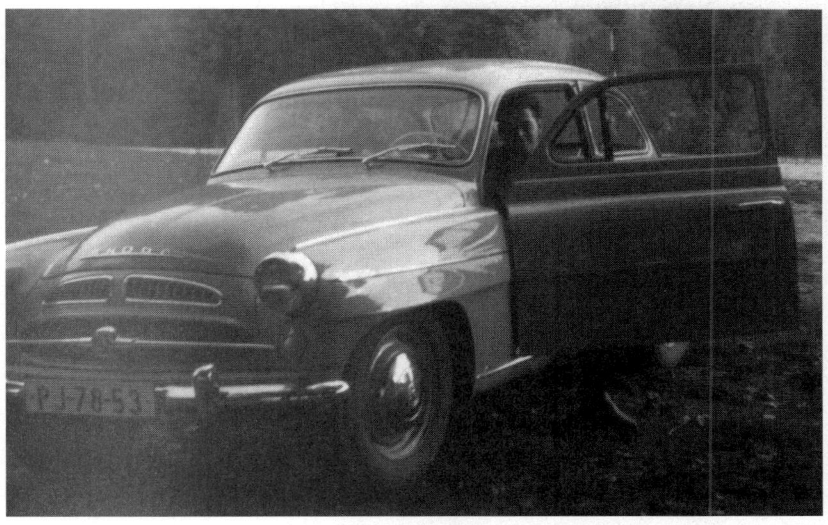

Jan behind the wheel of his family's Škoda 440 "Spartak" sedan, 1962

We visited some beautiful historic sites along the way, mostly castles and fortified towns in northern Slovakia and Bohemia. It was one of the first extended drives I'd ever taken in a car. As we approached Mariánské Lázně, however, I braced myself—for despite our being engaged for nearly half a year before the wedding, Jan had brought me to see his parents only a few times, and never for long. The couple had always been kind to me—Jan's father particularly—but now that we were married I wanted so much for them to accept me as their daughter-in-law. Jan's mother was a brilliant woman of strong character, and he had at one time let slip that she had always hoped her son would marry into wealth—something that I, of course, could hardly provide.

I felt a little guilty that we hadn't asked them to our wedding, even if it was just a brief civil ceremony held in the middle of a workday. But Jan didn't seem worried: his parents were open-minded and cosmopolitan, he said, and both of them were sure to respect me and welcome me.

Jan and I didn't have the opportunity to break the news to them immediately, because on the evening we arrived, his mother had arranged that we would join her friends for dinner at a neighboring hotel, and we arrived a little late. Only the next morning, over breakfast, did Jan announce we had been married. Jan's mother seemed very surprised, possibly shocked. But after a moment she merely expressed regret that she hadn't been able to invite their friends to the ceremony and hold a proper reception on our behalf.

While I was probably not the person Mrs. Vilcek had hoped her son would marry, and while she was surely surprised that Jan and I had married without including them (which was, in retrospect, rather thoughtless of us), I nonetheless had the feeling that she didn't dislike me. I was quiet and undemanding, which suited her, for she was colorful and loquacious. Also, she liked that I spoke Hungarian—although she soon revealed to me that I spoke it rather coarsely. Having learned the language from our housekeeper, Katka, who hadn't had much of an education, I apparently spoke with the accent, grammar, and vocabulary of a bumpkin. Both Jan's parents, by comparison, spoke Hungarian perfectly, with the fluency, accent, prose cadences, and specialized vocabulary of the Budapest intellectual elite. My accent, my odd turns of phrase, and my very basic sentence constructions in Hungarian would be an endless source of amusement to both senior Vilceks for many years to come.

Jan's father was friendly and easygoing. Throughout the breakfast he seemed delighted by me, and deeply pleased that his son had decided to marry me. I was very relieved to realize that, whatever their opinion of me, Jan's parents clearly adored him and only wanted him to be happy—and if I made him happy (clearly I did), I was very much welcome among them. As if to reassure me of that fact, Jan's father ordered a bottle of the local champagne, even though it was breakfast time, and we all raised our glasses to a happy marriage. It was a lovely gesture on his part, and a good way to begin our new life.

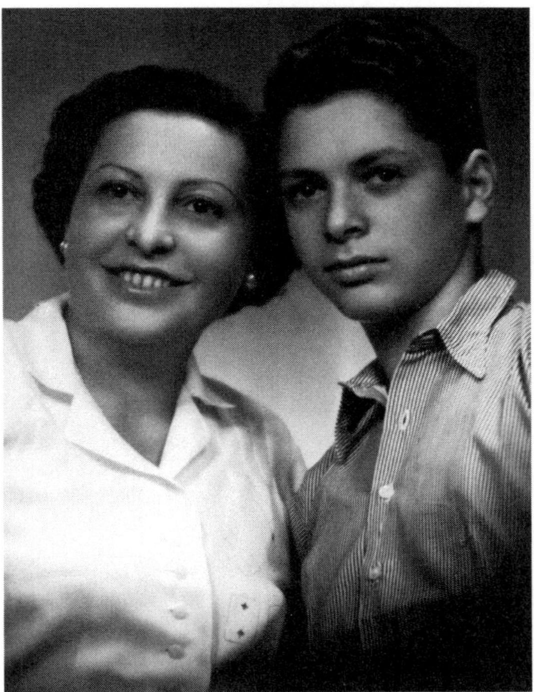

Jan with his mother, c. 1946

Once we had done some small renovations on the second floor of my father's house, my new life with Jan was a comfortable one. It was around this time that I sold my beloved piano to buy a refrigerator, thereby simplifying my shopping and cooking duties. Much to my delight, Jan felt no inhibition about helping with the cooking and the washing up. What a difference it made, to have a companion in that endless kitchen work! And how nice to have a husband who believed in sharing household chores with his wife.

We saw Jan's parents regularly too: every Sunday Jan's father would take the two of us to lunch at a restaurant, then bring us back to his home for dessert and coffee with Jan's mother. When, in time, I introduced my father to Jan's parents, I found to my surprise that they all got along quite beautifully. In part, this was because my father, thanks to his many years as a senior administrator of Hungarian-language schools, spoke a perfect and rather elegant Hungarian—something I had never realized or noticed, for we had not spoken Hungarian in our home since the end of the war.

Even as we settled into our new life together, though, Jan and I were quietly discussing how we might leave Czechoslovakia for the West. Knowing it would be dangerous to our extended family, we resolved to tell no one of our intentions. At the same time, we did whatever we could think of to make sure that no one in our family would be adversely impacted by our leaving—especially Pavol.

By 1963 Pavol was eighteen and had reached the end of his secondary schooling. His grades were such that a professional career hardly seemed possible, but he wanted to attend university—specifically, a technical university, since he was interested in mining engineering, mining being one of Slovakia's leading industries. By order of the Communist Party, however, anyone wishing to take this degree was required to spend a year working in a mine. As a result, Pavol had signed up to work in a salt mine near Košice, in easternmost Czechoslovakia, just ten miles north of the Hungarian border and sixty miles west of the border with the Soviet Union.

Pavol didn't realize until he arrived that the working conditions would be brutal. Workers were required to spend their entire workday underground, often standing in cold salt water up to their knees. Because waterproof boots were not available to them, most workers developed excruciatingly painful skin ulcerations and long-term infections. We were horrified by Pavol's swollen and infected legs and feet on his first visit home—he was in such pain he could barely walk. Thanks to Jan's connections we were able to get him immediate medical attention, and later a pair of waterproof boots. Subsequently Jan worked with his father (who, as I've mentioned, was a coal mining executive) to get Pavol transferred to an easier posting within the salt mine. By doing so, they may well have saved his life. At any rate, with his return to Košice, I sensed my years of looking after Pavol were finally drawing to a close.

7

From Bratislava to Vienna and Frankfurt

Thanks to his innovative research on interferons, Jan now had many professional friends in the international scientific community, and with those friendships came occasional invitations to travel. He was corresponding with scientists in Brussels, Paris, Zurich, Boston, Philadelphia, Baltimore, New York, and Washington, DC. In the fall of 1962, just three months after our marriage, he had taken a research trip to Brussels and then London. He came back feeling that either city might be a good place for us to live.

When he was offered a yearlong research fellowship in London, we had great hopes of moving there (if only temporarily), but the Communist government denied us permission to go. Needless to say, Jan and I continued to hope another opportunity might arise for us to spend time in Western Europe, and perhaps even remain there.

Working at the Slovak National Gallery kept me very busy, but in my free time I read about art and museum work in Western Europe and the United States. Our libraries were not allowed to purchase books on the subject of Western contemporary art, nor were professors allowed to teach the subject at Comenius. Like many young people, however, I was intensely curious about it, and the very fact that Western art was "forbidden" made it tantalizing. Through friends I had access to books and magazines on contemporary art in Europe and America—publications smuggled into Czechoslovakia that we shared secretly. We all felt trapped in our backward country and were intensely curious about what was going on elsewhere in the world. With access to Austrian television only, we relied mainly on books, newspapers, and magazines for such information. Through them we knew that Western Europe and the United States had dynamic, entirely uncensored contemporary art scenes. I particularly remember a little folder Ivan sent me from New York containing four full-color reproductions printed by the Museum of Modern Art: a Jackson Pollock painting, a Jasper Johns, and two works by Paul Klee. Although I lacked any information about them, I framed them and hung them in our home, feeling (as Jan too felt) that no government should ever be allowed to ban art, literature, or the free exchange of ideas and information.

In 1964, Jan's research laboratory, the Bratislava Institute of Virology, hosted an international conference at Smolenice Castle, a conference center thirty miles from Bratislava. Jan was very excited about it, since his interferon research was to be showcased, and many of the international virologists attending the conference were coming there specifically to meet him.

A few weeks before the conference, Jan and I invited Professor Hans Moritsch, the head of the department of hygiene and microbiology at the Vienna Medical School, and his wife, Edda, to stay with us for a few days. Like Jan, Hans Moritsch was both young and accomplished. Though only forty-one, he had been working for a number of years on possible treatments for tick-borne viral encephalitis, so he and Jan had much to discuss. Jan and I enjoyed the Moritsches' company, and they, ours. Shortly after the conference, they wrote inviting us to spend a weekend at their home in Vienna. With this invitation in hand, Jan and I applied to the Czechoslovak government for a travel permit.

While I was thrilled at the possibility of seeing Vienna's extraordinary museums, in fact Jan and I wanted to utilize this weekend pass for something far more life-changing: permanent escape from Czechoslovakia. Since the government had denied him the fellowship in London, Jan had become far more focused on leaving for good. Of course it would be an enormously complicated thing to do: we had no financial resources to draw upon, few acquaintances in Vienna, and only the most limited sense of how (or where) we might possibly make a life for ourselves in the West.

Now that the opportunity to leave was upon us, I found myself surprisingly conflicted. I felt tremendously guilty that my father would have no one to look after him. I was also worried that the ŠtB might retaliate by punishing him and seizing our home. Luckily Jan would hear none of it—he was entirely ready to go, and he strongly reminded me that up until this moment, it was I who had been pressing him most urgently that we leave.

We considered how we might manage it. While we would be granted permission to cross the border, neither Jan nor I would be allowed to take much money or clothing. I hadn't any jewelry—not even a wedding ring. And even if we had had something valuable to take with us, our luggage was bound to be examined very closely at the border. Nothing of value could be hidden in our overnight bags. Yet we would surely need money to continue our travels, for we could not stay in Vienna long. Partitioned Austria had become a free and independent nation only in 1955, and in order to achieve its statehood, the Austrians had been compelled to agree that it would not assist or harbor defectors from Warsaw Pact nations. Should we remain in Austria, we risked apprehension, incarceration, and ultimately deportation back to Bratislava, where punishment would inevitably follow.

If we were able to get from Vienna to West Germany, however, what would happen there? We had no idea if we would be welcome as refugees, since we would be without passports or official identification. Given our situation, how could we be sure that the West Germans would grant us temporary asylum? If not, what would happen?

In the days leading up to our trip to Vienna, I became increasingly agitated. I was fearful for myself and Jan, and also for my father—I wanted so much to warn him, even as I knew he would be better off if left ignorant of our plans.

Jan, on the other hand, felt compelled to tell his parents. I was initially against his doing so, because I worried they would try to stop him: after all, he was their only child. But much to my surprise, the evening we gave them the news, they were entirely supportive. Both my in-laws had come so close to being sent to the Polish death camps by the Slovakian nationalists during World War II (Jan and his mother had actually spent the last days of the war in hiding in a little village just twenty-five miles from Topoľčany) that they fully anticipated another holocaust would be likely during their lifetimes. For that reason they gave us their full and unconditional support. They even agreed to let us have their car, despite knowing that, should we be successful, they would probably never see the vehicle again. Their great enthusiasm gave us courage, as did their assurance that we would surely be reunited in just a few years' time.

On October 10, 1964, Jan and I drove his parents' Škoda to the Austrian border. The heavily guarded crossing lay just three miles from Bratislava. I had never seen the border crossing before and was chilled by the sight of it: watchtowers, gun emplacements, and minefields surrounded it, and an electric fence and razor wire stretched through the open fields on both sides of the road. The roadway itself was blocked by two gateway checkpoints, each manned by armed soldiers—the first Czechoslovak, the second Austrian. Since we were the only car at the checkpoint on that quiet Saturday morning, the Czechoslovak soldiers gave our travel permit a very long and thorough examination. They then instructed us to get out and had us open the car's hood and trunk.

They looked under the hood at the motor, then went around to the trunk of the car, removed our overnight bags, and looked through them. After a few minutes, having found nothing unusual, they returned the bags, handed us back our documents, gestured us into the car, and opened the gate to let us pass. The Austrian guards examined our papers and let us pass too. Then suddenly, much to our own surprise, we were speeding away through the open fields and pastures of Lower Austria!

As soon as he felt safe enough to do so, Jan pulled the car over and we got out and hugged. I remember having tears in my eyes, overcome by so many emotions. We were leaving everything behind—we had escaped—we were free!—and yet we were still in such terrible, terrible danger.

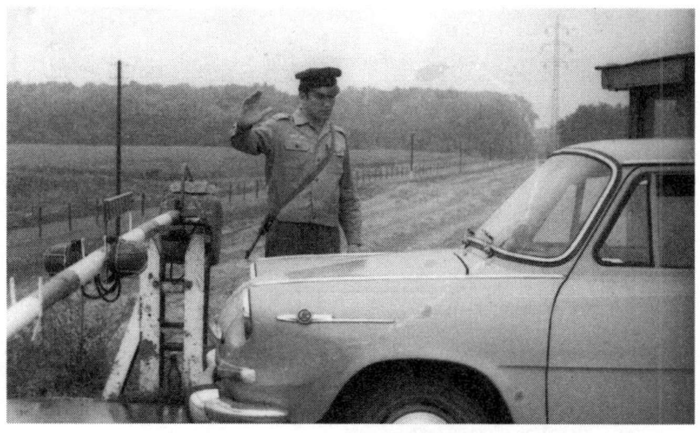

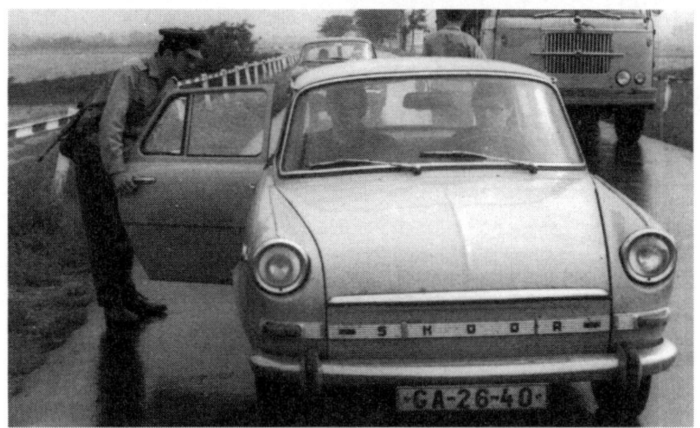

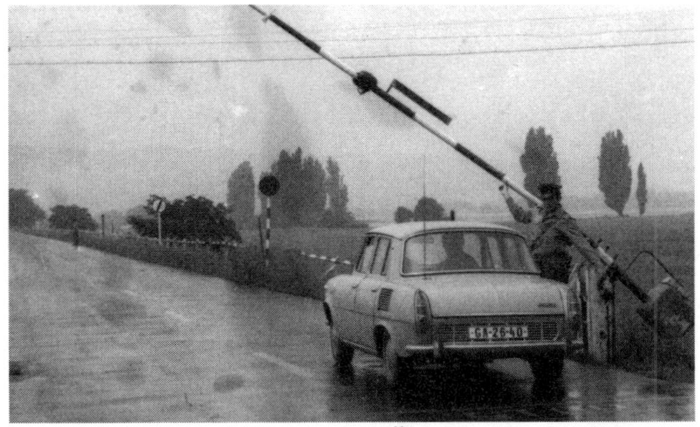

A border guard examining a Škoda at the Austrian-Czechoslovakian frontier just outside of Bratislava, c. 1964

Considering our agitation, Vienna and its many charms might easily have been lost on us. But they were not. One of the most beautiful cities in Europe, it is a treasure house of great art, extraordinary urban planning, and stunning architecture. It was also almost unbelievably lively on that radiant October weekend. I remember being dazzled by the beautiful, well-stocked shops on the Graben and the Kärntnerstrasse. The streets seemed to be thronged with the most fashionably dressed people I had ever seen. I remember the picturesque horse-drawn carriages, the chestnut vendors, and the beauty of the fall foliage. The Hofburg, the Kunsthistorisches Museum, and the Stefansdom were all so staggeringly impressive, as were the lively fountains and grand and solemn monuments, the beautifully tended public gardens and parks and public squares. Our hosts, the Moritsches, welcomed us into their home with great warmth and reassurance. Wanting to give us the best possible weekend, they had even bought tickets for Saturday night at the Vienna State Opera.

But even as I sat that night enraptured by the brilliance and beauty of *The Magic Flute*, I was trying to conceptualize how we might continue our escape. We needed money, contacts, and information—and we needed them *soon*. Jan had a few of his closest fellow research scientists to rely upon, but as for me, the only person I knew in the West was Ivan—and I had no telephone number for him, only his New York City address. As soon as we reached Vienna I sent him a note via airmail to let him know of our situation, and from the post office I made a phone call, asking the international operator for his phone number. After a wait, she told me that while that number existed, Ivan had chosen to keep it unlisted. In a moment of inspiration I realized I had one more option: sending a telegram. I wired him that we were out of Czechoslovakia, needed his help, and would be in touch again soon with more details.

On Monday morning the Moritches expected us to return to Bratislava. Instead, over breakfast, Jan told them that we had decided to defect. He then humbly asked if they might allow us to stay a few more nights in their home. We sensed Hans Moritsch's concern—and rightly so, since by harboring fugitives he might easily have harmed his reputation and career. But we also knew we had no alternative: compelled to surrender our passports and personal ID cards to the police before leaving Bratislava, we could not have rented a hotel room even if we had money to do so (which, of course, we did not). Luckily another contact of Jan's, the Belgian scientist Edward De Maeyer, stepped in and arranged for us to have a borrowed studio apartment for a week. We moved there immediately, not wanting to implicate the Moritsches any more than we already had.

Jan then attempted by telephone to secure a position on the faculty of medicine at Katholieke Universiteit Leuven in Belgium; his work had been much admired when he had made his presentation there over the summer, and he had been assured he would be welcome should he ever want a position there. With a firm job offer in hand, Jan would have been eligible to apply to the Belgian government for political asylum, and fully expecting to receive the offer, he went to the Belgian consulate, where he carefully explained the situation to an officer. But the officer was unsympathetic, threatening to turn us over to the Austrian police for deportation back to Czechoslovakia if we pressed him any further for assistance. Realizing that the possibility of getting asylum in Belgium was more complicated than we had anticipated, we began casting about for an alternative.

Thankfully, De Maeyer persisted on our behalf. Working through a friend at the American embassy in Brussels, he got us an appointment at the U.S. embassy in Vienna. The official there listened to us, then kindly told us that while he could do nothing for us in Vienna, he wanted to help. He advised us that the best thing for us to do would be to go to Frankfurt, where we could apply for asylum from the West German government. Once we had received refugee passports from the Germans, we would be eligible to apply for a U.S. immigration visa. Frankfurt's vast and bustling U.S. consulate general was the best place to make that application, he said, since it granted the largest number of the visas in West Germany and also offered the interviews that were a required part of the visa application process.

The American official then further advised us how to cross the border into West Germany: take the busy A8 highway from Salzburg to Munich, since most vehicles were simply waved through on that road. Should we be stopped by the West German border patrol, all we needed to do was tell them that we were Czechs entering the country to apply for refugee status. He also gave us contact information for American Friends of Refugees, an NGO in Frankfurt that would give us temporary housing and other forms of aid while we applied for the U.S. visas.

As we anxiously prepared to move on to Frankfurt, an American named Margaret Kunz, the wife of another colleague of Jan's, reached out to offer us even more help. Over lunch at the Griechenbeisl, a charming restaurant situated within Vienna's oldest inn, she promised she could help us once we reached the United States, since she had been born into a distinguished American family and had been raised just outside New York City, on Long Island. She assured us that, should we settle in New York, her cousin Helen Garrison would be glad to help us. Shortly thereafter, Margaret's husband, Christian (a virologist who ultimately achieved medical fame by developing the vaccine against tick-borne viral encephalitis), lent us two hundred dollars so that we might make our way across Austria and West Germany without undue financial worry. Two hundred dollars was a vast sum at the time, particularly to us. The loan was but one of so many acts of extraordinary kindness that we were to be shown in the coming year by people we barely knew. It was a generosity that Jan and I would never forget.

At the end of October, we drove from Vienna to Frankfurt. We stopped only for gas, even though it was a drive of more than five hundred miles that took about nine hours. We had no alternative, for we could not get a room without proper identification, and we dared not simply park and sleep in the car for fear of getting into trouble with the West German police. Once we reached Frankfurt, we went to American Friends of Refugees, where we were given a place to spend the night and promised permanent shelter in the days and weeks to come. The very next morning we began meeting with the West German authorities, with the aim of applying for refugee passports.

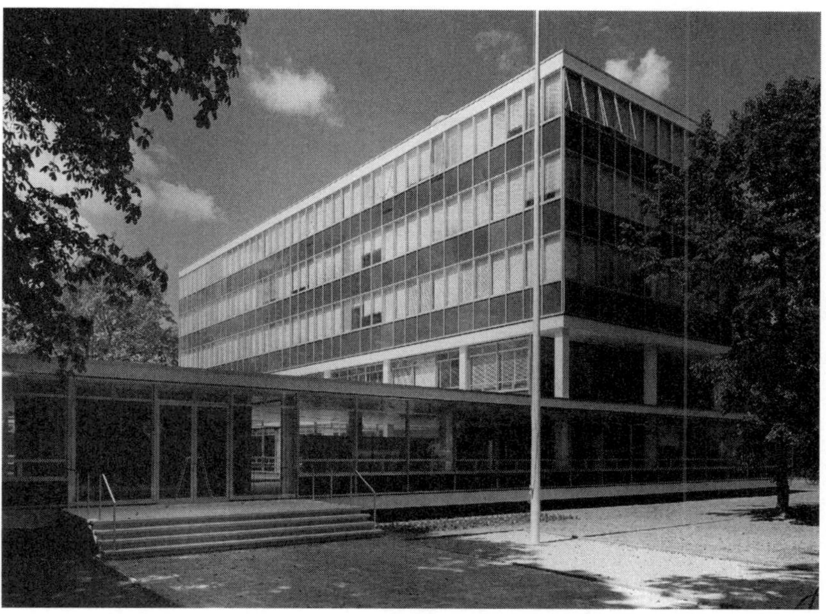

The U.S. Consulate in Frankfurt

It was a stressful time. Luckily Jan spoke fluent German—it was his mother's second language after Hungarian, and he had spoken and studied it all his life. The Germans who guided us through the asylum process were very kind about explaining the many things that we did not immediately understand. Tackling the paperwork over the next few days kept us very busy—which was actually good, since it kept us from fretting. The weeks of waiting that followed, however, were nerve-racking. Our finances were limited, our future so very uncertain. I remember that Jan and I spent a lot of time at libraries and museums that November and December, reading and studying. Being without daily work was new to us, and neither of us liked it: we felt anxious, powerless, and terribly disconnected.

From Frankfurt I was finally able to reach Ivan by phone. The telegrams I had sent had been slow to reach him because he had been enjoying a luxury vacation with a girlfriend in Mexico, but once I had him on the line I was able to fill him in on where we were and how we had started the immigration process. It was odd to be speaking to him after eight years. He cheerfully reassured me that he could provide whatever money or legal help we might eventually need, both in Frankfurt and New York. I was humbled to have to ask such an enormous favor from him, given that we had never been close. But Ivan had been in the same desperate circumstances just a few years earlier, understood our predicament completely, and was glad to be of service. To my surprise, he seemed genuinely eager that we might join him in New York.

December was cold and dreary in Frankfurt. The holiday season put us into a state of gloom, for we missed our homes and family and friends, and our spartan living conditions and limited belongings (each of us had basically a single change of clothes) made our quotidian existence even more grim. By now, too, we had become aware of the legions of Eastern European refugees camped out all around us in Frankfurt, getting by in similarly bleak circumstances, waiting for a U.S. visa interview. Many, I learned, had been seeking American visas for years and were living on next to nothing. Some days I woke up thinking we would never get to New York, that we would be stuck in Germany indefinitely, perpetually impoverished, unable to find work, make friends, or establish a permanent home.

Jan missed his work, his colleagues, his friends, and his parents. One afternoon, to cheer him up, I suggested we go out to the Christmas markets on the Paulsplatz and the Römerberg, those two great squares in Frankfurt's old town where people gather at Christmastime to drink, shop, and enjoy the holiday season. Nearly three-quarters of Frankfurt had been obliterated by Allied bombardments during World War II, and in fact most of the Altstadt's historic half-timbered architecture had been reduced to rubble. But the city had rebounded quite amazingly in the intervening twenty years. Some of the finest half-timbered buildings in the Altstadt had been restored and re-created, the rest replaced with relatively nondescript but perfectly functional new buildings. The music and the lights of the Christmas market, the fun fair, the gifts, the *Frankfurter* Würstchen, *heißer Apfelwein*, and *Glühwein*, and a seemingly endless assortment of Christmas cookies, cakes, and candies all combined to lift our spirits and reassure us of good times to come. And indeed, just a few days later, we had the greatest Christmas gift of all: a note from the West German authorities telling us that *die Fremdenpässe* (our "refugees' passports") would be ready for us on Christmas Eve.

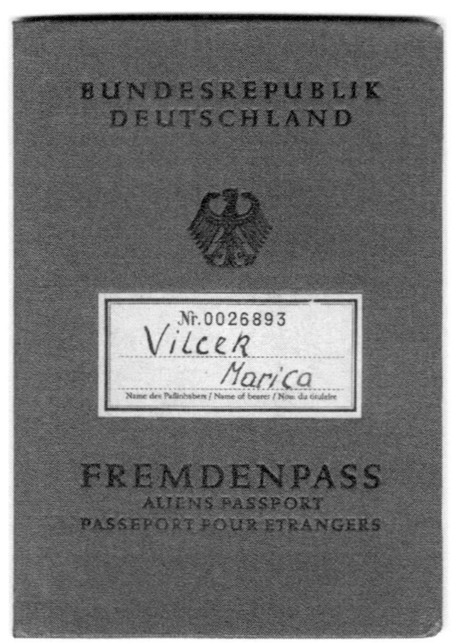

My Fremdenpass, or Refugee Passport

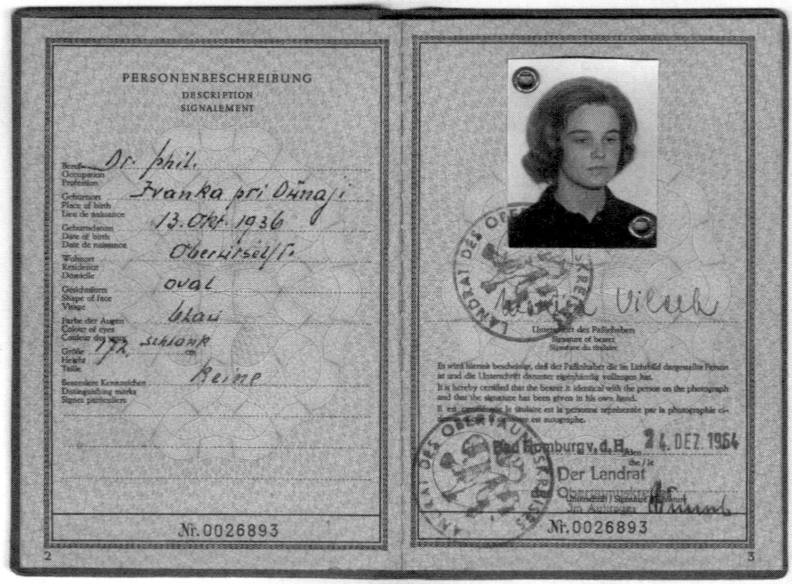

My Fremdenpass (interior)

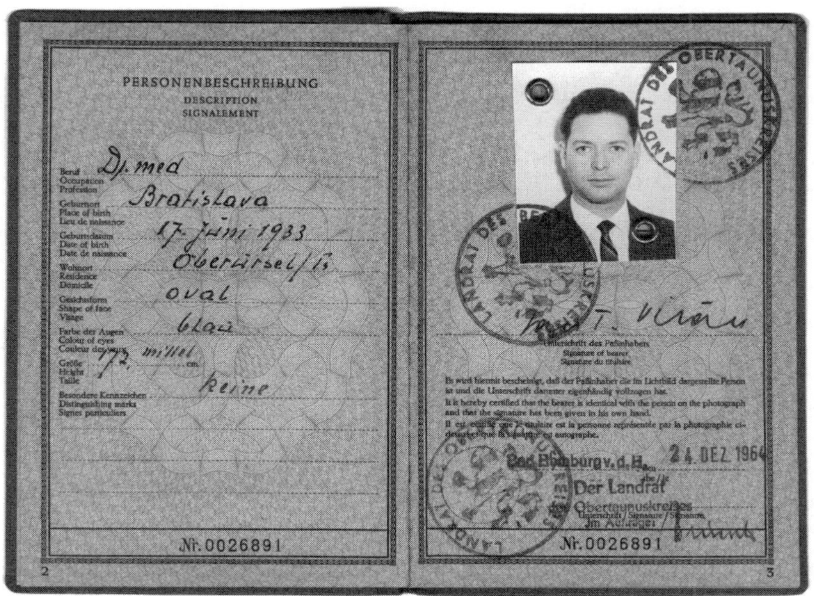

PERSONENBESCHREIBUNG
DESCRIPTION
SIGNALEMENT

Beruf / Occupation / Profession: Dr. med
Geburtsort / Place of birth / Lieu de naissance: Bratislava
Geburtsdatum / Date of birth / Date de naissance: 17. Juni 1933
Wohnort / Residence / Domicile: Oberursel/Ts.
Gesichtsform / Shape of face / Visage: oval
Farbe der Augen / Colour of eyes / Couleur des yeux: blau
Größe / Height / Taille: mittel 172 cm
Besondere Kennzeichen / Distinguishing marks / Signes particuliers: keine

Nr. 0026891

2

Unterschrift des Paßinhabers
Signature of bearer
Signature du titulaire

Es wird hiermit bescheinigt, daß der Paßinhaber die im Lichtbild dargestellte Person ist und die Unterschrift darunter eigenhändig vollzogen hat.
It is hereby certified that the bearer is identical with the person on the photograph and that the signature has been given in his own hand.
Il est certifié que le titulaire est la personne représentée par la photographie ci-dessus et que la signature est autographe.

Bad Homburg v. d. H., den 24. DEZ. 1964
Der Landrat des Obertaunuskreises
Unterschrift / Signature / Signature
Im Auftrage

Nr. 0026891

3

Jan's Fremdenpass

Our life situation in Frankfurt took a turn for the absurd when Ivan called two weeks later with a special request. He was now doing so well financially that he had decided to buy himself a Mercedes-Benz sedan. But a friend in New York had told him that he would get a significant discount on the car if he purchased it directly from the factory, which was near Stuttgart, and also that he could receive a substantial tax break on the car if it had enough miles on it to qualify as "used." So he requested that Jan and I please pick up the car on his behalf in Stuttgart and drive it around Germany, putting at least a thousand miles on it before dropping it off for shipment by freighter from Hamburg.

Touring Germany in the middle of winter, particularly given our limited finances, lack of warm clothing, and rather suspect refugee status, was not an immediately appealing idea. Jan was trying to keep on top of various developments in his research, and I was spending my days rather frantically trying to improve my English, a language I had studied only minimally in Bratislava. Both of us were tense about the immigration process, and we worried that we might well miss a vital summons while driving around Germany in Ivan's new Mercedes. But since we would be entirely dependent upon Ivan once we reached New York, I told Jan we should probably help my brother in any way he requested. And Jan of course agreed.

Although we had surrendered our passports before leaving Bratislava, Jan had retained his Czechoslovak driver's license, and with that and his *Fremdenpass* we were able to pick up the car in Stuttgart. We then spent three weeks seeing various sights by car: Karlsruhe, Baden-Baden, the Schwarzwald; Heidelberg and the Neckar valley; Wiesbaden and the Taunus; Nuremberg, Würzburg, Bamberg, and a number of picturesque small medieval towns in south Germany that had somehow escaped aerial bombardment by the Allies during those apocalyptic last weeks of the war. We also drove north along the Rhine, seeing Koblenz, Cologne, and then detouring to Aachen before turning back. As an art historian fascinated by medieval art, and despite my fretfulness and distraction, I was profoundly moved by the many treasures, churches, and cathedrals we saw. The innkeepers and restaurant owners, meanwhile, assumed us to be very rich thanks to our new Mercedes, which was amusing in its way. But the car meant little to Jan or to me (even though we were grateful for its comfort and warmth) and we weren't at all sorry to send it off to New York, where Ivan was so eagerly awaiting its arrival.

Because our visas were now pretty much assured, Jan and I faced a new quandary: what to do with the Škoda? The logical idea was to sell it, even if in Germany the car was not much desired—with its odd looks and top speed of sixty-five miles per hour, it really was something of an oddity on the German autobahns. But selling it turned out to be impossible, for the car had been bought and registered in his mother's name, and its title remained with her in Bratislava. Jan started to worry that if he were to be suspected of stealing his mother's car, he might be denied his immigration visa. After much deliberation, we asked the American Friends of Refugees to request that the local police return the car to the Czechoslovak border and hand it over to the Czechoslovak authorities. Amazingly, the Germans agreed to do so. Jan then sent word of its imminent arrival to his mother, who after proving herself its owner ultimately succeeded in reclaiming it.

During our last weeks in Frankfurt, Jan was also working to obtain a formal offer of employment from the United States, since having such an offer in hand would facilitate our immigration. By mid-January he had an offer (but only an informal one) from the Children's Hospital in Philadelphia. Another (also informal) came to him from the Cornell University Medical College in New York City. Ultimately, Ivan resolved the issue, having recently learned from a neurosurgeon colleague that the department of microbiology at NYU Medical School was seeking an accomplished virologist. Upon reviewing Jan's credentials, Milton Salton, the head of that department, quickly sent a formal job offer: Jan would be an assistant professor with a salary of twelve thousand dollars a year and the ability to establish his own independent laboratory and build his own research program. Jan thoughtfully asked me if I would be all right with living in New York rather than Boston or Philadelphia, to which I responded with an enthusiastic yes! Quite apart from the extraordinary opportunity it gave Jan, I sensed that New York was the most cosmopolitan city in America, and so would be the most open and welcoming to us as European immigrants.

Over the years, many people have observed that Jan and I had a relatively easy time gaining entry to the United States. It's true: many other refugees in Frankfurt had been waiting for their visas for much longer. Certainly in the years that have followed, so many would-be immigrants have been turned away. In truth, luck played a large part in our story: very few refugees from Communist Czechoslovakia applied for entry to the United States in 1964, for the simple reason that very few had been able to escape—and so the American quota for Czechoslovak refugees was unfilled at the time we made our application. Professional achievements also played a part, given that Jan and I both had advanced university degrees. But most important, Jan had a firm and specific job offer from NYU, and my brother had already filed an affidavit from New York pledging to support us financially, so there were no concerns among immigration officials about our ability to sustain ourselves upon arrival. Still, Jan and I remain grateful to this day that at a time when we had nothing, not even passports, the United States should have welcomed us and given us a home.

We had our oral interviews with the American immigration authorities in late January. Then there was a required medical exam, to determine we were both in good health. Perhaps the American authorities felt that the news of a distinguished scientist fleeing communism for American democracy would be good public relations. But whatever the reason, we were granted our visas without delay, and immediately began making our travel plans.

8

Arrival in New York

Jan and I finally boarded a Pan American Airways Boeing 707 from Frankfurt to New York on February 4, 1965. I had traveled by airplane only once before, in a little propeller plane on a short flight of two hundred miles from Bratislava to Prague. Of course Pan Am's transatlantic service on its flagship jet was an altogether different experience: a ten-hour flight with everything so elegant and stylish, even in economy class. The thrill and pleasure of flying was more than tinged with anxiety, though, since Jan and I still had only West German refugee passports, and no guarantee that upon presenting them to police and immigration officials we would be granted entry to the United States. Should we be denied, I didn't know what we would do—we had already borrowed so much money. With all our documents in a briefcase at my feet, I tried not to fret.

And then there was the question of New York itself: What would it be like? I really did not know. In Bratislava we had very limited access to information about the States: there were no American magazines, no American television, and few Hollywood films in circulation there, and none of our friends had ever visited. True, Ivan had been writing to me from New York for several years, but he wrote mostly postcards, because under communism every written document from the United States was checked over by the secret police and sealed letters were often intercepted or destroyed. On those few occasions when a longer communication from Ivan reached me, he had written only about the progress of his medical training. He had not wanted to get me in trouble with the ŠtB.

Ivan had been kind enough to send us the money to purchase our airline tickets. He had also assured us that he would be waiting for us when we arrived, just outside the passport and customs area. His voice over the phone had been very reassuring. Just knowing he would be there helped me remain calm.

When at last the plane began to descend, I caught sight of New York Harbor and just beyond it the island of Manhattan gleaming in the sunshine of a clear and brilliant winter afternoon. This city of my dreams—was it real, or just a fata morgana caused by hours of high-altitude air travel and week upon week of excitement and stress? The sight of this magic island of architectural madness floating at the confluence of ocean, rivers, and estuary was so breathtaking that the image of it remains with me to this day, a deeply spiritual visual memory.

When the jet touched down at JFK Airport, I thought we would immediately disembark; instead we had a very long wait, during which the chief purser told everyone to remain seated. When the plane's door finally opened, two men in military uniforms came down the aisle, stopped in front of us, asked us to identify ourselves, and then told us to gather our belongings and come with them.

I was terrified, almost numb, as we walked through the spacious modern terminal to what looked like a police office. Was this the American secret police? An official demanded our documents, then consulted our German-issued refugee passports and the visas that had been issued by the American consulate general in Frankfurt. Then he glanced over our health certificates. After taking some notes, he told us to follow the officers down the hall. Then suddenly we were in the brightly lit passport control area and the officers were telling the passport officials that we were clear to enter the United States.

That was it—we were in!

We retrieved our baggage from the carousel, passed through customs, and walked out into the crowded main hall. There Ivan stood waiting. I hadn't seen my brother in almost nine years but he was handsome as ever, grinning, and impeccably dressed—in fact, he looked very much like a country gentleman. I embraced him and introduced him to Jan. The two men shook hands and Jan thanked him for coming to collect us.

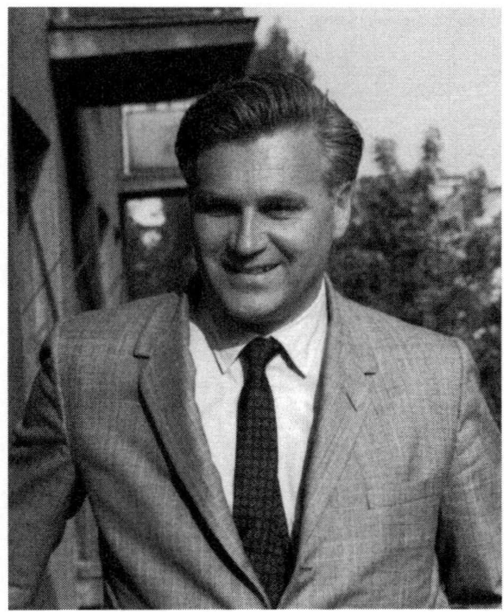

My brother Ivan in New York, 1965

I was dazzled by the vast, high-ceilinged, ultramodern Pan Am terminal, and by all the people milling about us, everyone moving so quickly. That was one of my first and strongest impressions of New York: the rapidity of everything—transport, language, business transactions, people in motion. Everything moved so much more quickly than back home.

We rode into Manhattan in Ivan's Mercedes, the car Jan and I had driven all over West Germany. The high-speed motorway into the city was terribly exciting, especially as the flat suburban expanses of Queens slowly gave way to a distant view of Manhattan. The buildings around us grew taller and taller as we approached. I remember how the Manhattan skyline stood out in silhouette against the brilliant midwinter sun. There were so many skyscrapers, the city was so enormous—it seemed hardly possible! After living all our lives in little Bratislava, population 260,000, whose tallest and most modern building was nineteen stories, we were now entering a city crammed with skyscrapers and a population of almost eight million.

For the first few weeks, we were going to stay at Ivan's apartment, a compact one-bedroom at 350 East Thirtieth Street, a block or so from the East River. He had chosen the place, he said, because it was just half a block from the NYU Medical Center, which was where he spent most of his time. The apartment was neat and tidy, but I immediately realized we would not be able to stay long there without inconveniencing him, for it was really an apartment designed for a single person.

That night we went to an early dinner at Marchi, a little Italian restaurant down the street. To our amazement we were served an elaborate, multicourse meal: antipasto, lasagna, a fish dish, two meat dishes, and two desserts—one of which, diced fresh cantaloupe, seemed utterly miraculous to me, for in Bratislava there was no such thing as a ripe melon in wintertime. The quantity of food we were served that night was overwhelming, all of it delicious. At first I assumed that Ivan had special-ordered everything on our behalf, and done so at great expense—but no: as he laughingly explained, this was the set menu every night of the week!

The following morning Ivan had a surgery scheduled, so Jan and I were on our own. By late morning, we had found our way down to the U.S. Immigration and Naturalization Service field office downtown, near City Hall. After presenting our identification documents, we applied for our green cards, the permits that allow a foreign national to live and work legally in the United States. It was all so incredibly simple, and the clerks were so patient and helpful. To our amazement, the green cards were simply sent to us by mail, arriving at Ivan's apartment by the end of the week.

Jan's work would not begin for six more days, so we decided to do some exploring. At first we kept close to the apartment and simply walked around the neighborhood, discovering the food markets, coffee shops, restaurants, and newsstands. Then, despite the frigid weather, we began walking all over Manhattan, because we were determined to learn our way around. Understanding the subway and bus systems took some doing. In fact, everything was so strange: telephone booths, grocery stores, the coinage and paper money. And the streets were bustling with people of every race and ethnicity.

I still have some snapshots taken by Ivan during our first few weeks—he was an amateur photographer, and on weekends he would take us to places he thought we might like to see. First we went to Lower Manhattan, to Wall Street and the New York Stock Exchange and the older parts of the city, including the Battery. For a nickel apiece we crossed New York harbor by ferry, going to Staten Island and back. From it I had my first sight of the Statue of Liberty. It brought tears to my eyes.

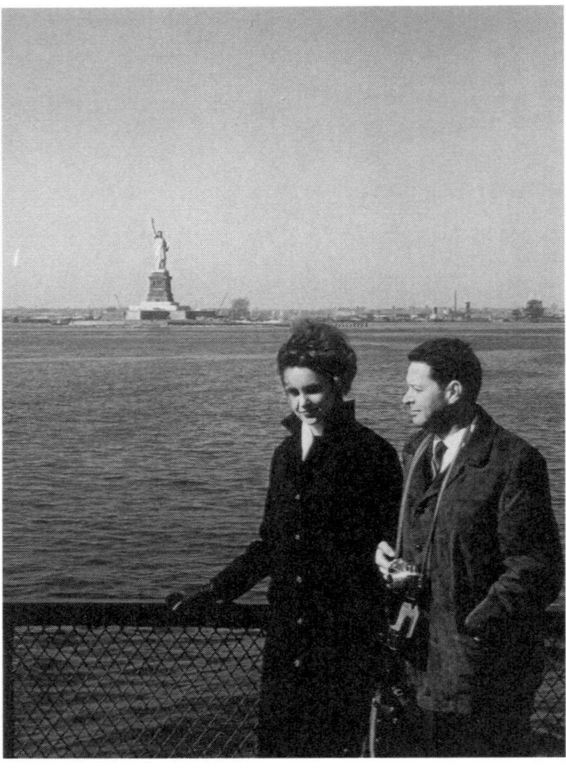

Ivan's snapshot of us with the Statue of Liberty, February 1964

I still have a number of photos that Ivan took that day as Jan and I gazed out at the harbor and the skyline. I remember how, on the return trip to Manhattan, the lights began to go on in the skyscrapers, and the city looked like an enormous piece of lace, all twinkling lights. As we came closer to Manhattan, the buildings regained their outlines, towering over us in the most extraordinary way. I recall thinking that there must be a person behind each and every window, marveling at the notion that I had no connection to any of them. My language, background, and experiences were all so foreign to everyone I had yet encountered; would I ever feel fully at home here? Could anyone here become my friend? It seemed hardly possible.

The following Sunday, Ivan took us uptown for lunch at the Palm Court restaurant of the Plaza Hotel. I was thrilled by the elegance of the place, fascinated by the beautifully dressed women at neighboring tables. After coffee Ivan suggested we take a stroll in Central Park, and we walked all the way up to the Metropolitan Museum of Art, wandering from one gallery to another there until the guards told us it was closing time. How miraculous an art collection, and how crowded and joyful the place was, compared to the Slovak National Gallery. So many people enjoying one painting after another!

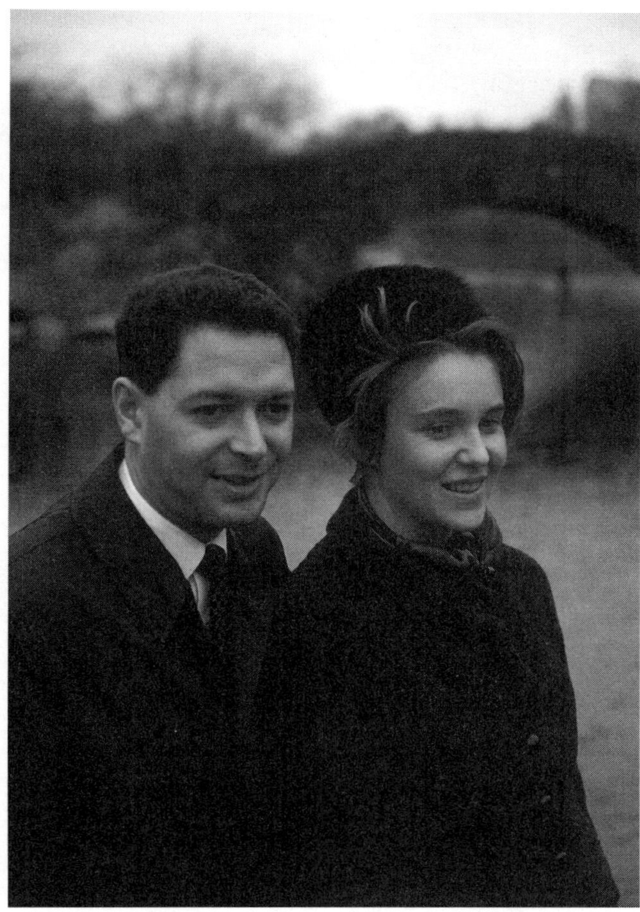

Another snapshot by Ivan, taken in Central Park

I was surprised by Ivan's liking the museum so much. He had changed in the years since our mother died. He was so nice to me now, so helpful, so full of ideas about how we might get started in our new life. And he seemed particularly happy that I had become an art historian and curator—since he, too, had recently developed an interest in art.

The thing that most astonished me about the Met was its size. There was nothing like it in Czechoslovakia. The only place I could compare it to was the Kunsthistorisches Museum in Vienna, which I had visited only briefly. Seeing so many world masterpieces in one place impressed me profoundly. Jan and I would eventually come to know the many other art museums of New York City—the Museum of Modern Art, the Guggenheim, the Frick, the Whitney, and the Brooklyn Museum among them—but it was the Met impressed me most. From that very first visit, I hoped to someday become part of it.

As the weeks passed, Jan began to spend more and more time at NYU—but not in the way he initially imagined. He expected to start working in the lab right away, but in fact he had a surprisingly difficult time tracking down Milton Salton, who had offered him the job. Salton was an Australian-born, British-trained bacteriologist who had only recently been appointed chairman of the department of microbiology. Jan had an equally confusing time with the personnel department, for they had received no direct instructions from Salton, and so were in no position to give him a work contract, much less his first paycheck. Jan didn't dare tell these people that we were living on borrowed money and extremely worried about our debts. Ivan had privately reassured us he would cover all our expenses until we could pay him back, but Jan and I felt more and more uncomfortable as days turned into weeks with no contract and no money. I think we both feared the job might never come through.

My brother's apartment wasn't large enough for the three of us, so even as I fretted about Jan's contract I started looking for a place of our own. It seemed a good idea for us to live near Ivan and the NYU Medical Center—we assumed Jan would be working long hours there too, and would appreciate the convenience of being so close to his lab. At that time apartments were far more widely available (and affordable) in New York City than they are now, so I soon found one that suited our budget and needs. It was two blocks from Ivan, at 250 East Thirty-second Street: a compact one-bedroom apartment at the back of the building, with a view of the Empire State Building. The newly constructed building was clean and secure, with a pleasant lobby and a full-time doorman. Because the management was having a problem finding tenants (the building was only half occupied) we were offered two months' free rent as an incentive for signing a two-year lease. Ivan lent us the first month's rent and the money for the security deposit; he also provided a letter of guarantee for our new landlord. We would live there for the next five years.

Our apartment was not large, but its cleanliness, modernity, and conveniences amazed me, given that it was all so different from my childhood home in Bratislava. The flat came with a dishwasher, built-in air-conditioning, and a laundry room in the basement that featured highly efficient washing machines and dryers. Along with our bedroom and living room, we had a well-laid-out kitchenette. I would do all our shopping, cooking, washing, ironing, and housecleaning for the next two years, long after I entered the workforce and began working from nine to five.

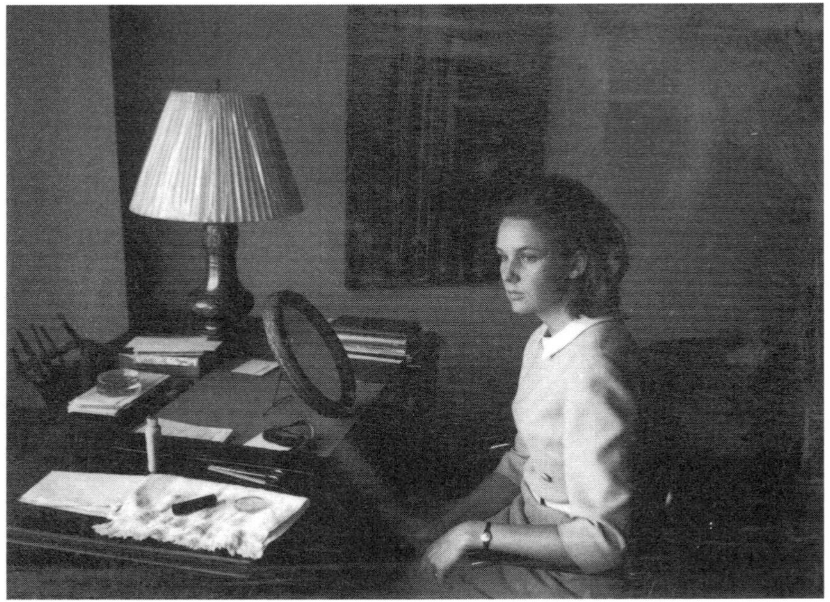

In our Thirty-Second Street apartment

NYU ultimately took six weeks to hire Jan officially, giving him the title of assistant professor. Three weeks later—more than two months after our arrival—he received his first paycheck. Only then were we able to open a bank account and start the long process of repaying my brother all the money he had loaned us over the past year. Since we were still short of cash, and since I was still unemployed, I told Ivan I would clean his apartment and do his washing and ironing for him, just as I had when we were younger. He was of course delighted with this arrangement.

As Jan settled in at NYU, he became extremely focused on his research. Beginning with little more than an empty room, he outlined several new projects and then lined up an able group of researchers to assist him. Six months after our arrival, in the fall of 1965, he submitted his first grant application, and by the spring of 1966 he was teaching microbiology at the medical school. Although he had never been interested in teaching, he found he had a knack for it—in fact, he soon grew to love it, largely because his students were so bright and highly motivated. One of his first and best students, Douglas R. Lowy, subsequently helped Jan write his grant applications, because the documents were very technical and, as a foreigner, Jan had no idea how such things needed to be done. After receiving his first grant (which came from the National Institutes of Health), Jan was able to buy the needed equipment. He had always been passionate about his work, but with the incredible new opportunities and substantial financial assistance made possible by NYU, his productivity skyrocketed. He was soon totally engrossed in a series of exciting projects, and routinely putting in twelve-hour days, often returning to his lab-office after dinner to work late into the night.

My own efforts, meanwhile, were focused on the more pragmatic and quotidian aspects of our new life in New York: creating and maintaining our home, paying off our debts, and learning to live on a budget while dealing with the surprisingly high cost of living in Manhattan. We had arrived with only one small suitcase apiece, so we needed to buy clothing—particularly clothes for warm weather, since all we had were the winter clothes we had taken to Vienna in our overnight bags. Jan particularly hated the shoes he had arrived in, pointy-toed things from Budapest that were both unfashionable and deeply uncomfortable, so that was the first item we replaced. I was slower to buy anything substantial; as I recall, I had only one dress and two skirts during my first two years in New York.

We had no furniture to start, so Ivan once again loaned us some money and we bought two beds. He also drove us out to Queens, to the Salvation Army, where cast-off furniture could be acquired for next to nothing. Only after several visits there did I find things I liked enough to bring home: a desk and chair for work, a small dining table with four matching chairs. I also invested in some plain new dishes, glasses, cutlery, kitchen utensils, and pots and pans. Obtaining a telephone took a bit of organizing. After three months we acquired a television. Jan and I rarely watched anything on it apart from the news, but I used it to improve my English-language comprehension—for I found American accents (and American slang) a great challenge.

Grocery shopping and cooking weren't easy for me at first, since I wasn't used to American foods, nor to the weights, measurements, and temperatures called for in American recipes (I had never worked with Fahrenheit before, and the gas marks common to European ovens had no equivalents on American stoves). I had no friend to tell me what foods here were good, and there was such an incredible variety of food on offer in the supermarkets—so many things I'd never seen in Bratislava—that I was often confused. I learned mostly by trial and error. Jan was very patient, though, and always very grateful for our home-cooked meals, however oddly they may have turned out.

To be honest, the biggest challenge I faced those first few months was loneliness: with Jan working all day and then again after dinner, I was alone nearly all the time. Unlike Jan, I didn't have important or interesting work to connect me to others. So far as my academic career was concerned . . . well, I hadn't been able to bring along my dissertation when we fled, and while I still hoped I might submit the work, it was simply impossible to focus on it now, for we were in debt and I needed a paying job. I also needed to learn English, a task made more difficult by the fact that I had no friends with whom to converse.

The people I eventually came to know were mostly associates of Jan's, but even then, I spent only brief periods in their company, and their talk was mostly on scientific subjects. I had no connection to anyone else, and no sense of how to make a friend. In fact it would be many years before I developed any close friendships in New York. At times, feelings of loneliness and disconnection completely overwhelmed me.

American English proved even more of a challenge than I had anticipated. New Yorkers, I found, tend to speak rapidly and informally, their speech peppered with an impossible number of obscure references and slang. Worse yet, none of the other languages I spoke were of any use to me in my new life; the only other language I heard regularly in New York was Spanish, a language I'd never studied. I did everything I could think of to increase my English comprehension, and diligently practiced speaking English every time I went out to the shops.

Despite the loneliness of those first months, I remember it as a time of great hope and wonder. Jan seemed well on his way to being a great success at NYU, and New York itself was a very exciting place to be. Every weekend we had some extraordinary experience in the city's many museums and galleries. Even as I was cut off from all family and friends, and struggling to accustom myself to listening to, thinking in, and speaking a language I had only just recently learned, I was intrigued by the new ways, new words, and new ideas that surrounded me. None of the customs, traditions, manners, and social expectations I had grown up with seemed to apply here, which was both terrifying and liberating. I literally had no idea what to expect from individuals I interacted with daily. But somehow, I was managing to enjoy myself, particularly when I was immersing myself in the city's cultural riches. I had a strong sense that if I could just keep my own anxiety from getting the better of me, I was going to be fine.

Only upon looking back on our first year in America do I realize what a significant year 1965 was, both in the cultural history of New York City and in the social history of the nation as a whole. After John F.

Kennedy's assassination in November 1963, his successor, Lyndon Johnson, had managed to pass the Civil Rights Act of 1964, outlawing discrimination based on race, color, religion, sex, and national origin. He also enacted his plan for the Great Society, a place in which "no child will go unfed, no youngster will go unschooled." Meanwhile his War on Poverty initiative proposed a broad range of social programming to better the lives of the average working American. Transit, housing, medical care, education, and environmental protections were all improved through federal actions funded by the extraordinary growth and wealth of the U.S. economy.

New York was hosting a world's fair when we arrived, with the U.S. pavilion celebrating the Great Society under the theme "Challenge to Greatness." Pope Paul VI visited New York eight months after our arrival to address the United Nations, celebrate mass at Yankee Stadium, meet with President Johnson, and visit the Vatican exhibit at the world's fair, where Michelangelo's *Pietà* was on display for the first time in the Western Hemisphere. Jan and I were not interested in seeing the pope, but we did make a point of going to the Queens fairgrounds to see the *Pietà*.

New York that year was a city of the future. A vast network of highways, tunnels, bridges, and parks had been constructed throughout the New York metropolitan area during the previous fifty years, including vast, lofty structures such as the George Washington Bridge, the Triborough Bridge, the Throgs Neck Bridge, the Bronx-Whitestone Bridge, the Henry Hudson Bridge, and the Verrazano Narrows Bridge. Impressive works of civic architecture had also arisen, including the United Nations Headquarters, built in 1952 and incorporating designs by Oscar Niemeyer and Le Corbusier, and Lincoln Center, built in 1965 with both Philip Johnson and Eero Saarinen as consulting architects. Many other major architectural landmarks had been constructed in Manhattan just before we immigrated or were being built as or soon after we arrived, including Mies van der Rohe's Seagrams Building (1958), Frank Lloyd Wright's Solomon R. Guggenheim Museum (1959), Richard Roth, Walter Gropius, and Pietro Belluschi's Pan Am Building (1963), Marcel Breuer's Whitney Museum of American Art (1966), and Kevin Roche and John Dinkeloo's Ford Foundation (1967). Roche and Dinkeloo would begin a massive renovation and reimagining of the Metropolitan Museum of Art just a few years later. It seemed to us a a city exploding with artistic and architectural dreams, projects, and ambitions.

Invigorated by the creative and artistic energy of the city, I was struggling with the question of my own future direction. Art history is not the most practical field for an immigrant, and establishing myself here as a curator or museum administrator seemed almost impossible, given the vast social and cultural differences between New York and Bratislava. What might I do instead? For a short while I considered returning to my first love, medicine. Ivan's success indicated to me that doctors were well respected in New York, made a good living, and had many job opportunities. I investigated the possibility of applying to an American medical school, but I learned that, in addition to improving my English, I would need to complete two full years of college-level science courses before I could even apply. Then, if accepted, I would need to borrow a great deal of money for tuition. Ivan might have loaned me some of that money, but he had already done so much on our behalf, and I knew it would be many, many years before I could afford to pay him back. So that line of inquiry reached a dead end.

Another possibility was motherhood, about which I was ambivalent. Much as I loved children, I had already spent so much of my childhood, adolescence, and young adulthood caring for Pavol. That responsibility had taken me away from my so many friends and experiences; I sensed that were I to have a child of my own, I would once again be isolated and frustrated. Had Jan felt very strongly about having children, I might have reconsidered. However his focus was on his work: he had little time or interest for anything else. Upon consideration, I returned once again to the project of finding museum work.

My first step was to send out cover letters, letters of inquiry, and my curriculum vitae to every cultural institution I could think of. In the weeks that followed I received several polite responses, there were no invitations to interview. It was very hard on my self-esteem. Of course, I was hardly surprised that the New York museum world had no pressing need for a Slovakian art historian whose specialty was Kremnica medals and whose work experience consisted mostly of cataloguing Communist-themed propaganda at the Slovak National Gallery! Still, I felt the rejection deeply, mostly because I had no friends or colleagues to reassure me of my worth, nor any connections within the New York curatorial world to counsel or advise me.

Being a practical person, and rather than giving way to self-doubt or despair, I began looking into alternatives. For a while I considered working in a supermarket or a department store—anything to improve our financial situation. I also took a long, hard look at my talents and abilities, which ultimately led me to expand my job search. Realizing I was good at managing information, organizing and maintaining records, and speaking foreign languages, I considered library work. It seemed hardly as attractive to me as museum work, but jobs were more readily available.

Oddly enough, my early life experiences now proved most valuable to me, for as lonely as I might have been, I was neither scared nor intimidated. Never for a moment did I lose hope about the challenges ahead. Having survived the wartime bombing of Bratislava, the horrors of life under the Slovak nationalists and the Nazis, the near destruction of our home by the Allies, the subsequent invasion of the Russian army, the Russian-sponsored Communist takeover of the country, the confiscation of our family's land and assets, and the blacklisting of our family, I was, at age twenty-nine, deeply confident that I would ultimately do well in America. To be unemployed and in debt in a strange new land where I had not yet mastered the language was neither easy nor comfortable; nevertheless, it was far from the worst thing that had ever happened to me. Jan and I were together in this new life of ours, and I knew that together we would thrive.

9

Starting Out in Curating

As we were settling into our new apartment, I continued sending out cover letters and résumés, this time to libraries as well as museums. While none resulted in an invitation to interview, a few responses were encouraging. For example, the director of the Frick Collection suggested that I revise and reformat my curriculum vitae to suit the American standard—and I did so immediately.

Ultimately, it was through a new friend that I got my first job. Helen Garrison, the cousin of Margaret Kunz in Vienna, had very kindly met with me to see how she might be of help. She turned out to be a generous person who had recently left her job at the Brooklyn Museum to have twin daughters. Knowing that the museum was always looking for volunteers, she suggested I contact a colleague there for an interview. I didn't initially want to be a volunteer, since I wanted to pay off our debts as soon as possible. But the interview was a pleasant one, and it resulted in an offer to work as a library volunteer. I began at the Brooklyn Museum Library in the late spring of 1965.

Prior to meeting Helen, I had not yet visited Brooklyn, much less its museum. The Brooklyn Museum is in fact New York City's second largest, with over 1.5 million objects in its collections and remarkable holdings in Egyptian, classical, ancient, and Near Eastern art. Its American collections were also exceptional. When I started, the museum's director was Thomas S. Buechner, a very young and energetic person who had revitalized the museum by updating its galleries and making many of its works available to the public for the very first time.

My daily commute to Brooklyn was quite an adventure. I spent an hour on the subway, changing trains twice—boarding the Lexington Avenue local at Thirty-Third Street, changing at Union Square for the express, and then, once in Brooklyn, transferring again, this time to the IRT Seventh Avenue line, at Nevins Street, and riding four stops to Eastern Parkway. On that ride I saw people from all corners of the world—Latin Americans, Asians, African Americans, Central and Eastern Europeans, Western Europeans, Middle Easterners—and was fascinated by their diversity. Everyone moved so quickly, whether on the sidewalks or stairwells or subway passages. From the exit on Eastern Parkway, I had just a short walk along Prospect Park to the Brooklyn Museum.

Unfortunately, my new job was not very interesting—just typing and filing. In those days before computers, all recordkeeping was done by hand, requiring constant updating and revision, and this sort of work fell to what was called a secretarial pool, a group of typists (all of us women) working on manual typewriters. There were no copy machines back then; and since copies were made with carbon paper, and corrections could be made only via strikeout, neatness and accuracy in typing were always of greatest importance.

I wish I could say that I was a fine typist, but I wasn't. For one thing, I was still adapting to thinking and writing in English. And while Slovak and Czech typewriter keyboards are roughly the same as American ones—they all use the Latin alphabet—my native language makes heavy use of diacritics, so I was used to employing combination keystrokes to compose certain letters of the alphabet. English does not have diacritics and, apart from that, my awareness of English spelling was limited. Therefore, I found myself making the same mistakes over and over, becoming terribly frustrated with myself. But years studying piano ultimately helped me with the required coordination, as did the sheer volume of typing work. My continued home study of English also played a part—every evening, after dinner with Jan, I would sit down with my English-language textbook and practice verb tenses, sentence construction, and vocabulary.

My work at the museum proved to be surprisingly lonely, since typing in even the most convivial of places is not a social occupation, and to make matters worse my desk was exceptionally isolated. I had hoped to meet some cultured people at the Brooklyn Museum, but as I soon discovered, the curators rarely interacted with the library staff. When they did, they tended to speak only with top-level librarians. Because the typing I was doing required no interaction with anyone apart from my supervisor, I spoke to no one, and due to the fact that I couldn't afford to eat in the museum's cafeteria, I wasn't able to practice my English with co-workers during my lunch break. I simply spent that hour alone at my desk.

However, I achieved a breakthrough the day my supervisor discovered my foreign-language skills. While my degree in art history was of little interest to her, and while my typing was not what it should have been, the library had a large number of foreign-language art history books, and many needed their titles translated into English for cataloguing purposes. Few of the librarians spoke a language other than English, so I was immediately given the job of translating titles from Hungarian, Czech, Russian, Slovak, Polish, French, and German into English and then entering those translations into the card catalogue. My supervisor was delighted with my abilities, and her delight made me feel so much better about myself.

My days at the museum passed quickly. Volunteers were not allowed to work more than five hours per day, so I often took a little time for myself in the museum before going home, walking through the galleries and learning about the collections. Simply to be in the presence of so many beautiful objects and artworks filled me with joy. I found myself most drawn to the American painting collection and early American furniture collection; I suppose this was because I wanted so much to know everything about my new country: its history, its cities, its art, and its culture.

Three months after joining the library, I was told that since the paid staff would be taking their vacations at the beginning of August, no volunteer workers would be needed until mid-September. I was urged to take a vacation myself. The idea was tempting, especially since it was one of the hottest summers on record in New York City. But Jan and I had work to do. I spent the end of the summer sending out more letters of inquiry for paid employment. Thanks to my volunteer work at the Brooklyn Museum, I had established myself as a competent would-be librarian trainee with significant and proven language skills. As a result, my inquiries met with a far more enthusiastic response. By the end of August I had my first real job offer: a position at the main branch of the New York Public Library, on Forty-Second Street and Fifth Avenue.

I was just about to take that job when I received another letter, this one from the Metropolitan Museum. A month earlier, through another introduction provided by Helen Garrison, I had spoken briefly with a curator who suggested that I apply for a job in the museum's cataloguing division. No jobs were available at the time, but I had filled out an application. Now the letter from the Met informed me that a job had recently become available—unfortunately not in the museum's cataloguing division, but rather in its Watson Library, its well-known reference library.

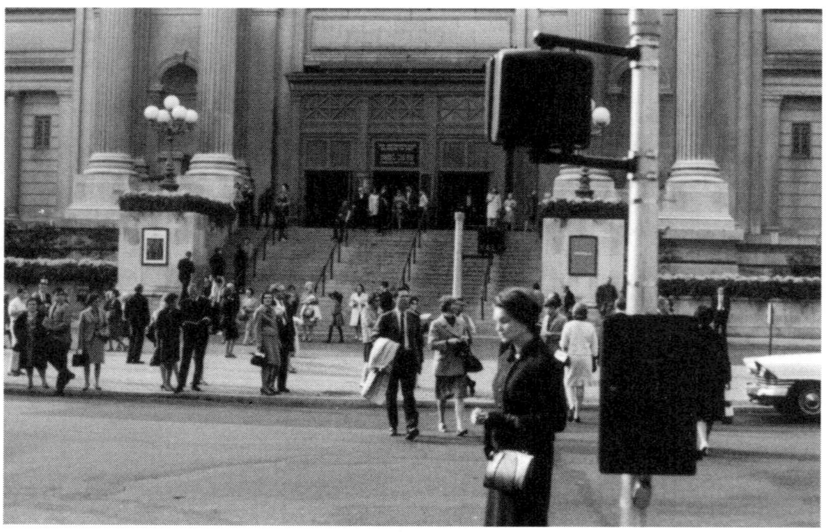

In front of the main entrance to the Metropolitan Museum of Art, 1965

While the Public Library had offered me a bit more money and a better job title, I decided to take the job at the Met because the Watson is one of the best art history libraries in the United States, and, perhaps more important, it was in the Metropolitan Museum. I knew my background in art history would prove more useful there, and of course I continued to hope that I might eventually move back into curatorial work.

The job on offer was simply that of a clerk-typist, very similar to the work I'd been doing in Brooklyn, and the salary and benefits were minimal—my gross annual pay would be just $3750, approximately two dollars per hour, which at that time was a mere seventy-five cents per hour above the federal minimum wage. (I would later learn that it was close to the lowest wage then offered at the museum.) But as I told Jan, it was two dollars more per hour than I had been making at the Brooklyn Museum, so I was clearly making progress!

I remember that on my first day of work I wanted so much to make a good impression. I was still very self-conscious about my mediocre typing skills and my heavily accented English. I was also self-conscious about my appearance, since my wardrobe was modest, and many of the women in the museum were beautifully dressed. As I soon discovered, though, my new position as clerk-typist was not one in which fashion would matter, for I would not be seen much. Nor did it require a high volume of typing. As for my accent, well . . . many people who worked at the Metropolitan Museum came from international backgrounds and had accents of their own. In fact, within a few days, my accent led Elizabeth Usher, the head of the library, to discover my language skills, and to recognize them as an asset. Once again, my knowledge of Russian, Czech, Polish, Slovak, German, French, and Hungarian proved something of a marvel to my co-workers, because the Watson (like all art history libraries) had a high percentage of foreign-language texts.

We clerk-typists worked very hard at the Watson, since there was always so much to be done. Elizabeth Usher required everyone on her staff to arrive promptly at nine a.m. and to remain without fail until five o'clock. Lunch hours and coffee breaks were strictly monitored, and during the workday we were always being checked on for productivity—I suppose because most of the work was so dull that most people would be inclined to linger over a lunch break or a chat.

However, thanks to my ability with languages, my job soon became far less dull. For example, when I was asked to double-check that a long list of foreign-language books ordered for the library were not already present in the library's collections, I found that many of them were indeed there—but because their titles had been improperly translated, they had been miscatalogued and misplaced. As my ability with multiple languages became known, various people would come to me for help with translations. Doing so was my pleasure: it made me feel valued and recognized—and in this way I began to meet many interesting people throughout the museum.

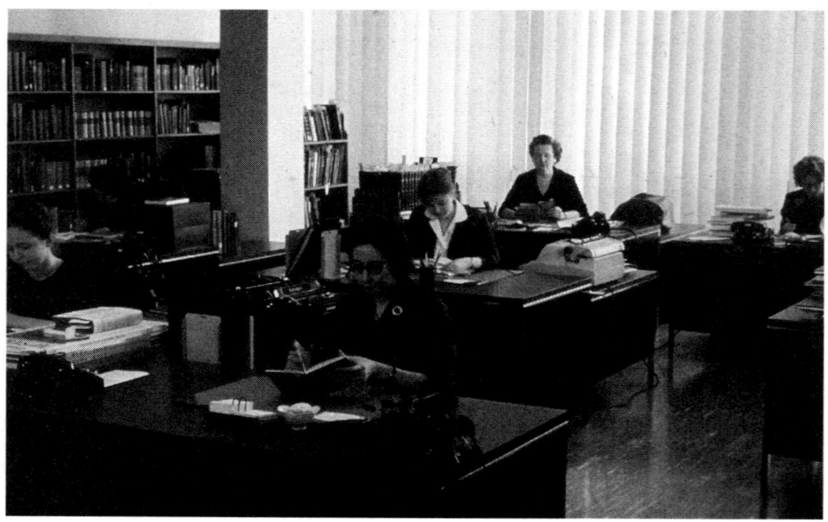

The Watson Library, Metropolitan Museum, 1965

My salary from the Metropolitan meant a great deal to me—not only because being paid is a form of personal recognition and an affirmation of one's worth, but also because I truly disliked owing money. While my brother Ivan had an unusually high income, and even though he repeatedly assured us that the money he had loaned us was immaterial,

Jan and I wanted to pay him back as soon as possible. By being very careful in our first year, we did—we were completely out of debt to him (and to the Kunzes in Vienna) by the early fall of 1966.

I should add, however, that the pleasure I took in my new job was never simply about the work or the pay. It was about belonging to the Metropolitan Museum, being part of its team. I was so tremendously excited to have become, in my very small way, part of this great institution. Every day as I walked the halls I knew I was working in one of the most privileged spaces on the planet—not only because it was a showplace and treasure house, but also because it was filled with such wonderful, dedicated people, committed to art, culture, scholarship, and civilization. To live and work among them would give me, in time, my greatest joy and my deepest sense of belonging.

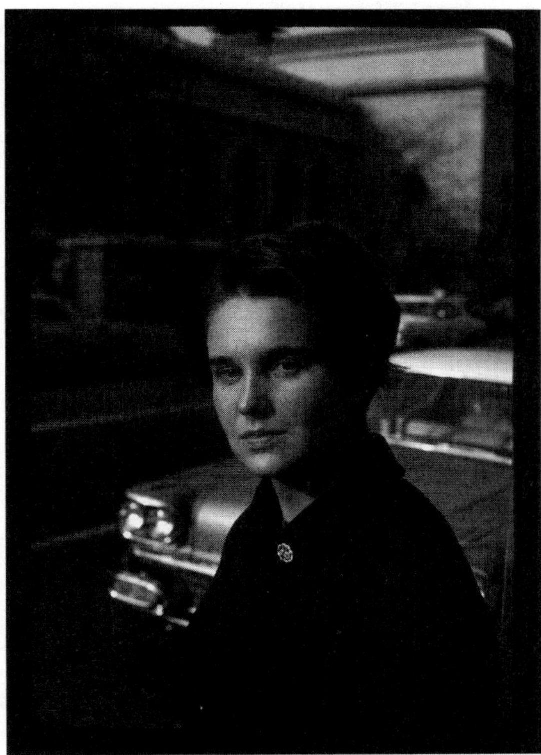

Outside the Metropolitan Museum, 1965

10

The Catalogue Department

Just a few months into my work at the Watson Library, in early 1966, I saw a notice posted on a bulletin board near the museum's employee cafeteria. A position was available in the Office of the Registrar and Catalogue Department for an art historian with foreign-language skills. I applied and was granted an interview with Marcia C. Harty, supervisor of the catalogue. The museum's registrar, William D. Wilkinson, joined us for the interview, explaining that he was doing so because Mrs. Harty, who had supervised the catalogue with great competence and wisdom for many years, was moving toward retirement. The interview went well—they liked me, and I came to them with a strong recommendation from the Watson Library, as well as from several curators. Shortly thereafter I was hired. My first day of work there was February 14, 1966. I clearly remember that the first items I catalogued came from the Department of Arms and Armor—a very new subject for me.

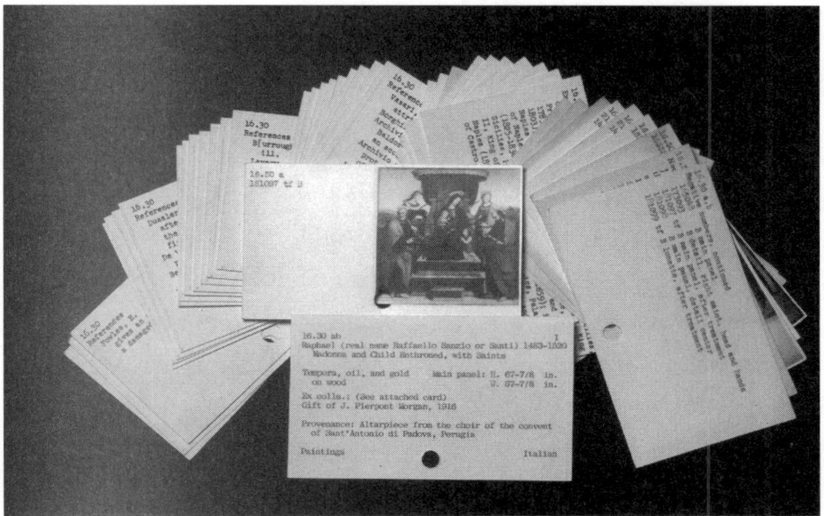

Catalogue cards, Metropolitan Museum

To those outside the museum world, my move from library work to cataloguing work may seem relatively unimportant: in essence, it was a move from one information-management department to another. But within the museum, there's a big difference between a librarian and a cataloguer, for the simple reason that the cataloguing of printed matter and the cataloguing of art objects are two entirely different endeavors. The cataloguing of unique and valued art objects is considered far more important than the management and organization of library books. Art objects are, after all, the heart and soul of the museum. Curators, the keepers and custodians of these art objects, are responsible for presenting these works to the public by way of exhibitions, publications, and didactic materials, and in order to do so they must have comprehensive information about each of the objects they work with. The vast store of information kept by the museum about its art objects and collections is therefore invaluable to the success of the institution and its exhibitions. So much so, in fact, that the maintenance of the catalogue is formally mandated in the Metropolitan Museum's collections management policy, which reads:

> The Museum, through its curatorial, registrar and conservation departments, shall maintain accurate, up-to-date records on the identification, location and condition of all objects in the collection, as well as of ongoing activities such as exhibitions, loans, research and correspondence with donors, artists and scholars. These records should be recorded in the Museum's [catalogue]. Any original paper files regarding the acquisition of objects should also be retained. [The catalogue will also] maintain coherent, organized records on accessioned, non-accessioned and deaccessioned works of art, departmental loans, exhibition loans, and works of art brought into the Museum for possible purchase or gift.

Because the central catalogue was (and remains) the definitive source of all information regarding the Met's works of art, the maintenance of that catalogue is endless, and the catalogue itself is best thought of as an endlessly ongoing work in progress. At the time I joined the department, the catalogue consisted of over five hundred trays of three-by-five-inch cards, a subject index of thirty-seven trays of cards, and many other indexes and glossaries, also on cards. If there were multiple cards for an artwork (as was often the case), the cards were bound together with string. A staff of six to nine cataloguers was constantly adding newly accessioned items to the catalogue and constantly updating existing entry cards. To comprehend the scale of the work, consider the museum's vast holdings: by recent estimation, more than two million works of art, artifacts, and cultural implements spanning fifty centuries of world culture.

Our group of cataloguers not only researched and composed the entries for the cards, but also typed several copies of each completed card, because the museum needed four complete copies of catalogue cards and their attached pictures. Two cards were kept in the curatorial departments, where curators were allowed to add their own handwritten notes. Two other cards were kept in our own department—one in the central catalogue, and one in the secondary catalogue known as the source file. Of the latter pair, one card was filed by the type of object (in the central catalogue), and the other was filed by accession number (in the source file). The cards kept in the central catalogue were available for general consultation; they did not have confidential information regarding such things as prices and the names of anonymous donors. That information, which was considered highly confidential, was kept only in the source file.

As part of my introduction to the Registrar and Catalogue Department, I learned all about its origins. The Metropolitan Museum had been founded in 1870 but only began registering and accessioning its items in 1906. In 1910, a librarian named Margaret A. Gash, working under the direction of Assistant Secretary to the Board of Trustees Henry Watson Kent, initiated the project of writing the museum's central catalogue. The data she included on those early catalogue cards was based upon an example set by the Victoria and Albert Museum in London.[2] In the years that followed, the Met's cataloguing system continued to develop, ultimately becoming one of the finest, best indexed, and most comprehensive art-object catalogues in the world. After World War II, three great American museums—the Metropolitan, the Smithsonian Institution, and the Museum of Modern Art—conferred frequently on the practice of cataloguing, for it was an evolving discipline in the

2 For information on how the catalogue was developed, see Winifred E. Howe, *A History of the Metropolitan Museum of Art*, vol. 2 (New York: Columbia University Press, 1945).

museum world, and each of these museums had been developing its own preferred formats and methodology.

For the first half of the twentieth century, the Metropolitan Museum's Catalogue Department was an independent entity, with offices housed on the top floor of the museum. In 1949, the department was combined with the Office of the Registrar, forming the Office of the Registrar and Catalogue Department. To facilitate coordination between the Office of the Registrar and its catalogue division, the catalogue was moved down to the main floor and situated next to the Registrar's Office. In 1954 its offices were again relocated, with both offices moving from the main floor to the ground floor. Our office was relatively simple: each cataloguer had a small desk, a posture chair, and a typewriter; and there was also a table used by visiting researchers. The cards used for tracking accessions and cataloguing were generated by a multilith, a small offset press used for duplicating office forms in the days before copy machines.

As I quickly learned, the Office of the Registrar handled the receiving and sending of art objects, the numbering of them, the accessioning of them, the measuring and marking of them, and the overseeing of their storage and care. It was also responsible for their classification, their risk assessment, and for any problems concerning their exhibition. Combining the Office of the Registrar with the Catalogue Department made good sense in 1949 because the two groups worked so closely together, particularly on accessioning and deaccessioning. We also had the general responsibility of maintaining accurate, up-to-date records on the identification, location, and condition of all objects in the collection, as well as tracking all ongoing activities regarding those objects: exhibitions, loans, research, and correspondence with donors, artists, and scholars.

Just in case anyone should doubt the thoroughness of the Met's accessions process, the workflow went as follows: when a new object was considered for inclusion in the museum's collection, the curatorial department interested in its acquisition sent a notice, called an Expected Notice, to the Office of the Registrar, letting the registrar know that an object was coming in. When the object arrived, a receipt was generated by the registrar and given to the deliverer of the object. A condition report on the object, known as an Examination Record, was then created for the registrar by the curator and related advisers. Once the Examination Record was complete, the curator wrote a recommendation form about the object to the trustees. That form was sent to the Secretary of the Museum's Office for inclusion in the next trustees meeting. When the trustees formally approved it, the object officially entered the museum's collection.

At that point a new set of records was generated. First came the Pink Card Record—the initial catalogue entry for the object—which was drafted by a cataloguer. After the registrar assigned its accession number (the unique number given to each new acquisition as it entered the museum's collection), that accession number was included on the Pink Card Record. Then a Blue Card Record was generated; this record containing the same information, to be entered into the registrar's numerical file (as opposed to subject file) of accessioned objects—the aforementioned source file. A carbon copy of this record was made, known as the Donor-Vendor Carbon, to be provided to the donor or vendor of the item. The source file card additionally included information on the price paid for the object (if any) by the museum. (The price paid for an object sometimes appears in the central catalogue record too, but only for entries dating up to 1955; after that, the price was kept confidential.) The Treasurer's Office and the Secretary were also given this confidential price information for their records. The Blue

Card Record also included information on the object's measurements, description, signature, marks, and inscriptions.

A cataloguer then created the initial draft of the full central catalogue record. (This first draft was commonly referred to as a Flimsie, because it was typed on thin, flimsy paper.) The draft was then sent to the designated, sponsoring curator to be checked over, and the curator was asked to provide any important additional information about the object. The draft including these curatorial additions was then checked over again by the cataloguers for inconsistencies or mistakes.

At this point the final central catalogue card was generated from the Flimsie. Its content varied according to object, but it always included a photo of the object. Along with that central catalogue card, a matching curatorial department catalogue card (and a duplicate of that card) was also generated, and those two cards were sent to the respective curatorial department for inclusion in its departmental catalogue or catalogues. A so-called Photo Sales Record photo was then created of the object, this time bearing abbreviated catalogue entry information on the verso—this was for both administrative use, and for use by the Photo Sales and Slides Department. Finally, information about the object was now added to various indexes within the central catalogue. These indexes included the artist index, the title index, the subject index, and the former collections index.

Because so much paperwork was involved, accession work was a labor-intensive process, full of many little details, all of which needed to be checked and double-checked at every step. Precision and accuracy were tremendously important, given that, for example, the transposition of even one digit or letter in an accession number could easily cause this essential information (and sometimes the valued object itself!) to be misplaced, misidentified, or, in the worst possible scenario, lost.

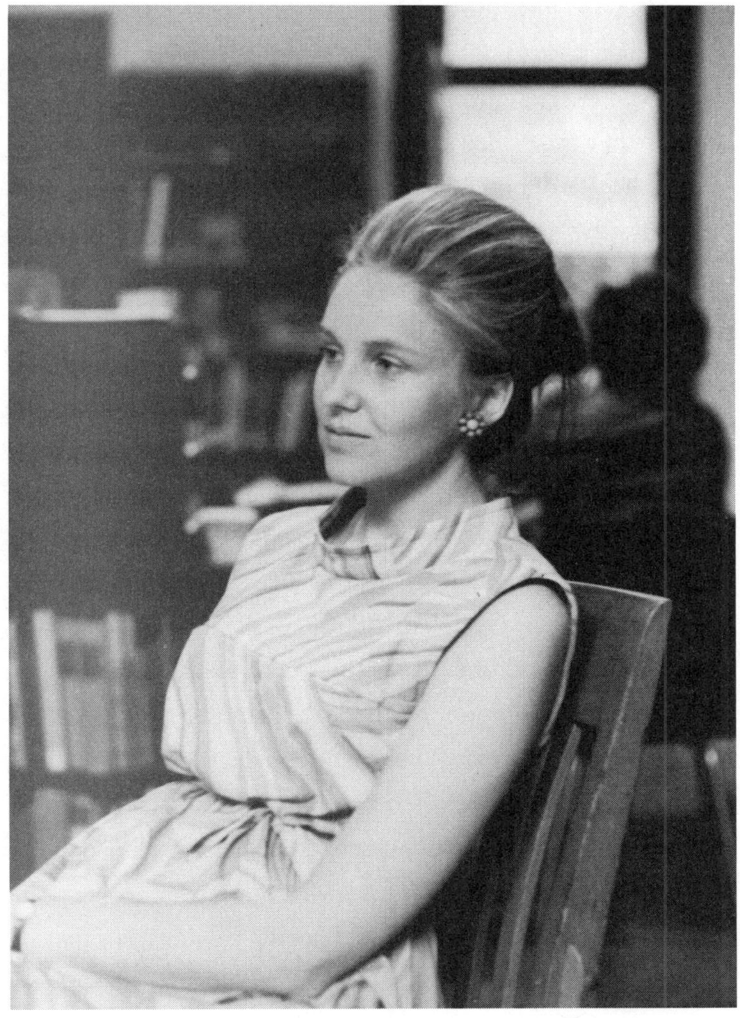

In the old offices of the Catalogue Department, September 1970

A few years into my work, I wrote a short piece for the *Metropolitan Museum of Art Bulletin* in which I attempted to explain to the museum's members what we did in our department, and why. It reads (in part):

People who picture the Catalogue Division of the Registrar and Catalogue Department as a place where brochures are stacked from floor to ceiling would be surprised to know that this division neither issues nor sells [exhibition] catalogues. Instead, a visitor, if patient enough to locate this office in the basement of the north wing of the Museum, would find a long corridor whose walls are lined with neatly arranged file cabinets. These cabinets house about a million catalogue cards, which contain descriptions and reference information relating to almost all the objects owned by the Metropolitan Museum of Art.

The Museum Catalogue . . . which in format resembles a library card catalogue, was an invaluable contribution by the Metropolitan to museum methods. Today we have one of the most extensive and comprehensive catalogues in the world. . . .

The cataloguers supplement th[e] basic information on the cards with a record of ex-collections, and notes on the history of the object's execution, on its relationship to similar pieces, and on its iconography. Whenever possible, they support their findings with extensive reference to publications, exhibitions catalogues, and archive documents. . . . What is included in the individual catalogue cards varies with individual objects. The information available on some archaeological materials may be so scant as to warrant only a few lines on a single card, whereas for the twelfth century Bury St. Edmunds ivory cross . . . it fills no fewer than 121 cards.

To serve their function as a central source of data on all Museum objects, the catalogue cards must be organized in a systematic fashion. For example, to find Claude Monet's *Garden at Sainte-Adresse*, one would first go to the section containing the cabinets for Western art and the series of drawers devoted to paintings. Within the subclassification Paintings, French, the cards for this work would be filed under the artist's name.

Accessibility of information is augmented by extensive cross indexing. Index entries include names of artists, titles, types of objects, subjects depicted, iconography, provenance, and ex-collections. The usefulness of the index is manifold. For example, works in different media by a single artist will not all be found under one category in the main catalogue. A look into the index quickly helps to locate cards for every work in the collections done by that artist. Or a scholar might want to study all works of art in the Museum representing one subject, for instance, "Perseus," or to locate one type of object, such as apostle spoons. He again would turn to the subject index for a quick answer.

Over a period of years, the Catalogue Division, which originally served merely a record-keeping function, has entered into much closer cooperation with curatorial departments. It is now staffed with nine research cataloguers, each one specializing in one or two areas of museum work. The cataloguers hold master's degrees or the equivalent in art history, and their academic qualifications for appointment are scrutinized by a curatorial committee.

The cataloguing process usually starts with a careful study of newly acquired objects in the Registrar's storeroom. The following stage involves an often-tedious study of literature and documents. Several weeks of research may be required to locate a single pertinent source. Controversial opinions may have to be clarified in consultations with specialists from inside and outside the museum. Only then is the accumulated information condensed into the format of catalogue cards and sent to the appropriate department for approval by a member of the curatorial staff.

I loved my new job, particularly because everyone in my department was wonderful, from the all-important registrar right down to the most junior cataloguer-typist. Their collective passion for art, art history, and connoisseurship inspired me, as did their humility, generosity, and hard work. In my previous job at the Watson Library, my job had been mostly clerical in nature, and relatively repetitive and dull, and the majority of my co-workers had had few ambitions beyond secretarial work. My work in the Catalogue Department, by comparison, was much closer to what I had aspired to in my university years. The work routinely involved researching art objects of exceptional beauty, value, and cultural significance, a fact that kept me mentally and spiritually invigorated. My colleagues shared this sense of excitement, as well as of mission and purpose. They had all worked so hard to be here: every one of the women (we were all women) had a master's degree, and many were on their way to their PhD. A good number of us had accreditation from leading institutions worldwide, including the Sorbonne and the École du Louvre. All hoped someday to curate or to teach, and many were interested in collecting. As a group, we were cooperative, industrious, and reliable. We were also cultured, well traveled, and well read. No wonder, then, that many of us developed close, lasting friendships.

As a team we were responsible not only for the cataloguing of objects and the preparation and proofreading of the catalogue's index cards, but also for helping *anyone* who came to the department to consult the catalogue. There was always some new person presenting us with a problem in need of a solution. The only real tension within the department concerned the vast backlog of work that awaited us every day. Along with the regular updating of the cards within the catalogue, the museum was constantly acquiring new works, and each newly acquired work needed its own new highly detailed catalogue card. Since there were literally tens of thousands of items waiting to be catalogued, there was never enough time to get caught up. We all worked as hard and as fast as we could, hoping not to fall further behind. As a result, most of us came into the office early, and all of us worked well past the traditional museum quitting time of five p.m.

There was no tension at home about my long hours, because Jan had a similar work ethic and he fully supported my career. In consequence I rose quickly through the ranks. While this happened in part due to my dedication and commitment, it was also the result of a series of departures (some expected, some unexpected) among the group's senior members. Our supervisor, Marcia C. Harty, retired in 1968. A senior cataloguer was then promoted to take the job of supervisor, but she quit on short notice several months later, seemingly overwhelmed by the job's demands. Another person then became supervisor, but she, too, decided rather abruptly to leave—in her case, to marry. Several other cataloguers then left to take better jobs. And that's how, in late 1968, two and a half years into my work there and much to my own surprise, I found myself promoted to chief cataloguer.

The new job title brought with it many of the administrative responsibilities previously undertaken by Marcia C. Harty, but I did not have the authority and independence that came with her title of supervisor. Instead, I was to report to the registrar, William D. Wilkinson (and upon his retirement to his successor, John Buchanan). Nonetheless, as chief cataloguer my new duties included coordinating and overseeing all the cataloguing going on within the museum, including accessioning and deaccessioning; this meant I was now not only doing my own work, but also supervising the work of many others. Approximately 55 percent of my time was spent assigning, coordinating, and supervising the work of the cataloguers who worked under me:

deciding upon the fields in which they were to specialize, training the newer cataloguers, and reading draft versions of everyone's catalogue entries—remaining vigilant for any possible errors, including errors of transcription (which were surprisingly frequent). I was also proofreading (and correcting) draft versions of articles written by the cataloguers for the *Metropolitan Museum of Art Bulletin*. Roughly 20 percent of my time was spent directly assisting the registrar, and the remaining 25 percent of my time I was answering inquiries by telephone or letter, assisting in deaccessioning, and doing my own share of the cataloguing and recataloguing, the tasks I loved best. When requested, I would prepare statistics and special reports for the administration. Finally, of course, I was required to oversee departmental personnel matters: sick leave, vacation time, and the like.

This new position of chief cataloguer challenged me for many reasons. It required curatorial and library skills and extensive knowledge of the museum's operations, but it also required a great deal of careful listening, on-the-spot problem solving, and gentle but firm diplomacy. Because I was in charge of the central catalogue, I fielded questions all day long from people throughout the museum—from the administration; from the Bookshop and Reproduction Department; from Conservation; from Education; from the library; from Photo Sales and Slides; from public relations and membership; from the Publications Department; and of course from all seventeen curatorial departments. On top of that, there was the general public (which included but was not limited to journalists, academics, collectors, art dealers, donors, students, and would-be bequeathers), who queried our department daily by telephone, in person, and via correspondence. As such, I appeared to many to be the de facto problem solver and answer person for anything to be found (or lost) within the museum—not an easy job, for sure. But I loved helping people, took great pride in doing it well, and considered myself incredibly lucky to have achieved a position of such trust and responsibility at the Metropolitan Museum of Art.

Amazingly enough, not everyone at the museum was convinced that the catalogue division was indispensable. I did not know it when I joined the department, but the museum's director, James Rorimer, had recently commissioned an investigative review that provided a detailed assessment of the many activities then taking place within the department. Significantly, this report, entitled "The Registrar and Catalogue Department at the Metropolitan Museum of Art: A Report on Its Functions, Responsibilities, Operations and Problems," pointed out that each of the seventeen curatorial departments within the museum maintained its own catalogue of departmental holdings. Those departmental catalogues held records on accessioned, nonaccessioned, and deaccessioned works of art, as well as records of departmental loans, exhibition loans, and works of art brought into the museum for possible purchase or gift. Some of the departments—for example, the Egyptian Department—held tightly to all the information contained within its own catalogue. The question then became: Was this doubling up of cataloguing activities really necessary? Or was it a waste of time, effort, and money?

Marcia C. Harty, who had hired me, was of course aware of this doubling up, and the suggestion of wastefulness that went with it. Just before retiring, she noted in a brief memoir that:

> because this department has often been considered an extravagance and a luxury, the idea of discontinuing it had to be fought by [its founder] Miss Gash all through her career, and by [our former registrar] Irma Bezold Wilkinson for many years. At

> one time it was proposed that each curatorial department do its own cataloguing [for the central catalogue], and the fact that each [department] would need to have a trained cataloguer was difficult to put across. The fact that there would be no uniformity of records, no central Subject Index of Western Art, no certainty that the correct information would reach the Photo Sales and Slides Departments and thence the scholars and public was finally recognized.[3]

As the person who had been in charge of maintaining the catalogue for several decades, Harty knew that an impeccably maintained central catalogue was an absolute necessity for the smooth functioning of the museum. And she further doubted that curators from the Met's many different departments should (or could) be entrusted with the significant (and surprisingly complicated) work of maintaining it.

The report to James Rorimer reached a similar conclusion. "Cataloguing is generally a curatorial function . . . [but] in a large museum with many curatorial departments, ten curators may develop ten different [cataloguing] systems. To maintain uniformity of records for such diverse materials as laces and arms and armor, [there is a demonstrated need for the] centralized cataloguing [of the] Catalogue Department, where each cataloguer [works] under the supervision of the respective curators." Only in that way, the report concluded, would the Catalogue Department remain the museum's central, indisputable, beautifully organized, and entirely reliable source of information concerning the entirety of its holdings.

One big question remained: If the cataloguers were doing work that was best left to curators, wouldn't the Met save money (and

3 Marcia C. Harty, "Some Notes on the History of the Department with Random Recollections on Happenings in the Museum, 1944–1966, as Written Down in Great Haste by Marcia C. Harty" (draft manuscript), Marica Vilcek Archive.

perhaps have a better-written central catalogue) if the cataloguers were dismissed and the curators alone wrote the entries? Possibly so; but, as the report cautioned, the integrity of the catalogue would then be at risk, for there was a great deal of detail-oriented housekeeping and tracking involved in maintaining the catalogue. The curators were already overworked; were they really up to the task? Moreover, the Catalogue Department was at that moment so far behind in its cataloguing of the museum's recent accessions—more than seventeen thousand objects had not yet had their catalogue entries researched or written at the time of the report, and were awaiting inclusion in the Met's records. Given that situation, dismissing the cataloguers seemed inadvisable, and Rorimer therefore made no changes to the system.

But then, just after I joined the department, James Rorimer died. Within the year Thomas P. F. Hoving was named the museum's new director, and a new era began. A self-described trailblazer, innovator, and iconoclast, Hoving immediately set out to streamline and modernize the museum's operations, and at the same time to boost museum attendance and revenues by essentially reinventing the museum-going experience. As part of that enormously complicated project, he too began to question the need for a Catalogue Department.

11

Hoving, the Centennial, and a Crisis

During most of my first year in the Office of the Registrar and Catalogue Department, the Metropolitan Museum was without a director. The trustees' eventual choice, Thomas Hoving, had begun his professional career in the Medieval Department; however, in 1965 he had taken a leave of absence from the museum to join the mayoral campaign of John V. Lindsay. When Lindsay was elected, Hoving stayed on with him to serve as his parks commissioner, a position that coincidentally made him a trustee of the Metropolitan Museum—because the museum, being situated within Central Park, is subject to the parks commissioner's oversight, and as a result, the commissioner has a seat on the board of trustees. While sitting in on these board meetings as parks commissioner, Hoving had learned a great deal about the various challenges the museum's director must face, including its financial challenges—and he had planned and strategized accordingly.

Hoving wanted to expand and popularize the institution in order to ensure its survival. He became its director on March 17, 1967, and in the months and years that followed, he authorized numerous highly publicized acquisitions, developed corporate sponsorships, mounted blockbuster exhibitions, and created an exceptionally profitable gift shop that pioneered the sale of museum-commissioned art reproductions along with museum-generated publications. All these innovations not only sparked publicity and boosted attendance, but also amplified the Metropolitan Museum of Art's name and reputation worldwide.

Hoving simultaneously reimagined the museum as a new kind of social center: he installed more restaurants and cafés, and he staged many more events there too. It was really a very exciting time to work at the Met, for Hoving was transforming it from a sedate old-fashioned treasure house into an international tourist attraction, public forum, and meeting place for people of all nationalities, backgrounds, and classes.

Behind the scenes, Hoving also developed a grand and comprehensive architectural plan for this newly imagined museum, using the firm of Kevin Roche, John Dinkeloo and Associates. Their first great project was to put the entire collection of Egyptian art on view, creating some thirty-eight galleries that were sponsored by Lila Acheson Wallace. (This was actually a long-term project that was first initiated in 1961 under Rorimer, and that reached completion in 1983, five years after Hoving's departure.) Other extraordinary additions, both during and after the Hoving years, include the Robert Lehman Wing (completed 1975), housing an extraordinary collection of old masters, as well as impressionist and postimpressionist art; the Sackler Wing (completed 1978), with its grand atrium for the Temple of Dendur;[4]

4 Egypt offered the Temple of Dendur to the United States in 1965 as a gesture of thanks for the $16 million American contribution for the rescue of the Abu Simbel monuments; it came to the Met on condition that the museum house the temple indoors. The Met's collection of ancient Egyptian art, meanwhile, consists of approximately twenty-six thousand objects of artistic, historical, and cultural importance, dating from the Paleolithic to the Roman period (c. 300,000

the American Wing (completed 1980), featuring twenty-five renovated period rooms and an extraordinary collection of painting and sculpture; the Michael C. Rockefeller Wing (completed 1982), displaying the arts of Africa, Oceania, and the Americas; the Lila Acheson Wallace Wing (completed 1987), displaying modern and contemporary art; and finally the Henry R. Kravis Wing (completed 1991), devoted to European sculpture and decorative arts from the Renaissance to the beginning of the twentieth century.

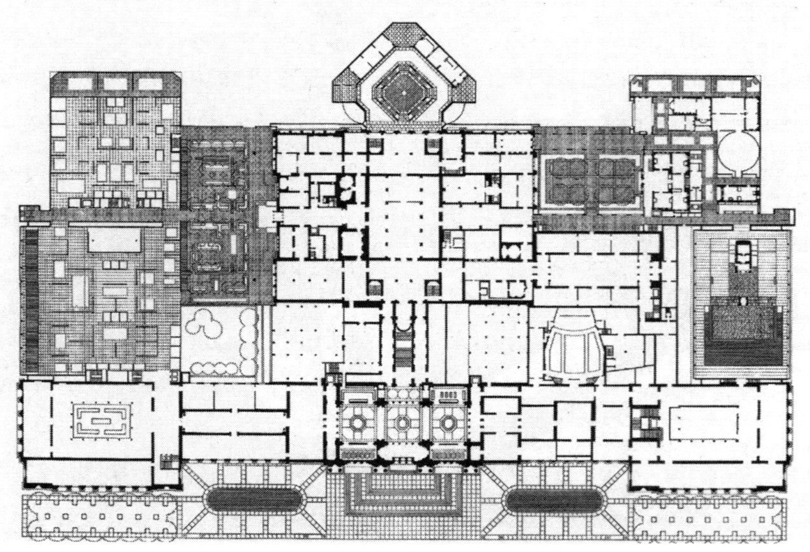

Kevin Roche, John Dinkeloo and Associates' master plan for the Metropolitan Museum, 1970

The Met's first fashion exhibition, "The Art of Fashion," took place in October 1967. The show juxtaposed noteworthy gowns of the nineteenth and early twentieth centuries with the work of top contemporary fashion designers, thereby establishing a mutually beneficial

BCE–fourth century CE), with more than half of the collection derived from the museum's thirty-five years of archaeological excavation work in Egypt.

relationship between the museum and the fashion industry that has continued to the present day. In 1971 the Costume Institute, led by the newly arrived Diana Vreeland, the former editor of *Vogue*, began mounting yearly exhibitions at the Met, and also began using the Met to hold its annual Costume Institute fund-raiser—an arrangement that injected glamour into the otherwise staid museum, even as the museum provided a palatial backdrop for a fashion-industry showcase. The first corporate sponsorship for a major exhibition, meanwhile, was Olivetti's sponsorship of "The Great Age of Fresco: Giotto to Pontormo," which opened to acclaim in the fall of 1968.

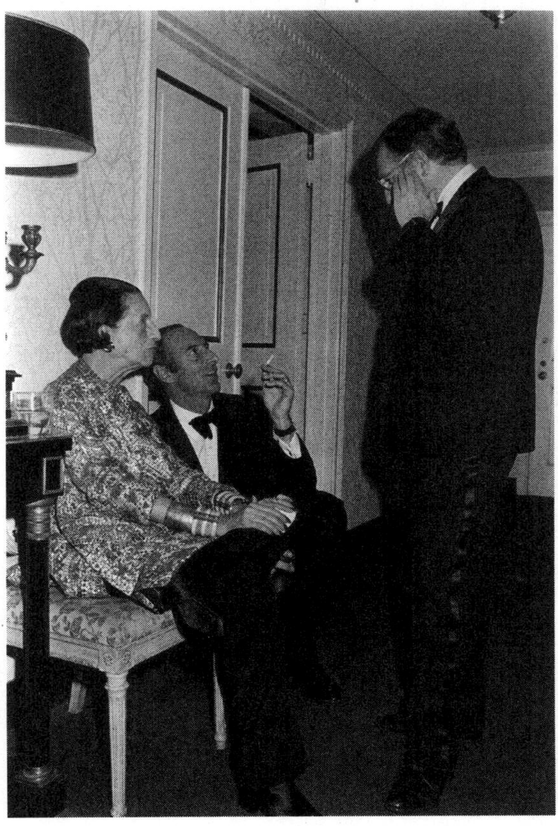

Diana Vreeland and Thomas Hoving

Not everyone who worked at the Met was thrilled by these new developments, which arguably threatened to compromise the museum's august name and reputation. Some even called such developments sellouts. But the connection to sponsorships proved lucrative. I remember when Hoving presented the rest of his so-called Comprehensive Plan for the Second Century to the assembled staff of the museum on April 10, 1970. In his talk, he laid out his ambitious schedule for expanding the Met and its collections even as he emphasized the need to broaden the museum's social outreach. Hoving felt, rightly I think, that the museum needed more visitors, supporters, and underwriters if it were to remain financially viable. He encouraged all of us working at the museum to adjust our outlooks accordingly.

When Hoving became the director of the museum in 1967, I had been working there for about a year. While I didn't often see him, I couldn't help noticing the many changes he was making. The museum was becoming an ever more visible cultural institution thanks to his bold changes in programming, exhibitions, and acquisitions. Before, museum openings had always been very quiet. Now, many people were attending, including young professionals and wealthy socialites. The most elegant young women began appearing at these openings and parties, wearing incredible and unusual outfits.

Probably the most extraordinary of these gatherings took place on April 13, 1970. The Centennial Ball was a grand black-tie affair attended by more than three thousand guests. Tickets for the main dinner-dance were far too expensive for Jan and me, but the museum had thoughtfully arranged a second, less expensive event, described as a "cocktail after-party," and tickets to that event were half price for all museum employees. Since we wanted to be a part of the ball, the main event of the museum's yearlong centennial celebration (the museum had been founded one hundred years earlier, in 1870), we stayed up well past our usual bedtime and dressed up in our finest for the fun.

Our after-party began around ten or eleven in the evening. The ball consisted of dances being held in four separate halls, with each dance evoking a different period in the museum's history—1870, 1910, 1930, and 1970. I remember so many beautifully dressed young people doing all sorts of wild dancing—for it was the 1970 discotheque that remained most popular late into the night. There were fashion models in décolletage so extreme as to seem half naked. It was all so different from the museum I knew in my everyday working life, and certainly very different from any museum function I had ever attended in Czechoslovakia. I was thrilled and delighted by it, because I had come to think of the museum as a sort of second home, and under Thomas Hoving this new home seemed more youthful and energized than ever before.

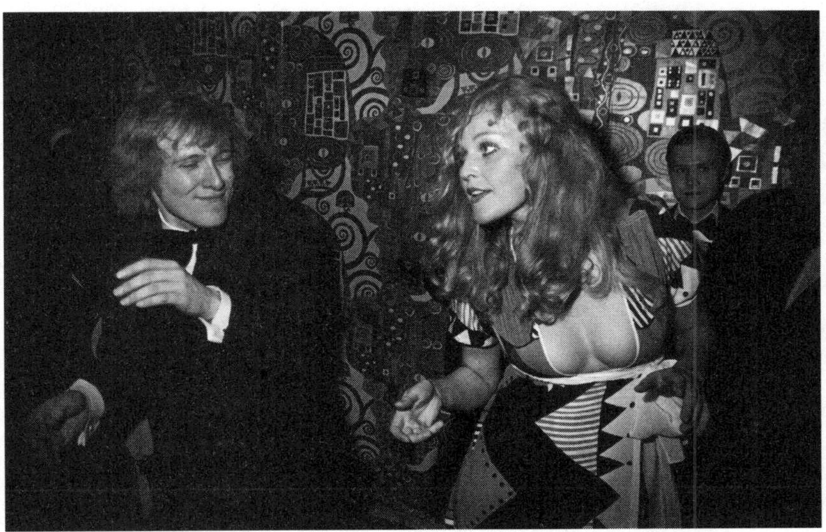

Garry Winogrand. Metropolitan Museum of Art Centennial Ball, New York, 1970

The centennial continued for more than a year, with symposia, concerts, lectures, special tours, and parties throughout that time. The centennial exhibitions began with "New York Painting and Sculpture: 1940–1970," a show establishing New York City's preeminence in postwar contemporary art. Then came "The Year 1200," exploring medieval art during the period 1180–1220; "19th-Century America," focusing on American painting, sculpture, and decorative arts; and "Before Cortés: Sculpture of Middle America," presenting three hundred works of art spanning three thousand years. The last and greatest of the centennial exhibitions was "Masterpieces of Fifty Centuries," displaying nearly five hundred artworks dating from earliest times to the present day.

Of course, these exhibitions took a huge amount of planning and scholarship, and the museum brought in many new people to mount them. The Met also published eighteen books about itself during the centennial, twelve directly related to the centennial, and the remaining six documenting various Metropolitan Museum collections. There were also centennial-related national television projects: "Masterpieces of Fifty Centuries," narrated by Sir Kenneth Clark; a one-hour program about the history of the Metropolitan Museum on NBC; and a series of reports on network television each evening of the week of October 6, 1969, in which each of the five centennial exhibitions was given an individual profile. The museum also sponsored a yearlong art history course consisting of thirty lectures and arranged special visits for members of other museums from across the United States. By the end of the centennial year, the Metropolitan Museum had established itself as a major tourist attraction for New York City and a recognized name in households across America.

Behind the scenes, there was so much more to do. While our charismatic new director was transforming and improving the museum, each of the centennial's special exhibitions—not only the five major exhibitions taking place within the museum, but also the many traveling exhibitions originating at the Met and going out to institutions worldwide—required a huge amount of additional logistics and paperwork. Risk assessment, packing, shipping, insuring, and tracking of all the art objects, whether they were being moved around the museum, moved from storage to the museum, or moved from our museum to other museums—all these responsibilities fell to the Office of the Registrar and Catalogue Department.

The centennial also proved so costly that, as it came to an end, the museum faced a severe financial crisis, with a 1972 budget deficit of $1.5 million. As a result, many of the new people hired by the museum could no longer be kept on the payroll. During 1972 alone, sixty-three members of the curatorial staff were let go. Demonstrations by these staffers in front of the museum—thirteen of whom subsequently accused it of unfair labor practices—created very bad publicity. That publicity threatened to worsen when a group of women working at the museum (including curators Clare Le Corbeiller, Jessie McNab Dennis, and Clare Vincent) filed a complaint with the New York Attorney General alleging sexual discrimination; it was obvious that, despite the high proportion of women employed by the Met, nearly all the top positions were occupied by men.[5] The most glaring inequality was in the catalogue section, where all the cataloguers were women. Our pay was exceptionally low, and the possibility of promotion into the curatorial ranks was historically rare.

As a result of this complaint, the administration grew more sensitive to the question of sexual discrimination. So far as the women of the Office of the Registrar and Catalogue Department were concerned, however, the proposed changes would not be to their

5 For more on the 1972 budget crisis and its related labor conflicts, see "Boomer of the Arts," *The New York Times*, Nov. 30, 1975.

advantage. Rather, the administration wanted the majority of the cataloguers to be let go, and for the museum's curators to take on the work of maintaining the catalogue.

In early spring of 1972, I was asked to coordinate with our new registrar, John Buchanan, on a report about the viability of doing so, and my response was not in favor of it. As I noted,

> The proposal [to sever the Central Catalogue from the Registrar's Office and transfer cataloguing functions to the curatorial departments] was first advanced as a solution to the frustrated desires of individual cataloguers to join curatorial departments. It was strengthened by the Museum's present financial crisis in the belief, possibly mistaken, that such a reorganization will save money. It is the thesis of this report that the disbanding of the Central Catalogue would be a serious mistake [and that furthermore] transferring cataloguing functions to the curatorial departments while at the same time attempting to maintain the Central Catalogue with a skeleton staff would seriously weaken the Central Catalogue and lead to its deterioration as one of the world's great art sources and possibly to its eventual abandonment.
>
> Should the responsibility for cataloguing be shifted to the curatorial departments? . . . The answer to this question should be an unequivocal no. If such a reorganization is carried out, it is quite likely that we will end up with seventeen different cataloguing systems. [Rather,] the integrity of the Central Catalogue should be safeguarded, and cataloguers should be given adequate recognition in terms of pay and status. . . . And the door should always be left open for the transfer—not

> promotion—of promising curatorial types [from the Catalogue Department] to curatorial departments.
>
> [As for saving money,] it takes a new cataloguer about a year to learn the necessary methods employed in the Central Catalogue. Curatorial staff, who perform other essential duties, are generally not familiar with the details of cataloguing methods. [Moreover, making them do their own cataloguing] would add to the[ir] duties [considerably]. . . . Curators at present are often far behind in approving draft catalogue cards. Given the proposed reorganization there is no doubt in my mind that the cataloguing of newly acquired objects would fall well behind schedule.
>
> [Cataloguing] is not a "glamorous" subject, and unfortunately in the eyes of many it is considered "drone-work." But it is vital to efficient operations and causes untold anguish and confusion when it is inadequate or not done properly.
>
> [In conclusion] if we cannot afford to operate the Central Catalogue at the present level, then I strongly recommend that every effort be made to maintain it at a level sufficient to wage a successful holding action, foreseeing the day when the Central Catalogue will be fully staffed and operating as normal.

In the end the department was split in two, with the Office of the Registrar becoming its own department, as it had been in the years before World War II. The catalogue section was given the new name of the Accessions and Catalogue Department, for all the major responsibilities that went into accessioning art objects would now fall to our department rather than to the Office of the Registrar. Even as we were given those additional duties, however, we were told that our staff was to be reduced to two—only Marian Harrison, a senior cataloguer, and I were to remain; all the others were reassigned or let go. This was traumatic news, to say the least, for up until that moment we had thought of ourselves as a team, united in our commitment to preserving and maintaining the central catalogue. I received a promotion at this time (as did Marian Harrison), but I was far from happy, given that I now faced a near impossible workload as well as the loss of my valued colleagues.

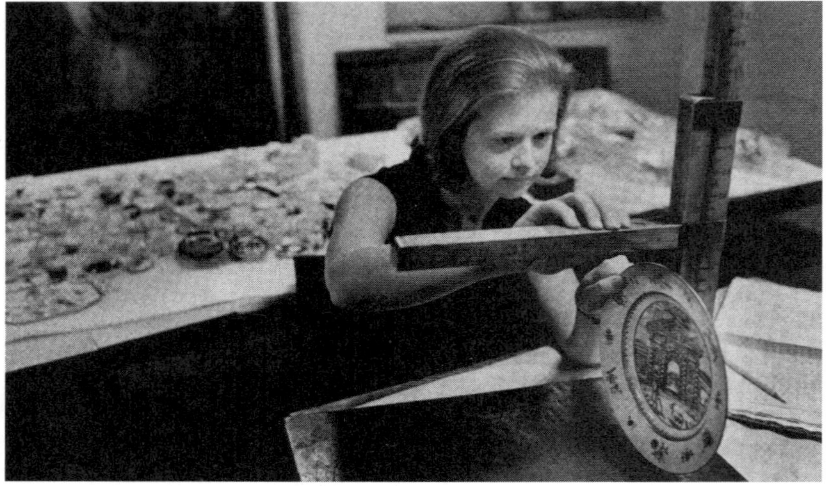

Marian G. Harrison, 1970

As the shock subsided, I reflected that even as the museum relied heavily upon our department—without a flawlessly maintained central catalogue, the institution could hardly function—its upper-level administrators apparently felt that its cataloguers were superfluous and expendable. Marcia C. Harty had warned me of the various movements to abolish the Catalogue Department during her tenure, as well as under the tenure of the previous Office of the Registrar and Catalogue Department head, Irma Bezold Wilkinson. Now it was happening.

I felt bad for my fellow cataloguers Katharine Brown, Hermine Chivian, Elsie Holmes, and Natalie Spassky.[6] Natalie Spassky was just then completing her PhD at Columbia University while cataloguing American paintings; Katharine Brown was working on her PhD at NYU's Institute of Fine Arts, with a specialty in medieval art; Hermine Chivian had a master's in European paintings (as did Marian Harrison, whose specialty was European sculpture and decorative arts); and finally Elsie Holmes was working on her PhD at Columbia, specializing in art of the ancient Near East. Now Katharine Brown was to be moved to the Medieval Department to do research. Elsie Holmes was not reassigned, but she left, subsequently married, and moved to Detroit. Natalie Spassky transferred as an assistant curator to the American Paintings and Sculpture Department, where she continued to work on a book ultimately published, in 1975, as *The Heritage of American Art: Paintings from the Collection of the Metropolitan Museum of Art*. While all of us had hoped someday to rise into the ranks of curators—including me—most of us would not. I would do so, but not in the way I had hoped, for although given the new title of assistant curator in charge, I was to remain in the Accessions and Catalogue Department.

I now had to reinvent the way in which Marian Harrison and I, the two remaining people in the department, handled the many daily requests for assistance coming from throughout the museum as well as from the general public. To do so, I created a Catalogue Department study room—a place where museum staff, graduate students, art collectors, and the interested public could make an appointment to look at the catalogue cards (and their related photographs) by themselves, under watchful supervision.

6 Three other cataloguers had departed around the time of the sexual inequality protest: Johanna Hecht transferred to the Department of European Sculpture and Decorative Arts (where she ultimately achieved the position of senior research scholar), Judy Nakamura Hecht (no relation to Johanna) transferred to the Department of Asian Art, and Nancy Dorfman Pressly moved to the Department of American Paintings and Sculpture.

To further ease our monumental workload, I began a program by which our department would accept high school students as school-year interns and summer interns. New York City regulations now permitted students who had already achieved enough credits to enter college to work as interns at various cultural institutions during their senior year. We soon had several excellent interns coming to us daily. (In time, some would return during their college vacations.) These interns assisted us from noon until five p.m. The program continued with great success until my own departure (and the closing of the department) many years later. Several of our interns subsequently rose to positions of prominence within the curatorial world. In general I found these young people a delight: motivated, intelligent, energetic, and passionate about art and culture. It was my great pleasure to work with them and help them learn and grow. Many remain my good friends to the present day.

One reason Thomas Hoving felt so confident in dismissing the cataloguing staff was that he had decided in 1970 that computers would soon become the museum's laborsaving tool of choice. Hoving had charged our registrar to start using computers for the registration and cataloguing process. The registrar in turn hired a young woman, Hanni Mandel, to tackle that challenge, giving her a small office down the hall from the central catalogue, where a computer was installed for her use. Mandel's first task was to digitize the version of the catalogue cards kept in the Registrar's Office, which were ordered by accession number, and contained only the most basic information about the artwork: title, measurements, price paid, material, classification, century, date, country, and how it was acquired. In creating the digitized version of those cards, Mandel consulted with the Museum of Modern Art, which was undertaking a similar challenge.[7] She ultimately found that her work was complicated not only by the lack of a reliable software program, but also by the museum's limited budget: she was the only person working on the project, she had only one computer terminal to work with, and the electrical wiring in our section of the museum was so antiquated that power surges and power outages threatened to destroy any information she stored on the terminal, meaning that registration cards had to be kept on an early form of a computer diskette. Given those circumstances, anyone seeking information from the computerized registration cards had to wait for access to the computer terminal, then learn how to use its primitive data-management software program, then hunt for the correct diskette holding the registration card, then find the registration card file on the diskette, and so on, and so on, and so on.

I was interested in the project, and I liked Hanni Mandel. As we got to know each other, she asked me for assistance with a new component of her project: she wanted to put a couple of the central catalogue's entries for European paintings on the computer, simply to demonstrate that doing so was possible and (potentially) useful. But by the time the two samples were completed in 1972, Mandel had decided to leave the museum to go to law school. Faced with her departure, the registrar discontinued the project, and all the materials that Mandel created were simply placed into storage.

Thomas Hoving had been prescient in realizing the importance that computers would eventually play in collections database management—today they are indispensable in museums the world over—but in trying to implement their use in the early 1970s at the Met, Hoving had been too early. He was right that computers were in the

7 Starting in the early 1950s, the Metropolitan Museum's registrar, Irma Bezold Wilkinson, had worked closely with Dorothy H. Dudley, registrar of the Museum of Modern Art, on the book *Museum Registration Methods* (New York: American Association of Museums, 1958) to tackle the enormously complicated problem of collections management.

museum's future, but at this early moment in computer technology, he was unable to come up with a viable replacement for the central catalogue and its admittedly old-fashioned card catalogue system. Even if he had been able to obtain a computer equal to that task, there was no software program capable of creating and maintaining a database as extensive and complicated as that of the Metropolitan Museum of Art's central catalogue.

In attempting to introduce computers, Hoving began a dialogue among curators that lasted for many years. A number of senior curators (most notably Dietrich von Bothmer and Morrison Heckscher) would express real alarm and opposition to the idea, believing that the transfer of so much sensitive information onto electronic media was risky and fundamentally wrong. Once uploaded, this precious information could so easily be lost, corrupted, intentionally altered, or even maliciously vandalized. Their rightful objections to the computerization of the central catalogue continued for two decades, even as department after department began installing and maintaining their own varied forms of collections management software independent of the central catalogue, simply to facilitate quick curatorial access to such information.

Those first months of the reorganization were very difficult—it was in many ways like being given command of a battleship, only to find I had a sole able-bodied seaman to help me run it: in my case, Marian Harrison. Given the vast amount of paperwork required for even a single accession, I wondered how on earth the two of us were to maintain and update the central catalogue's more than two million entries, much less process the tens of thousands of objects that were awaiting formal accession. Doing all that work had been difficult enough with a room full of cataloguers; managing it between two cataloguers was not possible. And yet by accepting my promotion I had essentially promised the museum I would somehow get the job done.

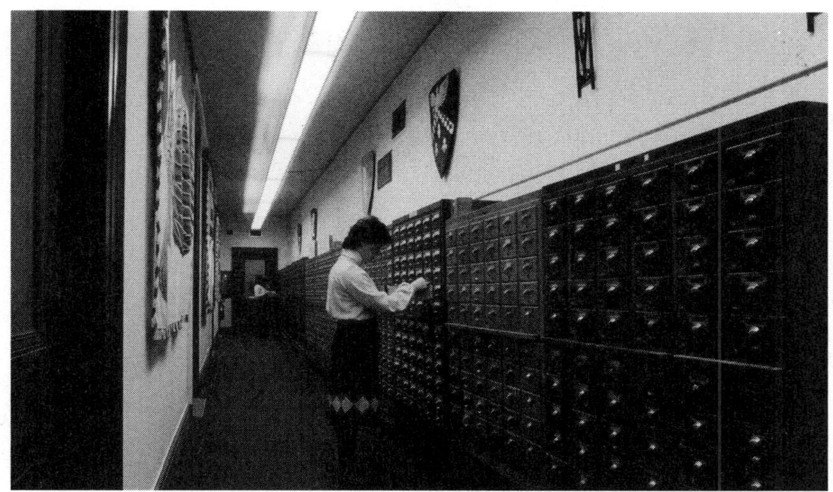

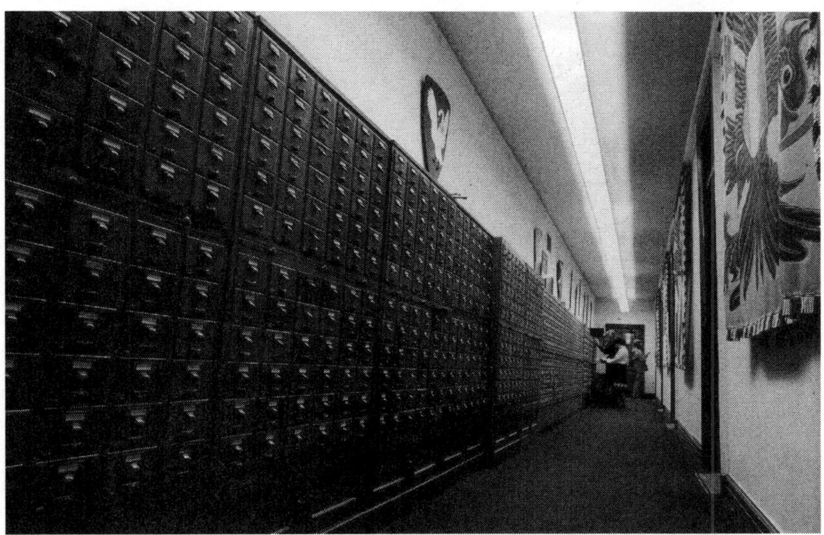

Two views of the Central Catalogue, taken in 1970

In the end, there was only one solution: outsourcing the work to the curators, an idea that was already being advocated by the museum's curator in chief, Theodore Rousseau. Of course, curators had long been part of the cataloguing process; but now they would be tasked to do nearly all of it themselves. Enabling them to do so, however, required that I take on yet another daunting initiative: namely, composing a complete set of detailed instructions on how to create, maintain, and update central catalogue entries for all the objects in the museum's very different collections, as well as how to navigate the accession process from start to finish. The result would be the only book I would ever write while employed at the Metropolitan Museum: an instruction manual addressed specifically to all its curators, explaining the process of cataloguing in precise and painstaking detail.

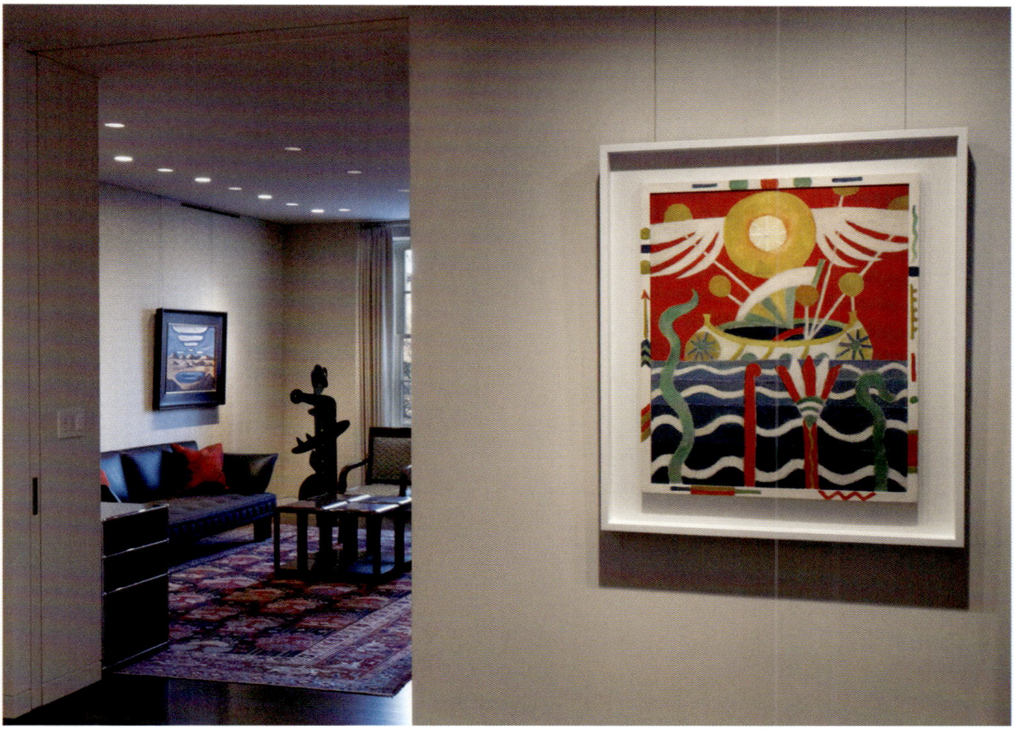

Vilcek residence, view from the entry hall to Marica's study

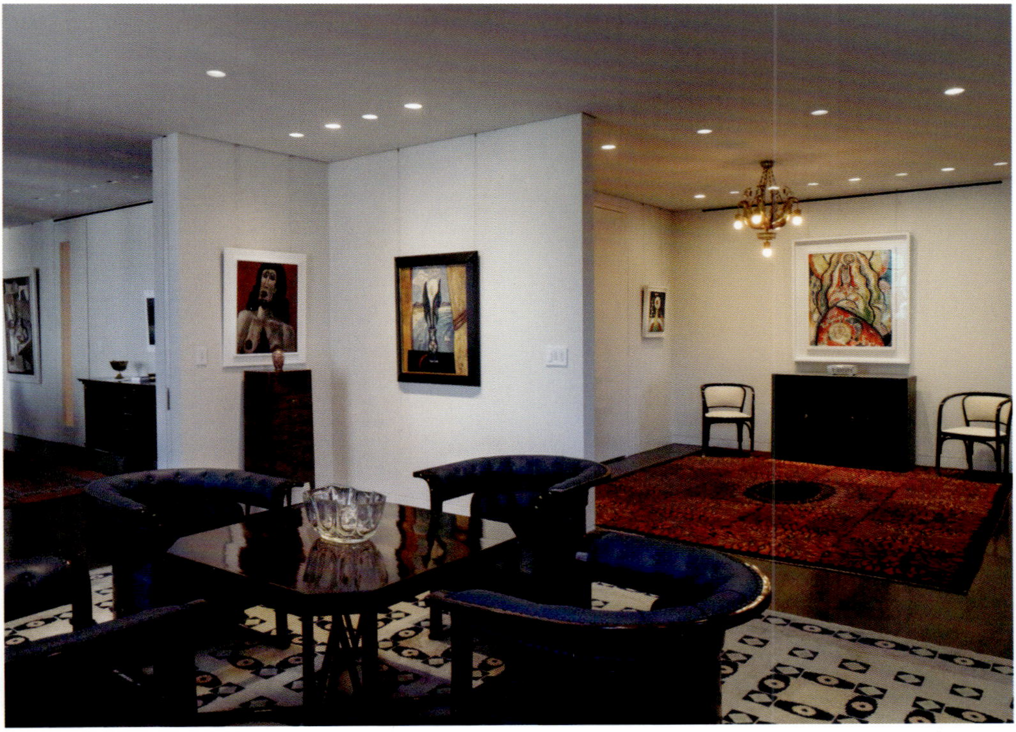

Vilcek residence, view from the living room to the entry hall

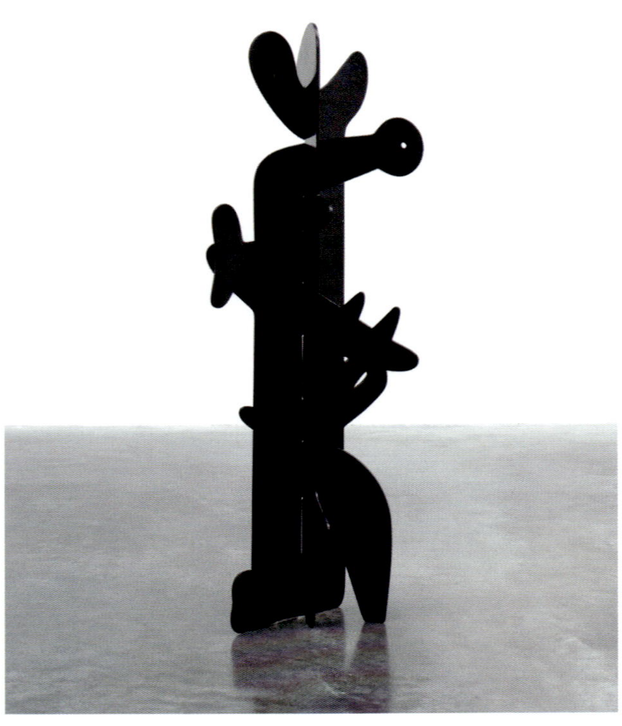

Isamu Noguchi, *Trinity* (1945/1988)

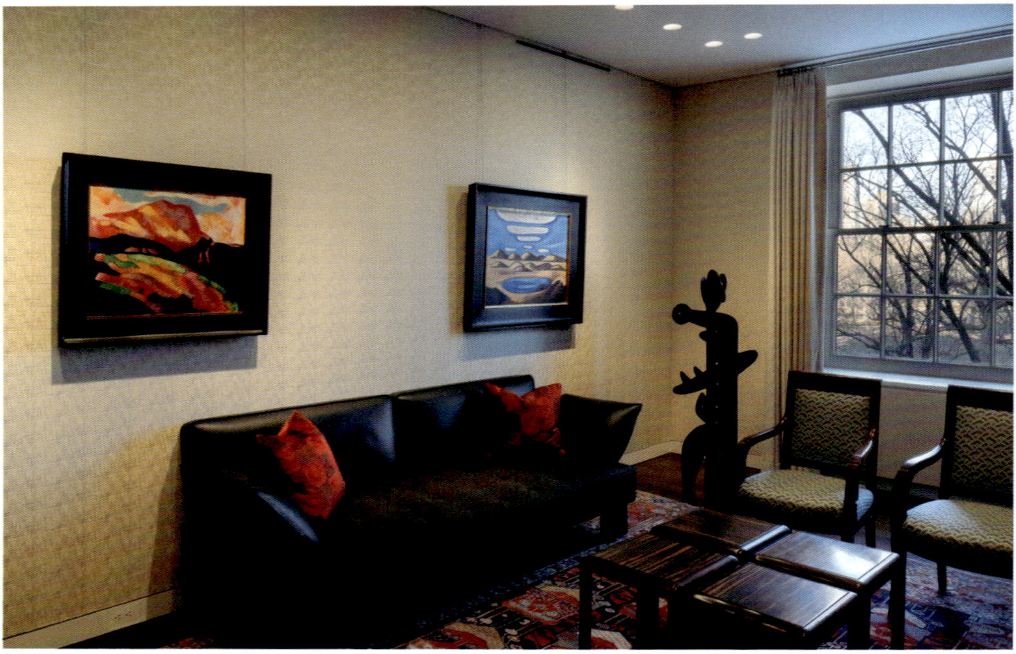

Vilcek residence, Marica's study

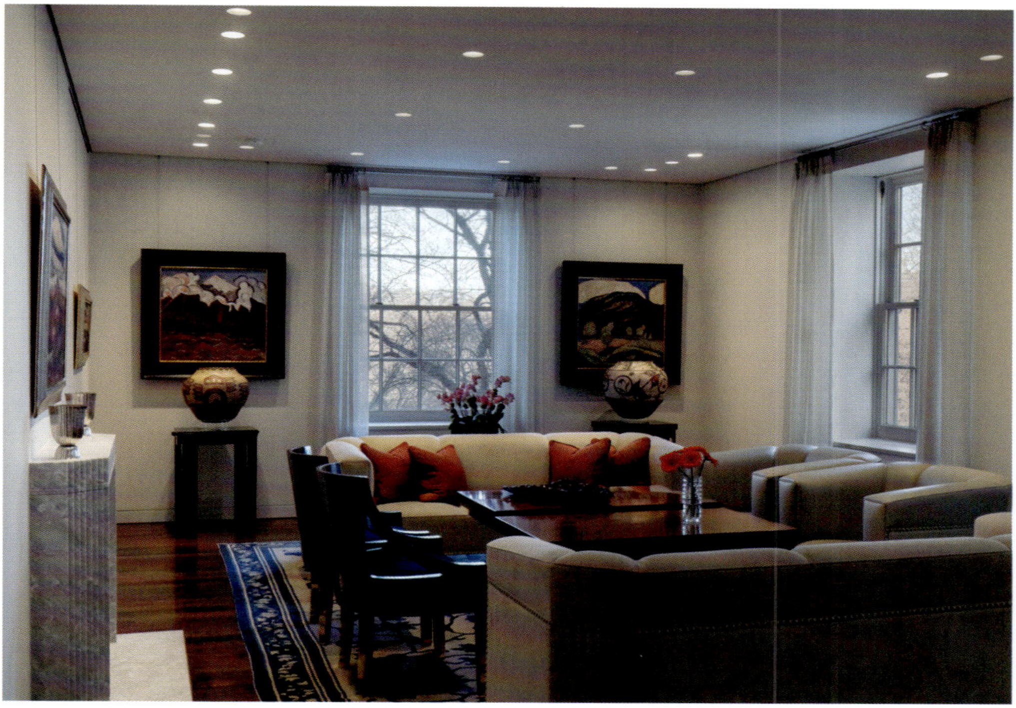

Vilcek residence, the living room (northwest view)

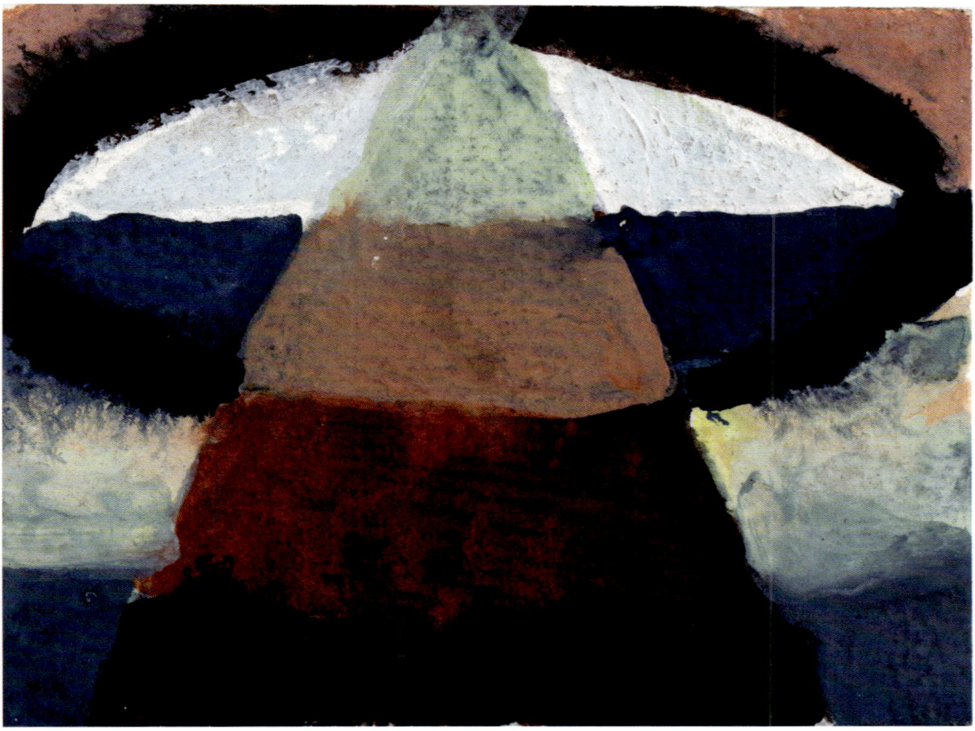

Arthur Dove, *Centerport XIV* (1942)

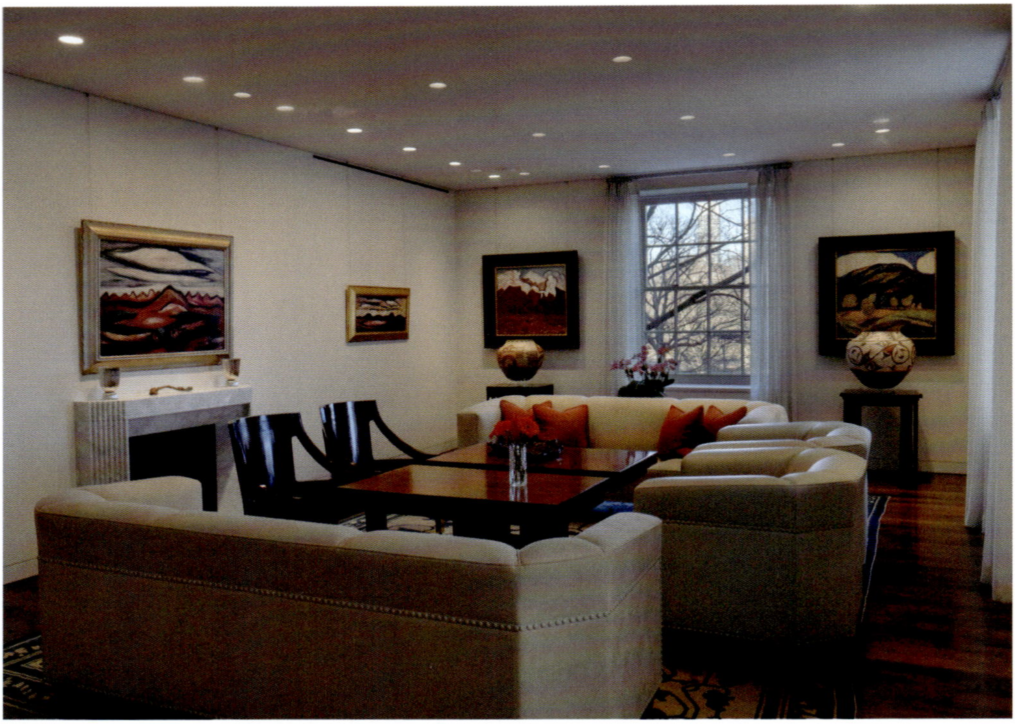

Vilcek residence, the living room (southwest view)

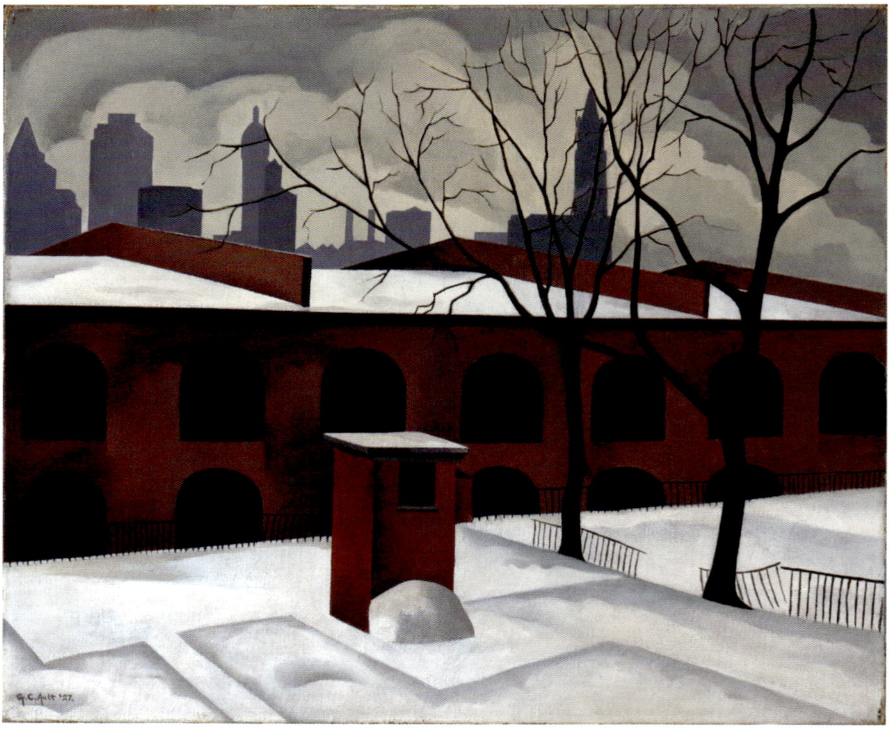

George Ault, *View from Brooklyn* (1927)

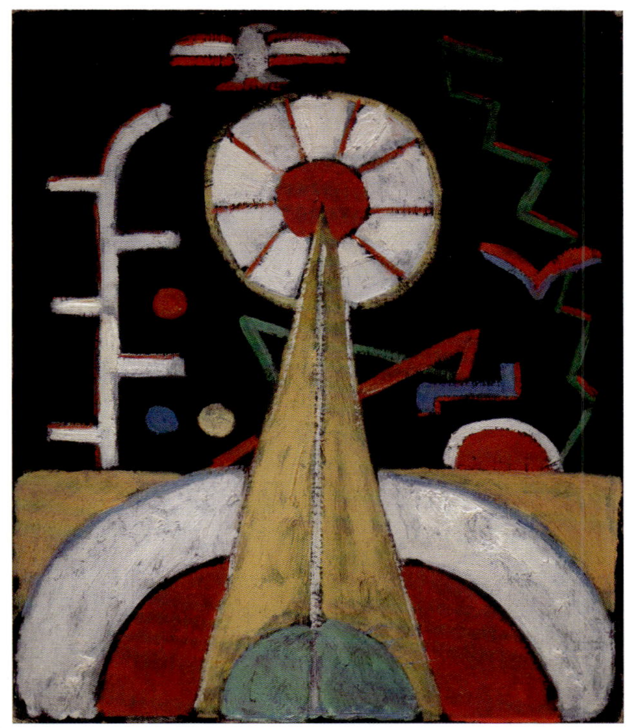

Marsden Hartley, *Berlin Series No. 1* (1913)

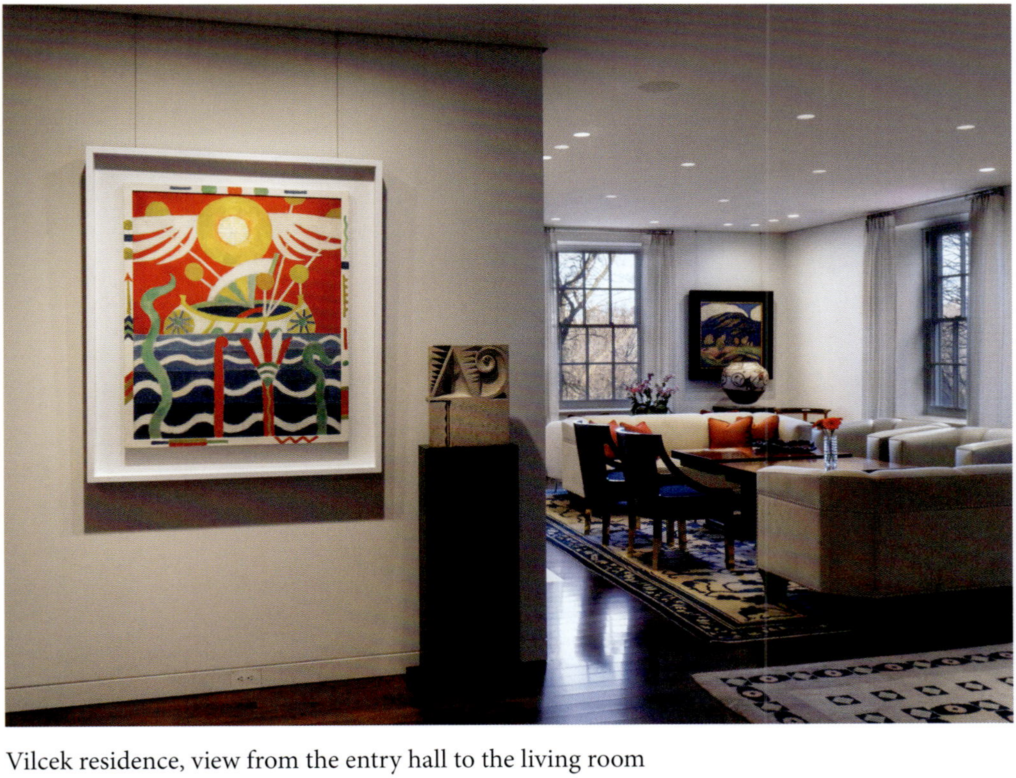

Vilcek residence, view from the entry hall to the living room

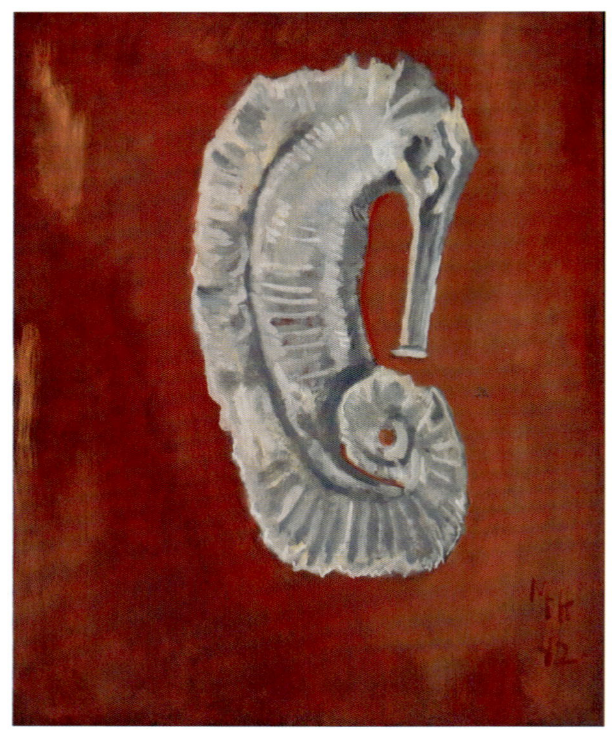

Marsden Hartley, *White Sea Horse* (1942)

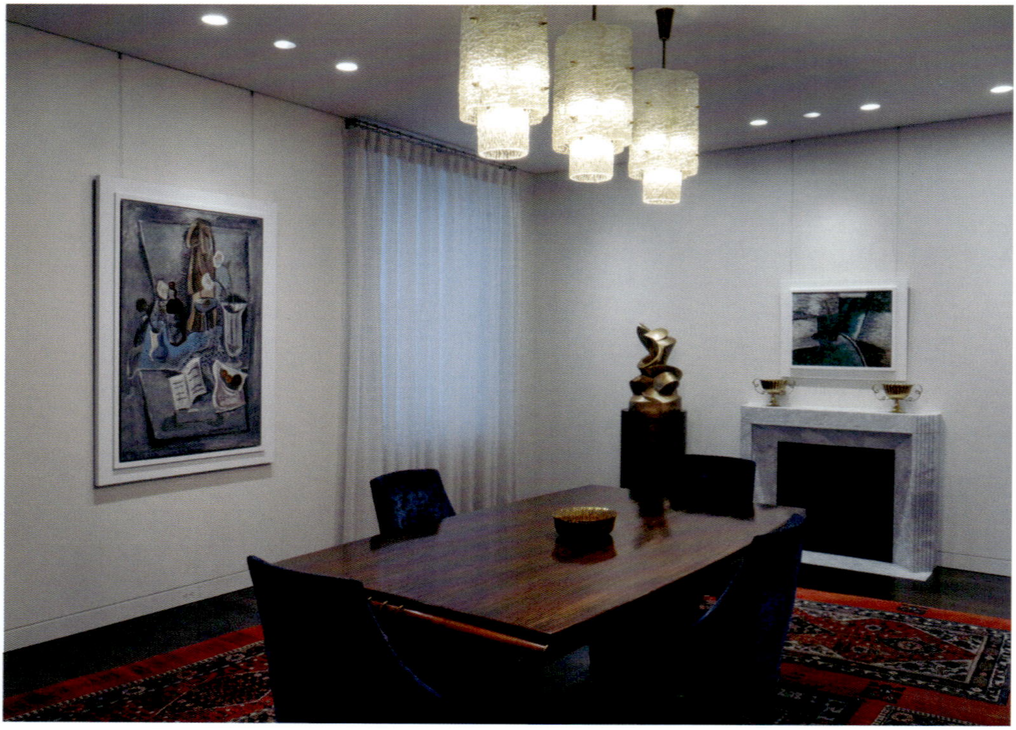

Vilcek residence, the dining room (northeast view)

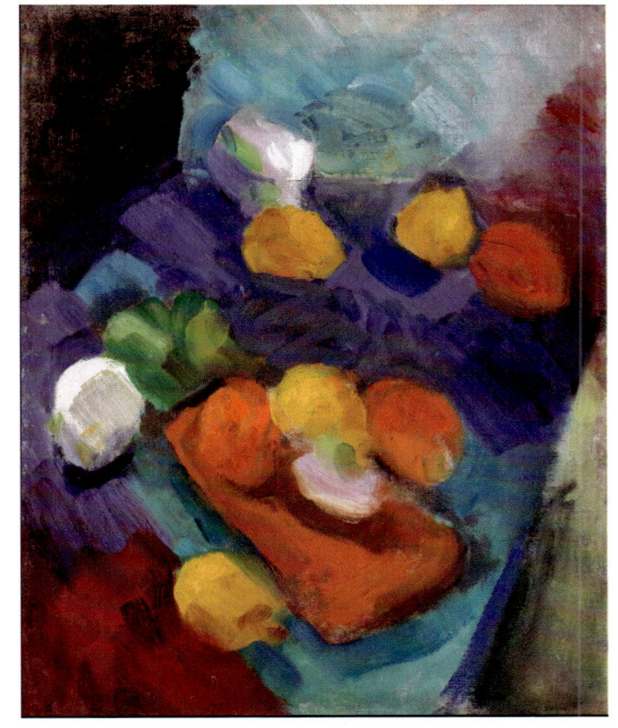

Morgan Russell, *Synchromist Still Life* (c. 1910)

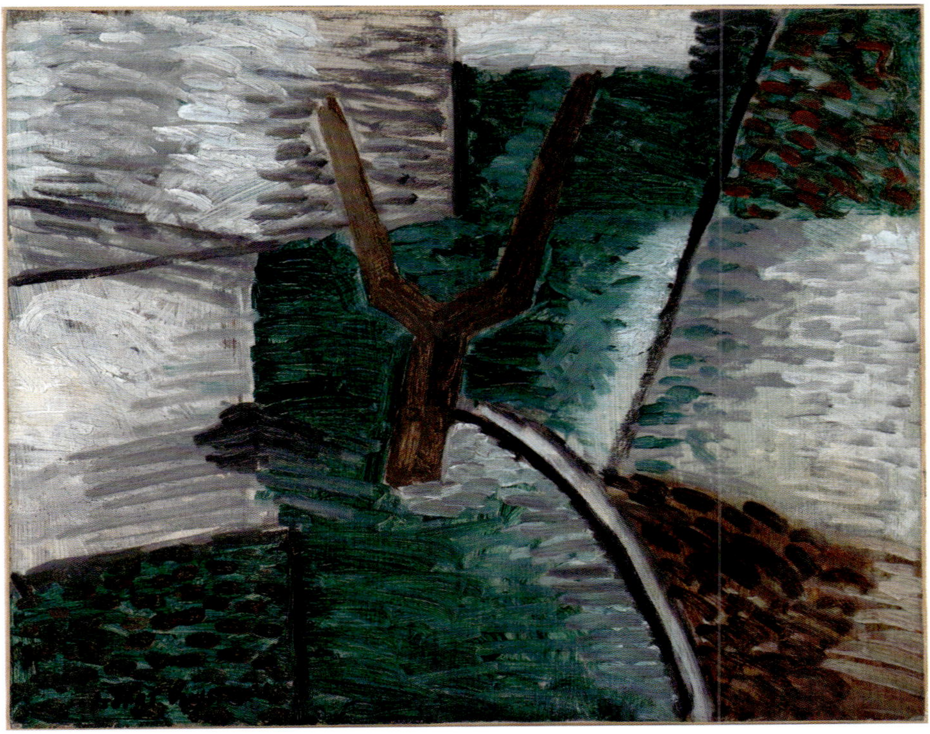

Stuart Davis, *Tree* (1921)

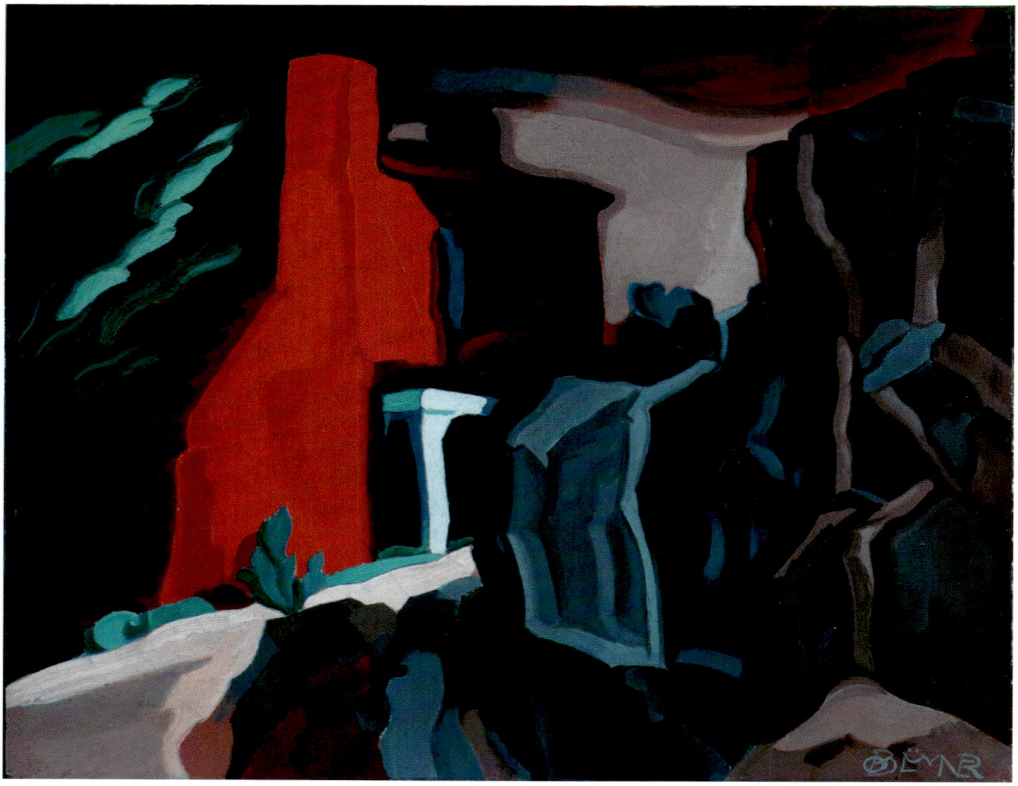

Oscar Bluemner, *Red Night, Thoughts* (1929)

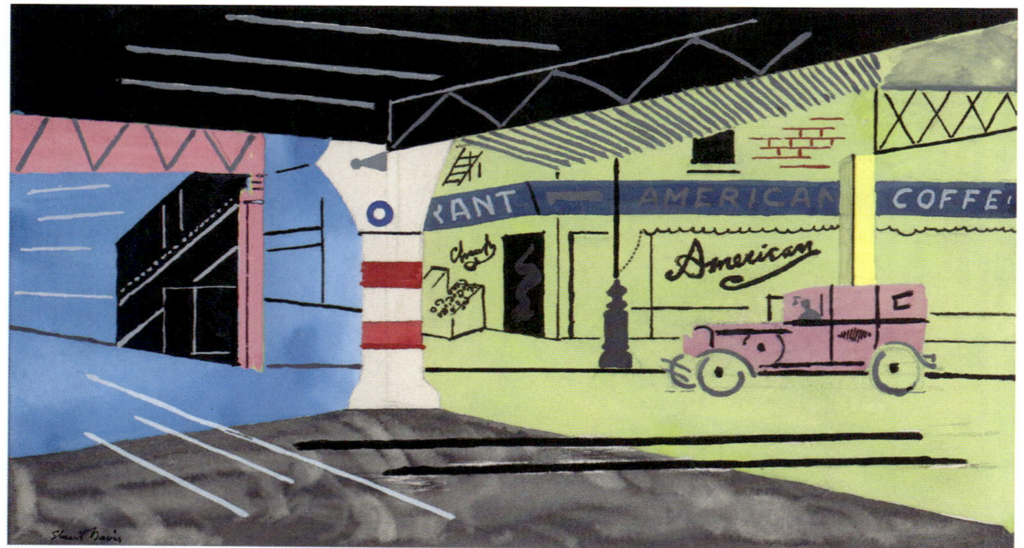

Stuart Davis, *Coffee Pot* (1931)

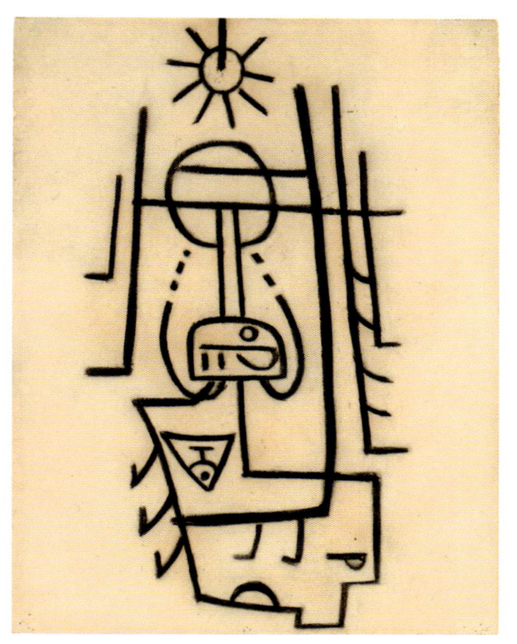

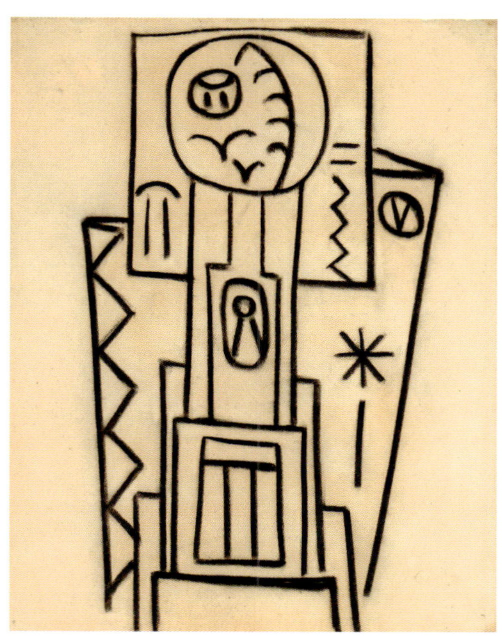

Marsden Hartley, *Symbol IV* and *Symbol V* (c. 1913–1914)

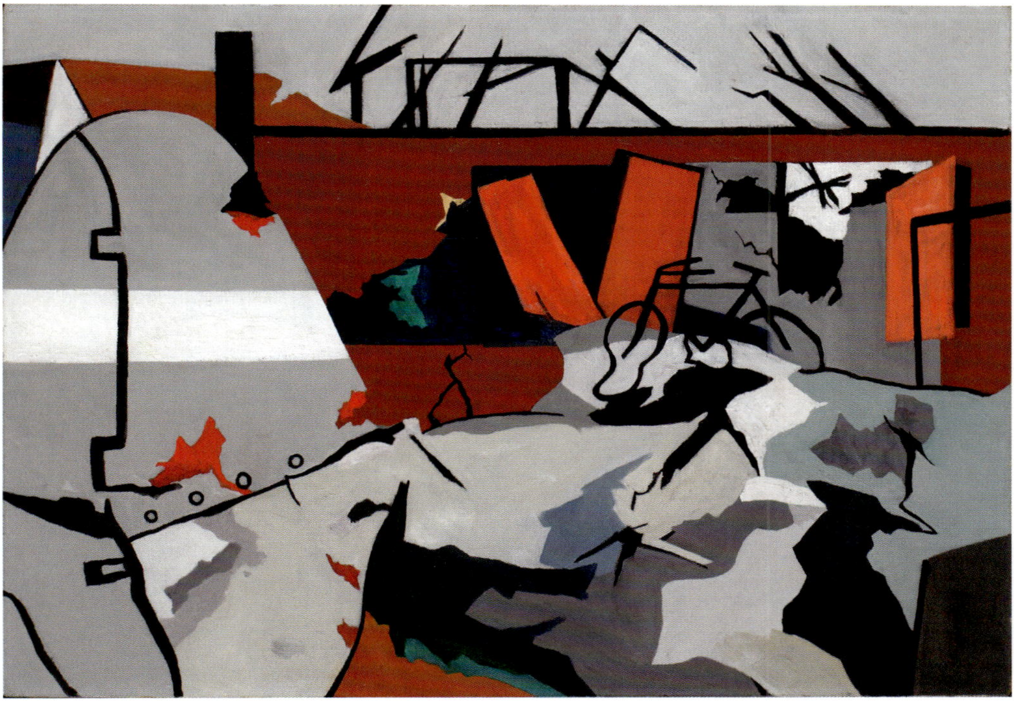

Ralston Crawford, *Bomber* (1944)

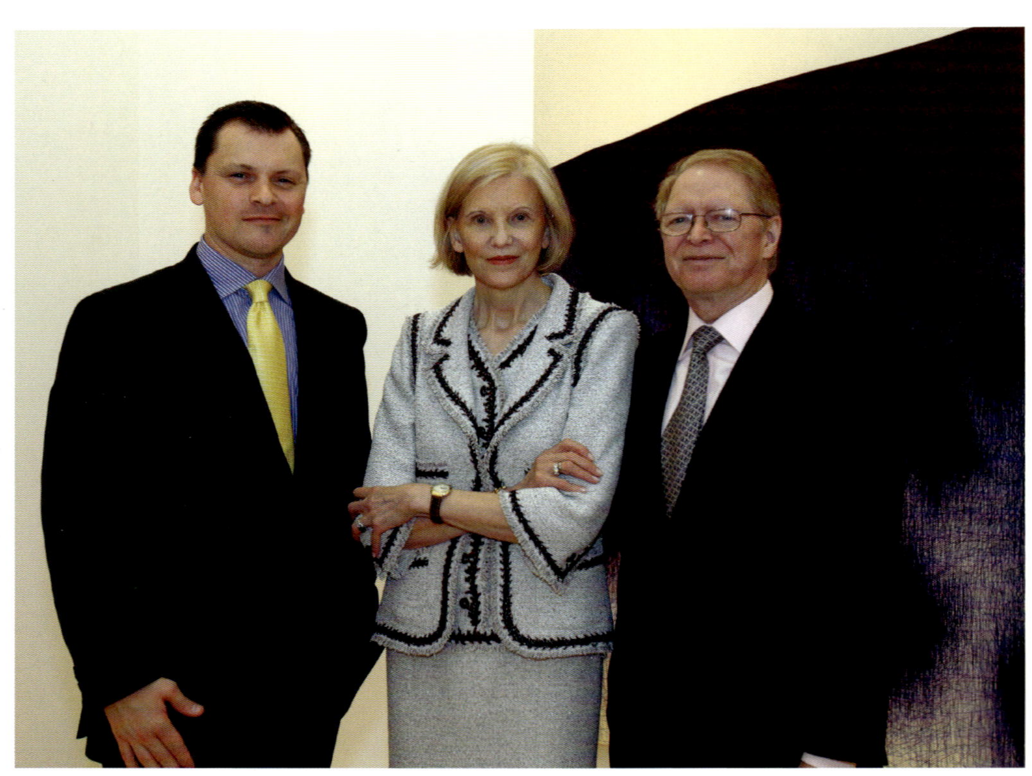

Rick Kinsel, Marica Vilcek, and Jan Vilcek at the Vilcek Foundation's inaugural exhibition "Il Lee and Pouran Jinchi" at the Vilcek Foundation Gallery, 167 East Seventy-Third Street, June 2008

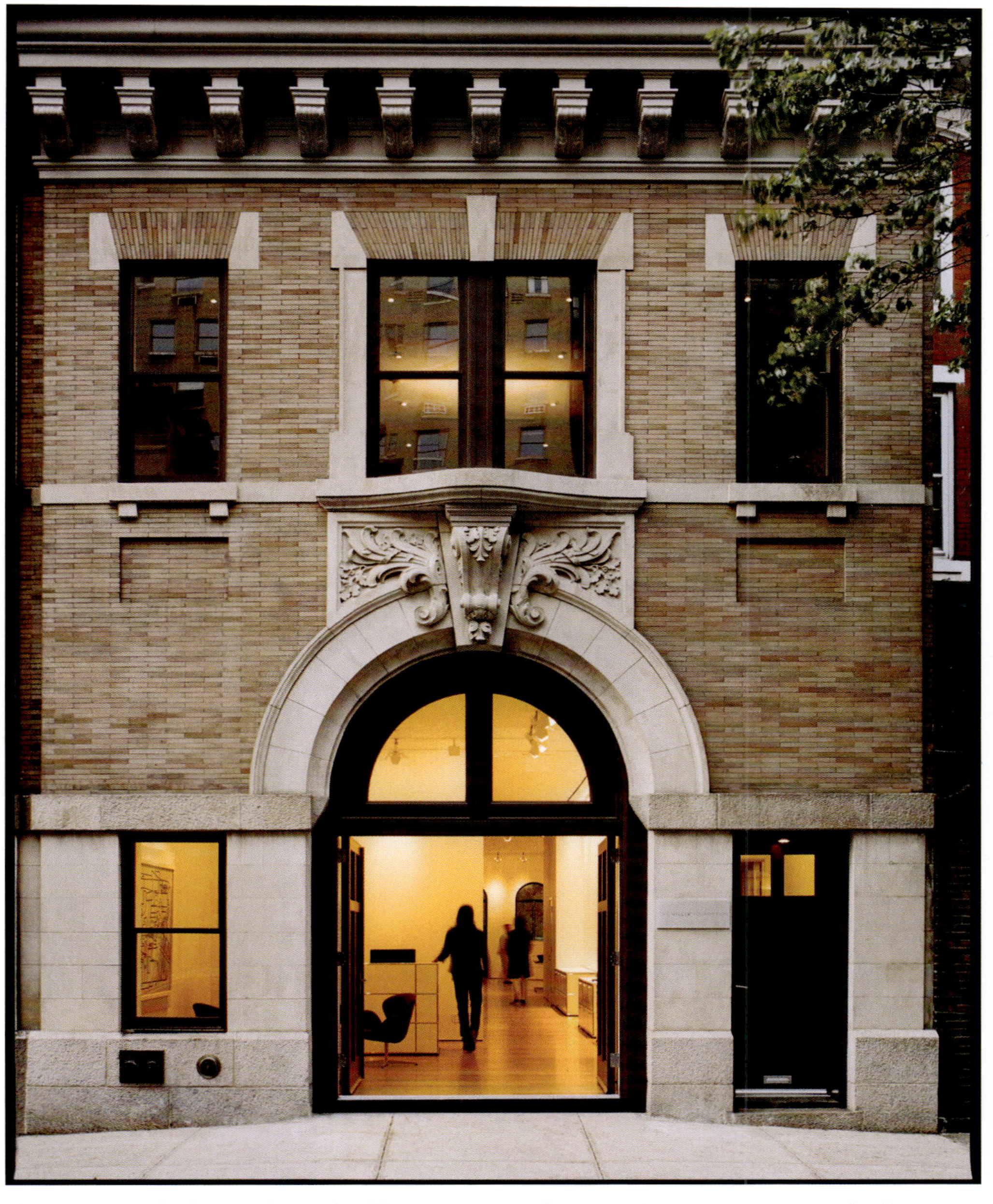

The original Vilcek Foundation building, a renovated garage at 167 East Seventy-Third Street

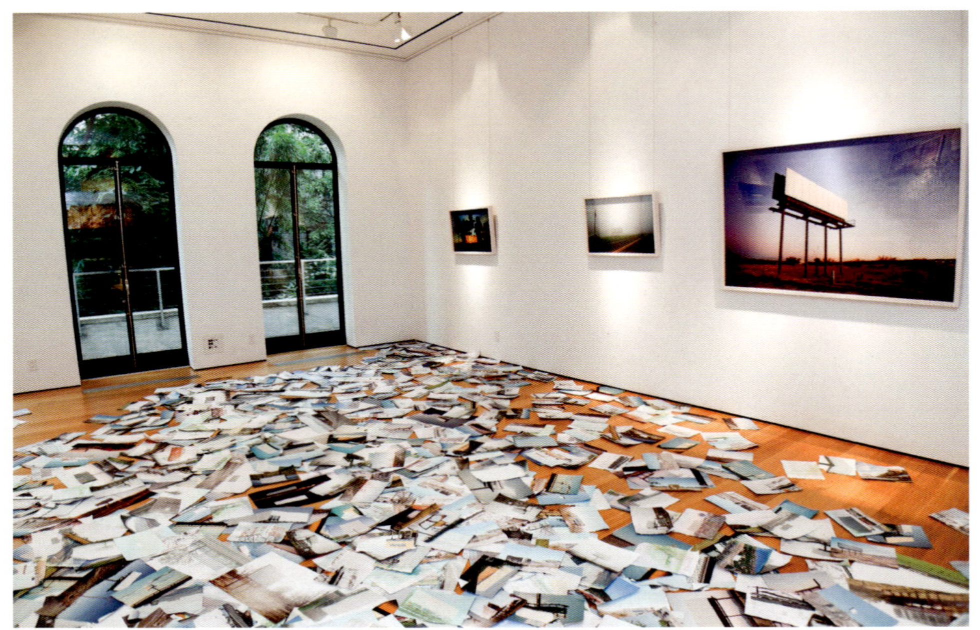

Installation view of the exhibition "O Zhang: I Am Your Mirror," held at the Vilcek Foundation Gallery at 167 East Seventy-Third Street, September 15, 2012 to Saturday, November 10, 2012

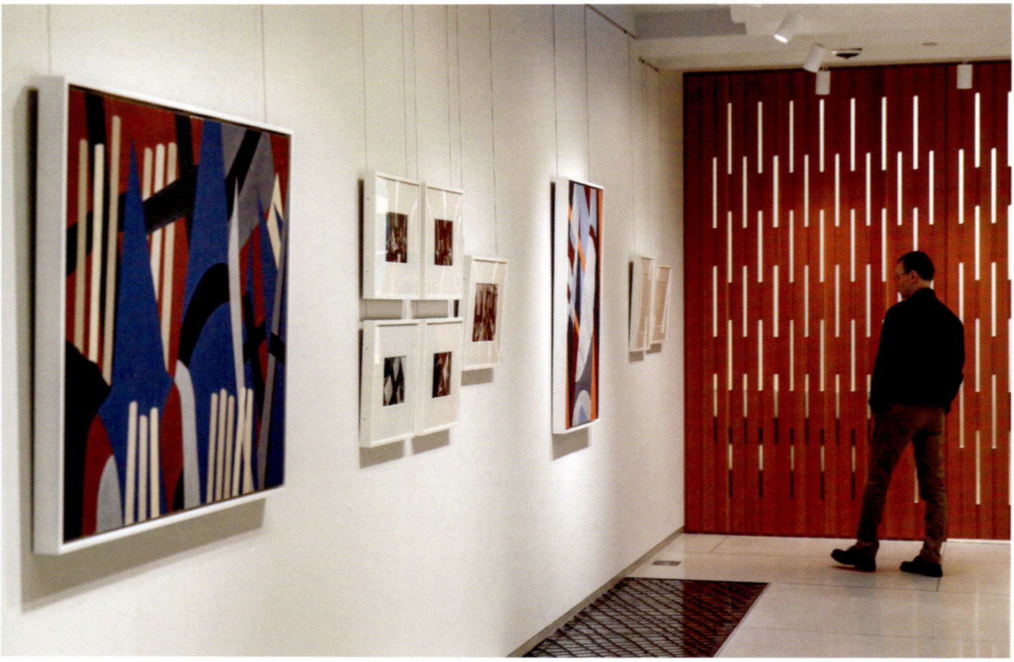

Installation view of "Ralston Crawford: Torn Signs," the inaugural exhibition held at the Vilcek Foundation Gallery, 21 East Seventieth Street. The exhibition ran from May 15 to November 13, 2019

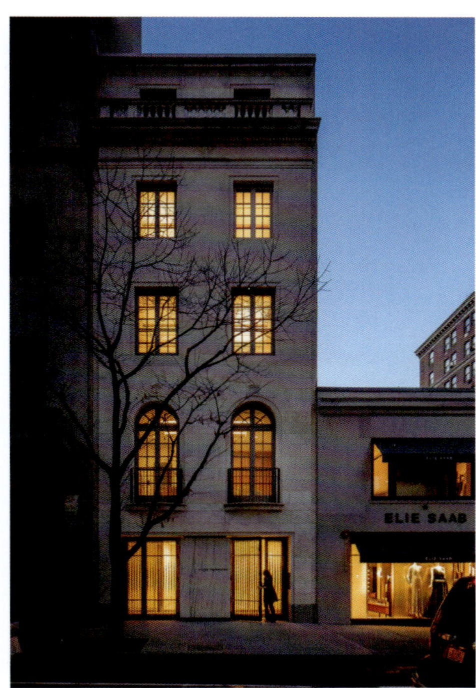

(above) Street view, the Vilcek Foundation building, 21 East Seventieth Street

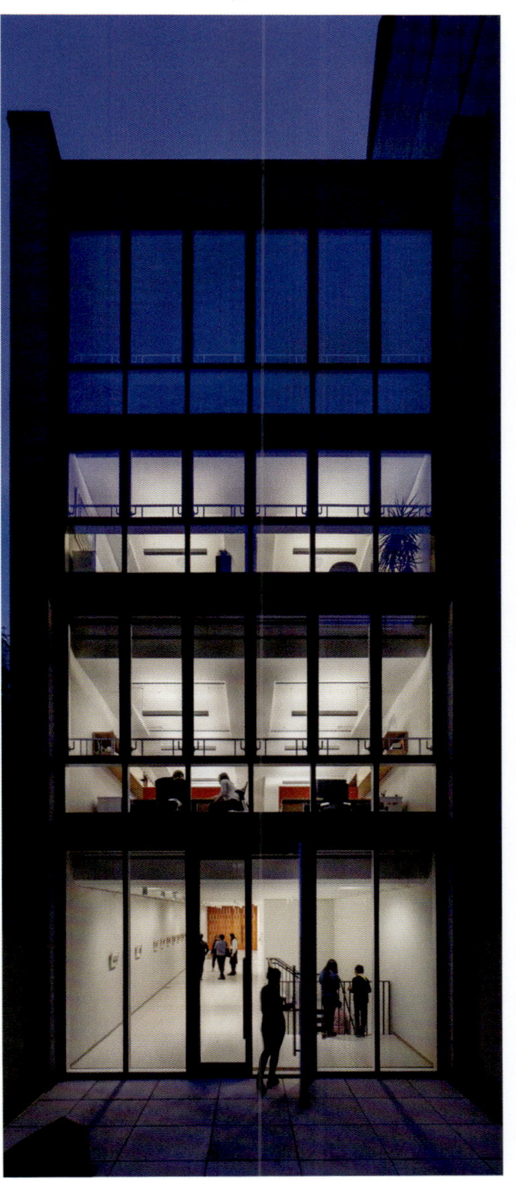

(right) Garden view, the Vilcek Foundation building, 21 East Seventieth Street

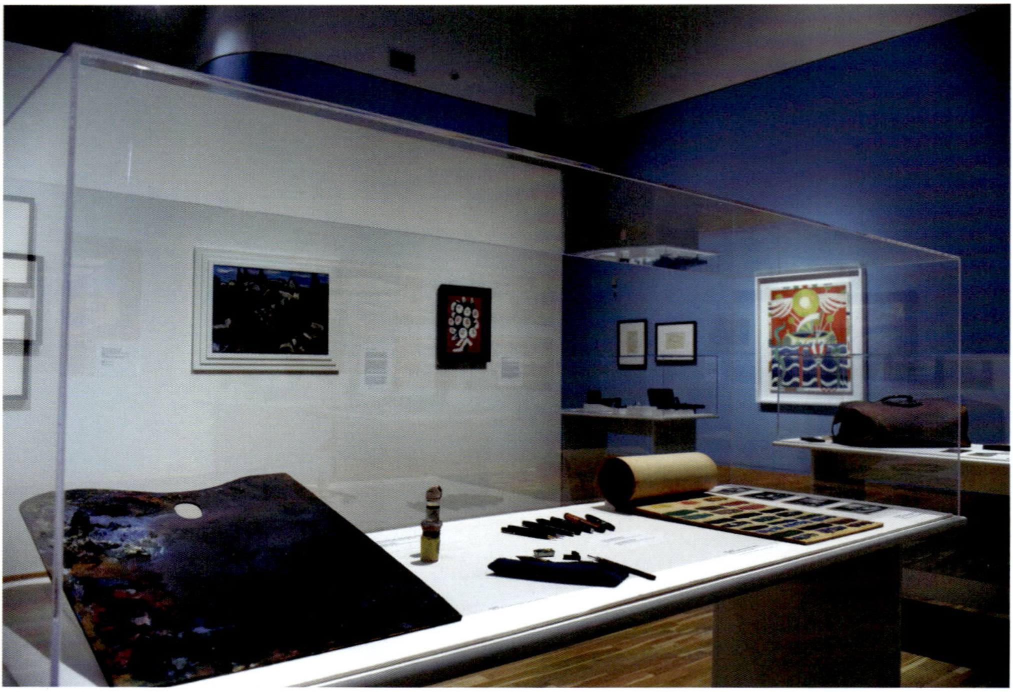

Installation view of "Marsden Hartley: Adventurer in the Arts" (Bates College Museum of Art, September to November 2021) showing a collection of Hartley's ephemera, including his palette, pen collection, and valise

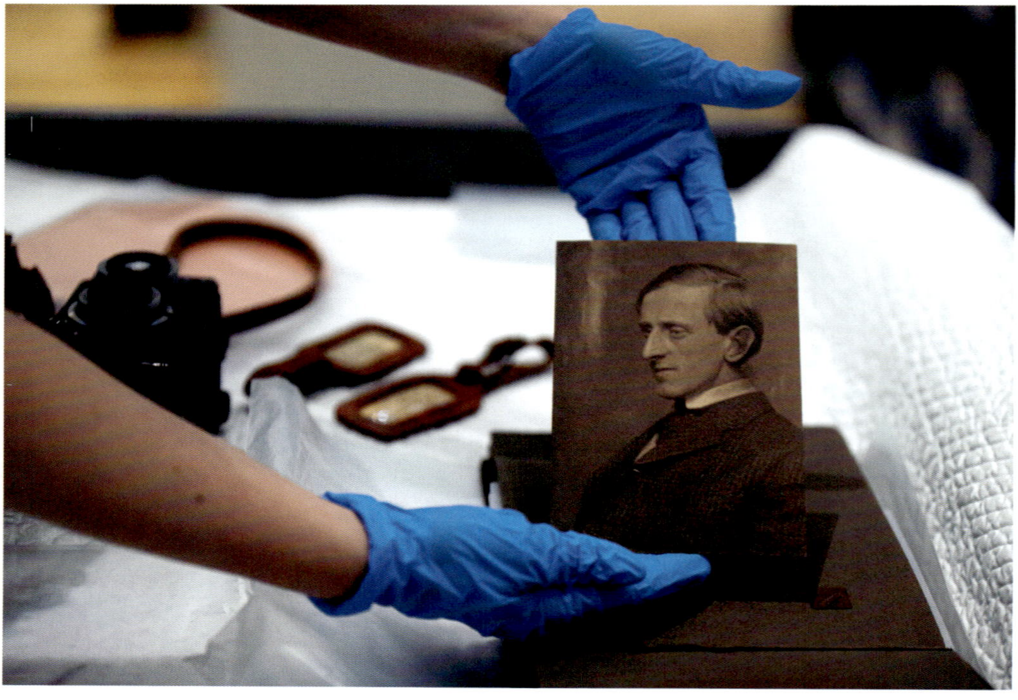

A curator installing a photographic portrait of Marsden Hartley for "Marsden Hartley, Adventurer in the Arts" (Bates College Museum of Art, September to November 2021)

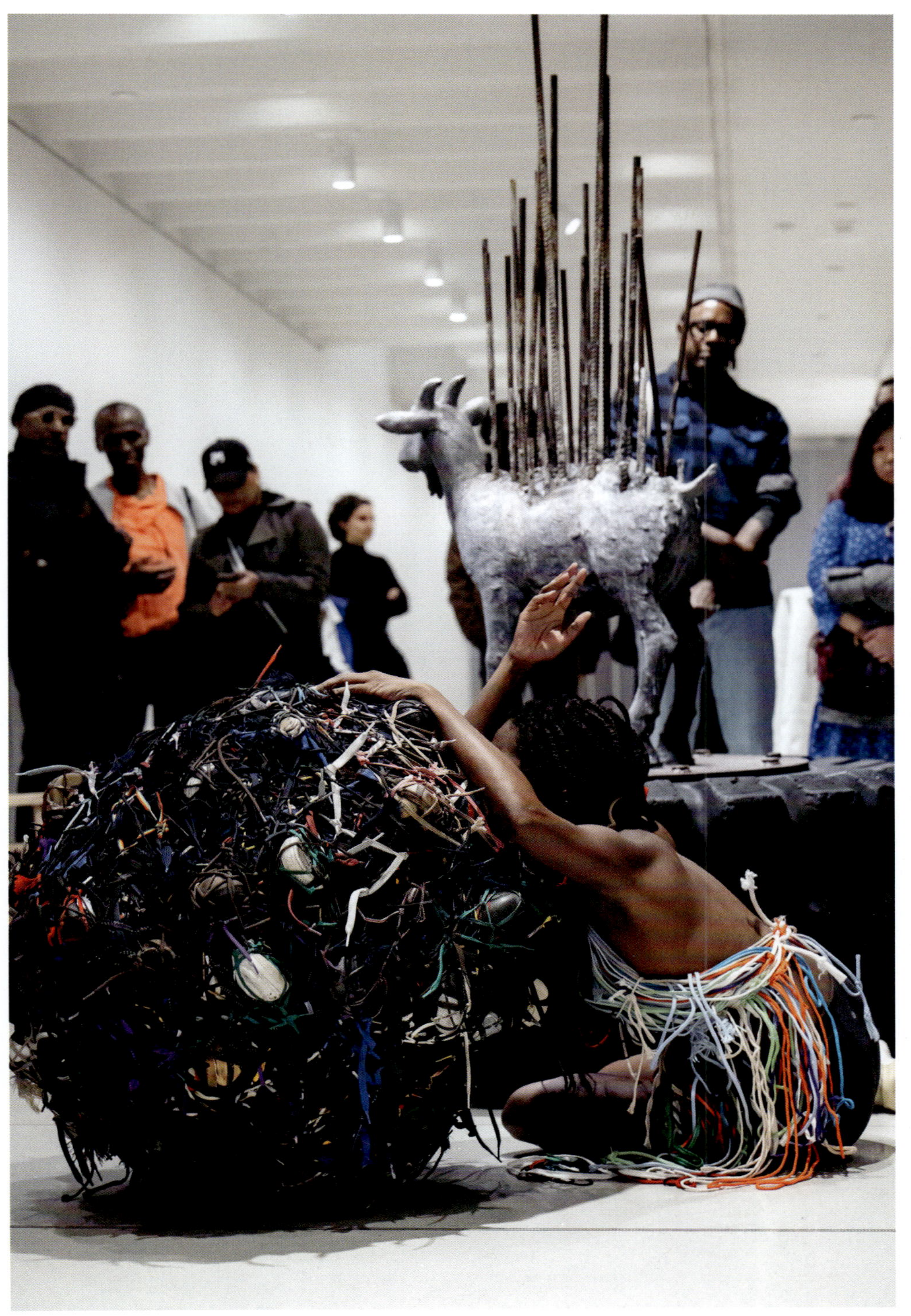

Dancer and choreographer Jessica Emmanuel stages a performance piece activating Nari Ward's sculpture *Tumblehood* (2015) as part of the Vilcek Foundation's exhibition "Nari Ward: Home of the Brave," February 16, 2023. The exhibition ran from May 31, 2022, to March 24, 2023.

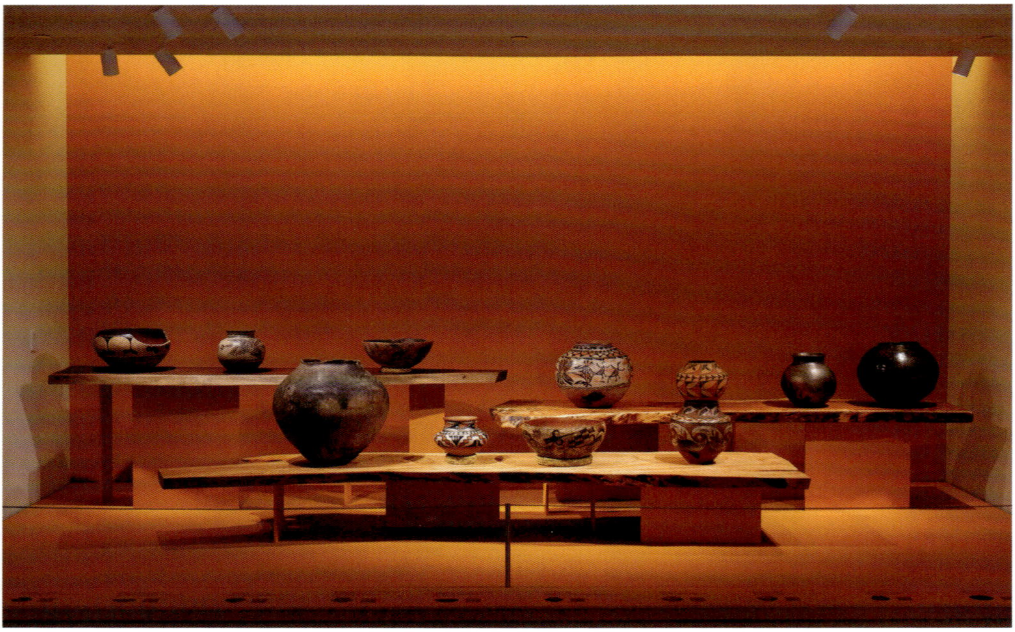

“Grounded in Clay: The Spirit of Pueblo Pottery,” curated by the Pueblo Pottery Collective and featuring works from the Vilcek Collection and the Indian Arts Research Center at the School for Advanced Research, Santa Fe, NM. Installation view, first floor, north wall, Vilcek Foundation Gallery.

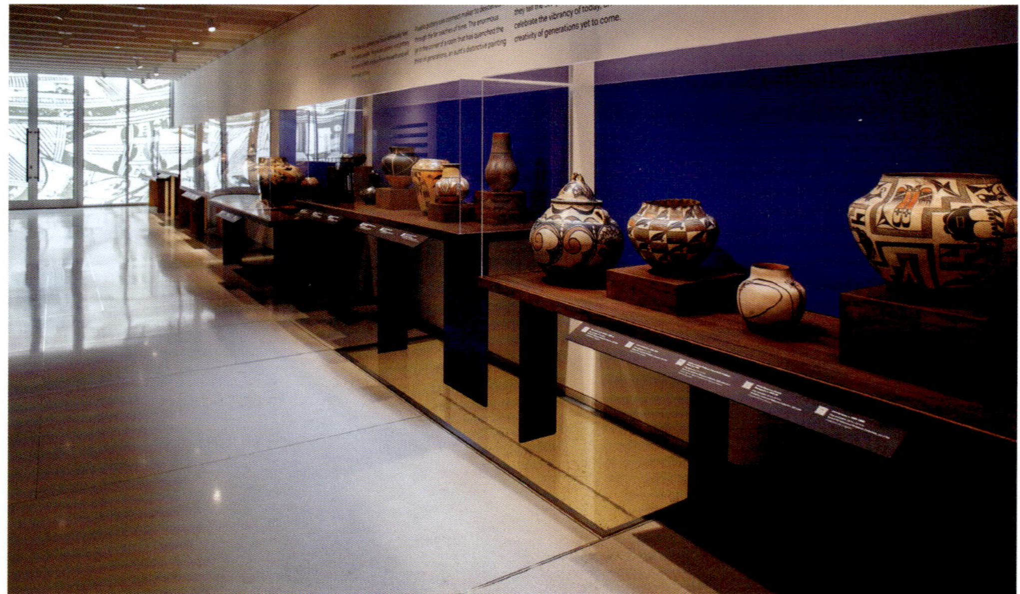

“Grounded in Clay: The Spirit of Pueblo Pottery,” curated by the Pueblo Pottery Collective and featuring works from the Vilcek Collection and from the Indian Arts Research Center at the School for Advanced Research, Santa Fe, NM. Installation view, second floor, east wall, Vilcek Foundation Gallery. “Grounded in Clay,” a joint presentation at the Vilcek Foundation and the Metropolitan Museum of Art, ran from July 13, 2023, to June 4, 2024.

12

Personal Affairs

While it is tempting for me to write endlessly about the Metropolitan Museum—so many amazing things happened there so soon after I settled into my work at the Office of the Registrar and Catalogue Department—I should pause to describe a few life events that were equally significant to me during the late 1960s and early '70s.

The first was a health issue. It began as a loud and persistent ringing in my ears. At first it came and went episodically, but within a few weeks that ringing soon worsened into a case of vertigo so severe that I could barely stand. Consultation with a specialist revealed that I had developed Ménière's disease, an affliction of the inner ear that creates episodes of severe vertigo, tinnitus, and hearing loss.

Throughout my childhood and adolescence I had suffered from ear, nose, and throat complaints, and the Ménière's was perhaps a further development of my inherent physical vulnerability. My mother also suffered from Ménière's, though her attacks occurred only once or twice a year. So possibly I had a genetic predisposition to it. In truth, no one really knows where the disease comes from or why.

At first my vertigo attacks lasted for only about twenty minutes, but they soon became much longer—lasting from several hours to half a day. Their severity increased as well: at their worst, I experienced a profound, nauseating, full-body dizziness, as if I had just stepped off an amusement park ride. I was only thirty years old at the time of my first attack, and I was in perfect health, so it seemed impossible to me that I should be so disoriented and incapacitated. But I could neither walk nor stand during an episode, and even remaining seated was difficult. The nausea was awful. If one began during work hours, my colleagues in the Catalogue Department would put me on the floor of our little office and cover me with a blanket, where I would lie still with my eyes closed until it passed. Despite my misery I was determined not to let illness interfere with my work. I never told anyone in the Human Resources Department about it, nor did I ever take sick leave due to an attack.

Through Jan's connections at NYU I was able to consult Dr. Noel Cohen, a specialist in Ménière's disease. He told me that during the entire course of his career he had had only one other patient with such an aggressive case. The disease affected just my right ear at the start, but it then spread to the other, and by 1975 I would require surgery. Four more surgeries, one of them disastrous, would follow in the decade to come.

Even as I was dealing with this unexpected medical problem, Jan and I faced a new challenge, helping Czechoslovak refugees. During the mid-1960s a number of reforms took place in Czechoslovakia, so much so that by 1967 Ivan had been able to return there for a visit. Starting in January 1968, Czechoslovakia seemed to be on the brink of Westernization, under the leadership of Alexander Dubček. The newly elected first secretary of the Czechoslovakian Communist Party initiated an accelerated program of democratization and economic decentralization, which included a loosening of restrictions on speech, travel, and the media, and in response the entire nation seemed to have spontaneously decided that the Soviet model of communism needed to be abandoned. (This entire period came to be known as the Prague Spring.) But the Soviets had other ideas. On August 21, 1968, they invaded Czechoslovakia with tanks, aircraft, and an army of half a million—the troops ostensibly drawn from all the Warsaw Pact nations, but clearly on orders from Moscow. With the country's movement for liberalization crushed, many Czechoslovakian professionals fled: seventy thousand people left immediately, and more than three hundred thousand would eventually go into exile. In New York, we had old friends and acquaintances from Bratislava suddenly showing up on our doorstep, penniless and desperate. Even though our apartment was small and our resources were limited, Jan and I resolved to do all we could on their behalf.

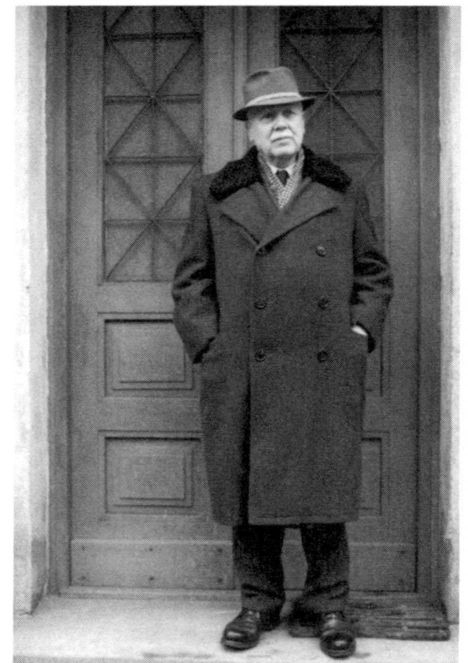

(right) My father in the doorway of our home in Bratislava, photographed by Ivan

(below) Ivan and Pavol, briefly reunited during Ivan's visit to Bratislava

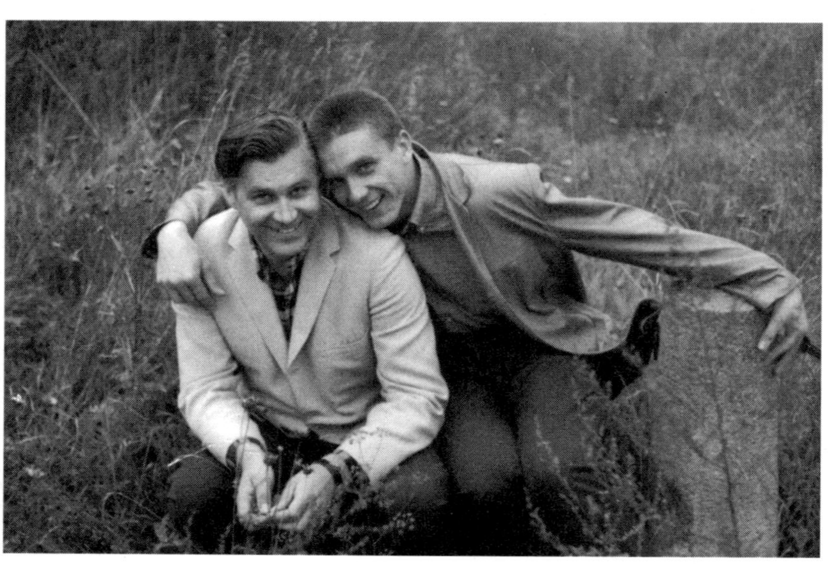

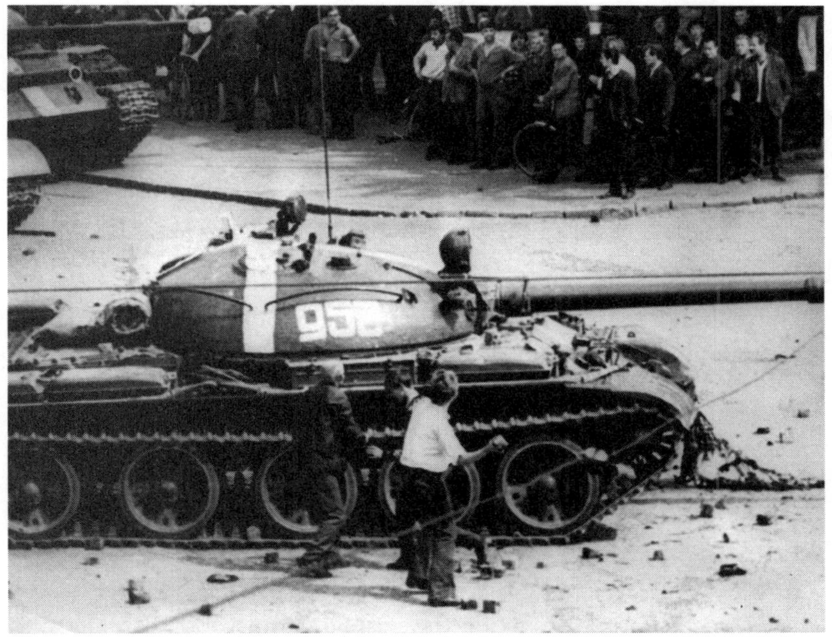

Czechoslovakians hurl rocks at Soviet tanks, Bratislava, 1968

We couldn't accommodate more than one or two people at a time, however, since the only place to sleep was the one sofa. Most stayed for a week, and none lingered more than three. But week after week we seemed to have some new person coming to us, and thus for several years our little apartment became a sort of transit lounge: a place where distant acquaintances and friends of friends would arrive, exhausted and confused, staying just long enough to gather themselves for whatever might come next. We welcomed the majority of these refugees during the period 1968–1972, but in truth we had people living on our sofa throughout the 1970s and '80s. Both Jan and I were fine with this new reality: after all, our own needs were few, and these people were desperate for help. Because just a few years earlier we had needed such help ourselves, we understood the depth of their needs.

At the same time, we could give our guests only limited practical assistance—and because Jan was always so busy with his publications, reports, or grant applications, much of the work of helping the newly arrived refugees fell to me. I found myself typing up résumés, offering job-hunting advice, and explaining various aspects of New York living to our guests even as I was serving up hot meals, changing sheets, and doing laundry. Money was their greatest need, of course. We gave what we could, sensing it would probably ultimately come back to us, but not really minding if it didn't. Back in Bratislava, life had been so difficult that offering even the most basic hospitality to our friends had been nearly impossible; now that we had enough to share, we shared. Along the way we discovered that helping others made us feel good about ourselves.

In the meanwhile I reestablished contact with my father, and was relieved to discover that while the ŠtB had come and searched our home after we Jan and I fled, and while they had interrogated my father repeatedly, they ultimately did not punish him. And while they confiscated a number of possessions from the apartment Jan and I had created on the second floor, they did not appropriate the house from my father, nor confiscate his belongings. Pavol was at that point doing a compulsory two years of military service, so he had been unaffected by our departure. My father assured me that Pavol looked well and was doing fine, and Ivan's photographs from his visit confirmed that. When Pavol completed his military service he was finally to enter his five-year program in mining engineering at a nearby technical university, and therefore would remain in my father's home.

I had worried my father would be incapable of living without me, since he could not cook and had never done any housekeeping. But he came to an arrangement with a dormitory of Comenius University that was situated near our home, for the man who was managing its dining hall was a friend of his. He bought his meals there every day, either eating them in the dining hall or else taking them home in a parcel. My mother's four sisters all lived in Bratislava, and they invited him regularly for meals. Best of all, he reconnected with an old friend he had known in the 1920s in Ivanka pri Dunaji, an attorney who now worked in Bratislava and loved to cook. Since the man's family lived about two hours away and he could visit them only every few weekends, he and my father now spent many evenings together, with the friend cooking for both.

I saw a good deal of Ivan during our first years in New York. He seemed to want to help me—I expect because I was the only family he had. He and I were very different: he loved nightlife, had many girlfriends, and enjoyed spending money on luxury items and fancy vacations. Nonetheless, we had some pleasant times together. For a while he kept a boat at a marina in Greenwich, Connecticut, and invited me to join him on it. On the drive home, he would encourage me to practice my driving skills on the Merritt Parkway, and with just that little bit of helpful instruction, I was able to pass my New York State driver's test. Ivan gave me other good help and advice. Much to my surprise, he urged me to be more attentive to my appearance, insisting that I find a good hairdresser and improve my wardrobe. His years in France had made him conscious of fashion. Also, being such a good-looking man, he knew firsthand how appearance can contribute to professional success.

He was particularly concerned with the state of my teeth. In postwar Bratislava we had very little dental care, and unfortunately it showed. My teeth were discolored and crooked, and as a result I rarely smiled in photographs. Ivan assured me that until I had them fixed, I would never flourish. So he took me to his dentist, who after a close examination informed me that I had seventeen cavities needing immediate attention, along with two bridges and a good bit of cosmetic dentistry. The estimate for the work was shocking—two thousand dollars, the equivalent of roughly seventeen thousand in today's money—and I thought at first of spreading the repairs out over several years to make it more affordable. But Ivan insisted I have it all done immediately. He would pay for it, he said, and I would pay him back whenever I liked. I remember feeling terribly embarrassed, but at the same time greatly relieved, for I wanted the work done. He was right too: my looks and confidence were much improved, and I began to smile much more often.

As my confidence increased, I decided to take Ivan's advice about improving my wardrobe. When I was still in Bratislava, Ivan had sent me packages from New York with pieces of clothing I loved and wore all the time—scarves, mostly; sometimes a blouse. They made me feel quite special. Now that we were in New York, Jan encouraged my interest in fashion. His support and approval kept me from feeling overly vain or self-indulgent, for in truth I was not in the habit of buying things for myself.

I should add that since starting to work at the museum my interest in good clothing had become much more focused, given that I was seeing exceptionally well-dressed women there every day. It therefore seemed to me that dressing well at work was just as important as speaking English properly, or having good office manners. One's own personal style is, after all, a projection of oneself—particularly so when working among people (such as curators and art collectors) who are highly visual. My new hope, as far as my wardrobe was concerned, was to give others a sense of my organization, consistency, correctness, and professionalism—and hopefully to do that with just a little bit of flair. Therefore I began to assemble a wardrobe that reflected these aspirations, doing it piece by piece rather than all at once. I wanted clothing that was well tailored and elegant, but not intimidating: my goal was to appear familiar, open, and approachable.

The basics of this wardrobe were assembled easily enough—much of it at Ohrbach's on Thirty-Fourth Street, which sold inexpensive copies of French designs. But for clothing that expressed a sense of material well-being, I needed to be more resourceful. Through a friend I discovered a fine consignment shop not far from the museum, Encore, at Eighty-Fourth Street and Madison Avenue. Founded in 1954, it was said to be the first of its kind: a resale shop featuring haute couture clothing, shoes, and handbags. Rich women on the Upper East Side would place these luxury items on consignment with the owner, a woman named Florence Barry. I started visiting after work to see what was available, and when I found something that suited me, I splurged. To this day I have two handbags that I bought at Encore, and three pairs of ankle boots once owned by Jacqueline Onassis.

Perhaps the most significant addition to my wardrobe was the smallest: a wedding ring. Jan and I had not thought rings necessary back in Bratislava, but I now decided it would be good to have one, mostly for the sake of convention. I chose a simple platinum wedding band. Jan considered getting one too, but his lab work required him to wash and rewash his hands all throughout the day, and because he worried he might lose it, he decided against it. I understood and didn't mind.

Even as I worked long hours at the Metropolitan Museum, I continued to think about how I might return to my dissertation, because (odd as it may seem) I still wanted my full candidate of sciences degree from Charles University—I was currently the Czechoslovak equivalent of the American PhD "ABD," or "all but dissertation." My first challenge in putting the dissertation back on track was, of course, recovering the draft of it, along with my research notes. I had necessarily left all those things behind in October 1964, when I departed for Vienna with only my overnight bag.

Luckily, I was able to reach out to my friend and fellow curator at the Slovak National Gallery, Eva Šefčáková, for help. While traveling to Canada to mount an exhibition in 1967, she stopped in New York for a three-day visit, bringing along the draft and all my research notes in her luggage. With those, I was able to continue my work on the project for the next two years. But even with my access to books and journals through the Watson Library, I had trouble getting hold of those very few, rare German and Hungarian books that had been published on the medals and their production in the Slovak mining town of Kremnica. To make matters worse, many of my handwritten research notes from my summer of 1958 in Kremnica had gone missing and needed to be re-created. Nonetheless by late 1969 I had completed the dissertation, which consisted of over 150 pages of text, followed by approximately 100 pages of a catalogue containing close descriptions of the medals and their makers, along with accompanying photographs. Making it into a finished document was both time-consuming and exceptionally costly (the photography especially), so I made only one copy. But along with the dissertation, I also prepared a much condensed version that I wanted to publish as a long scholarly article in *Ars*, the official journal of art history of the Slovak Academy of Sciences. I had a good relationship with Dr. Marian Váross, the editor of *Ars*, who had told me he would be delighted to publish it. I knew that doing so would be the fastest possible way of getting my scholarship on record, since having the dissertation read, reviewed, and approved would probably take upward of two years.

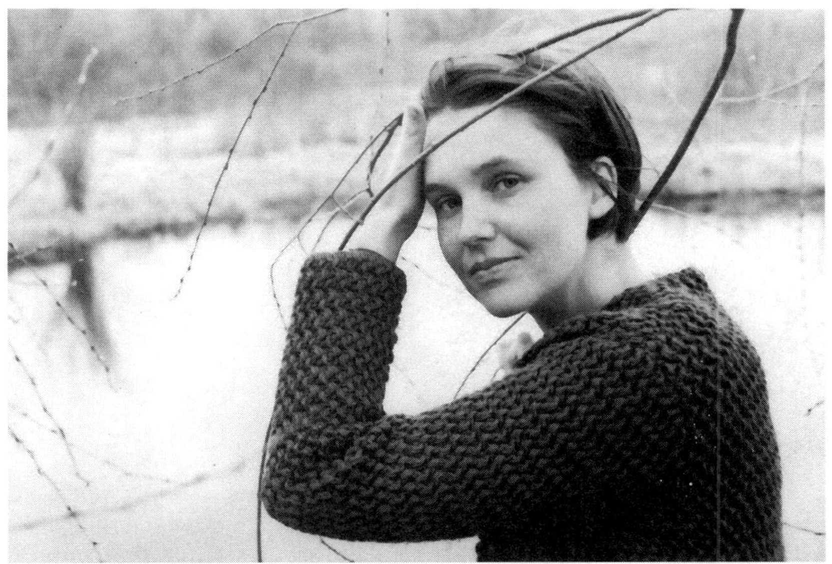

A photograph of me taken by Eva Šefčáková, Hillsdale, New York, April 1967

By this time, of course, the Prague Spring was over, the Russian-backed Communists had regained control of the country, and Czechoslovak society was as just troubled and backward as it had been before Jan and I left. As a result, I needed to find someone to deliver the package containing the dissertation and the article for *Ars* to Eva Šefčáková, because I dared not entrust it to the Czechoslovakian mail. In the end, it was my old friend Líza Aichová (now Líza Rajterová, since she was married to the celebrated conductor and composer Ľudovít Rajter) who did me that great favor. I gave her the dissertation during a brief reunion in New York when the Slovak Philharmonic Orchestra, of which she was now dramaturg, came to do a series of concerts.

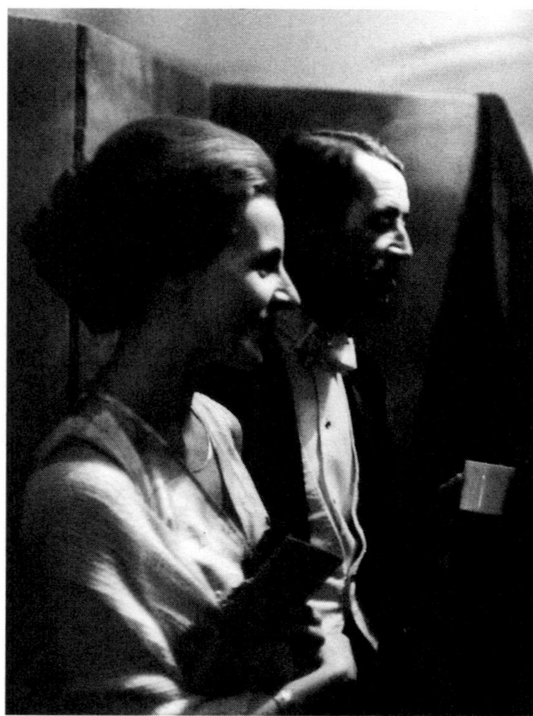

My old friend Liza Aichová, now Liza Rajterová, with her husband, Ľudovít Rajter, cofounder and first conductor of the Slovak Philharmonic

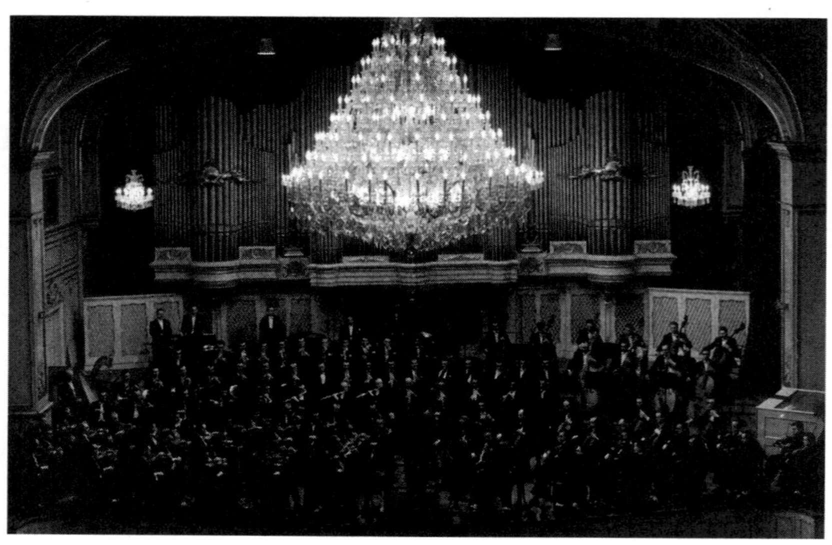

Ľudovít Rajter conducting the Slovak Philharmonic

Upon receiving the package from Líza, Eva Šefčáková hand-delivered the dissertation to the Slovak Academy of Sciences in Bratislava, for it was through this institution (rather than the university) that completed art history dissertations were to be registered and evaluated (the academy would choose the panel of three art history professors who would judge my dissertation). As one of the most well-established curators in the city, she was confident that her endorsement of the dissertation would assure it a careful reading, even though I had fled the country and was thus no longer considered a Czechoslovakian in good standing. She then gave the article based on the dissertation to Dr. Váross, who published it in *Ars* in 1970.

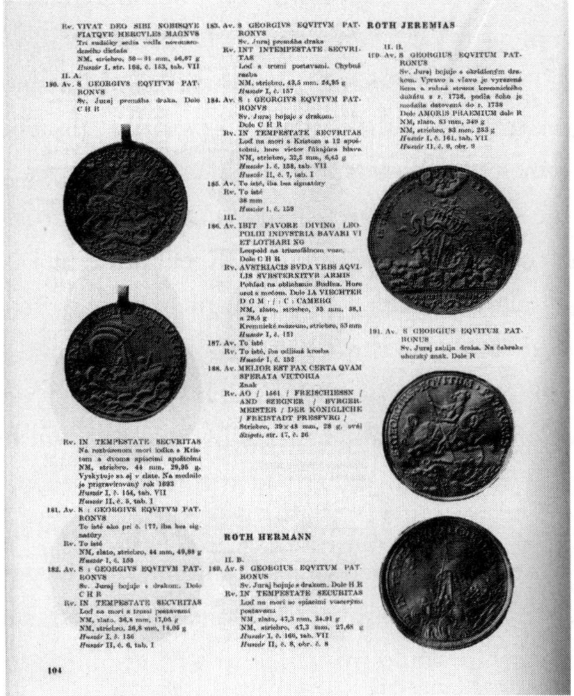

Rv. VIVAT DEO SIBI NOBISQVE FIATQVE HERCVLES MAGNVS
Tri sudičky sedia vedľa novonarodeného dieťaťa
NM, striebro, 58–31 mm, 46,87 g
Huszár I, str. 168, č. 153, tab. VII

II. A.

180. Av. S GEORGIVS EQVITVM PATRONVS
Sv. Juraj premáha draka. Dole C H R

Rv. IN TEMPESTATE SECVRITAS
Na rozbúrenom mori loďka s Kristom a dvoma spiacimi apoštolmi
NM, striebro, 44 mm, 29,35 g. Vyskytuje sa aj v zlate. Na medaile je prigravírovaný rok 1693
Huszár I, č. 154, tab. VII
Huszár II, č. 5, tab. I

181. Av. S : GEORGIVS EQVITVM PATRONVS
To isté ako pri č. 177, iba bez signatúry
Rv. To isté
NM, zlato, striebro, 44 mm, 49,88 g
Huszár I, č. 155

182. Av. S : GEORGIVS EQVITVM PATRONVS
Sv. Juraj bojuje s drakom. Dole C H R
Rv. IN TEMPESTATE SECVRITAS
Loď na mori s troma postavami
NM, zlato, 36,8 mm, 17,05 g
NM, striebro, 36,8 mm, 14,05 g
Huszár I, č. 156
Huszár II, č. 6, tab. I

183. Av. S GEORGIVS EQVITVM PATRONVS
Sv. Juraj premáha draka
Rv. INT INTEMPESTATE SECVRITAS
Loď s troma postavami. Chybná razba
NM, striebro, 43,5 mm, 24,95 g
Huszár I, č. 157

184. Av. S : GEORGIVS EQVITVM PATRONVS
Sv. Juraj bojuje s drakom. Dole C H R
Rv. IN TEMPESTATE SECVRITAS
Loď na mori s Kristom a 12 apoštolmi, hore vietor fúkajúca hlava
NM, striebro, 32,5 mm, 6,43 g
Huszár I, č. 158, tab. VII
Huszár II, č. 7, tab. I

185. Av. To isté, iba bez signatúry
Rv. To isté
38 mm
Huszár I, č. 159

III.

186. Av. IBIT FAVORE DIVINO LEOPOLDI INDVSTRIA BAVARI VI ET LOTHARI NG
Leopold na triumfálnom voze. Dole C H R
Rv. AVSTRIACIS BVDA VRBS AQVILIS SVBSTERNITVR ARMIS
Pohľad na obliehanie Budína. Hore orol s mečom. Dole IA VIECHTER D G M : / : C : CAMERG
NM, zlato, striebro, 53 mm, 38,1 a 28,5 g
Kremnické múzeum, striebro, 53 mm
Huszár I, č. 151

187. Av. To isté
Rv. To isté, iba odlišná kresba
Huszár I, č. 152

188. Av. MELIOR EST PAX CERTA QVAM SPERATA VICTORIA
Znak
Rv. AO / 1561 / FREISCHIESSN / AND SZEGNER / BVRGERMEISTER / DER KONIGLICHE / FREISTADT PRESPVRG /
Striebro, 39 × 48 mm, 28 g, uvál
Szigeti, str. 17, č. 26

ROTH HERMANN

II. B.

189. Av. S GEORGIUS EQVITUM PATRONUS
Sv. Juraj bojuje s drakom. Dole H R
Rv. IN TEMPESTATE SECURITAS
Loď na mori so spiacimi viacerými postavami
NM, zlato, 47,3 mm, 34,91 g
NM, striebro, 47,3 mm, 27,68 g
Huszár I, č. 160, tab. VII
Huszár II, č. 8, obr. č. 8

ROTH JEREMIAS

II. B.

190. Av. S GEORGIUS EQVITUM PATRONUS
Sv. Juraj bojuje s okrídleným drakom. Vpravo a vľavo je vyrezané liena a rubná strana kremnického dukátu z r. 1738, podľa čoho je medaila datovaná do r. 1738
Dole AMORIS PRAEMIUM dole R
NM, zlato, 83 mm, 349 g
NM, striebro, 83 mm, 283 g
Huszár I, č. 161, tab. VII
Huszár II, č. 9, obr. 9

191. Av. S GEORGIUS EQVITUM PATRONUS
Sv. Juraj zabíja draka. Na čabraku uhorský znak. Dole R

104

A catalogue page from my long article on Kremnica medallions, Ars, *April 1970*

After waiting nearly a year for a response about the dissertation, Eva began making inquiries with the academy. Since she was well connected within the Communist Party of Czechoslovakia, she expected a prompt reply—but she could get none. Finally, she went in person to ask why the dissertation had not yet been reviewed and accepted. She was told that there was no record of the dissertation being given to them. When Eva told them that she had brought in the manuscript herself, she was met with indifference. For years afterward, Eva tried to find out what had happened to the dissertation. But she never had a satisfactory answer, and ultimately, she decided it had been either intentionally misplaced or destroyed.

On learning the dissertation was lost, I became tremendously distressed. The project had taken me years to research and write. But as time passed, I was not altogether surprised. Political refugees are generally seen as traitors by the Communists, so the "disappearance" of my work seemed to be just as intentional as the disappearance of any civilian by the ŠtB. In retrospect, I ought not to have entrusted my only copy of the completed typescript to Eva, or to the Slovak Academy of Sciences—but then again, I never imagined that any scholar would intentionally discard or destroy a dissertation, particularly one about an art form unique to Slovak culture and history.

The loss of the dissertation marked a turning point for me. The incident brought back so many bad memories of the Communist system, where hardworking, well-intentioned people were routinely cheated or mistreated by party officials without possible appeal to the rule of law. I felt a tremendous anger and disgust. I had naïvely hoped that my scholarship would make a lasting contribution to Slovakian art history. But the disappearance of the manuscript brought an end to that hope, and made me sick and tired of all things Czechoslovakian.

From that day forward, I would no longer concern myself with Slovakian art history: I would stick to my new life in America.

Eva and I remained friends in the years that followed, and her continued inquiries about the dissertation were always a topic of our long-distance phone conversations. But in 1989 she was fired from the Slovak National Gallery for political reasons, and she could make no further attempts to locate the dissertation or advance my claim for the full candidate of sciences degree. But at least the publication in *Ars* of my thirty-four-page article, "Kremnica Medallions of the 16th and 17th Centuries,"[8] made a substantial portion of the dissertation research available to scholars and entered it (in an abbreviated form) into the historic record. More than twenty years after publication of the article, Susan Weber Soros, the founder and director of the Bard Graduate Center for Studies in the Decorative Arts, invited me to give a long, illustrated talk on the Kreminica medals in their lecture hall. With that accomplished, I was done with the project for good.

Thanks to our joint careers, Jan and I were beginning to have more money and could indulge in small luxuries. Among the first of these luxuries was sending out Jan's shirts to be ironed—since, while I love my husband, I love ironing far less. I then started sending out our sheets and pillowcases to be ironed as well, because our laundry did a very fine job with them. It would still be a few years, though, before I felt confident enough about our household finances to hire weekly cleaning help.

Our social life improved by increments. Jan and I would now occasionally go out to a Chinese or Italian restaurant, so that I might have a night off from cooking and dishwashing after a day's work at the museum. Occasionally we would be invited out by professional friends

8 M. Vilčeková-Gerháthová, "Kremnické medailérstvo 16. a 17. storočia," *Ars* 1, no. 2 (1970): 75–108.

of Jan's. I remember the first time we went to a friend's home for an evening, how surprised we were to be given dinner. In Bratislava there had never been enough food to share, and thus it was customary to have one's meal at home before going out. That first evening with our New York friends, we wanted to be polite, and so we ate a second dinner.

We also began enjoying weekend leisure time. Jan liked to work on Saturdays, but we kept Sundays to ourselves, and made a point of visiting New York's museums and cultural institutions to see the latest exhibitions. Since I worked for the Metropolitan, I had a pass that allowed us free entry at any museum in the city. Luckily Jan enjoyed museums as much as I did. I suppose it was through these outings that we began to think about the pleasure of living with art, which in time would lead us to collecting.

We made other outings too. The shops on the Lower East Side were open Sundays (most other shops were closed), so it was a good place to buy gifts to send to our relatives and friends back in Czechoslovakia. If for some reason Jan happened to be taking a Saturday off, we would browse the antique shops in Greenwich Village—not to buy anything, just to see what was out there.

One of the nicest things about our new life was having ready access to good, fresh food. Back in Czechoslovakia, you couldn't get good meat of any sort unless you knew the butcher and paid him something extra, and specialty cuts (such as lamb chops, calves liver, or veal) were impossible to find. Likewise fresh fruit: in Bratislava one could occasionally get oranges or bananas during the Christmas season, but even then, one had to line up and wait for them. During most of the year, even something as simple as a lemon could be difficult to obtain. Now, however, it was simply a matter of going into any grocery store and picking out whatever one liked: tropical fruits, fresh mushrooms, a porterhouse steak.

Another discovery was seafood. Because Czechoslovakia is landlocked, the only fish available were small freshwater fish or else farmed carp. Prior to our arrival in New York, neither Jan nor I had ever tasted anything from the ocean. My first experience of it was a shrimp cocktail at a friend's house. It was intimidating because I had no idea what they might taste like, or even how one ate them. But I found them delicious, and on that basis, I resolved to teach myself how to cook seafood. On any given day our local seafood market had shrimp, scallops, lobster, swordfish, flounder, tuna, oysters, clams, and mussels, so the possibilities were endless; it was simply a question of learning what was good, what one liked, and then (of course) knowing how to cook it.

By 1970, we were realizing that our neighborhood, while convenient, was not really where we wanted to live. There were no parks nearby, and the neighborhood was dull. Ivan had already found himself a very nice apartment on the Upper West Side, not far from Central Park. My work at the museum, meanwhile, had led me to appreciate the charms of the Upper East Side, which I thought might suit us better than either Midtown East or the Upper West Side. While we couldn't afford anything near the museum—it's possibly the most expensive neighborhood in New York City—there was an area by the East River called Yorkville that was much more affordable. So we looked there, and ultimately found an apartment on East Seventy-Ninth Street between First and Second Avenues. Yorkville had a substantial population of Czech, Slovak, Polish, and Hungarian residents, a fact reflected in the numerous Central European specialty shops and restaurants that lined its streets. We hadn't moved there for that reason—we had no great nostalgia for Czechoslovakia and were committed to becoming fully "American"—but the shops and restaurants were a pleasant surprise, for we still loved Hungarian, Austrian, and Czechoslovakian cooking.

Our new apartment, slightly larger than the previous one, was in a fine prewar building with a pleasant back garden.

We also experimented (but only briefly) with having a weekend home in the country. Doing so would never have occurred to us except that Ivan had decided that he wanted to ski—he had always loved winter sports. Since Jan and I also enjoyed skiing back in our Bratislava days (one could take a public bus to the ski area, as long as there was gas for the bus), Ivan proposed that we take a half share in a little old house he had found and wanted to buy. After some consideration, we decided to give it a try. The former schoolhouse was in Hillsdale, New York, just two and a half hours up the Taconic Parkway, and it cost very little. By splitting the purchase price fifty-fifty with Ivan, we were able to afford the monthly payments on the place. The Berkshire hills reminded us of Slovakia, and the air was fresh and clean. But the nearby ski area was very modest, and its ski season was terribly short. Ivan predictably took no interest in housekeeping or home maintenance, and so I soon found myself doing a good deal of shopping, cleaning, and cooking on my weekends, especially during the summertime. Jan, meanwhile, was compelled to mow the lawn. It did not suit him. Within a year, we had had enough. Jan preferred to spend his Saturdays in the quiet of the lab, or else polishing up his articles for scientific publications. I, too, had things I liked to do on Saturdays: reading, housekeeping, shopping, and errands. So Jan and I decided to leave the house in Hillsdale to Ivan and his new fiancée, and return to the life we preferred, as full-time urban residents of New York City.

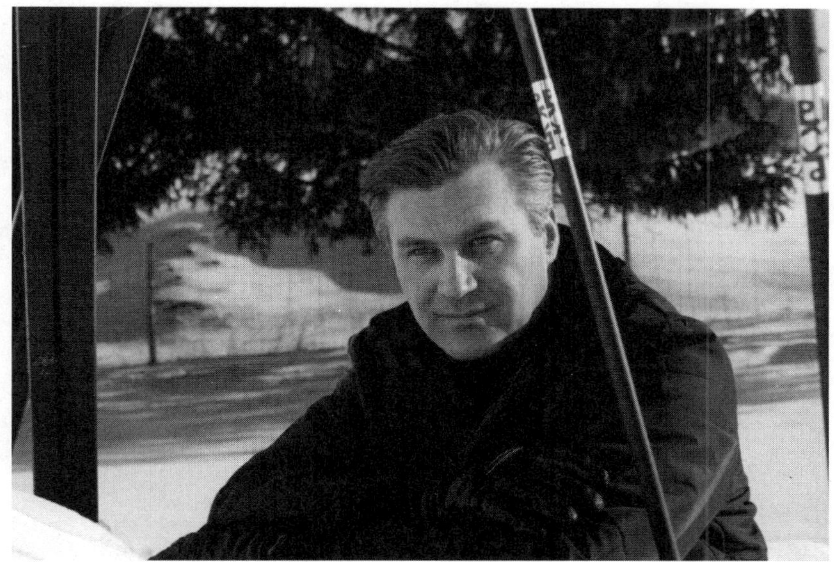

Ivan at the Catamount Mountain Resort, Hillsdale, New York

Ivan had met a fellow Slovakian, Eva Henslová, during the Prague Spring of 1968, during his first visit back to Bratislava since 1956. Like Ivan, Eva was a doctor. He was so enamored of her that he immediately invited her to come to the United States and live with him. I never got to know Eva well, because she was always very busy: working, studying English, and preparing for her American medical exams all at the same time. The few hours we spent together were in Hillsdale, on ski weekends. She was good-looking, had a forceful personality, and was very good at sports—in these ways she and Ivan were very well matched. The two married within a year. They seemed happy, but just a few months after the wedding, Eva committed suicide.

It was devastating for Ivan. He never returned to the house after that. When I went to spend time with him at his apartment, he seemed on the edge of a nervous breakdown, so I took a week off from work to sit with him and help him through it. He was so overwhelmed that

Eva should have chosen to end her life, especially since she had never mentioned being depressed. I didn't know what to say to him because I couldn't understand it, either. Nor did I know how to look after him, apart from keeping him company and making sure he ate something, had clean clothes, and his apartment was clean.

When the week came to an end, Ivan was still very unsteady. I suggested he spend some time up at the Metropolitan Museum, which he did. He would visit the various collections until noon, then meet me for lunch, when we would talk. I think being in the museum helped him: the building itself is so solid and reassuring, and the works of art at least distracted him. I think my company helped too.

Ivan was fragile for months afterward. As he recovered, he saw me less and less. He went back to work, began seeing his various old friends and girlfriends, and no longer called or visited. To overcome Eva's suicide he needed to distance himself from the whole affair, including from me and Jan, since we had known her, had shared the Hillsdale house for a while, and had been back there the weekend she died. In any event, we lost touch. A few years later he met a young art historian who was then taking a degree at the NYU Institute of Fine Arts, Zoe "Zoya" Neandra Švecová, and she became his second wife in 1974. The two began collecting contemporary art together. After they married they moved to Garden City, Long Island, and later to Los Altos Hills, California; as a result I never got to know her very well. Out west, Zoya (who had studied to be an architect) designed a grand new house in the shape of a pyramid, and it was there that they installed their growing contemporary art collection.

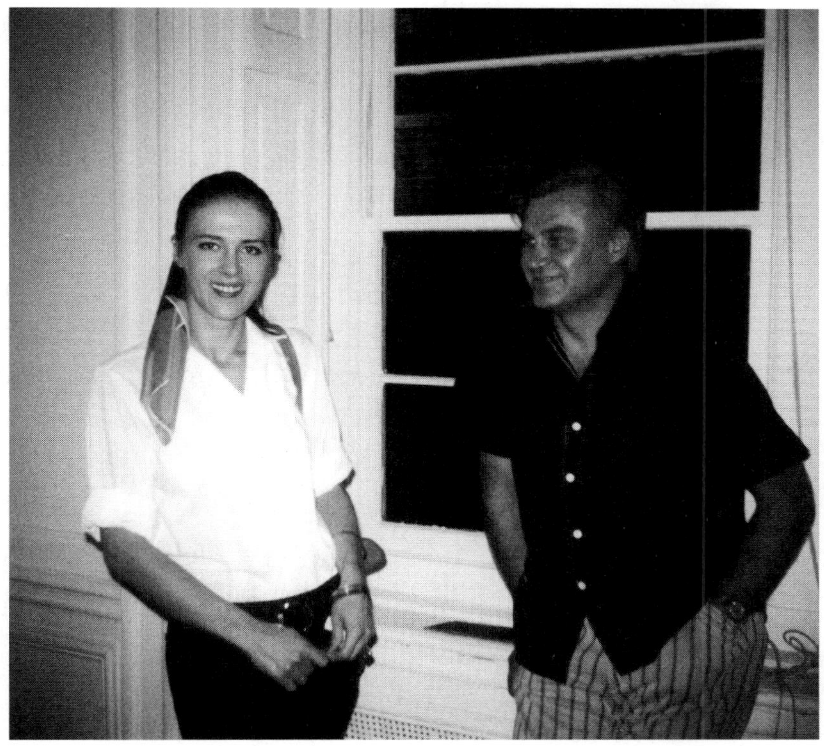

Ivan with Zoe "Zoya" Neandra Švecová, who would become his second wife in 1974

During my early years at the Metropolitan, I started to develop a truly fascinating circle of friends and colleagues, many of whom had started life in Europe. Perhaps the most charming among them was Helmut Nickel, head of the Arms and Armor Department. His offices were directly adjacent to those of the Catalogue Department, so I met him frequently, and he soon became one of my best friends at the museum. Helmut had been born just outside Dresden in 1924, where he had shown early talent as a cartoon artist. After serving in World War II, he had supported himself as a comic book artist and illustrator while taking his PhD in art history in war-ravaged Berlin. He left Germany and joined the Metropolitan in 1960, becoming head of the department in 1968. By then he was a leading authority on arms and armor. Apart from his abiding interest in medieval history, medieval literature, and heraldry, Helmut had a lifelong passion for adventure stories. He illustrated or else made comic book versions of many of them, including the Winnetou novels about Native American life by the German author Karl May. Both Jan and I had loved the Winnetou novels when we were children.

Since Helmut and I would take a coffee break at roughly the same time most mornings, we often sat together in the cafeteria and had a chat, and sometimes other distinguished curators would join us. Among them was Dietrich von Bothmer, who, although born and raised in Berlin and educated at Oxford, had finished his dissertation at UC Berkeley just before World War II. He joined the Metropolitan Museum in 1946 as a curatorial assistant, becoming a curator of Greek and Roman art in 1959, and was ultimately made the head of the Greek and Roman Art Department in 1973. Said to be the greatest connoisseur of Greek art of his generation, he was also the most important and productive classical curator of the twentieth century in the United States. His brother, Bernard, was similarly gifted: a curator, and later the chairman, of the department of Egyptian, classical, and ancient Middle Eastern art at the Brooklyn Museum.

Vera Ostoia, a Russian-born researcher in the Department of Medieval Art, would often join us for coffee. She had recently completed her book and exhibition *The Middle Ages: Treasures from the Cloisters and the Metropolitan Museum of Art.* Another exceptional curator, George Szabo, joined our group a little later. Born in Budapest in 1928, George had started his career as a curator of medieval archaeology at the Hungarian National Museum, but immigrated to the United States with his artist wife, Martha, in the late 1950s. He became a private curator for the great American collector Robert Lehman in 1963; after Lehman bequeathed his extraordinary collection of more than twenty-seven hundred objects to the Lehman Foundation, which in turn bequeathed it to the Met, Szabo was given the job of overseeing the transfer and installation of the collection into the museum's new Robert Lehman Wing, even as he was writing a comprehensive guide to the collection. To this little group of ours came a few other "regulars" as well—Stuart Pyrrh and Ann Willard from Arms and Armor, and Oscar White Muscarella from the Department of Ancient Near Eastern Art. I was glad to be part of this friendly group, which came to be known whimsically as the Kaffeeklatsch due to the preponderance of Central Europeans at its core.

13

The *Cataloguing Manual* and Its Reception

In *Making the Mummies Dance: Inside the Metropolitan Museum of Art*, Thomas Hoving's very entertaining 1993 memoir, our former director noted with regret that much of his work at the museum was taken up with "the burden of housekeeping chores." While planning and organizing exhibitions was great fun, he wrote, most of his days consisted of worrying about budgets, infrastructure, and personnel, as well as about somehow keeping the whole grand institution solvent and functioning, particularly during the great budget crisis that immediately followed the Met's centennial. I remember smiling with recognition at this idea of "the burden of housekeeping chores," because in truth all museum work—from that of the director to the lowliest cataloguer—bears comparison to housework: one is constantly keeping things tidy and in order, and one is always worried about appearances, budgets, efficiency, scheduling, and time.

Early in my career, while cataloguing prints at the Slovak National Gallery, I had quickly learned how closely curating resembled housekeeping, for there had been a vast backlog of prints and photographs that needed to be ordered, numbered, and stored. Now, at the Metropolitan, I was engaged in a recordkeeping variant of that housekeeping, only on a truly monumental scale. Home to millions of objects, the museum is a place where each work of art must have all its related information kept correct and up-to-date, from accession number to exhibition history, description, and item locator. Only by doing so can the collections be maintained. Nothing must ever be lost, forgotten, or misplaced.

To continue with this housekeeping metaphor, I will suggest that the 1972 changeover in our Catalogue Department procedures was something like the revolution in housekeeping that took place after World War II, when families no longer had a housekeeper and instead began doing all their own housework. So it was at the Metropolitan Museum after the budget crisis: with all the full-time cataloguers gone, the curators needed to do their own cataloguing.

Meanwhile I, to empower them, needed to reinvent and streamline the entire cataloguing process in a way that would enable curators from all the different departments in the museum to take on this complicated work. (Consider, for example, how different it is to catalogue a sixteenth-century fragment of lace, a late-seventh-century Tang horse, and a medieval donor portrait.) Curators would now need to write and update their own catalogue entries, and enter and track their own acquisitions through the accessions process, and they would need to do so with complete accuracy, so as not to compromise the integrity of the central catalogue and its related subcatalogues. The manual I was to write for them would guide them through each of these various complicated procedures, step by step.

Devising the plan by which curators would undertake the work of cataloguing took a long time. I consulted on the project with John Buchanan, our registrar, who in turn shared my initial draft of the plan with Dan Herrick, the museum's chief financial officer, with an additional copy going to Thomas Hoving. In his note to both, Buchanan (who had risen to his position as registrar through many years as an archivist) wrote, "I would be guilty of an injustice if I did not point out to all concerned the splendid efforts of Mrs. Marica Vilcek. A reorganization of this sort requires expertise and dedication, and Mrs. Vilcek's performance has been admirable and deserving of the highest praise. If the reorganization is successful—it appears that it will be—it will be in no small measure due to her untiring efforts."

Once the plan was approved, in June 1972, I began the transition by writing a detailed five-page memo to the heads of all the curatorial departments, outlining the expected changes and letting them know the new responsibilities that their curators would need to take on. In it, I briefly outlined the new, curator-driven system for updating the central catalogue. But I also let them know that Marian Harrison and I would continue to prepare and file "index" and "ex-collection" entries for the subject index of Western art that was a part of the central catalogue, since writing these entries was a distinctly complicated task. We would also process all photographic records of art objects, adding the accession and negative numbers to these photos, since doing so required specialist technical work. We would maintain the Deaccessioned File; we would continue to maintain and supervise the central catalogue study room; and we would continue providing consultation services on problems related to museum cataloguing. We were also tasked with giving lectures on museum cataloguing methods whenever they were needed, either within the museum or outside. Otherwise, though, the process of cataloguing was henceforth in the hands of the curators, right down to the required clerical and secretarial work. (I should note that in previous years, curators had often submitted handwritten notes that had then been reviewed, copyedited, and typed up by the cataloguers, which perhaps led many of the curators to consider us not much more than glorified secretaries.) "I realize that this change in the cataloguing procedure will not be without problems," my memo to the curators concluded. "Miss Harrison and I will do our best to get the new system underway. We trust that in close cooperation with the Curatorial Departments we will succeed."

The manual I wrote for the curators, entitled *Cataloguing Manual: Metropolitan Museum of Art,* took me many months to compose. Nearly a hundred pages long, it begins with a brief introduction describing the historic importance of the central catalogue to museum methodology. The fact is that many of our curators did not know that the Metropolitan Museum's central catalogue was the first of its kind in the United States, and by far the most extensive in the nation, or that since its inception it had proved an invaluable example for other art museums across the country, including the Smithsonian Institution and the Museum of Modern Art. I explained all this quite carefully because, as I then wrote, "it is in the interest of the Museum to preserve the integrity and uniformity of the Central Catalogue which has been painstakingly built for over sixty years. Whether we will succeed in achieving this goal depends to a large extent on the efforts of the curatorial departments."

The text that followed was essentially a highly detailed (and decidedly technical) manual of style, laying out standards for the writing, formatting, and design of all documents related to the cataloguing process, and outlining both general procedures and specific procedures for entering and maintaining entries to the central catalogue, as well as its various indexes and related files. The manual also included many illustrations—that is, visual examples of how the various sorts of index cards were to be organized and composed.

The rules for composing the catalogue cards are so complicated that I can hardly begin to describe them here; suffice it to say that they are concerned with not only the placement of the information on the cards, but also the technical and taxonomic descriptors (and other terminology and numerics) that are required to keep in order the entirety of the Met's collection—which, of course, runs to more than two million art objects created all over the world over the course of several millennia.

The inclusion of these descriptors was crucial because, amazingly enough, in 1972 there was no standardized nomenclature for museum cataloguing. At that time, the effort to standardize museum nomenclature was well underway, but it would not be officially codified until 1978, when a structured and controlled list of object terms organized in a rigid classification system was published, thereby establishing an international framework for the indexing and cataloging of all collections of human-made objects. After 1978, art museums around the world readily adopted this standardized classification and controlled vocabulary, which would facilitate a curator's (or administrator's, or scholar's) ability to search, use, and share museum collections data between institutions—whether doing so for purposes of research, collections management, or exhibition planning. However, back in 1972, the only structured and controlled list of object terms our curators had to work from was the Metropolitan Museum's own central catalogue terminology and related hierarchical classifications. This terminology and classification system, devised by the museum itself starting in 1910, had evolved organically over the sixty-two years that had followed and was unique to the Met.

Learning the necessary rules and terminology for composing catalogue cards had, in my own experience, taken each new cataloguer the better part of a year, so I worried that our curators would never be able to pick up such complex protocols on the fly. After all, they were working full-time at curating. I also worried that our extraordinarily precise and well-ordered central catalogue was in imminent danger of being forever compromised. In fact, these worries sometimes gave me actual nightmares.

But we had no choice: full-time, highly trained cataloguers were now a thing of the past at the museum, and the curators would need to do the best they could on their own. In my moments of greatest worry, I comforted myself with the knowledge that by writing the cataloguing guide, I had at least articulated all the procedures, terminologies, and rules for these curators from start to finish. However inexperienced, each curator now had a book-length manual describing what to do and how to do it. My other great comfort came, of course, from knowing that the museum's curators were just as passionate about maintaining their records as I was: as guardians and custodians of the Met's myriad treasures, they knew the profound importance of concise, accurate, organized, and up-to-date recordkeeping, given that they relied heavily on it daily.

One very nice thing about publication of the *Cataloguing Manual* is that it made me better known within the museum, simply because it was immediate and required reading for every single curator working there. Naturally enough, many of the curators had questions about the procedures, so they came to consult with me in person. In this way I met a great many curators I had not yet had the opportunity to interact with during my many years working in the catalogue section. It was a very social period in my career.

The administration kindly recognized me for my work. On December 22, 1972, Director Thomas Hoving wrote me a memo describing the *Cataloguing Manual* as "a fine job." He and other top administrators at the museum now knew me, by name and by face, and would often say hello to me—whether in the hallways, at staff meetings, or (more informally) in the staff cafeteria.

The work I did during this period of enormous transition—overseeing the disbanding of the department while keeping the department going, writing the *Cataloguing Manual*, assisting the curators' transition to curator-generated cataloguing information by working both as their instructor and overseer—kept me exceptionally busy. But I loved the work: I felt more vitally connected to the curatorial side of the museum than ever before, and I seemed to be establishing new friendships with the most magical people every day. Meeting and working with curators from every department gave me such pleasure, especially since solving complex problems is something I have always enjoyed.

The only thing that really troubled me was the lingering memory of the many fine scholars and would-be curators who had been so coldly dismissed from the Metropolitan during the financial crisis. Museums are wonderful places, but the archivists, curators, and administrators who work there have little in the way of job security. Most work exceptionally long hours at low wages. Yet the competition for these jobs is so keen that they are pushed to publish, fund-raise, and produce exhibitions even while spending an enormous amount of time interacting with the public. Art museums, meanwhile, almost always struggle financially: despite having holdings worth many millions of dollars, most have a hard time meeting their operating costs. Indeed, operational finances are often so precarious that institutions must periodically let go of their staff, just as the Met had done (and would, sadly, do again, in the not-too-distant future). I had survived the most recent purge, but I felt a survivor's guilt, even as I was all too aware of the continued precariousness of my position.

As I became more and more at home with various curators and curatorial departments, I was sometimes called upon to sort out problems caused by cultural misunderstandings. In 1973, for example, a group of Russian curators arrived at the Metropolitan Museum to install "From the Land of the Scythians: Ancient Treasures from the Museums of the U.S.S.R. (3000 B.C.–100 B.C.)," an exhibition featuring 197 priceless works of ancient gold, carvings, and textiles from the Soviet Union. The show, which had taken five years to negotiate, was the brainchild of Thomas Hoving and Charles Wrightsman, a wealthy collector who sat on the Met's board of trustees, after both men had been moved by the ancient treasures they came across in the Gold Room of the Hermitage Museum. Because these objects were of such fragility, age, and cultural significance, the Soviets had insisted that they be handled only by the Hermitage's curators, who were sent to New York to do the installation themselves.

Few people at the Metropolitan could communicate with these curators upon their arrival, since none of the Russians spoke English. The American curators could not comprehend why their Soviet colleagues were so cranky and disgruntled. Eventually a call went out to find someone who spoke Russian. As it happened there were only three people on the curatorial staff who were fluent in it: Olga Raggio, the chair of European Sculpture and Decorative Arts, whose parents had fled the Ukraine for Italy at the time of the Russian Revolution;

Natalie Spassky, my former colleague, now a researcher in American Paintings, who had grown up in New York speaking Russian at home; and myself. Of the three, I was the only one who had ever done any curating behind the Iron Curtain.

I was asked to find out why they were so unhappy. I expected they were suffering from jet lag and culture shock, but soon realized the issue was something far more elemental: hunger! With little Soviet money to cover their daily expenses, and no freedom to walk around the city on their own, they had been unable to find anything to eat. I immediately brought them to our staff cafeteria and arranged for them to have their meals there, apologizing that we hadn't organized it sooner.

That night, I baked a quiche. I remember how the next morning my colleagues thought my bringing a quiche to the museum was exceedingly funny, even bizarre—particularly our registrar, John Buchanan. But while it may have seemed to him "above and beyond the call of duty," I knew from my own experiences under communism that hunger—*real* hunger—is no laughing matter. Nor is the humiliation one feels at experiencing hunger in front of those who are well fed. So I swapped a few anecdotes with the Hermitage curators while I sliced it up and handed it out, and had a bit of the quiche myself, just to be sociable, and in a few minutes everyone's mood improved dramatically. A day or two later I was told that the Hermitage curators had become far easier to work with, and I quietly congratulated myself on having done my part for U.S.-Soviet détente.

My encounter with the Russian curators brought with it a related development: the museum's upper administration began to feel that, thanks to my ability with European languages and customs, I could be relied upon to meet, greet, and entertain nearly any overseas dignitary. It was, in a sense, a great compliment. But the simple truth was that our director often needed to get these distinguished visitors out of his office so that he might get on with his own pressing work. As a result, Hoving or his secretary now made a habit of suggesting to these visiting dignitaries and VIPs that they adjourn to the Catalogue Department for a glimpse of the fabled inner workings of the Metropolitan Museum.

The guests would then be led down to the study room. After greeting them and making them comfortable, I would briefly explain the history of our recordkeeping system, show them the vast cabinetry housing the central catalogue, provide some impressive facts about the museum's vast holdings, and answer whatever questions they might have. If there was real interest, I would even demonstrate how to locate a work of art and decode the information in its catalogue entry.

At that point, like the director, I too would need to get on with my work, and so I would bring my visitors over to the staff cafeteria to offer them coffee and cake, which was always gratefully received. Over time, I would meet a great number of extremely important people in this way, including directors and curators from the Louvre, the National Gallery in London, the Rijksmuseum, the Uffizi, and the Vatican Museum. Celebrities and politicians, too—so many important people passed through the Metropolitan Museum over the years as VIP guests, all of them grateful for coffee and cake at the end of all my little talk.

But even as the Met was relying on me for my European language skills, Jan and I were moving in the opposite direction at home. We became American citizens in 1970 (the process had taken five years) and while we occasionally visited Europe to attend Jan's various conferences, see his parents, and visit museums, we no longer spoke Slovak to each other. Instead we spoke only English, having mutually decided in 1968 that this would help us transition more fully to our new lives in the United States. Some might consider this a radical step—for language is so elementally connected to thought, to feeling, and to one's own sense of oneself that it seems almost impossible to abandon the language of one's childhood and youth. But Jan and I were determined to make this transition. Although at first we struggled, the change drew us closer, since it was like stepping through a doorway together, moving from one reality to another with only each other for company. I am sure that doing so as a couple was far less traumatic than doing such a thing alone.

However, this changeover to English was much more difficult for me, because Jan had been speaking English from childhood, whereas I had come to it as my fifth fully fluent language, having been introduced to it only in my late twenties. Now in my early thirties, I sometimes despaired that I would ever master it. But I took comfort in a notion that Jan once expressed to me: namely, that in changing from Slovak to American English, he and I were consciously dismantling one cultural reality and exchanging it for a new one that was far more welcoming and inclusive.

By 1973, I was far closer to proficiency in this endlessly variable, idiosyncratic, and complicated language than I had thought possible. In fact I no longer translated Slovak thoughts to English before speaking; instead, I was thinking in English—occasionally dreaming in English too.

With my promotion to associate curator in charge on July 1, 1974, I found myself invited to take part in more curatorial endeavors. The most enjoyable of these was writing, editing, and reviewing articles for our museum publications. One such article, "Cataloguing in the Metropolitan Museum of Art, with a Note on Adaptations for Small Museums," drew extensively on all the work I had just completed with the

Cataloguing Manual; but it was designed specifically to help smaller art museums understand and adapt our cataloguing methodology for their own use. I was so pleased to work with my former boss, Marcia C. Harty, on this particular piece. I drafted and wrote most of it, since she was retired and working only in an advisory capacity, but in speaking with her about our respective challenges over the years, I grew closer to her and learned a great deal about her life and career at the Met.

That same year, I was invited to join the editorial board of *Metropolitan Museum Journal*, a position I held until 1976. *Metropolitan Museum Journal* had been established just a few years earlier, at the time of the museum's centennial, for the publication of scholarly articles on the museum's collections. As a board member, I was tasked with reading submissions, voting on our accepting or rejecting them, and assisting in the editing of the accepted articles. I also participated in decisions regarding the *Journal*'s appearance and distribution—and while this was rather time-consuming committee work, I found it enjoyable simply because of the good company of my fellow curators.

Some of the curators who stand out for me as I think back on those busy, happy times include my good friend Marilyn Jenkins Madina, from the Islamic Department, who had started curating at the Met in 1964; Christine Lilyquist, the head of the Egyptian Department, who had done such brilliant work with Thomas Hoving and Kevin Roche on the new Egyptian galleries; Joan Mertens, curator of Greek and Roman Art; Katharine Baetjer, curator of European Paintings; and Morrison Heckscher, curator of American Decorative Arts. To be in the company of such wonderful scholar-curators was a privilege, and to be considered their colleague truly an honor.

Unfortunately, right in the middle of this very busy time in my life, I had a significant worsening of my Ménière's disease. Because I was more and more incapacitated by it, my specialist at NYU felt that surgery on the right ear was the best (perhaps last) option for me. In October 1975 I had the surgery, technically described as a labyrinthectomy. But it failed, destroying my balance center on my right side and eradicating all hearing in that ear. To make matters worse, my problems with Ménière's disease continued, and in 1977 it started affecting my left ear very badly as well, causing me even more balance, vertigo, and hearing problems.

The sadness I felt at losing half of my hearing (and I lost it in both of my ears, which is rare) is something I don't often mention to others. But the grief I experienced was considerable, since this new loss limited my ability to interact easily with people, and created in me a new shyness about speaking, given that I was no longer sure that I was speaking at the right volume. Nor could I be sure of what others were saying, particularly when I was in a noisy environment. My foreign accent had always been a cause of apprehension and self-consciousness, and now this apprehension intensified. But as there was nothing to be done about it, I reconciled myself to accepting this new condition and focusing instead on something I could actually control: my appearance. I reasoned that if I couldn't communicate easily through speaking and listening, I could at least communicate *visually*—by looking my best, in a way that projected both intelligence and approachability. Perhaps as a result, most people at the Metropolitan Museum who knew me probably perceived me as rather more reserved and *comme il faut* than previously—but also (hopefully) rather more accessible too. Luckily, the majority of my work concerned written communication and data management, activities that did not require constant verbal interaction. Had I been a full-time curator charged with lecturing and mixing socially with donors and patrons, my situation would have been impossible.

In late 1975, Jan and I decided to move to a larger and better apartment. We liked our Yorkville neighborhood so we didn't move far; in fact, just two blocks west, to be closer to Central Park and the museum. Our new home was in an eighteen-story prewar cooperative at 180 East Seventy-Ninth Street—technically placing us in Lenox Hill rather than Yorkville. The apartment was larger and airier, with better light, and because we had a little more space, we were more able to indulge in some furniture collecting. I liked that my walk to work was now shorter: I was now just seven blocks from the Metropolitan Museum, and could get there in a mere ten minutes, rather than the previous fifteen.

Because I had worked for ten years at the museum, I received a letter in March 1976 from Philippe de Montebello, who was then the vice director of curatorial and educational affairs, informing me that I was eligible to apply for tenure. I did so. The curators making the decision were Dietrich von Bothmer, Frances Gruber, Colta Ives, Clare Le Corbeiller, and Helmut Nickel. Some were good friends, others simply acquaintances, but all of them knew and liked me from our decade of working together. They reviewed my work history, considered my various accomplishments, and cast their votes. In June 1976, Ashton Hawkins, secretary and counsel of the museum, wrote me with the happy news that I had been granted tenure by unanimous consent.

Jan and I were used to our friends and colleagues receiving tenure—it was a common occurrence among Jan's many research associates at NYU Medical School—so we didn't celebrate the occasion. It's never been our style to engage in self-congratulation. Our life simply continued as always. I continued to work at least eight hours a day at the Museum, from nine to five, Monday to Friday, and often stayed longer since it was easier for me to concentrate after everyone else had left. I usually returned home around six, with Jan returning from his own busy workday at NYU around seven. After dinner he would return to his desk, because only in the quiet of the evening could he fully concentrate—his teaching and research life being taken up, as mine was, with so many interruptions. I often brought work home too, for I did my best writing between dinner and bedtime.

Jan was happy that I had received tenure, knowing that my work there could now continue without threat of layoff. Job security probably meant more to me than to others, given that—starting with my work at the Slovak National Gallery many years earlier—I had never had any such assurance, ever. Money was not the issue, because Jan was earning well in his position at NYU, and we had few expenses. Rather, it was the sense of acceptance, inclusion, and security that the tenure decision provided. I had never really experienced such security before, anywhere. To be totally honest, even within my family I had often felt expendable and unwanted. Now, however, according to the Metropolitan's curatorial regulations, I could work at the museum for the rest of my professional career.[9] After years of relative anonymity, I had been assured a job for life!

An honor of a very different sort arrived on my desk that same month as my tenure: the most beautiful thank-you note I have ever received, handwritten by former First Lady Jacqueline Kennedy Onassis.

During the previous year, Mrs. Onassis had requested my assistance in locating and identifying Russian works of art within the Metropolitan Museum's collections for inclusion in the first book she was ever to edit. Her *In the Russian Style* was to be published to accompany Diana Vreeland's exhibition "The Glory of Russian Costume," which was to run at the museum from December 1976 to August 1977. The

9 More precisely, I could be dismissed only if I exhibited "unfitness or refusal to hold the position or carry out the responsibilities of the position" or committed "a felony or any misdemeanor other than a traffic violation." For more on curatorial tenure at the Metropolitan Museum, see "Regulations for Curatorial and Educational Employees, Originally Adopted by the Board of Trustees on November 14, 1972 [and] Amended May 14, 1974 and September 10, 1974," Metropolitan Museum Archives, Watson Library (quotes from p. 14).

Met had partnered with Mrs. Onassis's publishing house, Viking Press, to produce this lavish picture book.

Our director, Thomas Hoving, had asked Mrs. Onassis to help plan and research "The Glory of Russian Costume" starting in early 1975, inviting her to travel to the USSR with Diana Vreeland and himself to select items from the great Russian museum collections. The combination of Mrs. Onassis and Diana Vreeland dazzled the Soviet curators and helped facilitate the loans; news of her travel there had also caused a growing excitement about the exhibition across the United States and Europe. Mrs. Onassis subsequently chaired the Costume Institute gala for that year, which of course boosted attendance and publicity for both the gala and the exhibition. How could it not? At that moment she was universally considered the most beautiful, most fashionable, most talked-about woman in the world. Everyone wanted to see her, to know her, to emulate her style.

Mrs. Onassis's book, meanwhile, was to feature photographs and illustrations drawn from numerous private and public sources, but it would also draw heavily upon the Met's own holdings. There was only one problem: as she explained to me, for the past six months, "everyone" had told her that there was nothing Russian in the Metropolitan Museum!

I would very gladly have welcomed Mrs. Onassis into the study room and then explained to her how the central catalogue was organized so that she might undertake her own research. But as it happened, our section of the museum was just then under construction, and the study room was filled with noise and dust. Knowing that she could not possibly function in such an environment, and also sensing her special need for privacy, I did the bulk of the catalogue research on her behalf, delivering all the relevant catalogue entries to the museum's main information desk, where she could pick it up whenever she liked.

My fluency in Russian, as well as my knowledge of Russian art and culture, made the research relatively easy for me, and I was delighted to discover that there were indeed an extraordinary number of fine Russian works of various sorts in the museum's collections.

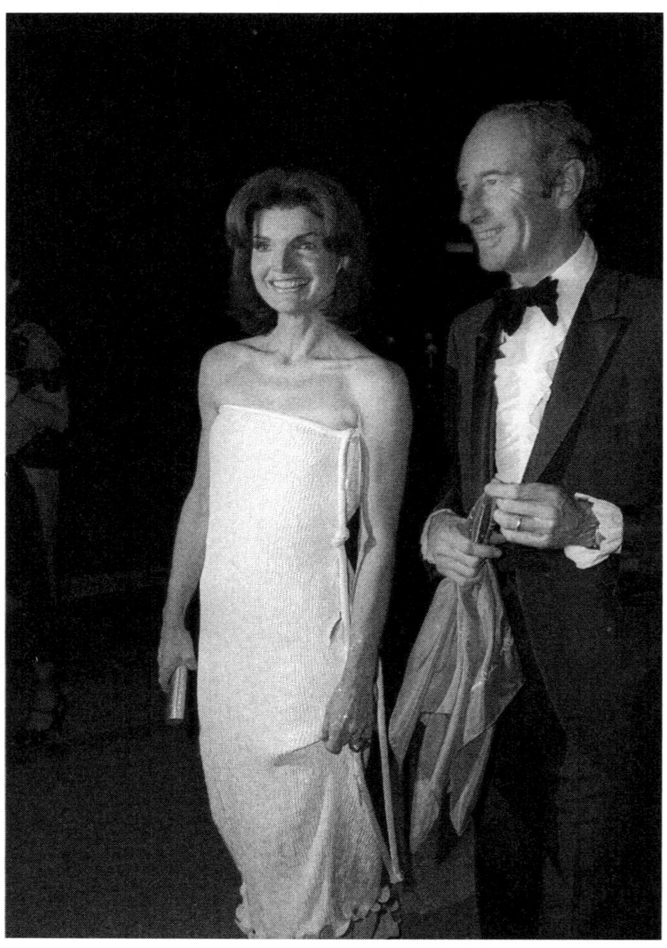

Jacqueline Kennedy Onassis and Thomas Hoving at the Metropolitan Museum's Costume Institute Ball, 1976

Once I had delivered the materials to Mrs. Onassis, she did an extraordinary amount of organizing in record time, bringing together a dazzling selection of treasures (paintings, furniture, decorative objects, clothing, and jewels) that had long been buried in museum storage. Their photographs were included in the book along with a far larger selection of Russian works from around the world, all of which were then accompanied by her text, which was written with exceptional grace and refinement.

The handwritten note I received from her several months later, in June 1976, said so many nice things that I would love to quote it in its entirety, but her estate has requested that I do so only briefly. Here is the passage I find most charming:

> *Now that I have seen how a great museum works—that you are the vital heart of it—the center without which it could not function—I am mortified at our imposition, and doubly, triply grateful . . . you appeared, with your magic wand and your generous spirit, and look at the infinity of treasures you cast before us!—Like stars—*
>
> *With my deepest, deepest thanks,*
> *Most sincerely,*
> *Jacqueline Onassis*

It was around this time, as well, that Jan and I made our first targeted financial donation to the Metropolitan Museum. In November 1976, a high school student named Ina Gallon was accepted into the catalogue division's internship program, but I was subsequently told that there was no money left in the museum's yearly budget to pay her stipend. (I had started the intern program three years earlier, in September 1973; our first intern, Anne Havemeyer, was already an undergraduate at

Yale, where she would subsequently take a PhD in art history.) Rather than disappoint Gallon, Jan and I decided to pay for her internship ourselves. We couldn't afford to pay for the full stipend all at once, so I paid the $250 in two installments, sending one check in mid-November and another in late December. The museum's vice director, Richard Dougherty, sent a note of thanks for both—but of course, the greater reward lay in giving this deserving young student a chance to work at the Met.

14

Mid-Career Years

The year I received tenure many other changes took place at the Metropolitan Museum—especially since Thomas Hoving decided that he would leave to head a new branch of the Annenberg School of Communications, through which he hoped to make films and television programs about fine art. Our new director was Philippe de Montebello, who had already spent most of his professional life working at the museum. He started in the Department of European Paintings in 1963, and left the Met only briefly, in 1969, to run the Museum of Fine Arts, Houston. He returned in 1974, serving as vice director for curatorial and educational affairs under Hoving.

When the trustees named de Montebello the new director, they also split the director's job in two, creating a new position of museum president. The idea was to free the director to concentrate on programming and education, leaving the burdensome business-oriented work to the president. Our first president was William H. Macomber, who would serve in that position for the next nine years. This new development helped to stabilize the museum's finances and to ease the challenges of the directorship.

Many of the great expansion projects initiated under Hoving reached completion under de Montebello, and with so much expansion and renovation came a good deal of recataloguing and accessioning. When the Robert Lehman Collection opened to the public in the new Robert Lehman Wing in 1975, for example, all the roughly three thousand works in that collection needed to be given new accession numbers beginning with "1975." But even while undertaking such projects, I was working to improve the accessibility of the museum's cataloguing records by transferring specialized information from various departmental catalogues into the central catalogue. During 1977 we amended over fifteen thousand catalogue cards, and we continued to do so, at a similar volume, every year for the coming decade. I was also kept busy overseeing the study room, which by 1977 was being used by more than six hundred museum staff members, scholars, students, and interested members of the public (that number of visitors would more than double in the coming decade). Whenever required, I would also offer guidance and assistance to smaller museums and private collectors seeking information on registration and cataloguing procedures for their own collections.

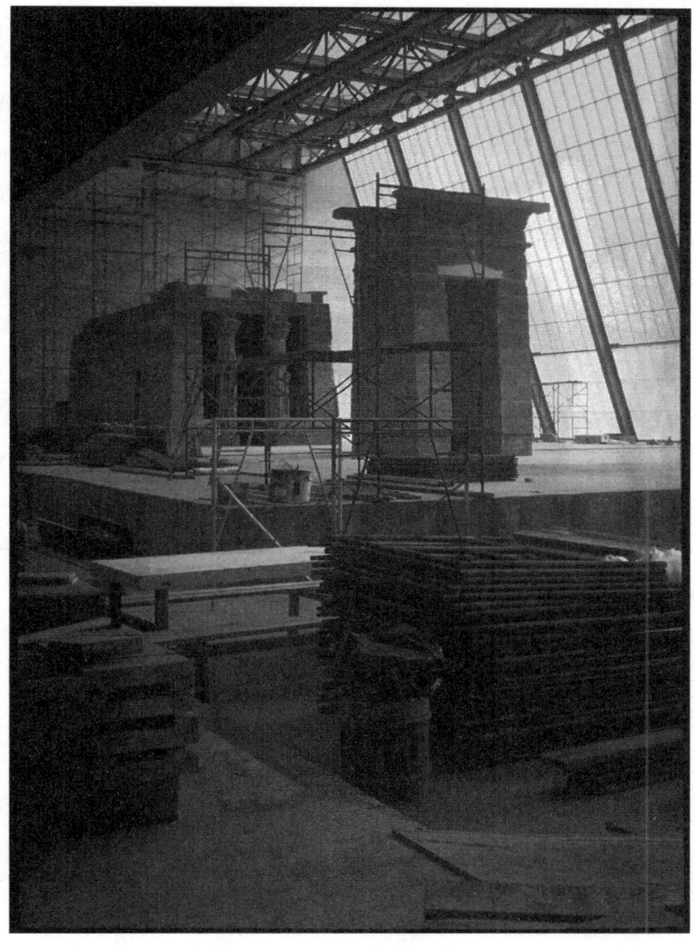

Reassembled Temple of Dendur, Metropolitan Museum, 1978

Because of this increased volume of work, our high school interns became more and more vital to the smooth functioning of our group. The department now consisted of myself, two other full-time workers, and one part-time worker. Our very first high school intern dated back to 1973, but starting in 1978 we had two or three interns per year, with many of them returning during college breaks to work for us part-time. They came from many different backgrounds: the ones born and raised in New York were of various races and ethnicities; others came to us from Brazil, Czechoslovakia, France, Germany, Japan, Peru, Taiwan, and Switzerland. While my records are incomplete, I know for certain we had at least forty-seven such interns during my years at the museum. Many would go on to significant careers in the arts while others took careers in business, teaching, or law. Only one has remained with the Met after all these years: Lisa Pilosi, who came to me in 1983 and is today the head of the museum's Department of Objects Conservation. She worked for me part-time throughout her college years (coming back on every break and vacation) before deciding to study art conservation at the graduate level. She returned to the Met to work in conservation immediately upon earning her degree. To this day we remain the very best of friends.

In 1979 we undertook two new initiatives. The first involved photographic documentation of works of art in the museum's collections. We obtained, processed, and distributed about eleven thousand of these photographs in our first year, for they served as a much needed supplement to the written descriptions in both the central catalogue and the departmental catalogues. Because curators and scholars valued these visual records so highly, we continued to add and process them throughout my time at the museum. And in fact today, many of those photographs can also be accessed by the public via the internet, on the Met's superb website. Our second initiative was to improve the recordkeeping of the Department of American Paintings and Sculpture. To do so, we created triplicate copies of all of its central catalogue entries, thereby enabling the department to have a far more satisfactory recordkeeping system of its holdings within their own offices.

We began accessioning the Nelson A. Rockefeller Collection that year too. Although the bulk of it had been promised as a gift to the museum in 1969, it was only accessioned a decade later. Nelson Rockefeller had created this collection with the help of René d'Harnoncourt, the Austrian-born art curator who had been director of the Museum of Modern Art from 1949 to 1967. Rockefeller, the longtime governor of New York who served as Gerald Ford's vice president, had housed the collection from 1954 through 1976 in his own Museum of Primitive Art in New York. The transfer of this vast collection (417 works from Africa, 1068 from Oceania, and 1054 from the Americas) to the Metropolitan Museum necessitated both the creation of a new department—the Department of the Arts of Africa, Oceania, and the Americas—and the construction of a new wing in which to display it. The Michael C. Rockefeller Wing was named in honor of Governor Rockefeller's son, who had died in New Guinea in 1961. Because each item in the collection had been formally gifted to the museum in 1979, each required a new accession number beginning with "1979"—so that year, too, was a busy year in cataloguing.

In 1980, we began yet another initiative: reviewing and refurbishing those catalogue cards and photographs in the central catalogue that were either worn, damaged, or missing some crucial informational component. (Wear and tear to the cards and their related photographs was hardly surprising, for many dated as far back as 1910, and most had been handled by generations of curators, administrators, and members of the public, incurring various sorts of damage and loss along the way.) That year, too, we transferred a good deal of information from the central catalogue to the numerical file. In all, we handled or filed approximately 18,000 new cards and processed approximately 13,500 documentary photographs. We also made a special project of updating the subject indexes for European art, American art, Far Eastern and Islamic art, and tribal art.

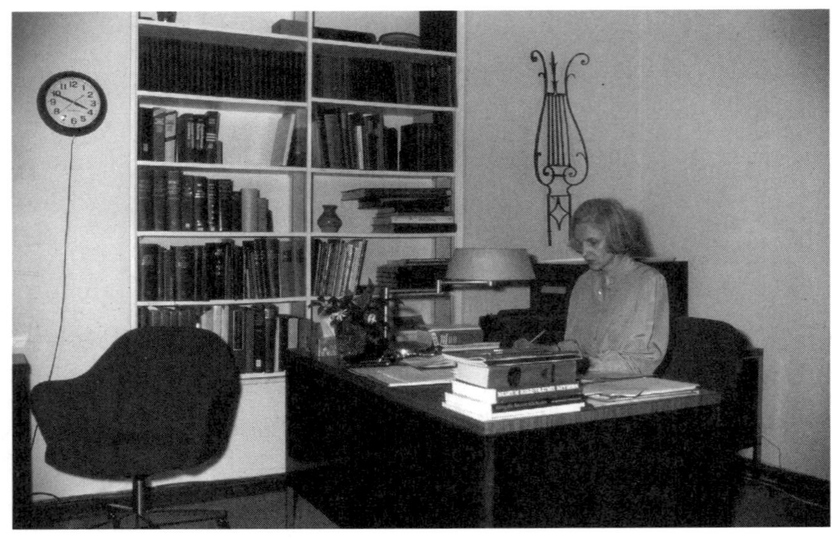

At my desk in the Cataloguing Department, Metropolitan Museum,1982

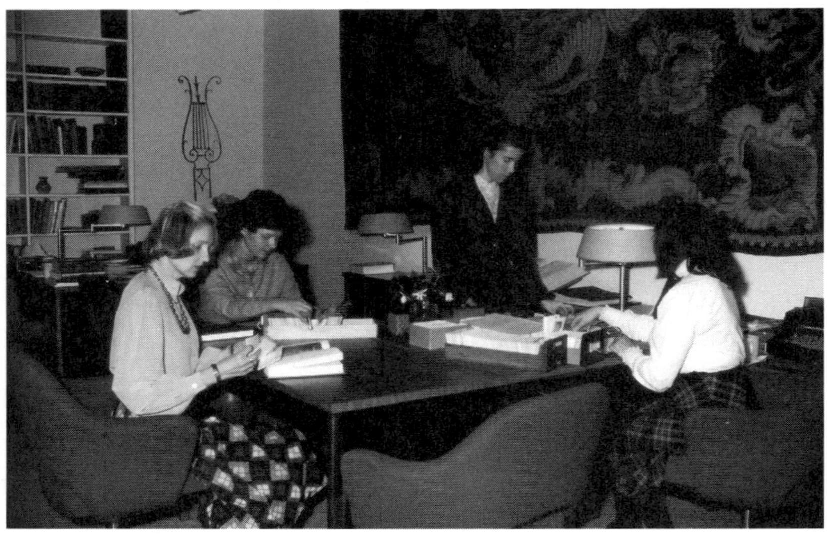

Working with interns in the Cataloguing Department, 1982

Amid these various cataloguing projects, Jan surprised me with some big news. After visiting a colleague at the medical school of the University of Geneva, he had been offered the chair of its department of microbiology. Accepting it would mean relocating permanently to Europe.

Jan was far more tempted to move than I. He found Geneva remarkably clean, orderly, and civilized, and the university had a top-level microbiology department. With the new position would come many opportunities for professional and scientific advancement, as well as substantial remuneration.

In discussing the offer with me, Jan pointed out how deeply troubled New York had become. Starting in the early 1970s many middle-class and upper-class New Yorkers had fled the city for the suburbs, prompting a steep drop in tax revenues. As a result, the city was shockingly dirty, disorderly, and run-down. Carrying more than $11 billion in debt, the local government was unable to borrow more from the credit markets and so was facing bankruptcy. Though ultimately bailed out by various state and federal loans, it had to cut many basic services, including policing. In 1977, a massive summertime electrical blackout prompted riots and looting, with more than three thousand people arrested in just a few days. At that point, many people felt the city was trapped in a death spiral and would never recover. And in truth, even our very nice neighborhood was now being menaced by criminals and defaced by vandals.

Still, I opposed moving to Geneva. I was not unaware of the beauty, charm, and orderliness of European life, because Jan and I had been traveling to Europe on short, work-related vacations yearly ever since receiving our American passports, and of course we loved our visits there. By now we had visited Amsterdam, Athens, Budapest, Helsinki, Lisbon, London, Madrid, and Paris and also returned to Frankfurt and Vienna.[10] I had not yet visited Geneva, but then I had no great interest in it: despite Switzerland's reputation for beautiful scenery, Geneva seemed awfully small and provincial in comparison to New York. More to the point, I loved my work at the Metropolitan Museum and knew it would be difficult for me to find a workplace more interesting. Our art-focused life in New York was one that I cherished, and I cherished my friendships here too. So together we decided against the move. In years to come, Jan would receive several more job offers from top microbiology departments, but whenever we discussed it, we always came back to the simple fact that we loved New York far too much to leave.

Thoughts of immigration remained on my mind in May 1979, when my brother Pavol emigrated from Czechoslovakia to the United States. He defected via Austria, along with his new wife, Denisa, a dentist. The couple needed to wait nearly seven months in Austria for their U.S. visas, but that December the documents finally came through. They arrived in New York just a few days later, planning to remain with us for an extended stay. (Luckily our new apartment had a spare bedroom and bath.) Pavol was going to seek work as a mining engineer, but he knew that finding such a job would take time, so in the meantime he took a job at a sporting goods store. Denisa faced a much more difficult adjustment, since she spoke only Slovak, German, and Russian and had no family here. She seemed very intimidated by big-city life.

When Pavol ultimately found an engineering job in Denver, Jan and I helped him purchase a modest suburban home. A year and a

10 In Hungary Jan and I visited the Museum of Fine Arts Budapest and the Museum of Applied Arts; in the United Kingdom, the British Museum, the National Gallery, the Victoria and Albert Museum, and many others; in the Netherlands, the Rijksmuseum, the Van Gogh Museum, Mauritshuis. and Kroller-Muller Museum; in Finland, the National Museum of Finland and Sinebrychoff; and in France, the Louvre, Versailles, the Pompidou Center, the Musée des Arts Décoratifs, the Cluny Museum, and many others.

half later, he and Denisa had a son, Pavol Jr. From all Pavol told me, they seemed to be settling in; he was making a good salary, Denisa was studying for her Colorado dentistry license, and they both liked the mountains and the climate. But as we later discovered, Denisa failed several attempts to gain her dental accreditation, in part because she was struggling with English. Lonely and discouraged, she began pressuring my brother to move back to Europe, where she felt certain she would be able to practice dentistry again. At last he agreed, and in January 1982 they left Denver for a new life in Berlin.

Witnessing their struggle, I realized that not everyone can adapt to life in America. Immigration is itself a major challenge, but then after arriving, one faces so many other challenges: gaining fluency in the language, learning new customs, understanding American politics and manners and social norms—all of which are so very different from those of Europe. I was sorry that Pavol and Denisa hadn't been able to rise to the challenge. But in thinking about their decision, I remembered all too well the crushing isolation I had experienced in my first months here. I had managed because New York is one of the most welcoming cities in the world, and because Jan and I were both so focused on our professional lives. Pavol and Denisa, by comparison, had felt no connection to their neighbors in suburban Colorado.

With their return to Europe, I felt less and less of a connection to my family. Ivan and I rarely spoke these days, because he and his new wife, Zoya, had moved by then to Long Island, and in their free time they were collecting contemporary art, a field that did not interest me much. My father, meanwhile, rarely wrote to me, for he had always been a man of few words, and he hadn't much news to share in old age. I hadn't been to Bratislava since a brief trip in the summer of 1978. When my father died in 1984, I was denied a visa and could not attend the funeral. But with my father and brother gone, there wasn't much left there for me. Ivan and I decided that my father's house and possessions should go to Leonka, my mother's half-sister, given that she and Ivan had always been close, and she had been good about looking after my father in his final years.

Starting in the early 1980s Jan's research work at NYU became far more pressing. He had been working on interferon for more than twenty years. Many people thought that interferon might ultimately cure cancer, and Jan was one of the world's great experts. Interest in interferon escalated further in 1981, when a devastating new illness emerged that would ultimately be known as AIDS.[11] Large amounts of interferon were being found in the blood of AIDS patients, leading researchers once again to seize upon the idea that interferon might somehow be the key to finding a cure. (Ultimately it wasn't a cure for AIDS, or for cancer either, but it did help in developing a treatment for hepatitis C.)

Because New York City quickly became the epicenter of the AIDS epidemic, Jan found himself working among of a network of brilliant, highly motivated, and politically astute scientists and clinicians keen on finding the cause of and a cure for AIDS. Among these many talented clinicians and scientists was the NYU dermatologist Alvin Friedman-Kien, whom Jan had first befriended in 1965. Jan was also in contact with the outspoken Sloan Kettering research scientist Mathilde Krim and the unconventional infectious diseases specialist Joseph Sonnabend, who (like Friedman-Kien) often worked in Jan's lab. Sonnabend and Krim would, in time, cofound the American Foundation for AIDS Research (amfAR). But even as Jan found himself tangentially drawn into AIDS research and HIV prevention, he was focusing upon a remarkable new substance that had

11 On July 3, 1981, *The New York Times* published Lawrence Altman's groundbreaking article "Rare Cancer Seen in Forty-One Homosexuals"; one month earlier, the Centers for Disease Control had published the first "official" recognition of HIV/AIDS in the United States.

a powerful effect upon the immune system. Jan's work on understanding this substance, called TNF or tumor necrosis factor, and on utilizing TNF derivatives to influence the immune system, would ultimately lead him to the development of the monoclonal antibody infliximab (later known as Remicade)—a highly effective medication for the treatment of a large number of autoimmune diseases.

While Jan zeroed in on this vital research, I continued my cataloguing work at the Metropolitan. During the 1980s the understanding and interpretation of the museum's collections continued to evolve. As a result, the cards in the central catalogue were in constant need of updating and revision. Every single year of this decade, our department would add more than ten thousand references to the catalogue cards for previously acquired objects. We also worked from year to year on creating and improving several central subject indexes. And we continued our work of processing and distributing approximately thirteen thousand record photographs yearly to the many departments throughout the museum. We were also now hosting and tending to approximately thirteen hundred visitors annually in the study room.

As I look back, I am amazed that the museum's administrators took so long to incorporate computers and computing into our everyday working life in the Catalogue Department. Today the idea of data management without computers is unthinkable, thanks to their brilliantly efficient data-management software systems. Not until 1985 did the first personal computer—a Compaq Deskpro—arrive in our office.[12] And since there was no data-management software program

12 The Met's 1985 Annual Report notes that the "recent introduction of computer terminals into museum work may lead to the first major change in the storage and retrieval of information from the Central Catalogue." See *Annual Report of the Trustees of the Metropolitan Museum of Art*, no. 116 (1985), pp. 45–48; available at JSTOR, http://www.jstor.org/stable/40304922 (accessed June 15, 2023). Additional information on the development of custom software (1989 and after) comes from Rick Kinsel, email to Justin Spring, June 2023.

on it, our use of that personal computer was extremely limited. Indeed, only in 1988 would we start to map out the full scope of all the fields that might be needed for a data-management system of the collections. We then worked with programmers to build a custom software system specifically adapted to the highly specialized needs of the Metropolitan Museum. Ultimately a team of approximately seven people would work on that project and another, related project, a computerized accessioning system.

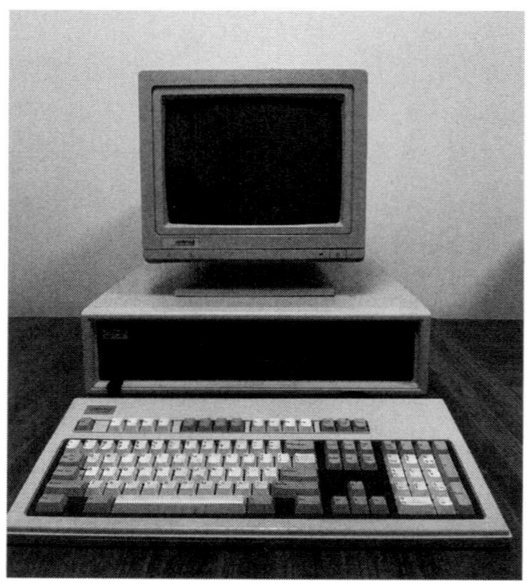

The Cataloguing Department's first computer,
a Compaq Deskpro, acquired in 1985

In these last years before computers became vital to our work, I was often approached by members of the curatorial staff to locate objects that were somehow "lost" within the central catalogue—to serve, in effect, as a human search engine for those who had exhausted all other options for locating the object or information they required. I remember once helping the young Andrew Solomon, who came to the Met as a high school intern in 1980 (and is today a distinguished author, fellow museum trustee, and friend) to locate some information about a photograph for the Costume Institute. He later praised my "figuring out how to categorize everything so that it could be found through minor clues."

The curator Penelope Hunter-Stiebel recently observed something similar, noting that during her years at the museum (1969–1983), I seemed to her "a sort of high priestess and guardian angel of the records of the museum's vast collections." Such a characterization seems excessively flattering, but her further observations point to an essential truth about our catalogue at the time:

> Marica's presence and lilting voice remain an indelible memory. . . . Back then there was no such thing as shared on-line information about the Museum's holdings. However there [was] the Central Catalogue where Marica presided, and where I spent many an hour. The curatorial departments tended to be fiefdoms and the information on their holdings was in effect proprietary, to be shared at curators' discretion. However Marica, together with her staff of cataloguers, saw to it that every new addition to the collection was meticulously described, measured, and had its basic data recorded on 3x5 cards before it left the Registrar's Storeroom on its way to the respective departments, along with copies of the cards—[which] meant one did not need to make an appointment with the curatorial department to access their information about a given work. Marica's contribution was not only her maintaining of an ironclad system of documentation, it was also the guidance that no "Finder" button could replace. When one did not know exactly what one was looking for, Marica, with

> her wide-angle view of art history and its manifestations in the Metropolitan's collections, often did, [whether the person seeking the information was] expert or novice.

On our free weekends, Jan and I found ourselves spending more and more time with his friend and colleague Dr. Alvin Friedman-Kien, since, apart from being very good company, Alvin shared our passion for art. He expressed his own creativity through collecting, a passion that grew substantially during the 1980s, perhaps because of the stress of his working with the first AIDS patients, so many of whom were dying quite suddenly while in his care. In July 1981 Alvin was the first researcher to publish on the prevalence of Kaposi's sarcoma and *pneumocystis* pneumonia among homosexual men; by 1987, he and his colleagues at NYU had documented more than a thousand cases of AIDS-associated Kaposi's sarcoma. Along the way he lost an untold number of patients.

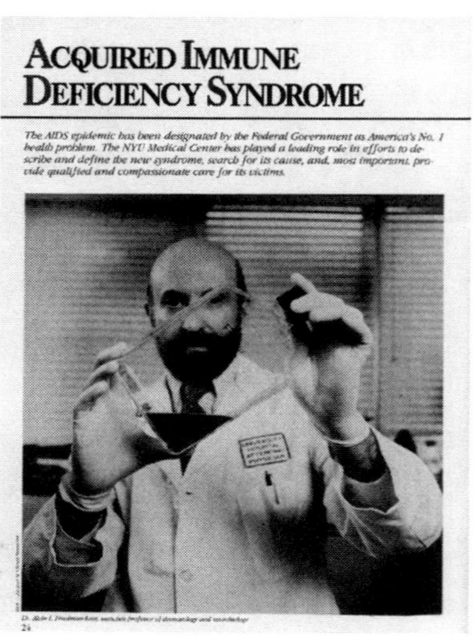

ACQUIRED IMMUNE DEFICIENCY SYNDROME

The AIDS epidemic has been designated by the Federal Government as America's No. 1 health problem. The NYU Medical Center has played a leading role in efforts to describe and define the new syndrome, search for its cause, and, most important, provide qualified and compassionate care for its victims.

24

Our close friend Dr. Alvin Friedman-Kien, who spearheaded early efforts to find a cure for AIDs

Then in his early fifties, Alvin was wonderfully enthusiastic about looking at art and buying it. Apart from collecting American art, he loved acquiring furniture, textiles, decorative objects, toys, games, and folk art. A day out with him in galleries and antiques shops felt like a treasure hunt: to his way of thinking, there was always something magical to be discovered and acquired. In fact, it was through him that Jan and I began to realize that collecting could bring great joy.

I should explain that up until this point in our lives, Jan and I had done a good deal of window-shopping, but not much actual purchasing, because our means were limited and our apartment was small. Of course, I had been picking up little things here and there since my early days in Bratislava, and that habit had stayed with me after arriving in New York: I always enjoyed poking through thrift stores, where one could usually find something—a piece of silver, a vase, a bit of old porcelain—that gave pleasure and amusement. Occasionally I would come across a fine old carpet. If it seemed really special and in top condition, I would take the plunge and buy it. Once properly cleaned and cared for, such textiles often revealed themselves as dazzlingly beautiful.

And in fact, that was how Alvin persuaded us to make our first substantial purchase: he had found and bid on a very beautiful eighteenth-century Persian carpet at Sotheby's, and only afterward realized it was too large to fit in his home. Not knowing what to do with it, he offered it to us on loan. For two years it lay on the floor of our living room, and since I liked it more and more, we finally asked if we might purchase it in installments. He was delighted to say yes.

By 1988, Jan and I were so fond of Alvin that when he suggested we take a trip with him to Santa Fe, we accepted. We spent our first days with him combing through the city's many galleries. Of course, there were museums to visit as well: the New Mexico Museum of Art, the Museum of International Folk Art, the Museum of Spanish Colonial

Art, the Wheelwright Museum of the American Indian, the Museum of Indian Arts and Culture, and the New Mexico History Museum. But we went out to an enormous open-air flea market early in the morning, which held items of every possible sort, including fine antiques and works of contemporary art. The experience was so dazzling—not just the objects, but the people, the scenery, and the bustle of the marketplace—that we knew we would happily return. I don't think Jan and I were quite ready to start collecting; we were content simply to watch Alvin purchase a wide variety of things, and to congratulate him on each purchase.

Alvin was having such a good time that he altered my sense of what it meant to collect. Since childhood I had enjoyed art simply by seeing it in museums. My aunt Eržika had demonstrated to me the pleasure one could take in acquiring and looking after beautiful things, and to some extent I had acquired some things too. I had never thought much about collecting—neither as a talent nor as a vocation. And to be honest, in my privileged position at the Metropolitan, surrounded by some of the greatest art in the world, I felt I was already living and working amid objects of great beauty and cultural significance. But Alvin suggested to me that the thrill of being a collector lay in finding, appreciating, and safeguarding beautiful or important works for generations to come. And I began to see the value in doing something similar. Having spent most of my career reviewing the history and provenance of artworks in the Met's collections, I expected that, given the right motivation and opportunity, I might in time develop into a discriminating collector. The only thing Jan and I lacked, of course, was the means! My salary was modest despite my seniority at the museum, and Jan, too, made only a comfortable living as a research scientist and teacher.

Not long after that first trip to Santa Fe, another person entered my life who would have an equally strong effect upon my future. Oddly enough, I met him at the Metropolitan Museum of Art bookshop.

During the mid-1980s several full-time employees came to work with me through the Metropolitan Museum's Human Resources Department who ultimately were not well suited to the work. As a result, I decided not to rely solely upon Human Resources the next time a position became available in my department, but rather to see if I could find someone of promise on my own. This was how I met Rick Kinsel. Then twenty-two years old, Rick was an assistant manager in the museum's bookshop. He had been interviewing for an entry-level position at the museum throughout the fall of 1989, having graduated with a bachelor's degree in art history from Ohio State University. But when no museum job was immediately available, he agreed to take a sales position in the bookshop to help with the holiday rush.

Not content simply to track down books for people—a difficult enough thing to do in those days before computers made bibliographic searches easy—Rick reorganized the shelving system throughout the store to improve its efficiency, impressing his bosses with his flair for organization and his good solid work ethic.

The first time I met him, I was impressed at how respectful, poised, and articulate he was. When he subsequently told me he was seeking curatorial work, I suggested he join me. That fall Rick received two other offers from within the museum—working with curator James Parker on French furniture in the Department of European Sculpture and Decorative Arts, or else training docents for the Education Department. But Rick felt that working in cataloguing would offer him the greatest opportunity for rising within the museum, so he joined me there, beginning part-time right after the 1989 Christmas holidays. And, just as I had anticipated, he proved exceptionally well suited to the work. Despite the difference in our ages, we soon became friends as well as colleagues.

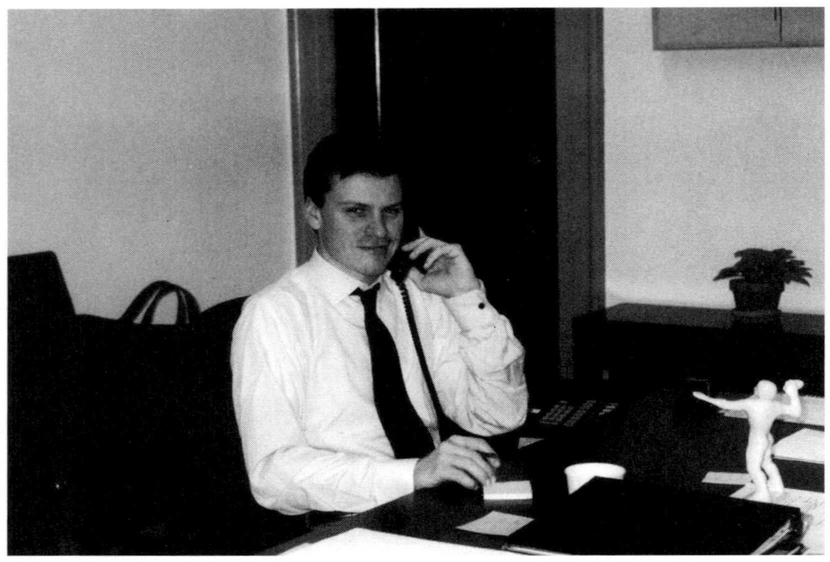

Rick Kinsel during his early days in the Cataloguing Department

Rick soon proved himself enormously capable at cataloguing and at working with interns. He was good at fielding queries from curators, collectors, and scholars. And he was far more familiar with computers and computer programs than I had ever been—so much so that he was the only person in the department who worked regularly on our one computer terminal. By 1991 he had been promoted to full-time work in the department. The next year, we began the conversion of accession numbers into a computer format, a complicated process that required a great deal of preparatory work. In order that it go as smoothly as possible, I prepared a manual detailing the rules and regulations of the accessioning process, along with complete instructions for assigning numbers and recording information on accession cards. By using this manual, Rick and the programmers were able to develop and implement a basic computer accessioning program.

Another new worker, Danka Andraško, joined us in December 1992. Danka was conscientious, hardworking, and multilingual. Half French and half Czechoslovak, she had come to America from Czechoslovakia with her husband, a paintings conservator who worked at the Met. She had taken a law degree in Prague, but was glad to find work at the museum—for she and her husband were raising a young daughter and struggling financially. The work also enabled her to apply for permanent resident status in the United States.

In May 1993, I received a memo from Philippe de Montebello informing me that the responsibility for the maintenance of the accessions files and for the assignment of accession numbers was soon going to be transferred from the Registrar's Office to the Catalogue Department. Because the accession-card file served as the central record of objects owned by the museum, this was a major new responsibility, and because of these changes, the accessioning of newly acquired objects became one of our most important activities. Every member of the department needed to become thoroughly acquainted with the rules and regulations concerning the assignment of new accession numbers. We began the work with an enormous backlog of items awaiting accession, with several new objects being added every day. We also faced a vast backlog of work relating to our newly implemented computer accessions program.[13] To further facilitate our transition to computers, Andraško and another employee were now being given computer training, and Kinsel was selected to coordinate the computerization of the central catalogue's subject index.

Even as we began this work, however, I worried that the museum

13 For more on this situation, see "Accessions and Catalogue Department." *Annual Report of the Trustees of the Metropolitan Museum of Art*, no. 124 (1993), p. 51; available at JSTOR, http://www.jstor.org/stable/40305017 (accessed June 15, 2023).

was not making a coordinated effort at data management. Rather, different departments had adopted or rejected various software programs for their own collections management needs. The Department of American Paintings and Sculpture had extremely expensive custom software; the Department of Photographs employed the ZIM database; the Department of Modern and Contemporary Art had another, different, completely customized (and very expensive) software system; the Department of Musical Instruments had a low-cost but limited software system; the Lehman Collection had two databases, SNAP and Q&A; the Department of Egyptian Art had recently rejected the Superbase database to work instead with the Access database; the Loans Department used a database called PARADOX; the Department of Greek and Roman Art, the Department of Ancient Near Eastern Art, the Department of Islamic Art, the Department of Asian Art, and the Department of Medieval Art and the Cloisters all used Dataperfect, but the Department of European Paintings used a more advanced (and much more expensive) system called Argus. Clearly there would be a great deal of work needed if we were someday to pull all of these various incompatible systems together into one, centralized catalogue database!

During this great data-management challenge, one very good thing happened: Rick was accepted into the master's program at the new Bard Graduate Center for Studies in the Decorative Arts. Founded by Susan Weber Soros, it was one of the best possible graduate-level institutions for advanced degrees in the decorative arts. I knew that the Metropolitan Museum of Art was offering a partial tuition reimbursement to any employee accepted into its program, so I had strongly urged Rick to apply. He had very limited financial resources and told me he was worried about going into debt, but I urged him not to be intimidated. Simply go step by step in the application process, I told him, and we will see what happens. I wrote him the best possible recommendation, and in the end things worked out in his favor. Even though it would take him nearly seven years of part-time study to gain his MA, he had at least made a start toward doing the work he most wanted to do: curating.

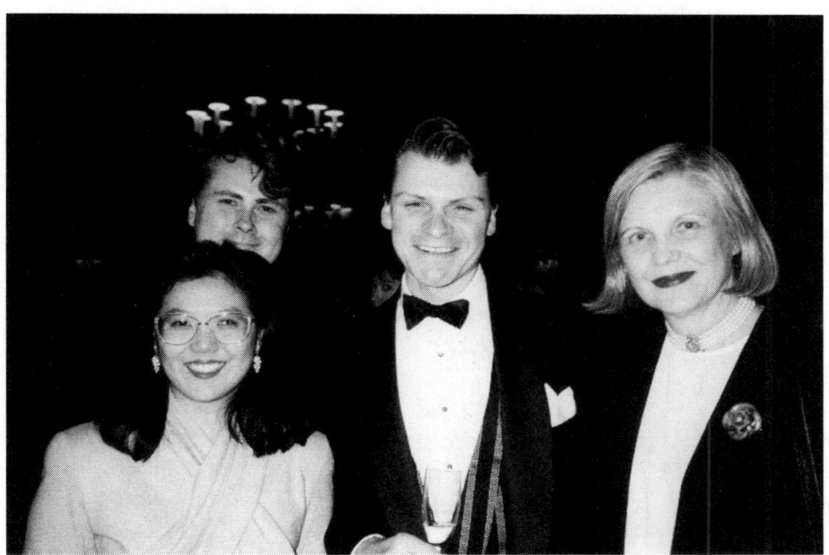

With Rick Kinsel, Museum of the City of New York Winter Ball, early 1990s

Looking back at my last decade at the Metropolitan, I think perhaps I have focused a little too much on describing my work and its challenges, and I worry that I have created a false impression that my life there consisted of endless toil and not much pleasure. But in fact, I really did love my work and I had a good time doing it. While it is true I worked many long hours, including nights and weekends, I also had a very active social life through the museum, and so did Jan. I frequently attended the openings of exhibitions curated by friends—both at the Met and other museums and galleries—and in doing so over the course of many years, I developed friendships and acquaintanceships with a great many people of similar interests. When Jan and I were not working, we went to parties and get-togethers, and had quite a few of our own. Our life was busy and full.

Particularly during the years that we lived on Seventy-Ninth Street, I would regularly cook dinner for friends. We occasionally gave larger parties too—especially during the holiday season, when we invited friends from all walks of life, and would hire in helpers to assist. Jan's research associates and top students from NYU would be there, along with my friends and former interns from the museum. We also invited recent immigrants who had just arrived in New York and didn't yet know anyone. Because of my own early experiences, I was always sensitive to the possibility that people were lonely and struggling and in need of inclusion and support. For that same reason, I always tried to have simple foods on hand at our parties—just in case people felt overwhelmed or confused by food and drink that was too fancy or unfamiliar.

Rick was wonderfully helpful at times like these, because he knew I wanted the apartment to look its best when having company, and there was always so much that needed to be done. He and I would work together to get everything in order. He would even use a special floor polisher, waxing and buffing our hardwood floors until they gleamed. In the meantime I had a lot of shopping, ordering, and cooking to do. For many years, I would poach and decorate a large salmon as the centerpiece for the buffet, and prepare several good side dishes too, creating a sort of smorgasbord. At other times, I would roll up my sleeves and spend an afternoon making authentic Hungarian stuffed cabbage or something similar—*plnená paprika*, stuffed peppers, or *kapustnica*, a spicy pork and sauerkraut soup.

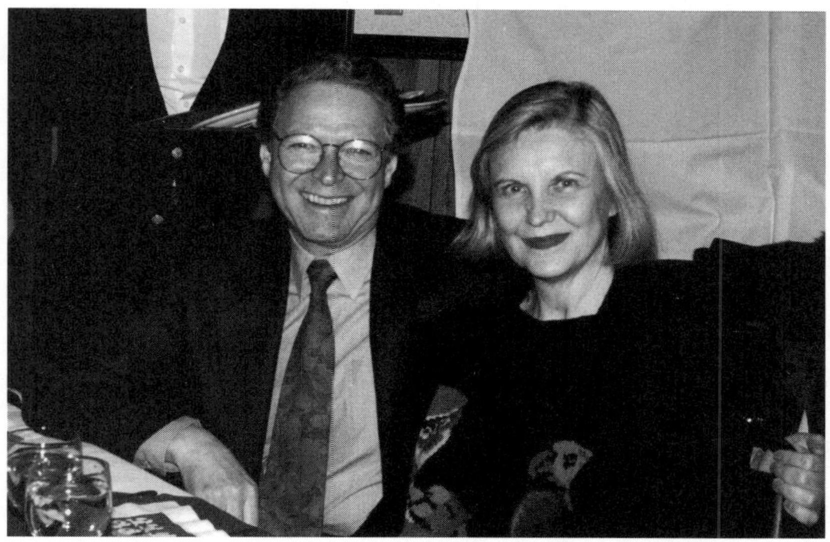

At a party with Jan, in 1994

For the most part, though, I depended on the many delicacies from those wonderful specialty shops of the era—Balducci's, Dean & DeLuca, the Silver Palate—and of course Zabar's for the finest smoked salmon, pâté, cheese, and Jan's favorite, sourdough bread. Much to our delight, our guests would sometimes arrive with dishes they had prepared. Since many of Jan's associates were from Europe and Asia, these buffets took on a truly international air. The pleasure that such entertaining gave me was profound. Back in Bratislava, I had never been able to show hospitality to friends. Doing so now was a joy, for it made me feel wonderfully connected, appreciated, and loved.

15

An Unexpected Development

With our department's new accessions duties, our workload doubled. To help with that workload, Gwen Alston joined us full-time from the Registrar's Office. But we were also struggling with a problematic co-worker, whom I'll call D. in the pages that follow. D. was becoming ever more difficult and unpredictable, often provoking arguments with Danka Andraško, Rick Kinsel, and occasionally even the interns. It was unlike anything I'd ever before experienced at the Metropolitan Museum, and it made me worried—especially regarding the interns, who were young, impressionable, and defenseless.

In retrospect, I understand that D. felt threatened by both Kinsel and Andraško, for both were better qualified than he, and both had better prospects for advancement within the museum. Since D.'s arrival in the Catalogue Department in 1985, I had worked hard to help him move forward in his career. For example, when the Met decided in 1986 that all those seeking advancement would need graduate degrees, I suggested he apply to the Parsons/Cooper-Hewitt History of Decorative Arts program and I wrote him a recommendation for it, as well as a request to the museum that he receive a partial tuition reimbursement. But after being accepted to the program and receiving the reimbursement, D. quit graduate school after only two weeks, complaining to me that there was too much studying and homework required.

So far as I could tell he was not interested in art history or curating. He rarely if ever attended exhibitions within the museum. Since his scholarship and writing skills were not good, I wondered why he remained within the department, given that our pay was relatively low, since he would have earned far more at a corporate job. Few such secretarial workers stayed on for long at the Met because their opportunities to advance were limited. But D. had remained and over the course of a decade he rose by small degrees in both title and pay grade, ultimately reaching the title of senior cataloguer in 1994.

By then, however, his violent outbursts were increasing, especially toward Rick Kinsel. Kinsel was focused, well organized, and authentically interested in art and art history; he also attended exhibitions, wrote art reviews, and had even begun collecting art on a very modest scale. When I was asked to oversee the conversion of our manual accessioning system to a computerized one, I relied upon Kinsel to help me, because he was the only person in the department with proven computer skills.

D.'s jealousy of Kinsel and Andraško was such that he insisted on taking charge of the new accessioning work. I sensed he might not be good at it but allowed him to do some accessioning in the two weeks before he left on a brief travel grant. While he was away, however, I reviewed his work and found that he had made more than two hundred mistakes in his transcription of accession numbers. This was a disaster, since it threatened the integrity and accuracy of the catalogue.

When D. returned, I presented him with the mistakes he had made. He apologized but nonetheless insisted on continuing with the work. When I resisted, he grew confrontational, and so I agreed to let him try it one more time, on the condition that he work with Gwen Alston.

The arrangement lasted less than one day. By midafternoon he had accused Alston of engaging in unwelcome physical contact, an accusation he could not prove and that Alston vehemently denied. A loud argument followed his outburst against her, after which both workers filed reports with the Human Resources Department. The two never reconciled; Alston ultimately quit.

In November 1993, after evidence of his dyslexic mistakes seemed to me irrefutable, D. agreed to give up accessioning and concentrate instead on indexing work. But his outbursts continued. The interns now avoided interacting with him, and one quit outright rather than face this daily unpleasantness. When D. began shouting at me too, I realized something needed to be done. I made an appointment with the museum's associate vice director, Jennifer Russell, who listened to me with sympathy but would not agree to transfer him out of the department. If an employee was known to be difficult, she explained, museum policy forbid such a transfer.

D. then began making complaints about me to Human Resources. During one such meeting, he told the deputy administrator of human resources that he expected to be promoted to my position when I retired. When the administrator told me this, I couldn't quite believe it, because I had no intention of retiring anytime soon, and furthermore I knew D. was altogether incapable of doing my job.

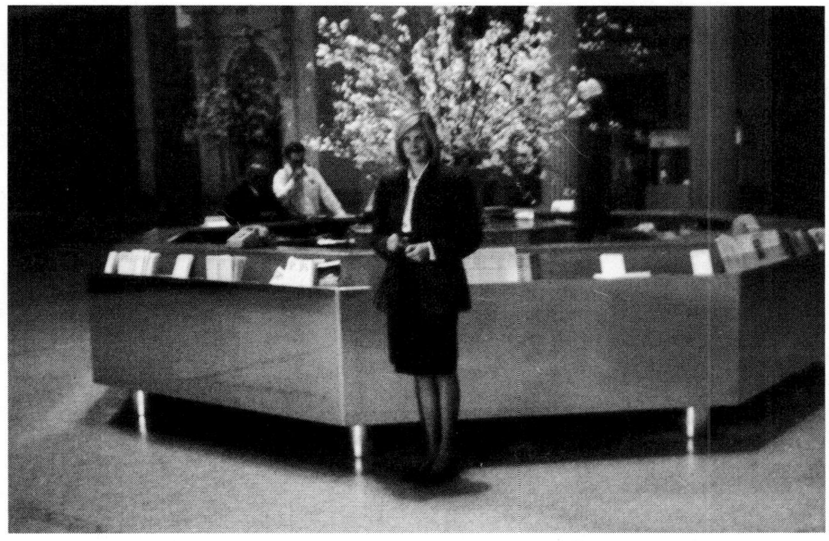

*At the Information Desk in the Great Hall,
Metropolitan Museum of Art, 1996*

In the weeks that followed, he began sending memorandums to me asserting his importance to the department: in one, he stated that he had developed the new subject index computer program that Rick Kinsel had in fact created. In another, D. claimed to have single-handedly completed the entire Islamic paintings subject index. I told my contacts in Human Resources that he was engaging in a disinformation campaign.

In April 1996, Jennifer Rusell left her position of associate vice director. She was succeeded by Doralynn Pines, a librarian at the museum's Watson Library with no apparent experience in museum administration. When I consulted her, Pines told me to give D. a low raise as a way of expressing my dissatisfaction with his performance.

Upon receiving news of his low raise (and the mildly critical job review that I filed along with it), D. filed a series of formal grievances against me and other members of the department. From May through

July of that year, he and his lawyer (who was also known to us as his domestic partner, for they frequently attended parties and museum events together) filed eleven such grievances. In one instance the two called a joint meeting with the museum's Human Resources Department and its Office of General Counsel.

In a grievance letter of June 26, 1996, they accused Kinsel and Andraško of doing freelance work on the job, of taking long periods of time away from the office, and of offloading their work onto others. The letter also accused me of showing preferential treatment toward Andraško and Kinsel. In another grievance, they complained about the low salary increase and accused me of lying on the job performance review. In yet another, they stated that Andraško and Kinsel had been given undue amounts of vacation time and personal days off and noted that, by comparison, D. had not been given the one vacation day he had requested.[14]

The implied threat of imminent legal action, combined with the repeated accusations against other members of the department, led Doralynn Pines to call an early-morning meeting with me on August 12, 1996.

Both the time and location took me by surprise, for I had just returned to New York from a weeklong collecting trip to Santa Fe. I remember thinking that Pines was going to advise me on how to handle this employee.

Instead, she told me that the museum was closing the Accessions and Catalogue Department and letting everyone go. Our last day of

14 This abbreviated account of the events of 1993–1996 has been reconstructed from extensive documentation in my archive, which consists of personal records I kept during this period (and in fact throughout my museum career), along with records and documents that were given by the museum to my attorney in late 1996, as well as my own lengthy communications with my attorney from that time. Supplementary information was provided by Rick Kinsel, who experienced these events with me. (Note: I have written a far more detailed, exhaustively documented narrative of these events, which can be found in my archive.)

work would be October 31. There would be no transfers of employees into other departments within the museum. Pines gave me no outright reason for the decision, merely directing me to Human Resources—where, she said, several separation documents were awaiting my review and signature.

I was too shocked by the decision to question or protest. But my being terminated in this way was, I knew, simply not possible—as a tenured associate curator I could not be let go by the Met without cause. Moreover, closing the department made absolutely no sense at a moment when thousands of works of art were awaiting accessioning, and when so much maintenance was needed on the central catalogue and its various indexes. Had a computer database already been set up to replace the catalogue, closing the department might have made sense. But the transition to computers was in its very earliest stages and no reliable or comprehensive database program had yet been found for the central catalogue. So closing the department in this abrupt way was, to my mind, entirely illogical.

Pines wanted me to believe that the decision was based on some sort of unspecified wrongdoing within the department, but my intuition immediately told me that something else was involved—that perhaps the administration was closing the department to achieve two goals at once: namely, to rid itself of our troublesome (and possibly litigious) staff member, and at the same time to trim the museum's operating costs.

At Human Resources I was presented with a separation agreement and a series of general releases which the head administrator, Carol Cantrell, asked me to sign right away. I did not. I told her I would read through them in consultation with my lawyer. I gathered the documents and returned to my desk.

Back at the study room the three young interns[15] were terribly upset. Kinsel and Andraško were in shock—like me, they had been presented with termination agreements. But unlike me, they had been given a limited amount of time to read and sign the documents and had been threatened with losing what few remaining benefits were being offered to them if they refused. In addition, both had been told that they would not be provided with any sort of favorable employment reference, merely a statement of the dates of their employment with the museum. No reason was given for this brutal treatment.

Even more incomprehensibly, Doralynn Pines had apparently told all the interns that they too were fired—which of course was not possible, since they were volunteers, not employees. I was immediately concerned for one other intern in particular, Edelgard Winands, who as a German national needed to retain her internship at the museum in order to keep her visa. I told her I would do what I could to see that she was transferred to another department—and in fact I was eventually able to get her an internship in the Department of European Sculpture and Decorative Arts, where she remained until May 1997.

I don't remember much more about that day, apart from feeling such shock and nausea that I could not think or speak without great effort. I vaguely recall phoning Jan and a few very close friends within the museum to tell them what had happened. Everyone was as baffled as I. Lisa Pilosi, the former intern of mine who now worked in the Department of Objects Conservation, immediately set up a drinks date for the end of the day. At five p.m. she came to my office with Christine Lilyquist, the head of the Egyptian Department, and the three of us walked out of the museum together. Lisa had not wanted me to face

15 These interns (Vidhya Ananathakrishan, Mira Azarm, and Allison Beesley) all wrote notes of sympathy and thanks to me shortly afterward, one of which said, "You are a wonderful person! I am sorry about the situation in the department, and I want you to know that you will be in my prayers (along with Rick and Danka). Thank you again!" I forwarded copies of these notes to Doralynn Pines on August 23, 1996.

that difficult moment of leaving the building on my own. We went to Demarchelier, a favorite restaurant on Eighty-Sixth Street, where we had a glass of wine and spoke of happier times.

The next few weeks were full of confusion. Ashton Hawkins, who had informed me in 1976 that I had received tenure and who was now the museum's executive vice president and counsel to the trustees, wrote a note to Doralynn Pines informing her that I was a tenured associate curator and could not be fired without cause. Jan and I meanwhile consulted with our lawyer, who quickly established to his own satisfaction that I had been wrongfully dismissed. In discussing the matter with us, he suggested that while a lawsuit would surely find in my favor, he could also simply begin a discussion with the Met, one that would result in a settlement that would achieve much the same result as a court case, without any significant exposure or expense. The matter was perfectly clear to him: as he saw it the museum had made a grave error, but having recognized it had done so, it would do what was needed to correct the error.

That September, October, and November, I continued to report to the museum, where I was now expected to train the Watson librarians in the management of the central catalogue. While I had the right to work at the museum until my retirement, I clearly could not continue to do my job, since with the Accessions and Catalogue Department now closed, that work was no longer supported. I was bemused, meanwhile, to discover (via memo) that the work of accessioning would now be managed by legal staff of the Secretary and General Counsel's Office—an odd budgetary decision, considering that the museum's lawyers earned exponentially more per hour than any cataloguer ever had or would.

There were then some discussions of my staying on for the next four to five years to work in an advisory capacity, since neither the Watson Library nor the Secretary and General Counsel's Office was at all experienced in the many cataloguing and accessioning duties that were suddenly expected of them. But it was extremely awkward all around, and destined not to work out, not only because I was angry about how I had been treated, but also because Doralynn Pines had explicitly forbidden me to speak with anyone else working at the museum without prior authorization from her. I was also told I needed to take all my lunches and coffee breaks alone. It seemed to me a form of petty tyranny. Pines also made it her daily business to record my comings and goings from the museum—presumably because one of the few grounds for termination of a tenured curator is not showing up on time for one's job. Considering that I had arrived on time for my job for more than three decades, usually staying well beyond closing time, not to mention working nights and weekends, Doralynn Pines's apparent decision to micromanage my hours felt unjust, unnecessary, embarrassing, and degrading.

This went on for a month. Then, on the day before Thanksgiving, toward the end of the afternoon, Pines appeared at my desk accompanied by two museum guards. She informed me that this would be my last day at the museum and that the guards were here to escort me off the premises. I was instructed not to touch anything on my desk or to take any of my personal possessions: everything needed to remain just as it was.

The four of us walked in silence to the Eighty-Fourth Street exit of the museum. It was terribly humiliating for me. Outside it was pouring with rain. Pines said she did not want to go any further because she didn't want to get wet. She instructed the guards to walk me across the parking lot to the exit gate and pulled the door shut behind her. It was terrible to be ejected from the museum in this publicly shaming way after more than thirty years of dedicated service.

Jan was very concerned about me in the weeks and months that followed, because he knew that my work had always been central to my self-esteem. But I was suffering in other ways too, since I could no longer speak to the many wonderful curators, art historians, and administrators who were among my closest friends. To make matters worse, the separation agreement I was now being asked to sign specifically prohibited me from *any* future relationship with the museum other than attending its exhibitions or using its library.[16] I simply did not understand how or why I should have been cut off in this way from everything that I loved and had worked for, or why I should be treated with such brutality by my employer just a few years before my retirement. I don't think I have ever felt so deeply wronged. And now, with Jan at work for most of the day, I suddenly had no idea what to do with myself, what had happened to me, why it should have happened, or why it had happened in the way that it had. On some mornings, I wasn't even sure who I *was.*

In late December, Jan and I began to learn a little more about what had been going on behind the scenes at the museum, for I received a letter from the lawyer-partner of D., my problematic employee, who was now making wild accusations against William Luers, the president of the museum, and his wife, Wendy. This letter alleging fiscal impropriety and corrupt practices at the Metropolitan Museum had been sent to eighteen other people as well, most of them administrators at the museum or board members of Wendy Luers's Foundation for a Civil Society—but copies were also sent to U.S. President Bill

16 Confirmation of this prohibition can be found in a July 29, 2015, letter to me from Sharon Cott, the Metropolitan Museum's senior vice president, secretary, and general counsel (Marica Vilcek Archive).

Clinton and Arthur Ochs Sulzberger, the president of the New York Times Company.

I should note that William Luers had been the American ambassador to Czechoslovakia before joining the Metropolitan as its president in 1986, and that his wife, Wendy, ran a small, New York–based foundation dedicated to promoting Czechoslovakia's transition to democracy. I had no particular friendship with either of them, nor did I have any interest in contemporary Czechoslovakia. But it was the lawyer's contention that Luers had compelled two employees in the museum's Catalogue Department (Danka Andraško and me) to translate documents from Slovak and Czech on company time—thus engaging in the misuse of federal, state, and city museum funding for the benefit of Ms. Luers's foundation. He further contended that when a worker (presumably his domestic partner, D.) had "blown the whistle" on this corrupt practice, he had been fired.[17] A squib in *New York* magazine's "Intelligencer" gossip column would repeat these spurious allegations (without attribution, and incidentally drawing a grotesque caricature of our department) several months later.[18]

All of this was nonsense, and to my mind nothing more than a smear campaign against the museum. But it was also a good indication of the various strategies the lawyer was now apparently utilizing on his domestic partner's behalf to press for a financial settlement as compensation for D.'s dismissal.

By this time, my lawyer had already worked out my own separation agreement with the museum based on my tenured status. I received the estimated earnings, benefits, and pension I would have received at an expected retirement age of sixty-five, and my separation was officially designated as a retirement, with all the additional

17 This letter was addressed to Lloyd Cutler, a member of the foundation's board, and was cc'ed to eighteen others, including myself (D. to Cutler, December 23, 1996, Marica Vilcek Archive).

18 "Intelligencer," *New York*, June 2, 1997, p. 10.

privileges (retirement gift, identification card) that came with it. Because the problematic staffer and his lawyer had brought a legal complaint against the museum, there were additional clauses in the agreement stating that the Met had investigated his allegations against me and determined there had been no wrongdoing on my part, and also that, should a suit against the museum go forward, the Met would indemnify me against any legal action.[19]

For the benefit of my reputation and self-esteem, my lawyer placed an additional clause in the agreement enjoining both Doralynn Pines and Carol Cantrell (the Human Resources administrator) not to disparage me in any way, nor to discuss the circumstances surrounding the closing of the Accessions and Catalogue Department. He also arranged that the museum release to him the documentation surrounding the closing of the department—which is how those additional documents eventually came to me, and how I have been able to reconstruct the events for this memoir and for the longer account of the incident in my archive.

I was traumatized by what the Metropolitan Museum had done to me and to the good people who worked under me. In retrospect I understand that its administration was probably attempting to protect itself against a civil lawsuit and related reputational harm. We in the Accessions and Catalogue Department were, in a sense, collateral damage in that larger legal and financial battle. Still, in discussing with Jan the hurt that had been done to me, I decided that I wanted nothing by way of financial compensation. True, I had been wronged professionally and personally, and my career had come to an ugly end; but to my way of thinking, no dollar amount could compensate for the way in which the museum administration had both traumatized me and tarnished my name and reputation. Only a full apology could do

19 The action, complaint no. MNEN-96-10002541-E, was filed with the New York City Commission on Human Rights.

that—and few institutions will ever apologize to a wrongfully terminated employee, for doing so can brings with it a renewed financial liability. I know that for many people, money can stand in lieu of the desired apology. But Jan and I wanted none of it—neither a lawsuit, nor the money. I had not worked for the Met for thirty years solely for money; I had worked there primarily because I believed so strongly in its mission. The great gift that the museum had given me over the years was a vital sense of *belonging*—something so precious, especially to an immigrant—and now it had ripped that gift away from me in the ugliest and most insulting of ways.

And so, on my lawyer's advice, I focused instead on forgiving the Met, and on making plans for my future. The question of course was: after more than thirty years at the museum, where could I possibly go, and what could I possibly do?

The year that followed was bleak. Cut off from my friends at the museum, I found myself unwilling to attend its exhibitions out of fear that I would run into colleagues who, not knowing what had happened, were probably making wrongful assumptions about my dismissal—assumptions that I was legally barred from correcting. As a result, I kept mostly to myself. Jan and I continued to see exhibitions in other museums, and to see our friends outside the Met, particularly Alvin Friedman-Kien.

I remained in close touch with Danka Andraško and Rick Kinsel because I was deeply concerned about both of them. Andraško lost her visa as a result of being fired, and was forced to return to Czechoslovakia on November 14, 1996, just two weeks after the official closing of the department. The move was particularly traumatic for her young daughter, who had been doing so well in the New York City school system. The little girl now had to communicate in Czech, not English, and had no friends at her new school. Worse yet, she was physically separated from her divorced father, who had remained in the United States. Andraško was already an accredited lawyer in Czechoslovakia, and she had a top-level degree from Charles University, so she soon found work in Prague. But she hadn't wanted to leave America, and neither had her daughter. The two of them missed New York very much.

Rick Kinsel, meanwhile, was scrambling. Having been let go by the Metropolitan without a reference, he could not find a job at another museum, nor at a gallery or auction house, and so instead he was doing freelance curatorial work for several collectors—including Alvin Friedman-Kien, who had recently decided he wanted his vast collection catalogued. Kinsel also worked part-time for various art dealers, doing art handling and clerical work. He expected he would need to drop out of graduate school since he could no longer afford the tuition and had lost all educational support from the Met. But Susan Weber Soros, who founded the Bard Graduate Center in 1993, already thought so highly of Kinsel that she allowed him to continue at the graduate center tuition-free. It was an extraordinary act of generosity on her part.

As for myself, I took several months to recover from the shock of being let go. Life at home didn't suit me, though, so I began sending out job inquiries and résumés. I hadn't applied for a job in more than thirty years, and clearly my work was rather specialized. Still, I assumed that with all my experience, background, and skills, I would eventually find museum work. I got two job interviews, one at the Morgan Library and the other at the Frick, but no work was ever offered to me, and in fact I received no follow-up communication from either institution. No other museums responded to my queries.

Apart from my lack of a reference from the Metropolitan (by the terms of our legal agreement, it would only confirm the dates of my employment), I was facing another handicap: age. I was sixty and I was officially retired from the Met, so how many working years did I have left to give my new employers? Apparently, not enough for a job offer. Could it really be possible, I wondered, that I was unemployable?

In late 1997, Rick Kinsel found a position as director of cultural affairs at Coty, the French American beauty company. His job was to organize and curate exhibitions of its historic collection of custom-made fragrance bottles and beauty-product packaging, which had been in production for more than ninety years. At his invitation I volunteered there to catalogue this significant collection. Doing so opened my eyes to the beauty of industrial design, for the earliest of these fragrance bottles had been created by no less than the great René Lalique. (Coty had subsequently championed the mass-marketing of these extraordinary bottles as a means of asserting the luxuriousness of its fragrances.) The work exposed me to corporate art collecting and corporate collections maintenance, which is very different from standard museum work. While I very much enjoyed learning about perfume bottles, and also about corporate art collections, I was most grateful simply to be working again among people who were kind to me. Every day when I arrived at Coty, an administrative assistant would come downstairs to greet me and thank me—for never before had Coty had a volunteer! It was during this time that I realized more strongly than ever before that to work, to be of use to others, can itself be life-affirming.

Kinsel combined his work at Coty with his graduate studies at Bard, ultimately writing a master's thesis called "Designs of the House of Coty," which received honors. The thesis then was privately published within the Coty organization. He was very clever in combining his graduate work with corporate work, and good at public relations as well. When I congratulated him on his success, he happily confided that his starting salary at Coty had been five times more than he had ever earned at the museum, and he was now being given new raises all the time. I could not have been happier for him, for he deserved it—his character, intelligence, and work ethic were all of the highest order. Since Jan liked him too, we now found ourselves spending more and more of our time with him, often having dinner or attending art exhibitions. Despite the great difference in our ages, we began to think of him as a very close friend.

In 1996, I received a letter from Líza Rajterová in Bratislava, alerting me to the fact that her young friends Peter and Jadranka Važan were moving to New York, and asking me to help them if possible. They arrived in the United States a month after my dismissal from the museum, and we had them to dinner a month or so later. Jadranka was a longtime friend of Líza's son and daughter; the three had sung in the same youth choir and studied musicology together at Comenius University. Peter had received a Fulbright to study psychology at the New School, and Jadranka was enrolling in the ethnomusicology program at the CUNY Graduate Center. I don't think they realized how complicated or expensive life would be here.

I was glad to get to know the Važans, not least because they put me in closer touch with Líza Rajterová and the music-oriented life I had left behind in Bratislava. Líza was now quite distinguished: from 1961 to 1988 she had been the dramaturg for the Slovak Philharmonic, researching, selecting, adapting, editing, and interpreting scripts, libretti, texts, and printed programs, as well as managing its public relations. She then became director of the entire Slovak Philharmonic in 1992 (and was, in fact, the direct successor to my first husband, Ladislav Mokrý, who had been its director since 1968). She also edited two fine Slovak music publications, the popular magazine *Hudobný život* (*Musical Life*) and the journal *Slovenská hudba* (*Revue for Music*

Culture). Over the course of her career, she had edited and translated into Slovak many books and monographs on music.

Líza's husband, the conductor and composer Ľudovít Rajter, was thirty years her senior. He had begun his directing career with the Hungarian Radio Orchestra, directing it from 1936 to 1946, then returning to Bratislava in 1946 to conduct the Czecho-Slovak Radio Orchestra. He founded Bratislava's Academy of Performing Arts and cofounded the Slovak Philharmonic, becoming its first conductor in 1949 and remaining with it until 1961, after which he returned to the Czecho-Slovak Radio Orchestra, which he conducted through 1976.

Because Jan and I are such great music lovers, we were always delighted to see Líza on those rare occasions when she traveled to New York. And because Jadranka and Peter returned yearly to Bratislava on their summer vacations, we now heard much more about Líza, her family, and her work.

In this way, a good friendship developed between us and the Važans. They came to us often to share traditional Slovak meals—things like *bryndzové halušky,* a potato spätzle with sheep's cheese, *makovník,* a poppy roll pastry, or *orechovník,* a walnut roll pastry. And we always saw them during the holidays: Jadranka made very good traditional Slovak Christmas cookies, and both she and Peter loved my *kapustnica*, a spicy sauerkraut soup with pork that is traditionally served on New Year's Eve.

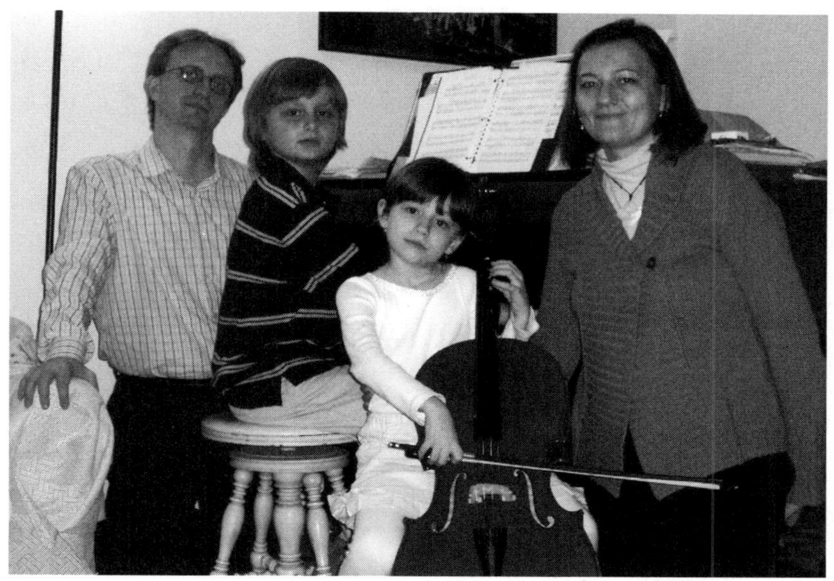

The Vazans

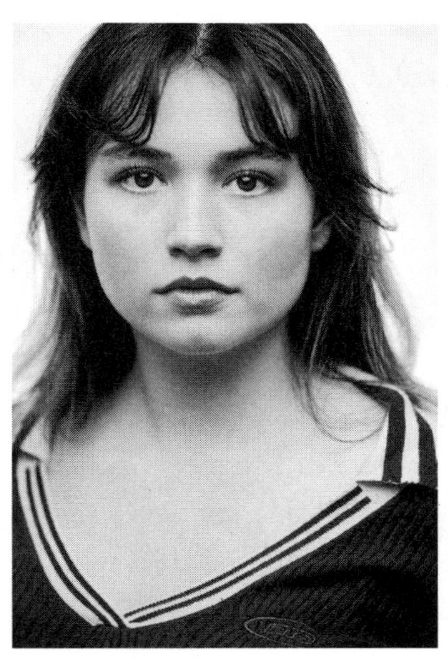

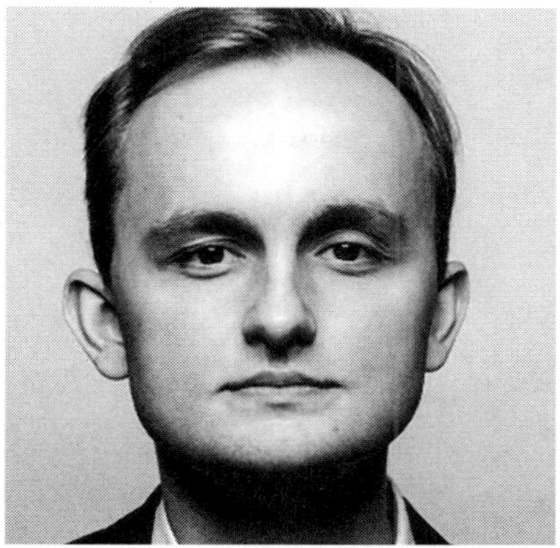

(left) Terezka Vazan
(above) Chris Vazan

It was lovely to watch this young couple start a family. They had their first child, Christopher, within a year of moving to New York, and their daughter, Terezka, followed several years later. By the age of three, Chris was reading, doing mathematics, and playing the piano. Seeing that he was gifted, I urged Jadranka and Peter to get him into a good private school. As recent immigrants they were largely unaware of how the school system worked, so I guided them through the application process. By helping and advising them in this manner, we became, in essence, Chris and Terezka's foster grandparents, and have happily remained so to this day.

When Chris reached fifteen, his interests shifted away from mathematics and back to music. I may have played a role here, since—apart from providing him and his sister with music lessons (Terezka played cello)—I often invited them to join us at the opera. So Chris had an extensive early-life exposure to this otherwise costly and largely inaccessible art form. After each performance, Jan and I would discuss with him what we had seen and heard, both the overall production and the individual performances.

By the time he was halfway through high school, Christopher had decided to become a conductor. I was initially very concerned—for, like his parents, I wanted him to have a full and happy life, and the world of classical music is both underpaid and highly competitive. But he was exceptionally talented, and so, with his parents' blessing, I helped him to enter the New York Youth Symphony's conducting program. From there, he went on to the National Youth Orchestra as a conducting apprentice. Rather than attend an American university, he decided to go straight into conducting, operatic vocal coaching, and operatic accompaniment, enrolling at the University of Music and Performing Arts, Vienna. It was a bold decision for so young a person, but

Chris is very gifted. Now twenty-seven, he has completed his master's in piano and conducting and is working as an assistant conductor at the Meiningen Court Theater in Germany.

16

Becoming Philanthropists

During my years working at Coty, I slowly got back in touch with a few close friends from the Metropolitan Museum and was relieved to learn I had their sympathy and support. One such friend was Dietrich von Bothmer, the former head of the Department of Greek and Roman Art, who was kind enough to give me a copy of the letter he had written to James R. Houghton, a trustee who sat on the Board's professional committee, after the committee had abruptly announced the closure of the Catalogue Department. Von Bothmer expressed in no uncertain terms how saddened he was by not only the committee's decision but also its subsequent execution, particularly since none of those in the department had been given the option of a transfer elsewhere in the museum—as they had been during the reductions made under Thomas Hoving. Von Bothmer hadn't written the letter on my behalf—rather, he had written on behalf of his fellow curators, for whom the central catalogue was a scholarly resource of the most vital importance. But he was kind enough to share a copy of the letter with me, and to express to me in private his consternation at how suddenly and unreasonably the entire department had been terminated.

Von Bothmer knew few of the particulars of my dismissal; none of my colleagues at the museum did. Since I could not discuss it—such were the terms of my settlement—I was never able to say a word to anyone in my own defense. No wonder, then, that my former colleagues hesitated to reach out to me, and I to them.

Angry and hurt as I was about what had happened, I was also very concerned about the catalogue, for having spent thirty years caring for it and maintaining it, I knew how vulnerable it was to mismanagement. While its care and maintenance were now the responsibility of the staff of the Watson Library, they were not well schooled in its many complexities and idiosyncrasies.

In 1999, three years after I left the Met, the museum adopted a powerful new cataloguing software called TMS. This electronic database and information-management system enabled the museum slowly to transition away from its own unique and idiosyncratic card catalogue system. Instead, the new TMS (an acronym for "The Museum System") made the Met just one of countless museums, archives, universities, libraries, and galleries utilizing this standardized software.

Transitioning into this system took more than a decade, however, and during that time, many of my curator friends told me they found its limitations deeply problematic. Even today, a quarter century after the implementation of TMS, the old, index-card-based departmental catalogues and the central catalogue are still in place at the Met. Researchers hunting for lost information still turn to the old system because these old-fashioned card catalogues often hold facts and figures that have never been (and perhaps cannot be) integrated into the TMS database.

Similarly, the museum's accessions procedure was the responsibility of its legal department for six years starting in 1996. In 2002, the museum adopted an efficient new accessions numbering format and protocol, one that has remained in place ever since, with cataloguing becoming once again the responsibility of the Office of the Registrar.

I remained deeply interested in the Metropolitan Museum. While my separation agreement very clearly stated that I might never work there again—not even in a volunteer capacity!—I was still free to visit: my retirement package came with an ID card that granted me a lifetime's free admission, suggesting (in a way that the separation agreement did not) that I was welcome any time. I hesitated, though, because I didn't want to run into my former colleagues. Had I been able to discuss what had happened to me openly, the entire situation would have been far less awkward. But I was not.

To make matters worse, I was no longer sent invitations to exhibition openings. Apparently, someone had struck my name off the museum's database after my termination. I was sorry not to be invited, for many of these exhibitions had been years in the making, and a number of them were curated by friends, so the openings were always a time of celebration and congratulation. Accordingly, Jan and I now made it our practice to visit the Met only on weekends, when we were far less likely to bump into curators or administrators. But we never gave up on the museum—we loved its exhibitions and collections, and we would not be without it in our lives.

In private, however, I had many sleepless nights, since I was struggling with shame, anger, and hurt at how I had been treated. I simply could not understand how the museum's administrators could do such a thing to me. I had worked at the Met for almost thirty-one years and been tenured for twenty of them. The injustice of their actions resonated against similar experiences I'd had throughout my childhood and youth, when I had been unjustly blamed and punished for events over which I truly had no control.

Ultimately, however, I had to let go of my anger. Having survived the Nazis, the Slovak fascists, the Allied bombardment, the blacklisting of my family, the Communist takeover, and even ejection by my father from my Bratislava home—not to mention the challenge of starting my entire career over again in a new country, speaking a language I had never studied, doing so without friends or family or connections—well, I had no doubt that I would survive an early retirement with full benefits.

At the same time, to be rejected by a person or place that one loves is never easy. And I really did—I really *do*—love the Metropolitan Museum of Art. I think what remained within me, after my anger lessened, was a lingering mix of melancholy and confusion. How could things have ended so badly with a place I had loved so much?

For the next two years I sought to reinvent myself by volunteering at Coty, during which time I learned a great deal about the perfume business and the history of perfume-bottle design. But then, quite unexpectedly, our life circumstances changed—and in fact they changed quite drastically. With that change came my return, ironically enough, to the Metropolitan Museum.

There is really no other way to put it: in 1998, Jan and I became very, very rich. It happened because Jan had been studying the protein known as tumor necrosis factor, and in doing over the course of seventeen years, he had ultimately developed a promising new drug he called infliximab. A chimeric monoclonal antibody, infliximab proved highly effective in the treatment of autoimmune diseases. As its official co-inventor, Jan held the patent on the drug.

NYU, meanwhile, had signed an agreement with a biotech firm named Centocor, by which NYU granted Centocor the right to develop and market any of the drugs invented in Jan's NYU laboratory. In exchange, Centocor had granted NYU a royalty on the sale of the drugs—and Jan's contract with NYU gave him a guaranteed percentage of those NYU royalties on any drug for which he held the patent.

In 1997, just a year before Jan patented infliximab, Centocor was acquired by Johnson & Johnson, the multinational pharmaceutical and medical technologies corporation. Seeing the great promise of the drug, Johnson & Johnson lobbied hard with the FDA for its immediate approval under its new name, Remicade. When the FDA granted that approval for the treatment of two widespread autoimmune diseases, Crohn's disease and rheumatoid arthritis, Remicade proved highly effective. In fact, many clinicians declared it a wonder drug because their patients showed stunning improvement. When subsequently approved for use in several other autoimmune diseases—including ulcerative colitis, ankylosing spondylitis, psoriasis, and psoriatic arthritis—sales of Remicade skyrocketed.

These drug sales yielded such massive profits that in 1998 Jan's drug royalty income surpassed his yearly salary. In 1999 the forecasted sales for the coming year were astronomical. The income generated by such sales, meanwhile, was already beyond our wildest dreams.

Jan and I were happy of course—but also bemused, since neither of us had ever coveted or pursued wealth per se. At the same time, the amount of wealth remained uncertain and unpredictable, for no one really knew the long-term prospects of the drug: if it turned out to be unexpectedly toxic, for example, it would be withdrawn. Similarly if a more effective drug were to come along, Remicade would no longer be widely prescribed, and sales would drop to nothing.

For the time being, though, we had far more money than we needed or knew what to do with. Never before had we needed to consider how to manage our money, but now, clearly, we had to look after the money as well as decide what to do with it. As a result, Jan sought advice.

I remember that at a certain point, faced with this vast inflow of money, Jan asked if there was anything in life that I wanted that I did not yet have: a country house? a diamond ring? a mink coat? But there wasn't. I had only to think of my brother Ivan, with his lifelong love of fine clothes, automobiles, sailboats, and country estates, to realize that none of these things had ever really made him happy; nor had any of them ever appealed to me.

I told Jan that I had always enjoyed our travels, especially if our destination was Santa Fe. Our visits there brought us to galleries and museums, gave us beautiful scenery, and allowed us wonderful nights at the opera. I also remember telling him that, after so many years of cooking our dinner each night after a long day at the museum, I would certainly appreciate dining out from time to time, or having someone help with the cooking. My only other interests were dressing well, looking after my health, keeping up with my friends, and maintaining a beautiful and well-ordered home.

As we continued to turn the matter over, Jan and I came to realize that our greatest pleasure in life had always been in helping others. Whether I was helping curators with art-historical research, assisting newly arrived immigrants with adjusting to life in America, or encouraging my interns to discover the joy of museum work, I had always felt best when aiding, sharing, and mentoring. Jan understood that feeling entirely, for after years of laboratory research, he too knew the fine feeling that comes from working with promising young students and researchers and helping them to realize their dreams and ambitions.

So we discussed starting a foundation. The idea was one I had been thinking about for some time. When I worked at the museum I sometimes lunched with a friend named Alice Mary Hilton, who suggested to me one time that even a small foundation could make a big difference. Hilton was about ten years older than me, and a distinguished academic—she had read classics and mathematics at Oxford, and held additional degrees from the University of California, the California Institute of Technology, and Columbia University. Throughout her career she had published on logic, computing, information technology and automation, but she also wrote about and taught art in the context of history and science, which is how she had come to lecture at the Met for nearly forty years. Over one particular lunch she mentioned in passing that she was creating a small foundation through which she hoped to raise enough money to publish her lectures in book form. The idea led me to wonder if I too might someday create a foundation, one through which I might help young people (such as my interns) make a start in curating. At that point Jan and I hadn't much money, so nothing came of the idea. But the notion had stayed with me.

When I mentioned the idea of a foundation to Jan, he was immediately interested, especially since he had received many foundation grants over the years. Moreover, several of his friends, including Alvin Friedman-Kien, had recently started small private foundations of their own. But Jan's first thought was that the foundation ought to fund medical research, not the arts. After all, he reasoned, his financial success owed so much to foundation funding. While I could hardly argue that point, I nonetheless continued to feel that there were so many young people in the arts (just as I had been, so many years ago in Bratislava) for whom even the smallest amount of financial help would make an enormous difference. And I became determined that, if possible, we should ultimately help people in the arts too.

We set up our foundation working from the kitchen table in our Seventy-Ninth Street apartment. I knew a little bit about foundations, for by this point in my life I was acquainted with any number of people in the art world who either funded them, administered them, or received grants from them. Even so, I had a great deal to learn about the nuts-and-bolts aspect of operating a foundation, since the finances, activities, and practices of private foundations are very carefully regulated by the state. We consulted with a number of legal and financial advisers who helped us to understand the way in which a private charitable foundation may operate within the United States.

While looking at various financial strategies, we came to the realization that by signing away a percentage of Jan's future royalty stream for Remicade, the taxation on our personal income would be far less, and the bookkeeping would be simplified as well. So it seemed a good idea, particularly because the donation to the foundation would thereby remain forever in proportion with the income Jan was receiving from the Remicade drug patent. Ultimately, that was what we did.

We initially called the foundation the Friderika Fischer Foundation, naming it after Jan's mother—in part to honor her, and in part to maintain a degree of anonymity for ourselves. We established the foundation on December 1, 2000, as a tax-exempt charitable corporation with 501(c)(3) status; its mission was to support research into treatments for chronic inflammatory autoimmune diseases. To maintain our nonprofit status, we needed to appoint a board of directors to serve as the foundation's governing body. (Jan was to be our president, and I would serve as secretary, but we needed three more people.) Our first choice was Bruce Cronstein, a distinguished colleague of Jan's from NYU, who told us he would be happy to join our board. Jan was impressed by the nonprofit work that Rick Kinsel had been doing recently as part of his for-profit work at Coty, and particularly by a far-reaching collaboration Kinsel had put together involving Coty and NASA (the National Aeronautics and Space Administration/Johnson Space Center), so Jan reached out to him. We also invited Jennifer Olshin, a former colleague of mine from the Met, since she too was now working in the private sector, as an art dealer.

Jan and I then spent 2001 and 2002 announcing the availability of funds, calling for projects, reading through project proposals, voting on allocations, and finally distributing the year's funds to the scientists and programs we thought would do the best job at researching chronic inflammatory autoimmune disorders. We also made a few anonymous institutional grants. It was a lot of work, but also a pleasure to see the money put to good use.

The foundation might well have continued in that manner to the present day, but on September 11, 2001, nineteen Islamist terrorists hijacked four commercial airliners and used two of them to destroy both towers of New York's World Trade Center. Americans responded with outrage, with many expressing hatred toward all immigrants. At the same time, the federal government responded to the threat of further terrorism by making the immigration process infinitely slower and more complicated for those applying lawfully for green card status. Witnessing so much anger and prejudice, and seeing so many qualified, well-meaning would-be immigrants unduly penalized, Jan and I remembered our own difficult experiences and decided that these people newly arrived or arriving in the United States were the ones who needed our help most. Accordingly, we began to make adjustments to our foundation's goals and mission.

There was another reason we made this decision: we discovered that first year that the nationwide funding of autoimmune research was already quite substantial, and that our money was making very little difference in that research. By comparison, funding for talented immigrants starting out in the sciences was truly scarce. So we decided to create a program specifically for promising foreign-born scientists (and, later, for foreign-born people working in the arts) to get a better start in America. We hoped to provide these promising young people not only financial support, but also public recognition, which is so important when first establishing oneself. These awards would also (we hoped) provide the secondary benefit of raising public awareness about the significant contributions made to America by foreign-born scientists and creative minds.

Jan and I were inspired here by our friends Paul and Daisy Soros, who in 1997 had founded an academic fellowship program for young immigrants. Paul was an engineer, inventor, and businessman who had started out in New York in 1948 as a penniless immigrant from Hungary. In later life he recognized that attending the NYU School of Engineering had been vital to his success, and wanted other young immigrants to have a similar opportunity. Their foundation awarded thirty such fellowships yearly, giving up to $90,000 to pay for graduate education. If we could do something similar, I thought, giving the money to young immigrant scientists and arts professionals . . . well, it might have a life-altering effect.

Even as we came up with this new idea for the foundation, however, Jan wanted to give directly to the medical research programs at NYU. So just before the end of 2002, we began the process of giving NYU an irrevocable gift of a percentage of the royalty stream for Remicade, along with a lump sum in cash and a trust fund. The three combined held an estimated value of approximately $105 million. These funds were to be specifically dedicated to four projects: endowing a chair in the department of microbiology; supporting research into microbial pathogenesis; endowing fellowships for graduate students, PhDs, and postdoctoral fellows in microbiology; and supporting research and recruitment into the department of otolaryngology—this last, because it had been so helpful in treating my Ménière's disease. This massive gift to NYU took some time to be finalized and was only announced to the public three years later, in 2005.

We have ultimately donated nearly $300 million in philanthropic gifts to NYU Langone Health—$277 million personally and $18 million in grants from our foundation. (I should also add that NYU Langone has received well over $1 billion in royalties from Remicade, which is roughtly the equivalent to 400 research project grants or 135 program project grants from the National Institutes of Health.) Our funding has helped every aspect of the NYU Langone health system, but the largest of these gifts have gone toward establishing the Vilcek Institute of Graduate Biomedical Sciences; helping the NYU Grossman School of Medicine become a tuition-free medical school through the Jan T. and Marica F. Vilcek Scholars program; and giving much needed accommodations for students through the construction of the Jan T. and Marica F. Vilcek Residence Hall. The funding has also created fellowships and professorships; advanced innovative research projects; renovated laboratories and major capital spaces; and supported the strategic recruitment and retention of faculty and staff, including deans and CEOs. Along with all we have given to NYU Langone, we have also given approximately $9.5 million to other areas of NYU, primarily to NYU's Institute of Fine Arts.

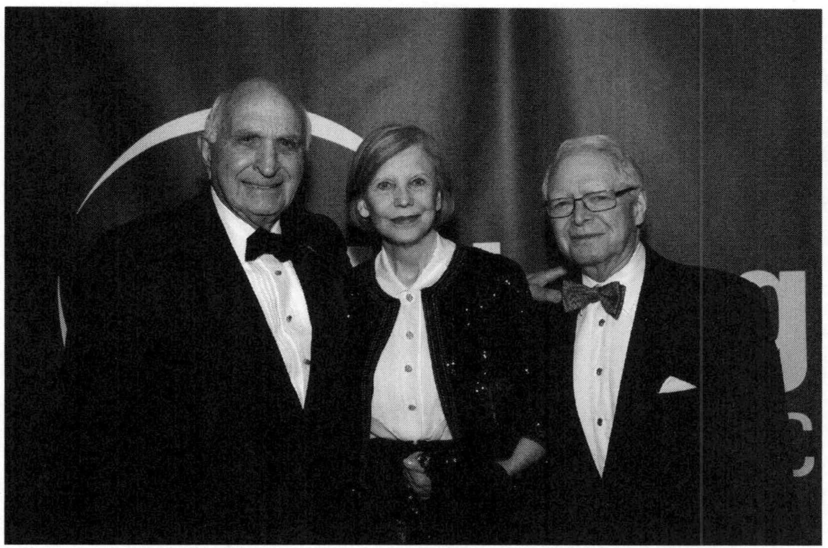

With entrepreneur Kenneth Langone (left)
another great donor to NYU's medical schools, 2015

Jan and I decided to rename our foundation the Vilcek Foundation around this time, since Jan's success (and mine too) was important to the foundation's mission of demonstrating that immigrants can contribute substantially to American science and the arts.

Rick Kinsel left Coty to join us full-time in 2003 as our executive director. In doing so, he took a reduction in pay, for he had been doing very well at Coty. But he liked what we were doing, felt the foundation had enormous potential, and wanted very much to be part of its future. Rick's arrival on the scene was a godsend because, while I am no stranger to hard work, by 2003 I was feeling overwhelmed. I had been handling nearly all the foundation's organizational work on my own for more than two years: sending out announcements, receiving and logging proposals, reading and judging proposals, writing memos, issuing checks, organizing board meetings, publishing the minutes, and so many other things. I was busy from morning to night.

I continued to do that work through 2006, but now I had help. And I was comfortable with Rick; having worked with him for ten years, I knew he could assume all the duties I could no longer manage, as well as undertake many new ones. As I was learning, the challenge of developing, initiating, and administering a foundation—particularly a foundation that was developing a major prize-giving program—required an extraordinary leader. I sensed we had found that person in Rick.

Within his first year, Rick proved to be a capable executive, spokesperson, and administrator, and the foundation thrived and grew under him. We started to focus on strategic planning for the foundation's future, and to conceptualize and then implement all sorts of new programs and events. With his help we managed the annual budget and oversaw the foundation's finances; its programs, operations, grants, donations, contracts, and payments all needed constant monitoring and review.

Because of his corporate experience at Coty, Rick could do all these things for us. He also generated yearly performance reports for our board meetings that ensured all the trustees knew exactly what the foundation had accomplished, as well as what it had cost. Finally, and to everyone's great delight, Rick used his love of design to develop a visual aesthetic for the foundation. Through his creativity, all our published materials, awards, trophies, logos, signage, and web pages looked entirely polished and professional.

With wealth, our life was changing rapidly—but far from living a life of leisure, we were busier than ever before! The foundation was expanding rapidly, so we had to create a proper headquarters for it, leading me to start looking at real estate. At the same time, Jan and I decided we wanted a more substantial home for ourselves—for, comfortable as we were in our apartment on Seventy-Ninth Street, we simply did not have enough space and light there to hang the significant works of art that we were beginning to acquire.

I felt very strongly that both the foundation headquarters and our new apartment needed to be in the same neighborhood, preferably in the one we had come to think of as home. After much searching I found a beautiful new apartment at Fifth Avenue and Seventy-Third Street, facing on Central Park. Its greatest asset was a series of finely proportioned main rooms—a reception hall, living room, dining room, and study—ideally suited to the hanging of paintings. The east- and north-facing windows, meanwhile, gave us an even, filtered natural light for much of the day—perfect for the paintings in our collection.

Shortly thereafter, using the same real estate agent, I discovered a former garage featuring a number of elegant architectural details and a high-ceilinged main floor. Built in 1920, it stood just a few blocks from our new apartment, at 167 East Seventy-Third Street, between Lexington and Third Avenues. Its quaint charm made it seem a perfect future headquarters for the Vilcek Foundation. The landmarked garage door was broad enough and high enough to accommodate large-scale sculpture installations, which was important because we envisioned the main floor as a combination of administrative offices and exhibition space. (We were now hoping that some of the young immigrant artists to whom we had given fellowships would have their first American exhibitions with us.) On the floors above, we installed a multiuse space with catering facilities as well as two roof gardens—one at the front, one at the back—for various-sized receptions. The street itself was charming, leafy, and old-fashioned, sitting just within the Upper East Side Historic District.

Renovation of this historic space required its complete reconstruction, as well as applications for permissions and variances. Ultimately the permitting and remodeling took nearly two years and cost nearly as much as the building did—but the end result was absolutely superb. Once again, Rick amazed us with his ability to handle the project, overseeing nearly everything: site management, interactions with architects and contractors, negotiations with the New York City Landmarks Commission, surveys of environmental controls, construction audits, utilities upgrades, and every single aspect of interior design, right down to the smallest detail.

It was during this time, in the spring of 2003, that I became involved once more with the Metropolitan Museum. It started when Julie Jones, an eminent scholar and curator who headed the Department of the Arts of Africa, Oceania, and the Americas, contacted me and asked me to join the Friends of the Department. By now I was feeling all right about visiting the museum during working hours, so I decided to accept.

I knew from a former colleague that this Friends group wanted to start a foundation to support the department, and I assumed I would be asked to donate to it. After so many years of not being included in any Met activities or exhibition openings, I was happy enough to be asked, and happy as well to contribute—for the foundation was, after all, a good cause. And I had known Julie for many years: she had started at the museum in 1975. In this way I began the long, slow process of rapprochement with the Met.

As the Vilcek Foundation began its next phase of awarding yearly prizes, Jan and I realized that we needed someone to be the public face of the organization, for our public relations initiative required a capable and energetic spokesperson. Jan and I were fine with giving an occasional speech or accepting an occasional prize for our philanthropy. But neither of us is accomplished at public speaking, and my hearing loss makes large gatherings particularly difficult for me.

Rick gladly assumed these duties in our place. Apart from accepting honors and awards on behalf of the foundation, he was skilled at giving talks about the foundation's various initiatives and goals. In doing so, he began developing relationships with other philanthropic organizations through which he discovered new ways in which our foundation's money might be put to good use. At the same time, he was good at deflecting those who made direct, in-person appeals for foundation money—something I always found awkward. The Vilcek Prizes for Creative Promise also helped us in this regard, since they are a juried, regulated, merit-based way of giving, awarded specifically to younger immigrant research scientists and arts professionals.

As we began the Vilcek Prize competitions, we discovered that giving away money is a complicated business. Consider, for example, the judging process. The prizes we offer need to be decided upon by qualified jurors, and since the disciplines in which the prizes are awarded change yearly, new jurors need to be selected yearly, and periodically we needed to bring in new advisers simply to help us find jurors. Also, because the reading, judging, and voting upon these prize applications can be tedious work for the judges (particularly when there are a very large number of applicants), locating and securing a commitment from conscientious, well-qualified jurors can be a challenge. Once the right jurors are enlisted, and once they read through and judge all the applications, we need to bring them together to debate and vote on behalf of the various candidates. That process, too, could be contentious, and so it needed to be overseen. Rick handled all of these matters, as well as such details as the design and manufacture of the trophies that accompanied the cash prizes, and the organizing and staging of the awards ceremony dinner.

Our first prize dinner took place in 2006, with several hundred guests gathered at the rooftop restaurant of Manhattan's Mandarin Oriental Hotel. It was a very glamorous venue—high in the sky overlooking Central Park, Columbus Circle, and the northern reaches of the Times Square theater district. Both Jan and I helped out a great deal behind the scenes—there were so many little details that needed to be decided upon at the last minute. It was a happy gathering, and by all accounts a great success. We have staged similar awards ceremonies every year since then. Each one has been a delight.

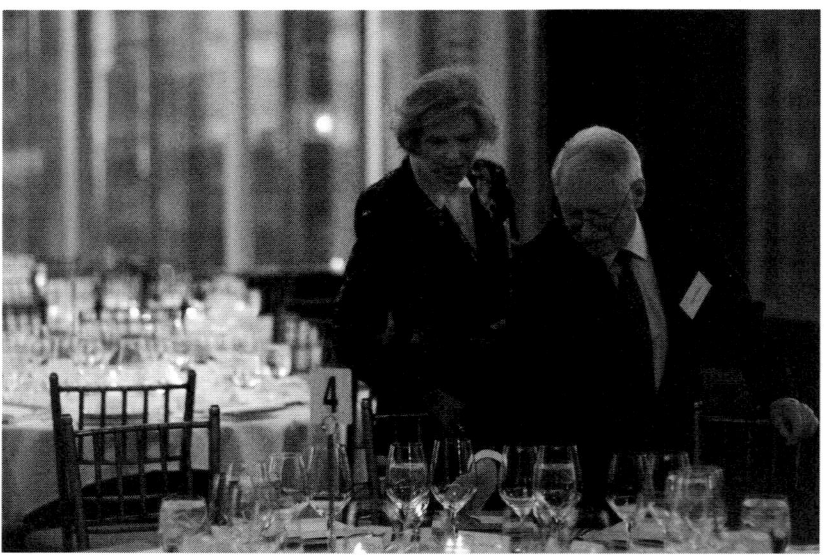

Tending to last-minute details at one of the Vilcek Foundation Awards Galas, held yearly at the Mandarin Oriental Hotel, New York

Over the years the work of administering the foundation has grown, for the foundation has grown. Today we have twelve full-time employees, two part-time employees, and three yearly interns divided among six departments: operations and administration, art curation, human resources, events and programs, public relations, and facility management. We have also moved the foundation headquarters to 21 East Seventieth Street, a far larger building with a two-story exhibition space, office and conference space, and extensive storage as well for the foundation's ever-growing art collection.

Jan and I confer regularly with our board of directors, which has likewise grown with the foundation. It currently consists of two senior arts administrators, two distinguished scientists, and Rick, who became the foundation's president in 2016. (Jan has become CEO and chairman, and I am now vice chairman and secretary.) Led by Jan and advised by Rick, our board reviews our strategic planning yearly, periodically reassessing the foundation's mission and overall vision in order that it may change with the times. (Such reassessment was particularly necessary during the years of the Covid pandemic, when many arts organizations were facing bankruptcy.) Together we manage the foundation's endowment and its annual budget. With the help of professional advisers, we administer the finances for all the foundation's programs, operations, grants, donations, contracts, and payments. And every year we assess the impact of our foundation's grants, programs, and activities, occasionally modifying them to make the Vilcek Foundation ever more effective in its mission. It is truly a great deal of work.

With the passing of years, Jan has received many honors. He holds the Albert Gallatin Medal from NYU and has been given three honorary degrees: one from Comenius University, one from the CUNY Graduate Center, and one from NYU. He was also given the J. E. Purkyně Honorary Medal from the Czech Academy of Sciences, and the Outstanding American by Choice Award from U.S. Citizenship and

Immigration Services. NYU Medical School, meanwhile, has named several programs, chairs, and facilities in our honor. In 2005, the Crohn's and Colitis Foundation of America recognized us as Humanitarians of the Year, and in 2011 we received the Outstanding New Yorker award given by the Center for an Urban Future. In 2012, I accepted the Steven K. Fischel Distinguished Public Service Award from the American Immigration Council in Washington, DC.

I too have received many honors and appointments because of our work in philanthropy. I have served as a consultant to several nonprofit organizations: the Commission for Art Recovery of the World Jewish Congress; the Jewish Museum in New York City; and the Jordan National Gallery in Amman. I am also a board member of the New York Youth Symphony and the Foundation for a Civil Society. But most important, I have become deeply involved once again with the Metropolitan Museum. My doing so might never have happened, had it not been for a chance remark made by Jan.

Jan and I were invited to lunch one afternoon in the late spring of 2012 with E. John Rosenwald Jr, a Met trustee, and the museum's president, Emily Rafferty. By this point we had endowed several curatorships at the Metropolitan and had made clear that we expected to give more in the future. As the lunch ended, Rosenwald asked whether Jan might consider joining the board of trustees.

It was an odd moment for us, for Jan had lived through my wrongful dismissal from the museum in 1996 and had experienced firsthand the anguish it caused me. He grew quiet for a moment, then demurred, saying he was too caught up with his work on the board of NYU Medical School. But a moment later he suggested the Met would be much better off having *me* on their board, since after all I had worked there as a curator for more than thirty years.

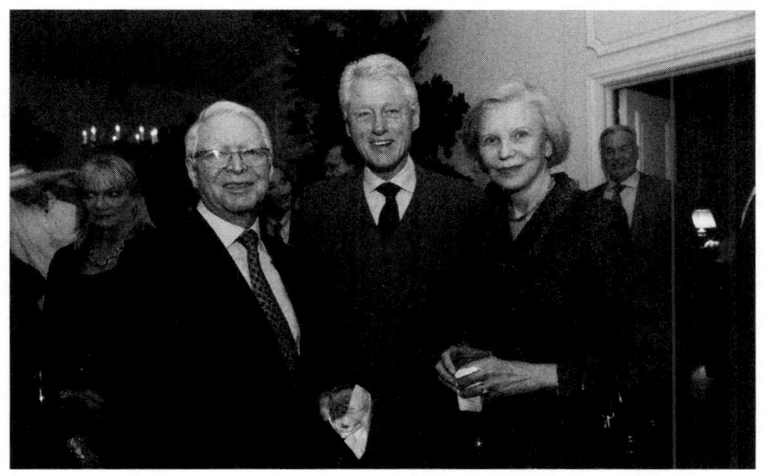

With former president Bill Clinton at a private reception in New York, 2013

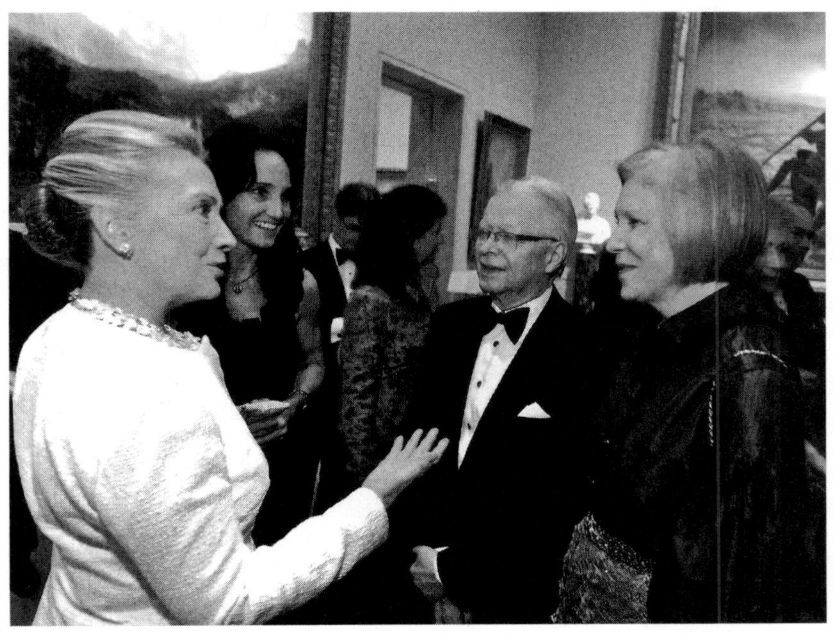

With Hillary Rodham Clinton at the opening of the Met's new American Wing galleries, January 2012. Beside her is Carrie Rebora Barratt, the museum's deputy director.

Rosenwald and Rafferty looked at me in surprise. While both had been affiliated with the museum when I left it in 1996, neither remembered that I had once been associate curator in charge of the Accessions and Catalogue Department. Rosenwald asked me if being an honorary trustee was something I might consider.

I froze, then hesitantly told him there might be a complication, since I had been pushed out of the museum, and had subsequently come to a settlement with it over wrongful dismissal. Both Rosenwald and Rafferty listened, then assured me it would make no difference—if I was interested, they would nominate me. I told them I was. When we parted, they promised I would hear from them soon.

I left the meeting shaken, for although more than fifteen years had passed since being forcibly escorted off the premises by Doralynn Pines and her security guards, the feelings of shame, humiliation, and anger remained with me. How could it be, I wondered, that without ever offering so much as an apology, the Met now wanted me back as a trustee? I told Jan I was very confused. Jan said nothing but he squeezed my hand. Our life had changed significantly, he said at last. Should I ever care to return to the museum, I would surely be welcome.

Just a few months later, on September 11, 2012, I received a letter telling me that the board's nominating committee had proposed me as an honorary trustee. The nominating committee included the same James R. Houghton who had overseen the closing of the Catalogue Department in 1996. Other members of the committee included Emily Rafferty, Thomas Campbell, and Daniel Brodsky, a very amiable trustee who had recently become board chairman.

I was then invited to the November 13 board of trustees meeting. My nomination was announced, after which I was asked to wait outside while the trustees voted on my election. A few minutes later, I was invited to rejoin, and was welcomed as a new honorary trustee.[20]

My work with the board, which began immediately, brought me into regular contact with Sharon Cott, the Museum's secretary and general counsel. Cott had overseen my departure from the museum in 1996, even though the particulars of the wrongful dismissal settlement had been handled by her subordinate. As such, she was one of very few people on the board who knew that upon my departure I had been compelled to sign an agreement stating that I might never again work for the museum. (Doralynn Pines, who had engineered my dismissal, left the Met for good in 2009.) The only other person on the board who remembered me from my days in the Catalogue Department was Andrew Solomon, whom I had first met when he was a high school intern for the Fashion Institute in 1979. To everyone else on the board, my long history with the museum was essentially invisible.

Three years after becoming an honorary trustee, I received a note from Sharon Cott to clarify the unique and valued position I now held at the museum. Although the agreement that I signed in 1996 discouraged and prohibited my having any future relationship with the Met, she wrote, the museum was mistaken to have included such a provision in my termination agreement, and it now waived that provision, rendering it null and void. She concluded by writing that the Met wished to express its gratitude to me for all that I had done while employed by the museum, and for all that I continued to do as an honorary trustee. While this letter was not quite an apology, I nonetheless welcomed it,

20 I should note here the difference between an honorary trustee and a "regular" trustee. Section 6 of the Met's by-laws explains that honorary trustees are chosen from persons eminently qualified in one or more aspects of the museum's activities and interests, and that while they share the honor and privileges of trustees, they do not attend meetings of the board of trustees unless specifically invited, are not counted in determining a quorum, do not vote and do not have the duties, rights, and legal responsibilities of the board of trustees in the conduct of the affairs of the museum. They may however be invited to serve in an advisory capacity on any committee of the board of trustees.

and responded in a note of my own, telling her how grateful I was that the prohibition had been waived, and how much I looked forward to continuing my relationship with the museum.[21]

In the years following my election, my duties as an honorary trustee included serving as chair of the Visiting Committee[22] to the Department of Objects Conservation, headed by Lisa Pilosi. She has been a close friend to me ever since she was my intern, so it was (and remains) a pleasure to visit her department and see the extraordinary work that it accomplishes. I have also been a member of the Visiting Committee to the Department of Arms and Armor, the Department of Paper Conservation, the Department of Textile Conservation, and the Education Department. Because I have a thirty-year knowledge of the inner workings of the museum, I have a better awareness than most of the trustees of which departments are particularly in need of financial support. Knowing this about me, the curators and department heads are always glad to have me on their committees!

It is not easy for me to tally the many bequests and endowments I have given to the Metropolitan Museum over the years. As mentioned earlier, starting in the 1970s I regularly contributed small amounts of money to various causes, including paying the stipends for my own interns. But over the years, thanks to our good fortune, the size of these gifts has grown far larger, and the biggest gifts are easy to remember. The largest of these have endowed four curatorial positions—two in the American Wing, one in the Department of Drawings and Prints, and most recently, one in the Department of Arms and Armor. In the American Wing, we made Amelia Peck the Marica F. Vilcek Curator of American Decorative Arts and Supervising Curator of the Antonio Ratti Textile Center. We also made Thayer Tolles the Marica F.

21 Paraphrased from Sharon Cott to Marica Vilcek, July 29, 2015, and Marica Vilcek to Sharon Cott, August 5, 2015. Both letters are in the Marica Vilcek Papers, Vilcek Foundation.

22 Visiting Committees are groups of trustees who visit various departments of the museum to learn of their projects and activities, usually with the aim of offering financial assistance.

Vilcek Curator of American Paintings and Sculpture. In the Drawings and Prints, we made Carmen Bambach the Marica F. and Jan T. Vilcek Curator. In Arms and Armor, we endowed the position of curator John Byck. In an effort to be as accurate as possible in the writing of this memoir, I recently requested that the museum provide us with a lifetime giving report. Although they were unable to provide me with figures previous to 1980, their report showed that from 1980 to the present, Jan and I have given the Met a total of $23,832,984.46. That figure does not include gifts of works of art or the valuations of those gifts. The Vilcek Foundation, meanwhile, has given an additional $125,750.

My position as honorary trustee has been renewed every five years since 2012. Despite my various health concerns, I have remained active at the museum to the present day.

Just a year after being made an honorary trustee of the Met, I became involved with another organization I have always admired: NYU's Institute of Fine Arts. I have known the institute well for decades, since many of my curatorial colleagues at the museum studied there, as indeed did many of the Met's top curators and administrators. Just down Fifth Avenue from the museum, it is one of the nation's leading graduate programs in art history, archaeology, and theory and practice of conservation. Joining its board was a pleasure because I believe so deeply in the institute. To my surprise, my fellow board members have included two former colleagues from the Metropolitan Museum, Jennifer Russell and Philippe de Montebello. In October 2015, after two years as a trustee, I succeeded Stephen L. Lash, the chairman emeritus of Christie's Americas, as the institute's board chair. Patricia Rubin, director of the institute, very kindly noted at that time that I brought "a wealth of museum experience and understanding to this role, as well as a passion for supporting higher education."

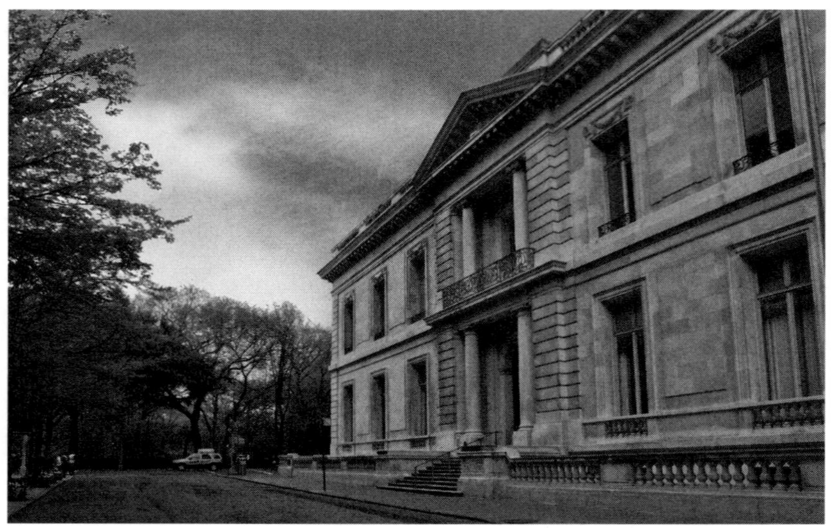

The NYU Institute of Fine Arts, formerly the James B. Duke Mansion, 1 East Seventy-Eighth Street, New York

Helping young scholars of promise find their way into the complicated world of museum curating has always seemed crucial to me, for as a young woman curator I struggled mightily to break into museum work, and I have witnessed many others engaged in similar struggles since my arrival at the Met in 1966. Moreover, the memory of my curatorial struggles in Bratislava remains with me to this day. In the hope of making a difference to young curators, Jan and I gave the institute a gift of four million dollars to endow the Jan and Marica Vilcek Curatorial Program, which provides funds for two PhD candidates per year to work with curators in a museum (one at the Metropolitan Museum of Art) and also funds a yearly series of museum-based courses taught by prominent curators from the Met, the Museum of Modern Art, the Frick Collection, the Solomon R. Guggenheim Museum, and similar institutions. I'm delighted to report that the program has proved an enormous success—so much so that in 2021 the institute surprised me by renaming the great hall of the James B. Duke House in my honor. I had always thought that this main room of the institute's glorious 1912 mansion on Fifth Avenue (which was donated to NYU by Doris Duke) was one of the most beautiful interior spaces in New York. Today, much to my delight, it is known as Marica Vilcek Great Hall.

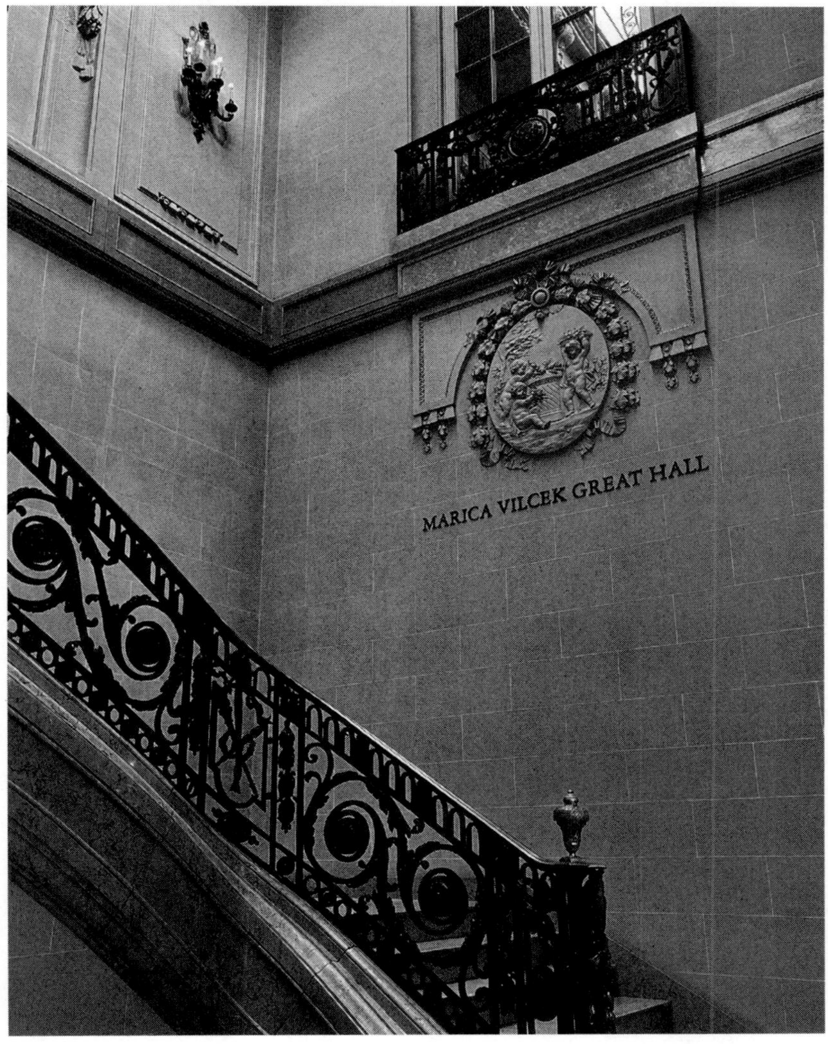

The Marica Vilcek Great Hall, NYU Institute of Fine Arts

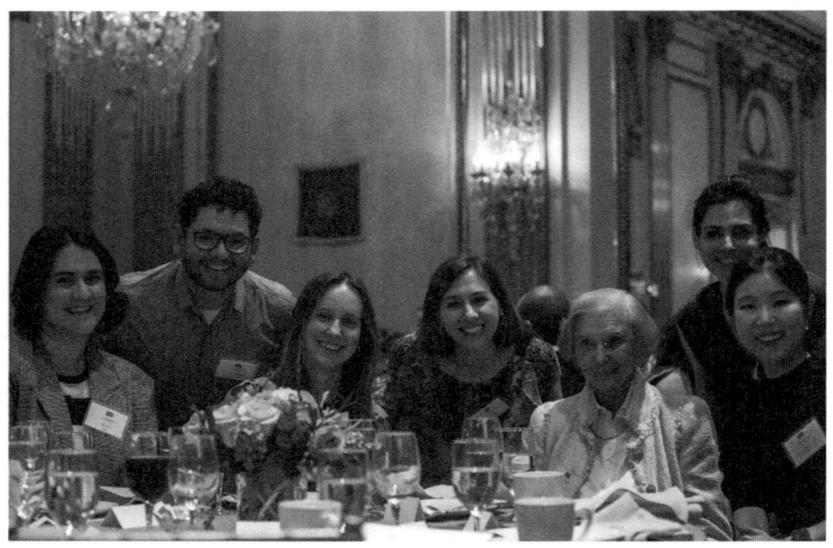

Celebrating with the Marica Vilcek Fellows at an Institute of Fine Arts luncheon in May 2023

In 2025 the board of the Vilcek Foundation surprised me by creating an art history prize in my name. Its purpose is to recognize professionals in art history, museum work, art conservation and preservation, or any other art history profession. Known as the Marica Vilcek Prize in Art History, it recognizes my lifelong dedication to art scholarship and museum work, even as it fosters appreciation for all those who work on behalf of the visual arts. The Vilcek Foundation plans to award three such prizes of $100,000 every year: in it's first year, we awarded three of them. Unlike the other prizes awarded by our foundation, these honors are not limited to recent immigrants, but are instead given to scholars worldwide. Recipients are currently chosen at my discretion, with the review and approval of Jan Vilcek, Rick Kinsel, and the Vilcek Foundation board.

Of all the many letters I have received in the past few years, the most meaningful has been one that I received on August 15, 2022, from the president and CEO of the Metropolitan Museum, Daniel H. Weiss. After a series of discussions initiated by board chairman emeritus Daniel Brodsky with Sharon Cott and Daniel Weiss concerning the events surrounding my termination in 1996, Weiss wrote:

> *Dear Marica,*
> *It has come to my attention that the circumstances surrounding the completion of your service as head of our catalog department were disrespectful to you and did not acknowledge your many contributions to the Museum. Moreover, these actions were entirely unprovoked. I am writing to express to you, on behalf of the Museum staff and the Board, our sincere apology. For a great many years, you have been a beloved, respected, and dedicated employee and friend of this Museum and an essential member of our family. If I could change the past this would never have happened.*
>
> *We are all grateful to you for your dedicated service and for your selfless care and support of the Museum and our community.*
>
> *Sincerely yours,*
> *Daniel H. Weiss*

I was so amazed by this letter that upon first reading it, I could not speak. I reread it three times before its meaning sank in. It was so kind of him to write to me about those terrible events of twenty-six years earlier. Sharing it with my husband, I told Jan I'd never received such a thoughtful, kind, and affectionate note from anyone.

To be honest, the letter helped me to let go of feelings that had troubled and saddened me for years. Of course, even without this apology, I had been happy enough to become a member of the Metropolitan's board—because Jan and I always loved the museum and believed in all it stands for. At the same time, whenever I remembered how my career had ended, I became terribly upset. As a result, even after becoming an honorary trustee, I found myself torn between contentment at being part of the museum "family" and anger at how badly it had once treated me—a very odd mix of emotions, to say the least.

It took me about three days to absorb the significance of Daniel Weiss's letter—for in doing so, I had to admit to myself how hurt I had been, and how meaningful and healing his apology had been. I wrote him this note of thanks:

> *Dear Dan,*
> *Thank you very much for your extremely kind letter. I agree that the circumstances of the closing of the catalogue department and the termination of my service were not handled properly by the administration at the time. Your extremely thoughtful letter will help me to draw a closure to this painful episode.*
>
> *I never talked to anyone about my difficult experience and I'm surprised you heard about it.*
>
> *Warm regards,*
> *Marica Vilcek*

I also wrote to Daniel Brodsky, since it was through his intervention that Weiss's apology on behalf of the museum had been generated. Although I had met Brodsky only a few times, I knew his charming wife, Estrellita, for she too sat on the board of the Institute of Fine Arts, and I have always liked her.

As I later learned, a mutual friend had informed Brodsky of the particulars of my dismissal, and upon learning them, Brodsky had volunteered to take action on behalf of the museum.

After thinking for several days, I wrote him:

> *Dear Dan,*
>
> *I believe you are aware of the fact that I received a very thoughtful letter from Daniel Weiss in which he addresses the events of many years ago leading to the closing of the Catalogue Department and my departure from the Museum. I understand that this letter was the result of a conversation you had with Daniel Weiss and Sharon Cott and I want to express my sincere appreciation to you. Daniel Weiss' letter means a great deal to me as it has helped to put a closure to a painful chapter in my relationship with the M M of A. While I have always loved and appreciated the museum for the many years it nurtured me, I could not help but feel sad about the circumstances of my final working days. Your kind intervention has helped me to resolve these issues once and for all.*
>
> *Sincerely,*
> *Marica Vilcek*

17

The Vilcek Collection

During our early years running the foundation, Jan and I were thinking more and more about collecting art in a serious manner. Having spent my entire professional life in museums, I loved the daily experience of looking at art, frequently taking my break time or lunch hour to visit the latest exhibitions or installations. Moreover, throughout my many years in the Catalogue Department, the cataloguers had been allowed to select and hang various works from the Met's collection in our study room and to change them out when we liked. (The fact that we were allowed to hang only lesser works of art, or works specifically accessioned for installation or study purposes, was of course perfectly understandable.) When my time at the museum came to an end, I found myself craving something similar—that is, to be in the daily presence of artworks that moved me.

On some level, I had been daydreaming for years about having a substantial work of art in our home. Jan knew this was something I wanted—and luckily for me, it was something he was open to, now that Remicade had left us without financial worries. After so many years of looking at art together in museums and galleries, we were more and more ready to acquire it and live with it. Our friend Alvin Friedman-Kien loved collecting and living with art; and of course so did many of my colleagues from the museum. Even my brother Ivan had begun collecting contemporary art after his marriage to Zoya, herself a graduate of the Institute of Fine Arts—her taste ran to younger artists, and in fact she was an early and discerning collector of Jean-Michel Basquiat.[23] (As a result, for a while their pied-à-terre on the Upper West Side became a storage place for a number of iconic Basquiat paintings she had purchased, which today are worth vast sums.)

Art collecting is, among many other things, a process of self-definition. While pursuing, choosing, and acquiring works of art, whatever they may be, we are constantly asking ourselves questions such as: Why do I want to collect? Why this type of work? Why choose this painting above all others? And also larger questions, such as: In what do I believe? In what do I find value? So when we started thinking about collecting art seriously, Jan and I wanted to be sure of what we would be collecting, and why.

We didn't immediately arrive at American modernism. In fact my first impulse was to acquire medieval sculpture, which I had loved, admired, and written about while attending Charles University in Prague. The sinuous, elegant devotional figures of the late Middle Ages had always captivated me. But by the time I saw the Metropolitan Museum's 2000 exhibition "Tilman Riemenshneider: Master

23 Most of Ivan and Zoya's collection remains with Zoya, but to give an example of its value, one of their Basquiat paintings, *Untitled (Yellow Tar and Feathers)* (1982) sold at auction in 2013 for $25,925,000.

Sculptor of the Late Middle Ages"—possibly the greatest exhibition of late medieval sculpture ever held in the United States—I realized that collecting such sculpture *well* would be very nearly impossible. The Riemenshneider masterworks were of course beyond compare, but truly great works of gothic sculpture by any sculptor are very rare on the world market, and highly sought after by museums. So I let go of the idea, comforting myself that I would always be able to see world-class exhibitions of medieval sculpture close to home at places such as the Met, the Morgan Library, and the Cloisters.

Jan, meanwhile, had begun to take an interest in pre-Columbian art, including works from Mexico, Central America, and South America. Our first pre-Columbian acquisition was a birthday present I bought for Jan in 1993: *Olmec Mask Fragment with Engraved Headband* (1000–500 BCE). That haunting fragment, which sits in Jan's study, remains a favorite piece to this day, in part because it memorializes the start of our adventure as art collectors.

As we were learning about and collecting pre-Columbian art—Jan would ultimately be far more caught up in it than I—we found ourselves drawn more and more to what ultimately became our second area of collecting: Pueblo pottery. For reasons we could not easily explain, both Jan and I felt an immediate sense of connection to these ostensibly utilitarian ceramic objects made by the Pueblo tribes of northern Mexico, New Mexico, and Arizona. They have extraordinary character and presence, and the more time one spends with them, the more interesting they become—something I have come to understand through the experience of living with them in our home. Built entirely by hand, these ancestral pots are subsequently fired in an earthen pit and then decorated by hand. The simplest of them carry minimal decoration, while other, more significant or ceremonial works are painted with abstract or representational motifs. Pueblo peoples think of them as living repositories of cultural memory, with some even considering them not so much objects as family members.

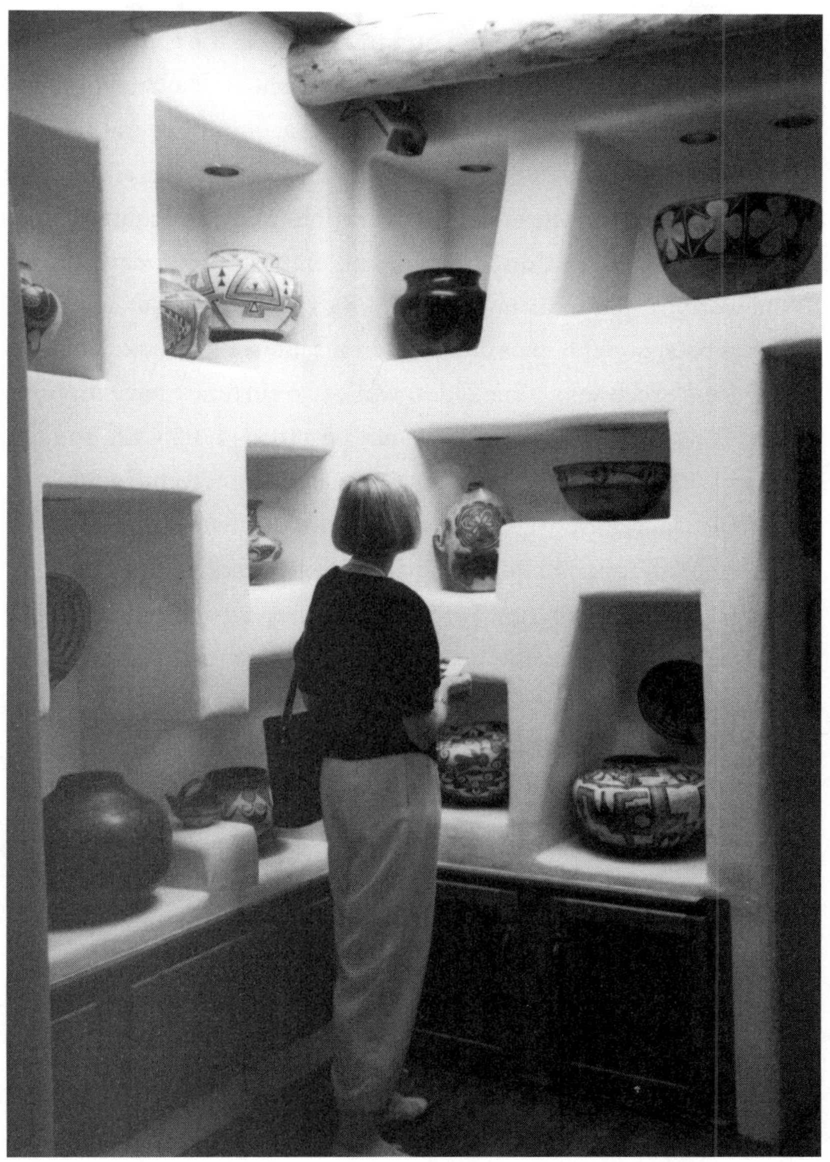

Admiring Native American pottery in Santa Fe, c. 1991

While such pottery has been made for millennia—the Pueblo culture originated approximately seven thousand years ago—most surviving Pueblo pots date from 750 CE. They have been avidly sought by non-native collectors for more than a hundred years, so the field has a well-established literature and is supported by substantial scholarship. When we first started collecting it, we might have acquired several masterpieces—but because we were new to collecting, and overly cautious, we missed that opportunity. In the years that followed, Jan acquired other major works with great discernment and enthusiasm. Today the best of the work offered to us in the late 1990s is unavailable at any price, for it has been bought up or donated to museums. But our collection is nonetheless exceptional. The oldest work (we currently have fifty-one pieces) is *Mogollon-Ancestral Puebloan Jar* (1050–1300 CE). The rest date from 1720 onward, with the majority being nineteenth century.

Many people have asked how we, Czechoslovakian-born collectors, could be so interested in Pueblo pottery. While we came to it gradually (and admittedly late in life), Jan and I had been curious about Native American culture for many years. As children we read and loved the adventure novels by the German author Karl May (1842–1912); his tales of Winnetou, a young Apache, were wildly popular throughout Germany and Central Europe starting at the turn of the century. While our first attraction to Pueblo culture and art evolved out of Karl May's Europeanized and romantic notions of Native American life, that attraction subsequently developed into something far more considered: a sincere admiration of the work itself, and deep curiosity about the culture from which it evolved.

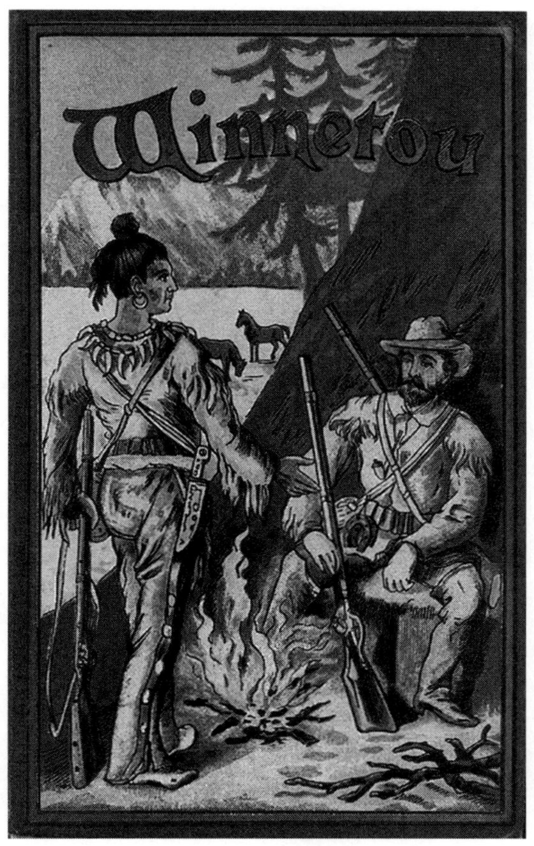

Cover illustration for Karl May's Winnetou trilogy (1893 edition)

As we immersed ourselves in collecting—for collecting is not simply a matter of assembling objects, but rather of understanding these objects in the context of history—our Eurocentric notions about Native Americans evolved into a much fuller and deeper appreciation of the Pueblo peoples and the historical, aesthetic, and spiritual significance their pottery holds for them. It also endowed us with a deeper compassion for Native American peoples and all they have endured. With that growing appreciation and compassion, Jan and I decided that we would acquire, preserve, protect, and make available these breathtaking works of Native American art and culture for present and future generations. We love our collection, but know that we are merely its caretakers.

Because Jan had approached the field of Pueblo pottery with all the zeal and brilliance of the world-class research scientist that he is, our collection recently served as the basis of the Native American exhibition "Grounded in Clay: The Spirit of Pueblo Pottery," curated by the Pueblo Pottery Collective, a group that includes sixty Native Americans of diverse ages, backgrounds, and professions, and representing twenty-one source communities. Other masterworks in the exhibition came from the Indian Arts Research Center of the School for Advanced Research in Santa Fe. When it opened in New York, the exhibition was held jointly at the Metropolitan Museum of Art and the Vilcek Foundation galleries. The show was a great critical and popular success, and as a result, a traveling version of the exhibition will appear in museums nationwide for years to come.

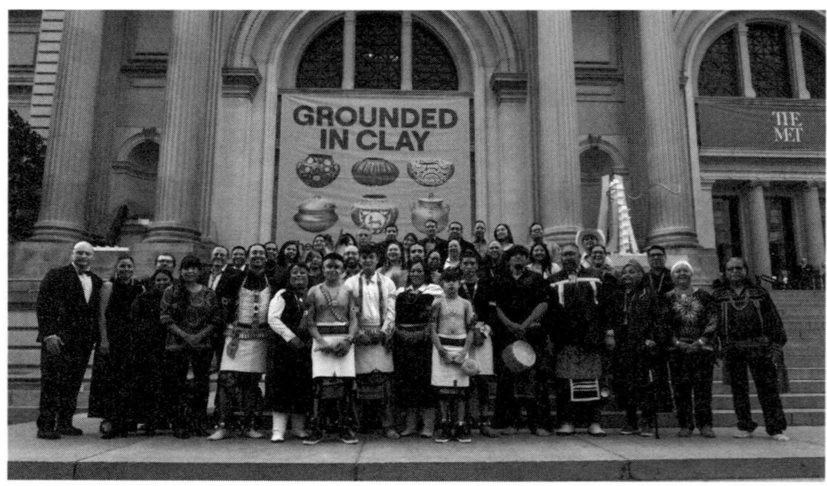

Rick Kinsel with the Pueblo Pottery Collective on the steps of Met, celebrating "Grounded in Clay: The Spirit of Pueblo Pottery," held July 13, 2023–June 4, 2024 at both the Metropolitan Museum and the Vilcek Foundation Gallery.

While Jan focused on Pueblo pottery and Pueblo culture, I renewed my acquaintance with American modernist art of the early to mid-twentieth century, which I had admired long before we ever thought to collect it. The Whitney Museum had always been the greatest champion of American modernism, but during our years in New York, good exhibitions had also been held at the Metropolitan Museum, the Museum of Modern Art, and the Brooklyn Museum. And while working at the Met I had been involved with the cataloguing of the Alfred Stieglitz Collection, a group of paintings, drawings, prints, sculptures, and photographs that had been given to the museum by Stieglitz's estate in 1949. The collection demonstrated by example the interactions between American art and the international modern movement during the first decades of the twentieth century, making it a good starting point for subsequent reading and research.

Before settling on American modernism, however, Jan and I did some serious thinking about European modernism. Modernism's radical reimagining of beauty had an energy and excitement to it, particularly when, early in my curating career, I had viewed it in comparison to the dreary twentieth-century state-funded art I was compelled to work with at the Slovak National Gallery. The Communist ideologues who had overrun our nation in 1948 so thoroughly condemned modernist art that we, as members of the younger generation, immediately sensed it must be work of great power and importance. Through smuggled art books and magazines from Europe and America, Jan and I recognized in modernism the unfettered creativity so valued by the progressive West, and so lacking in the tired propaganda being endlessly promoted as "art" by Czechoslovak apparatchiks.

I think, also, that Jan and I had always taken pride in thinking of ourselves as modern people. After all, we had lived our lives in accordance with Ezra Pound's celebrated modernist injunction, "make it new." By fleeing Czechoslovakia, we had broken with our pasts and radically reimagined our future, just as the painters, sculptors, musicians, and writers of modernism had done in their art. Leaving the Old World and its traditions behind, we arrived in New York, where we created lives for ourselves that were radically different and far more beautiful, interesting, and unpredictable than anything possible in Bratislava.

While collecting European modernism was a meaningful possibility, ultimately it didn't work out. In part, this was because by the time we started collecting, the European modern art movements of the twentieth century that most interested us—fauvism, cubism, expressionism, and futurism—had already been so heavily collected worldwide. Further complicating the matter were the rising number of legal and provenance issues related to European works that had changed hands during World War II and the Holocaust. More important, though, we considered ourselves Americans—so, more and more, we kept thinking, why don't we collect American art? Jan and I both liked the idea of collecting modernist work made here in this country.

Santa Fe also played a role in our decision, for many leading American modernists had visited or settled in the region, including Georgia O'Keeffe, while others had spent extended periods of time seventy miles north, in Taos, at the home of the arts patroness Mabel Dodge Luhan. As a result, American modernism was strongly represented in the Santa Fe galleries, and American modernist masterworks were often on display in that city's museums—including the Georgia O'Keeffe Museum, which opened just a few years after we started our collection.

Seeing American modernist works while experiencing one of America's most exhilarating landscapes—the Santa Fe region, with its high desert mountains and seemingly endless vistas of desert and sky, is itself so deeply, even breathtakingly beautiful—led us into an enhanced appreciation of the artists, for many of them had been equally captivated by Southwestern color and light, and sought to capture the majesty of the landscape in their work.

Oddly enough, our appreciation of American modernism also had a musical dimension, because many American modernists felt that painting and music were sympathetically aligned. Jan and I are passionate about music, and we had some extraordinary musical experiences in Santa Fe, thanks to its summer opera season, a world-class event comparable the great European opera festivals held in Salzburg, Glyndebourne, Parma, and Bayreuth. During our years there, operas by Gluck, Mozart, Strauss, and Wagner brought us back in touch with our European roots. When the open-air Crosby Theater opened in Santa Fe in 1998, its natural backdrop of sky and desert gave each opera performance a larger-than-life visual aspect. Similarly, we would sometimes conclude a long day by attending concerts of the Santa Fe Chamber Music Festival, which often featured pieces by such European composers as Schubert, Brahms, Mendelssohn, and Chopin.

Our study of American modernism led us to discover that many of the artists in Alfred Stieglitz's circle—most notably Arthur Dove, but also Marsden Hartley, John Marin, and Georgia O'Keeffe—were very much inspired by music. Arthur Dove had worked from the idea of synesthesia, the production of a sense impression relating to one sense or part of the body by stimulation of another sense or part of the body. Stuart Davis, meanwhile, was influenced by jazz and swing. Two other artists we later came to collect, Stanton Macdonald-Wright and Morgan Russell, had gone so far as to launch the short-lived art movement called synchromism in Paris, asserting that harmonious colors might be arranged in an abstract painting in a way similar to the way in which notes, keys, or motifs are arranged by a composer in a musical composition. Jan and I were intrigued by, compelled by, and sympathetic toward these theories and influences—particularly so since, after losing so much of my hearing during the 1970s and '80s, I had come to love and appreciate music ever more deeply, and to wonder ever more at its mystery.

During our first years of art collecting I was at a transitional moment in my life. Having left museum work, I was still hoping to maintain my connection to the museum world. Through collecting I now found a way of centering myself, and of redefining myself outside of the role of curator. In my previous life, museum work had connected me to the world. I had loved that I was making myself useful and participating in something greater than myself: the preservation and sharing of great art. As an immigrant and outsider, I particularly cherished this feeling of connection and inclusion.

And I needed to work—for work has always been at the center of my life, and to be without work did not feel right to me at all. In my new occupation as a collector, I found I had work very similar to the work I had done at the Metropolitan Museum: researching, organizing, cataloguing, and caretaking, all of it done in the service of art. Now, however, the work became especially interesting, because the collection was ours alone.

Jan and I enjoyed a certain advantage as collectors, for we could make our decisions quickly. Even the Met, powerful as it is, cannot acquire a work without significant deliberation. Museums can, with effort, fill gaps in their collections, but the decision-making process can be agonizingly slow, since funding from within the institution is nearly always limited, and there are always various factions within a museum that disagree on its collecting priorities. As a result, most museums build their collections through donations or legacies.

When Jan and I began collecting, we chose to do so in a more active, hands-on, and resourceful way than most. After years of looking at American modernism in museums and galleries, I had a strong sense of the historic importance of the movement and its major artists. That historic awareness made me feel the movement was undervalued. Rick Kinsel, who knows the various art markets far better than I do, confirmed me in that hunch.

When we began collecting seriously, American modernism was considered a sleepy, niche market—a field far more appealing to art historians and museums than to deep-pocketed private collectors, who tend to enjoy the flash and excitement of contemporary art. The works weren't fetching big prices at auction, nobody was amassing or speculating on works, and only a few top collectors were making substantial purchases. Therefore, Jan and I were able to seek out what we loved and wanted, and we could do so with unusual freedom. We solicited no external opinions, because we needed no one to advise us—we already knew the field, and we were answerable only to ourselves. We were drawn not to safe or conservative works, but rather to the most powerful expression of an artist's particular style. Even more than Jan, I was drawn to work that was gripping, engaging, and emotionally intense. But to my great relief, Jan was always supportive of my choices. Rick was too.

Ultimately, I think our greatest advantage lay in the fact that there were so few other major collectors actively collecting. As a result, we had an unusual amount of latitude with dealers and estates. And I should add that we were not satisfied simply to survey the available market: Rick and I did our own investigative research to track down works, contacting artists' widows and descendants, keeping an eye on estates going to auction, and often reaching out to galleries to solicit specific works they had handled in the past. In some instances we asked dealers to contact collectors who were holding substantial works we were interested in acquiring. Along the way, we let everyone know that we were soliciting these works not as speculators or middlemen, but as philanthropists intent on building and preserving a major collection of American modernism—and that, too, made an enormous difference. Through all this work, Jan, Rick, and I found ourselves acquiring treasure after treasure. We made a highly effective team of three.

Another aspect of collecting, and one that fell largely to me, was the installation and documentation of these works in our home. Several of my former colleagues have teased me over the years with the suggestion that my home is as beautiful, orderly, and well documented as any gallery in the Metropolitan Museum. They are not wrong—it is. I love having everything perfectly in order. I suppose because that has been my lifetime habit, starting in earliest childhood. Drawing on my many years' experience at the Metropolitan Museum, I have done everything I can to record, document, catalogue, and safeguard these works. Every object in the collection has its own Vilcek acquisition number and Vilcek catalogue entry, which includes information relating to provenance and exhibition history, as well as detailed notes on the work's imagery, historical and biographical references, and critical reception.

This explains, I suppose, why my colleagues and I look after the collection with a passion few outside the world of collectors or curators can possibly understand. The attachment I feel for the works is profound. I am terribly proud of them and consider them, collectively, as an expression of all Jan and I believe in and hold dear. Throughout my life I have never hesitated to give away my possessions—I will gladly give a person in need the clothes off my back or the shoes off my feet. I am not a materialistic person. But I *do* take great pride of ownership in the Vilcek Collection.

Assembling works of real social, cultural, and art-historical significance was a new and shared adventure between Jan and me, and it drew us closer. I brought my lifetime of art-historical researching and cataloguing expertise to the project, while Jan brought his skills of observation and scientific inquiry, as well as tremendous positive energy and enthusiasm. As a result, we suddenly had so much to discuss with each other—and, indeed, occasionally to argue about. For better or worse, we were more deeply in conversation with each other than we had been in years, and learning about one another in the process.

There were a few things, however, upon which Jan and I were always entirely in agreement. First, we felt that the collection ought to remain intact. For a long while, we were not sure how we might do this. But at some point Rick suggested we make the collection a promised gift to the Vilcek Foundation.

The idea made perfect sense. Jan and I would have all the pleasure of collecting, assembling, and installing the collection, and also living with it, even as we had the assurance that the collection would not be broken up and dispersed by a museum, as so many collections given to museums are. Rather, when the time came, our collection would remain in the care of our larger philanthropic enterprise, to do with as the foundation saw fit.

Collecting *well*—that is, collecting wisely and strategically, with wisdom and knowledge and the help of trusted experts—is undoubtedly difficult work. But it is also work of the most pleasurable sort, for one sees so much and learns so much while collecting, and one does so in a way that is entirely different from the way one sees, learns, and understands art through visiting museums, attending art history lectures, or researching an article or book. As collectors, Jan and I have become far more critical and discerning about art than previously. But we have also allowed ourselves to be far more intuitive. We have been guided and helped by various consultants—curators, scholars, and art dealers—with all of them bringing their own particular form of connoisseurship and expertise to our project. But since ultimately it is we, the collectors, who must decide what to acquire and what to pass by, we take the work of collecting very seriously, and think very deeply about each work and what it means to us. So it is, in a sense, a meditative practice.

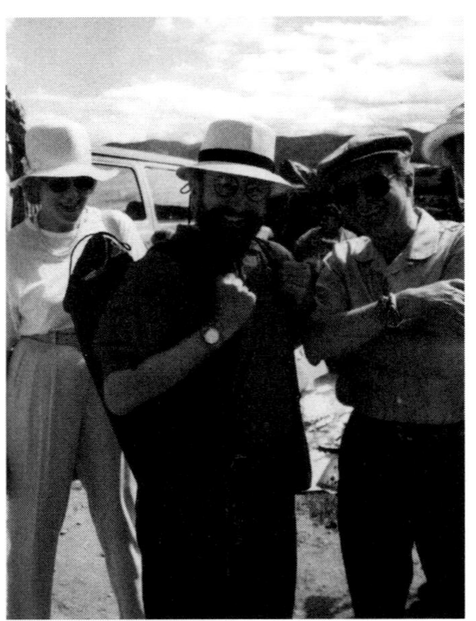

Visiting Santa Fe with Dr. Alvin Friedman-Kien

Another thing I have loved about our collecting is its social aspect, since to be in the company of like-minded art enthusiasts is a delight. Our early collecting trips to Santa Fe with Alvin Friedman-Kien, for example, were among our happiest adventures, in part because we met so many other collectors, curators, artists, writers, scholars, and dealers, many of whom became friends. Moreover, Santa Fe is a delight for art lovers. My memories are of a sunstruck town of adobe architecture with summer weather that was nothing short of glorious—dry, warm afternoons, cool evenings, and the high mountain air always so fresh and clean. When not attending the opera, we spent so many lovely evenings among friends and colleagues, discussing art, artists, and collecting.

When we first started going there, Santa Fe's many galleries, antique shops, art fairs, and flea markets allowed us to find our own way as collectors. In those days we were open to looking at just about anything and were attending exhibitions of contemporary art, folk art, self-taught art, art of the American West, Native American art and artifacts, African art, Asian art, and pre-Columbian art. (And because I had a long-standing interest in silver, textiles, and furniture, I was also looking at those things too.) During the course of a single day I might look at Navajo blankets, Olmec clay figures, and even an ancient sculpture from the Indian subcontinent before browsing contemporary art, nineteenth-century Iranian carpets, and turn-of-the-century American silver. Only through many hours of looking, evaluating, and deliberating did Jan and I come to an understanding about what we wanted very specifically to collect—and we had a very good time getting to that understanding.

I was initially drawn to the artists of the Stieglitz circle for their sense of color and design. The works by Marsden Hartley, Arthur Dove, Stanton Macdonald-Wright, and John Marin all gave me an immediate, visceral pleasure. But there were also a number of lesser-known artists of the period to whom I was drawn, some of them far better known in Santa Fe than New York. So Jan and I collected them too. Among our earliest purchases, for example, were evocative works by Howard Cook, Andrew Dasburg, and Max Weber.

Along with the Stieglitz group, I made a point of looking at artists who had either exhibited in or attended the 1913 Armory Show, the first great exhibition of modern art in America. To my surprise, Stuart

Davis was one of them—in fact, the youngest to exhibit at that show. It was the Stuart Davis painting *Tree* (1921), found at the Owings-Dewey Gallery in Santa Fe in 2001, that became our first major American modernist acquisition.

Jan and I thought about the painting for two years before finally making the purchase in 2003. One reason we hesitated was that we wanted to be sure in our minds about collecting American modernism. The other reason was that we wanted to define for ourselves the scope and ambition of our collecting, given that Davis came to maturity later than most of the artists in the group, and is not quite a leading figure (though he is certainly revered as a modernist artist and a great teacher of modernist art). But *Tree* moved me deeply, in ways I cannot easily explain, and in the end that response was the catalyst for the purchase. A cubist abstraction in green, white, and gray that is derived from the American landscape, the painting depicts a single bare tree against a background of what might be farm fields. The painting seemed to me to balance solitude with vitality, and starkness with promise. Perhaps because I had spent so much of my own early life isolated, yet had remained resilient, the image of the bare, leafless, solitary tree resonated deeply with me. I loved it at once—and still do.

Rick was most helpful to us as we continued to acquire, and in fact he has remained our most trusted art adviser to this day. Already in the late 1990s he had been tracking down various works he knew might interest us. Now he began to focus specifically on American modernism—not merely sourcing these works, but also doing preliminary assessments of their historical and cultural significance, their provenance and exhibition history, and their condition. After he had gathered this information, we would meet and discuss the work, go to look at it, then deliberate about it. If Jan and I agreed, we would then discuss the price being asked, and Rick would begin preliminary conversations with the dealer. In several instances when Jan and I could not come to an agreement on a work, we would ask Rick to cast the deciding vote. We found he was invariably correct in his assessments.

After *Tree*, we acquired a number of other works by Stuart Davis, both on canvas and on paper. Living with them spurred Jan's interest not only in Davis, but in American modernism as a movement, and he began reading about and researching it more deeply. We then revisited a number of museums, many of them in New York, to see major works by the artists we most liked. As our eyes became more discerning, our sense of what made each artist unique became much more specific, and our thoughts about how and what to collect became ever more focused.

We really had no master plan, however. While Rick helped us enormously by tracking down best-quality works that might fit within the parameters of what Jan and I had loosely agreed we would collect, Jan and I were determined to remain open-minded. Rick sometimes found and brought to our attention work that we might not otherwise have considered. Our spontaneous response to the works we were looking at was something we valued—we wanted to allow our hearts and our eyes to respond directly to these paintings and sculptures as we encountered them. So we had no "shopping lists" and made no instantaneous acquisitions. Rather, we visited (and revisited) a good many galleries and estates. We never worried too much that our collection could appear overly heavy in works by a specific artist. If today the collection has an arguably disproportionate number of works by Stuart Davis, Marsden Hartley, and Ralston Crawford, that's simply because they are artists and works that we particularly admire.

Despite my many years' study of collections management, I did not want to assemble a group of masterworks on the basis of their perceived importance. Nor did I feel we needed to be comprehensive or all-inclusive. To my mind, the good collector works from a strong basis in knowledge but remains attuned to an inner voice—and it is that dialogue, between the collector and the things collected, that makes every collection unique. Jan agrees with me here, since over many years of laboratory work he has learned the wisdom of working from an informed hunch. So that is what we do: we collect what we want to collect.

People sometimes ask about our decision-making process. Jan and I have a long-standing mutual respect, but we remain independent in our opinions. He has often said that he defers to my better judgment where art is concerned—and perhaps he does, but he will still sometimes decide on his own. And since Jan has always overseen our finances, I defer to him where expenditures are concerned. In other words, Jan has the ultimate say. But to be honest I can't recollect a single instance of his ever overruling me on an acquisition. I think this is largely because Jan is a far more avid, adventurous, and spontaneous art collector than I; time and again, it has been *I,* not Jan, who has objected to adding a work. He recently noted that, had he alone decided what we should acquire, the number of pieces in our collection would now be unmanageably large, and our collection far less coherent. I agree. I don't enjoy denying Jan something he wants, but at the same time, I do feel the need to point out to him that a particular work seems not to "fit," and in a few instances I have even told him that a potential acquisition is one I am sure he will regret. But I tended to say such things early on, in the days when we expected everything we collected to hang in our apartment.

As our collection has grown, that particular concern has essentially evaporated. We now have very good off-site art storage space. Works that we have already donated to the Vilcek Foundation are stored in the foundation building on Seventieth Street. And it may well be that my taste has grown broader and more accepting over time. For example, I did not want to collect Georgia O'Keeffe in the early days; her distinctive palette was simply not to my liking, and I was rarely moved by her imagery. But we now have several works by her that I quite like, and they fit in very well with the rest of the collection. In living with them my initial ambivalence has moderated; when the O'Keeffe Museum pressed us to sell them our O'Keeffe kachina painting in order to better their collection, I parted with it only reluctantly.

Thanks to living with our paintings, I find myself much more curious about the way in which works reveal themselves over time. Certain paintings, most notably the Marsden Hartley still lifes, become more and more fascinating to me the longer I live with them. Other paintings I look at less and less. We now allow ourselves the luxury of rotating works in and out of the apartment, and also occasionally rehang our favorites so that they can be appreciated from new angles, or in a different light, or in a new grouping. Our apartment has a marvelous built-in system of sliding hangers that allows us to move works almost effortlessly to any spot that we like. Moving the pictures around is a good way of renewing one's acquaintance with them and considering them from a new perspective. It is also a fine way of discovering new relationships, dissonances, or harmonies among various paintings in the collection.

One challenge in having significant works of art in our home has been that sometimes our home furnishings will distract from them, to the point that we need either to reposition those pieces of furniture or remove them. For most of our lives we had what I would describe simply as comfortable furniture, with carpets and curtains and decorative objects that, while loved, were not particularly valuable or rare, or even very interesting. As our life circumstances started to change in the 1990s, we realized our home environment needed to change a bit too.

I began the process by acquiring a few good examples of French art deco furniture. These pieces from the 1920s and '30s were becoming increasingly desirable during the 1980 and '90s, so a substantial amount were available. I liked art deco and thought it stylish—in fact I still do. Also it was modestly scaled, which is important when one lives in an apartment. The art deco pieces I liked best were well crafted and usually made of fine materials: rosewood, lacquer, ebony, figured mahogany. Furniture of this sort had been considered the height of elegance when I was a girl.

Within a decade of acquiring these pieces, however, I wanted something more subtle and refined, since this new furniture was somehow *too* stylish, even flashy, and as a result too much in competition with the paintings, sculptures, and pottery. So piece by piece I gave nearly all of it away, replacing it with furniture from the Wiener Werkstätte. We also began acquiring Wiener Werkstätte silver, textiles, carpets, metalwork, light fixtures, ceramics, and glass. The overall effect was exceptionally elegant and far more discreet.

Jan and I had long been admirers of Josef Hoffmann, Koloman Moser, and their workshop; the simplicity, functionality, and high level of finish to these beautifully proportioned works evoked the greatest cultural achievements of early-twentieth-century Viennese design. The objects we have collected (with the help of Rick Kinsel, a great fan of Wiener Werkstätte, who had fabulous adventures tracking them down in Vienna) have remained a delight to us, not only because they are so elegant, but also because they have served to reconnect us to our Austro-Hungarian roots. A perfect complement to the art collection, these pieces are works of art in themselves, and seem to me to make of the apartment a sort of *Gesamtkunstwerk,* in which furniture, paintings, sculpture, and decorative arts all come together in a unified expression of early modernist art and design.

Jan has become ever bolder about acquiring works as he has grown in expertise as a collector. Generally speaking, he tends to like work that is big, important, and impressive, while I find I enjoy smaller, quieter, more meditative works. I cannot say that I have a favorite painting in the collection, since my interest shifts among the works from day to day. But I do spend a good deal of time looking at Marsden Hartley's still life compositions, often composed of various sorts of bric-a-brac. (He, too, was a lifelong collector of objects, many of which are preserved in his archive at the Bates College Museum of Art in Maine.) During a period of poor health, I found myself returning again and again to a relatively recent acquisition, Hartley's very difficult painting *Christ* (1941–1943).

Jan's taste, by comparison, is probably best exemplified by the Marsden Hartley painting *Schiff*. Painted in Berlin in 1915, *Schiff* is uncharacteristically large for a Hartley, standing 40 inches tall by 32 inches wide, and it was painted during a period many consider Hartley's finest. It seems to me full of energy and joy. Originally one of a suite of six paintings called the *Amerika* series, it was composed during 1914–1915 in Berlin, the opening years of World War I. *Schiff* was the last survivor of that series to remain in private hands when it was offered for sale in 2015. Hartley's bold appropriation of ancient and Native American symbols and motifs, combined with a rich, vibrant palette inspired by Central European folk art (Wassily Kandinsky and Gabriele Münter had shared their folk art collection with him during a visit to their Russian-style home in Murnau that year), makes the work extremely bold, charming, idiosyncratic, mysterious, and charismatic. So, when offered for sale, Jan acted decisively, and the painting became ours.

While initially taken aback by the price Jan paid, I today consider the painting his most brilliant acquisition. *Schiff* is surely the greatest painting in our collection, and Jan's decisiveness in purchasing it was like his decisiveness at the time we fled Czechoslovakia—in both instances, he acted entirely without hesitation, and through his daring he forever changed our lives.

As we have progressed in our collecting, I have come to realize that many of the artists of the American modernist movement were not only in dialogue with European modernism, but also in motion between America and Europe. So as a collection, the works demonstrate the overall significance of international cross-cultural exchange to American cultural life, even as it establishes that many of the artists who were part of this broad movement were . . . immigrants.

Few people realize that a substantial number of the artists of the American modernist movement were immigrants—and before we became collectors, neither Jan nor I did, either. Only now, as we look back upon our collecting, does such a thing become clear to us. Alexander Archipenko, for example, was born in Ukraine, and while many think of him as Paris-based, he moved to the United States in 1923 and took citizenship here in 1929 and remained an American until his death in 1964. Oscar Bluemner was born in Prussia, but after moving to the United States as a young adult, he exhibited at the Armory Show, was given a solo exhibition by Stieglitz, and remained in the United States for the rest of his life. José de Creeft was born in Spain in 1884 and had a long career in Paris, but he moved to America permanently in 1929, and today his *Alice in Wonderland* is among the most beloved sculptures in Central Park. Andrew Dasburg was a Paris-born German émigré who lived in New York, Woodstock, and Taos; he exhibited at the Armory Show and with Stieglitz. Jan Matulka, born in Bohemia, immigrated to the Bronx with his family at the age of seventeen, and although during the 1920s he maintained a studio in Paris as well as New York, he ultimately chose the United States as his home. Joseph

Stella was born in Italy in 1877, moved to the United States in 1896, went back to Europe from 1909 to 1913, but then returned to New York and exhibited in the Armory Show, afterward becoming a fixture of the New York art scene. Max Weber, who migrated from Bialystok to Brooklyn at the age of ten, not only exhibited at the Armory Show but also became the greatest American proponent of cubism.

Among the American-born artists of the movement, Europe was always an inspiration. Howard Cook, Manierre Dawson, Marsden Hartley, Stanton MacDonald-Wright, and Morgan Russell were all influenced by their European travels—the last two developing their ideas about synchromism while living and working in Paris. Marsden Hartley grew up in Maine but tried for much of his adult life to establish himself in Europe, and only fate (in the form of financial insolvency and back-to-back world wars) kept him from settling permanently in Berlin. Howard Cook spent the 1920s in Paris before moving to Taos. Ralston Crawford, after enjoying an early success in pre–World War II America, lived and worked a lot in postwar Europe, exhibiting throughout his later life on both continents.

Looking back on our collection retrospectively, Jan and I have been delighted to discover that it supports our belief in the significance of immigrants to American cultural history. He and I will always think of ourselves as Americans first and foremost, and we will always be grateful that the United States took us in. But at this moment in our lives, we have also come to recognize the significance of our parents and our upbringings to the shaping of the Americans we ultimately became. No wonder, then, that I feel so at home among these many works of American modernism in our collection: they, like us, are a cultural blending of the Old World and the New.

18

Conclusion: Our Work Continues

While the Vilcek Foundation and its ever-expanding prize program required a great deal of our time and energy to launch, it produced an unexpected dividend: accomplished new friends and acquaintances from all walks of life. My favorites among them was the husband-and-wife artistic team of Christo and Jeanne-Claude. I had met them informally many years earlier, shortly after our arrival in New York, through Jan's colleague, Alvin Friedman-Kien (who was, I believe, their physician). But as we renewed our acquaintance with them, Jan and I felt a special connection to the couple too, since they were also immigrants (he from Bulgaria, she from Morocco), and their life journey was in many ways similar to our own. In fact, Christo had been living in Prague at the same time that I was attending Charles University—it was from there that he had managed to reach Vienna (and the West), thereby permanently escaping Communist Bulgaria. He then moved from place to place in Europe. After meeting and teaming up with Jeanne-Claude in France, the couple immigrated to New York and set up their atelier in SoHo in 1964, the year before Jan and I arrived. We awarded them the first-ever Vilcek Prize in the Arts, a sum of $50,000, just a few months after the debut of *The Gates, Central Park, New York City* (1979–2005), a work that Jan and I adored. Our admiration for them is such that we have continued to involve ourselves with their projects. Sadly, she died in 2009, he in 2020.

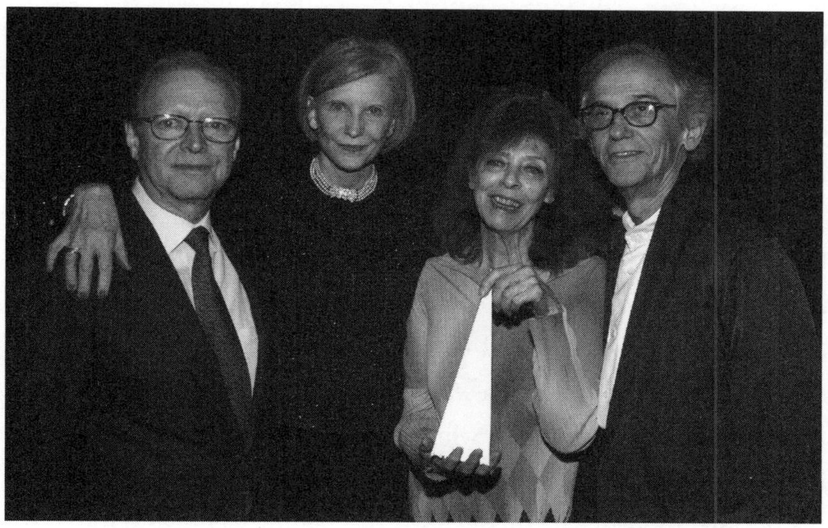

Jan and me with Christo and Jeanne Claude at the 2006 Vilcek Foundation Awards Gala, 2006

My continuing work at the Institute of Fine Arts and my work with Visiting Committees at the Metropolitan Museum have likewise introduced me to a number of exceptionally talented professionals—curators and art historians, mostly. While the work I do on behalf of these institutions is focused on financial and administrative matters, I treasure my interactions with these curators, scholars, and their students, since their creativity and vision is central to the life of the museum. Looking back at my own professional life, I realize that working alongside my fellow specialists at the Met was what I loved best, and that's because their passion, energy, and enthusiasm for art were so tremendously enlightening. I am very glad to say I was recently involved in the selection of art historian Joan Yee to head the Institute of Fine Arts; she is not only a fine scholar but a brilliant administrator.

At the Vilcek Foundation, meanwhile, our art collection continued to grow, as did our staff. Emily Schuchardt Navratil, who took her PhD at the CUNY Graduate Center, joined us in 2009 as our resident curator. Over the past decade she has worked tirelessly on the curating of our exhibitions, the writing of our exhibition catalogues, and the maintenance and organization of our holdings.

We began to add selected works of contemporary art to our collection starting in 2006 at the suggestion of Rick Kinsel. Up until then, we had collected only American modernism, but Rick felt that we ought to collect the work of up-and-coming contemporary artists too. Having done so much research on emerging and developing artists, we saw that there were many ways in which we could help them, and in doing so, hopefully to make a difference in the American cultural dialogue. We decided to formalize these efforts by creating a contemporary art-collecting and exhibition program, which is entirely separate and apart from our Creative Promise prize programs. After collecting the work of the Jamaican-born Nari Ward for nearly a decade, for example, we awarded him the Vilcek Prize in Fine Art (an unrestricted cash prize of $100,000) in 2017. Five years later we mounted an exhibition of his works, which are sculptural installations incorporating found objects and discarded materials. "Nari Ward: Home of the Brave" served as a mid-career retrospective for this artist. It ran for nearly a year at the foundation's gallery.

Because of his significant achievements in science, Jan has been the recipient of many honors over the past three decades. He and I were nonetheless astounded by a phone call we received from Washington, DC, in early 2013. Apparently, NYU had nominated him for the National Medal of Technology and Innovation, and he had won it. The call informing us of this great honor came from the White House. President Barack Obama would present Jan with the medal on February 1, 2013.

Because the ceremony was to take place at the White House, Jan and his fellow honorees were asked to present themselves a day early, so that staffers could instruct them on various protocols. I joined Jan the next day, the morning of the ceremony, accompanied by Rick Kinsel. Because we were allowed two additional guests, we asked Jan's friend and colleague, the virologist Douglas Lowy, to attend, along with his wife, Beverly. The deputy director of the National Cancer Institute, Lowy had been Jan's first assistant when we arrived in New York (and to our delight he would receive the same medal the following year, in recognition of his development of the vaccine against human papillomavirus). We were all so tremendously happy and excited for Jan on the day of the ceremony, particularly when President Obama singled him out by saying:

> One of the scientists being honored today is Jan Vilcek. Jan was born in Slovakia to Jewish parents who fled the Nazis during World War II. To keep their young son safe, his parents placed him in an orphanage run by Catholic nuns. And later, he and his mother were taken in by some brave farmers in a remote Slovak village and hidden until the war was over. . . . Today, Jan is a pioneer in the study of the immune system and the treatment of inflammatory diseases like arthritis.

I was so proud to see Jan's lifetime of hard work rewarded with such a high honor. As the president placed the medal around his neck, I felt tears come to my eyes. There are so many people like Jan—researchers, teachers, doctors—who work hard all their lives and receive no such recognition. They do so not to become wealthy or famous, but out of commitment to the common good. Jan hadn't become a virologist to receive a prize, and yet, miraculously, here he was, receiving the nation's highest honor in science from the president of the United States.

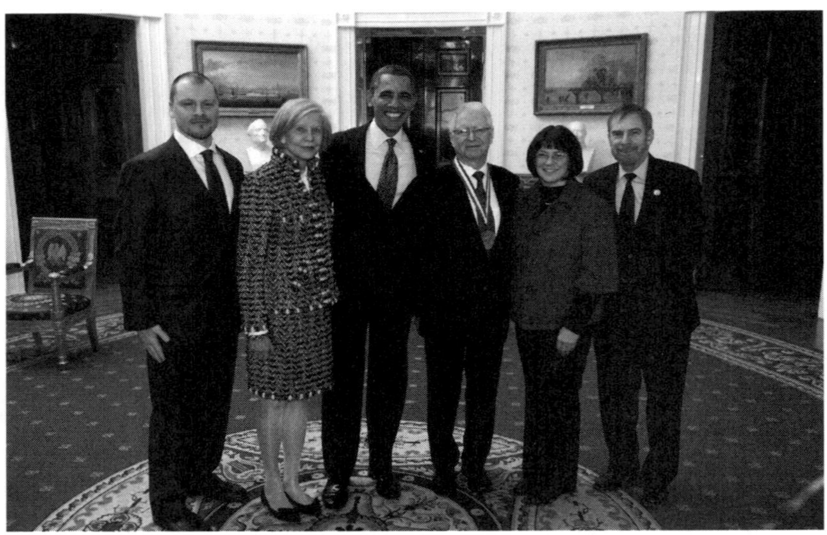

Our photo with President Obama in 2013, following Jan's being honored with the National Medal of Technology and Innovation. On the left, Rick Kinsel; on the right, Beverly and Douglas Lowy.

The presentation was followed by a photographic session with the president and a luncheon. I remember that Jan and I took advantage of being in Washington, DC, to visit several of the Smithsonian art museums, both that afternoon and the next morning, before returning to New York.

That same year, 2013, we published a book-length catalogue of our collection. We hoped that *Masterpieces of American Modernism: From the Vilcek Collection* would raise awareness of our holdings with curators, art historians, and museum administrators, as well as with the public. To our knowledge, many of the works had never before been included in a book, and we wanted very much to have them known. The book's central essay was by the curator and art historian William C. Agee, formerly the director of the Pasadena Art Museum and the Museum of Fine Arts, Houston. He was our neighbor in New York, teaching graduate art history just a few blocks away at Hunter College. Another fine independent curator and art historian, Lewis Kachur, composed detailed descriptions of the ninety-eight works featured in the book, and Emily Schuchardt Navratil contributed concise biographical sketches of the twenty artists represented in the collection. She also created a wonderful illustrated timeline about American modernist art, including many of the works in the book. The fine introductory essay by Rick Kinsel described how Jan and I had become interested in collecting American modernism, and how we had gone about assembling the collection.

Of course, we were in no way done with collecting. There were several notable additions to the Vilcek Collection in 2014: a 1913 study by Joseph Stella and an exceptionally handsome series of gelatin silver print photographs by Ralston Crawford. The next year, 2015, we purchased our third work by George Ault, *Night #2* (1921), and our second John Marin, *Yellow Sun, New York City* (1934). Most important, we acquired Marsden Hartley's *Schiff* (1915), doing so exactly a century after Hartley painted and exhibited it in Berlin. Bold, beautiful, alive with bright colors evocative of central European folk art and extraordinary symbols drawn from Native American and ancient Egyptian cultures, it is Jan's favorite painting, and it now occupies a central viewing position in our apartment, where we have the great pleasure of admiring it daily.

In June 2013, just a few days before his eightieth birthday, Jan began a significant new creative project: his memoirs. He had taken it up at the urging of Rick Kinsel, who felt very strongly that Jan's story needed to be thoroughly documented during his lifetime, and that doing so would be good for the foundation. Reliving the difficulties he had faced during World War II was a disturbing experience for Jan, but his later success as a young scientist and our subsequent escape from Communist Czechoslovakia were all much more enjoyable to recall—as was our new life in America, where his trailblazing work in virology and microbiology brought him so much international attention.

While much of the book is devoted to the specifics of his work as a research scientist, Jan also wrote about our private life. I expect most people will find his descriptions of the work involving interferon, AIDS research, and tumor necrotic factor far more interesting; but for me, his account of our life was a revelation, since never before had I experienced our courtship and marriage from his perspective. His words about me were full of love and respect. Likewise in the memoir's afterword he generously admitted that he had relied heavily on my memory as he had set about drafting the book. And indeed, we sat together often during the many months that he was composing the manuscript, trying to recall our past experiences, sorting out the dates and places and names and events—the experiences of a lifetime.

Particularly moving for me were his memories of our early life together, since they included incidents featuring his parents, my father, my aunts, and several of the very good friends we had been compelled to leave behind in Bratislava in 1964. I found myself thinking with great sentimentality about these people, for we had been forcibly cut off from them. Jan published the book as *Love and Science: A Memoir* with Seven Stories Press in 2016.

Much as we loved our foundation headquarters on Seventy-Third Street, I found by 2013 that we were growing short of office and storage space. The gallery began to seem limited too, given that the foundation was now expanding and evolving faster than we had ever thought possible—and so were our art holdings and art exhibitions. Much as I regretted the idea of leaving the beautifully renovated garage that Rick had worked so hard to transform into an ideal foundation headquarters, I realized we had to make plans for our future.

While looking at real estate in our neighborhood, I found a fine old town house at a perfect location, 21 East Seventieth Street—just a short walk from our apartment, on the street best known as the home of the Frick Collection. Seventieth Street between Fifth and Madison was also home to a number of historically significant art galleries such as Knoedler, founded in 1846. Since one of the previous tenants at 21 East Seventieth was the Hirschl & Adler Gallery, I was already acquainted with the building's main art-viewing spaces. But there were a few sitting tenants in the building, and as a result, the seller needed time to clear the title and conclude the sale. After the purchase went through, we discovered significant structural and materials issues that required our immediate attention—first among them, asbestos remediation. There was also a good deal of lead paint, and countless structural issues and building code violations. As a result, the gut renovation took three years, reaching its conclusion only in 2016.

Luckily the firm we had hired, Architecture Research Office (and specifically its lead architect on the project, Adam Yarinsky) were with us every step of the way. They were enormously committed to realizing our values, vision, and identity through their design. When we purchased the building, it had a landmark designation, but as we soon discovered, the actual structure was a mid-twentieth-century interior behind a 1919 façade. Our first task was to excavate some sixty feet down—a massive but necessary undertaking, since we needed a high-ceilinged basement level to house the elevator machinery, plumbing, heating, ventilation, air-conditioning and climate control equipment, as well as a series of sump pumps. This new basement also needed to be structurally fortified and comprehensively waterproofed.

We then needed to install an entirely new exterior featuring a ground-level entryway access for people with disabilities. We were sorry to see the landmarked façade dismantled, but the sleek new design vastly improved the building's interior light, and it gave the exterior a wonderful freshness and airiness. Inside, the renovated two-story gallery had a fine, north-facing light, thanks to the building's back garden. There were also three additional floors of administrative space, a roof deck, and a private apartment that could be used for entertaining. Completed a full eight years after we purchased it, the Vilcek Foundation at 21 East Seventieth Street immediately received the American Institute of Architects 2021 Interior Architecture Award for the most innovative and spectacular new space in America.

Public and institutional interest in our art collection grew considerably after the publication of our book, which in turn led to more proposals for collaborative exhibitions. Since then, we have done our best to create book-length catalogues for each major show. My favorite among them is *Marsden Hartley: Adventurer in the Arts*. The exhibition and its catalogue had their debut at Bates College Museum of Art during the Covid-19 epidemic, so few could see it. The exhibition's travel schedule also had to be postponed due to the epidemic. It finally had its next installation at the New Mexico Museum of Art in

2025. In the meanwhile the catalogue has garnered widespread critical interest and praise.

Since then, we have put together two very fine Ralston Crawford exhibitions and catalogues: *Ralston Crawford: Torn Signs* (2019) and *Ralston Crawford: Air + Space + War* (2021). The Vilcek Foundation was the sole venue for the "Torn Signs" exhibit, but "Air + Space + War" opened at the Brandywine Museum of Art in June 2021, then traveled to the Dayton Art Institute that October. Our most recent book-length catalogue is *Grounded in Clay: The Spirit of Pueblo Pottery,* created to accompany that exhibition.

In 2016, Donald Trump was elected president. In the months leading up to the election, Jan and I found ourselves increasingly concerned about the racial and ethnic tensions emerging on the American political scene, since we knew from our own personal history how quickly such feelings can turn deadly. We were even more disturbed by news of the Russian interference in the presidential election—interference of a similar sort had resulted in the Communist takeover of Czechoslovakia in 1948.

During the first year of the Trump presidency, nativist, anti-immigrant, and antisemitic sentiments were being openly expressed by Americans throughout the United States, often with implicit or explicit encouragement from the president. The "Unite the Right" rally in Charlottesville, Virginia, in the summer of 2017 was particularly upsetting, as neo-fascists, neo-confederates, neo-Nazis, and far-right militias converged on the city, inciting acts of mob violence that resulted in a murder and many serious injuries. We had always assumed that with our arrival in the United States in 1964 we had left such horrors behind: propaganda rallies, mob violence, nativism, and antisemitism had all, for many years, seemed to be something in our past. And yet here they were, happening again, right here in America.

In 2017 Trump signed a series of executive orders. One banned foreign nationals of seven predominantly Muslim countries from visiting the country for 90 days. Another suspended entry into the country of all Syrian refugees indefinitely. Yet another prohibited other refugees from coming into the country for 120 days. These orders were challenged in the courts repeatedly throughout 2017 and 2018, but Trump's stance against refugees, Muslim foreigners, and immigrants would continue throughout his administration. In late 2017 the administration also began separating refugee parents from their children along the length of the U.S.-Mexico border, a practice that subsequently evolved into the "zero tolerance" policy of 2018, in which undocumented asylum seekers were imprisoned and their children were taken from them and placed into custody. While this grossly inhumane treatment of families prompted widespread condemnation among most Americans, it nonetheless persisted for the duration of the Trump presidency.

Jan and I could do nothing to change these terrible new policies, and nor could our foundation, but we were relieved when several Vilcek prize winners spoke up in meaningful and inspiring ways in defense of immigrants—and Jan himself did the same. In a 2020 article published in *Science*, the magazine of the American Academy for the Advancement of Science, Jan wrote persuasively about the value of immigration to scientific achievements within the United States. He also signed an open letter with more than three hundred other scientists, pushing back against the Trump administration's new restrictive visa and immigration policies.

The growing visibility of American racism, meanwhile, prompted us to reconsider the way in which we operated our foundation. To support diversity and fight xenophobia, we worked with Rick Kinsel and the foundation's programs team to encourage greater diversity in prize candidates, reaching out to historically underrepresented communities to encourage nominations from those communities for our prizes. We also emphasized that immigrants who were DACA recipients and asylees were eligible to apply for Vilcek Foundation prizes. Several of the staff began taking racial equity and racial justice workshops with the organization Grantmakers in the Arts, and we offered these programs to our board members as well.

During all this political and social turmoil, I had sad news in May 2019 concerning my brother Ivan. Jan received a phone call from Ivan's second wife, Zoya Švecová, who told him that Ivan had died twelve days before at age ninety-one. We subsequently learned that Ivan had entered a nursing home and hospice in Portola Valley, California, four months earlier. The ultimate cause of his death was a blood marrow disorder, myelodysplastic syndrome, with coronary artery disease as a contributing factor. His final illness had lasted four weeks.

I was on good terms with Ivan but rarely spoke with him, so I was distressed Zoya had not thought to inform us that my brother had entered a hospice. I would have flown out to be with him if I had known his life was coming to an end. Ivan and I had not seen each other much over the past thirty years, but he was my brother and an important person in my life.

Upon marrying Zoya in 1974, Ivan had taken early retirement and moved out west, settling with her in Los Altos Hills, California, just a short distance from Stanford University. He had saved and invested wisely, and Zoya had family money (her mother owned a senior care facility), so they lived well. Jan and I had visited them there once, and were amazed by their incredible collection of contemporary art. The house was made largely of glass, shaped like a pyramid, and perched on its own little hilltop. Los Altos Hills seemed a fine place to retire, for the climate was invigorating and the countryside beautiful. Always an outdoorsman and sportsman, Ivan told me he hiked and bicycled often in the Santa Cruz Mountains, a greenbelt preserve that occupies the central section of the San Francisco peninsula.

Perhaps the distance that had developed between us was due to Zoya's dislike of me and Jan; but in truth, Ivan himself had never been very good at keeping in touch with me unless he needed something. He would sometimes call me from California to ask me to forward his mail from his Manhattan pied-à-terre, or else to pick up a package for him or do some other small chore. But he rarely saw me when he came to New York for a visit, and we were invited to his home in California only that one time.

When the catastrophic Covid-19 pandemic arrived in New York in March 2020, the Trump administration increased its anti-immigrant rhetoric and policies, scapegoating the Chinese for the introduction of the virus. At the same time, the administration failed to inform the public of the gravity of the pandemic. In January I had known from various news sources that the disease was spreading rapidly in Asia, and being elderly, I worried that Jan and I would be vulnerable if the virus were to come to New York—especially since I had been diagnosed with colon cancer the previous September. Though the tumor had been successfully removed, my doctor had told me that the continued preventative treatment would suppress my immune system.

Our sense of Covid-19 changed drastically in mid-March, when Jan attended a reception at the Metropolitan Museum for the exhibition "Photography's Last Century: The Photography Collection of Ann Tenenbaum and Thomas H. Lee." Ann Tenenbaum, a trustee at the

Met, had just given the museum the remarkable gift of her entire collection, and her parents, the philanthropists and art collectors Arnold and Lorlee Tenenbaum, came to the opening reception. Jan and I knew and liked the Tenenbaums, who were based in Savannah but kept a second home in Santa Fe, where we saw them often in the summer. Jan chatted happily with Arnold at the reception. On March 24, just two weeks later, Arnold was dead from Covid, and five days later Lorlee died of it too.

By this point the Met had shut its doors and canceled all programming. We canceled all the foundation's programming too, including the annual Vilcek Gala, which was only a week away. The spread of the virus was so rapid and so deadly that even Jan, despite his position in the field of virology, had had little advance notice of its arrival. The Trump administration further confused the public through its repeated assurances that the epidemic would quickly fade away of its own accord. Many lives were lost as a result.

Predictably, the epidemic set off a new wave of anti-immigrant sentiment, this time focused on Asian Americans. But other immigrants and refugees were also seen as potential transmitters of the disease, which helped bolster the administration's anti-immigrant policies and directives. Since the Vilcek Foundation is committed to supporting immigrants in the arts and sciences, we issued a statement that March condemning xenophobia. We also began sharing content by our prize winners working in the fields of virology and immunology—for many of these recent immigrants were on the front lines of the fight against Covid-19—as a way of demonstrating that many immigrants were working heroically on behalf of America's public health. Those we featured included the Iranian-born Pardis Sabeti, an epidemiologist and infectious disease specialist at Harvard Medical School, and the Bulgarian-born Silvi Rouskin of MIT and Harvard, who was just then charting the structure of the RNA genome of SARS-CoV2, the virus that causes Covid-19.

We also awarded Andrew Yang the 2020 Vilcek Prize for Excellence in Public Service. Our decision to give him the award came in response to his presidential campaign, since Yang was the first Asian American to run for president. But it was also in recognition of his philanthropy. We were so glad that in the months following his run for the White House Yang continued to speak out substantially on behalf of Asian Americans.

When the vaccine became available in late 2020, the foundation used its various social media platforms to inform the public of the many immigrant scientists who had contributed to its development, and to amplify the important work being done by immigrant scientists, doctors, and medical administrators to fight Covid. Early in 2021, we awarded the Vilcek Prize for Excellence in Science to the Hungarian-born Dr. Katalin Karikó, a vice president at BioNTech RNA Pharmaceuticals, whose research had led directly to the development of a safe and effective mRNA vaccine for Covid-19.

So far as our arts outreach was concerned, we did our best to help artists and arts professionals survive the Covid shutdown in the most direct way possible—by paying them. Many artists, curators, and arts organizations were faltering, some on the brink of ruin. Visual artists were facing the cancelation of gallery exhibitions, art fairs, and museum exhibitions; performing artists could not perform; and vast numbers of people working in the arts (including curators) had simply been laid off without pay. It was terribly stressful to receive so many desperate appeals for money from institutions and private individuals. We did our best to help as many as we could.

At home, meanwhile, our lives became very quiet. Advancing age, health problems, and now Covid meant that we could no longer invite guests into our home, nor could we leave our apartment. Many people urged us to evacuate to the country, but leaving Manhattan was simply not possible, for my cancer treatments were ongoing—and anyway, our New York apartment was the only home we knew. So, we kept ourselves as safe as possible by following the protocols issued by the National Institutes of Health. Maintaining a Covid-free home became especially vital to me when, in August 2020, approximately a year after my colon cancer diagnosis and six months into the pandemic, I learned that the cancer had metastasized into my lungs. I promptly had a surgery, and doctors successfully removed the tumor.

A month and a half later, Jan suffered a transient ischemic episode. The blood supply to his brain was briefly interrupted, giving him what seemed to be a stroke; luckily, however, it lasted only a few minutes. Three days later, on October 5, he had surgery to repair the source of the problem, a blockage in his carotid artery. The procedure went well, but he could not return home immediately. He was transferred to a rehabilitation facility, where he remained for the next two weeks. Despite the omnipresent danger of Covid infection, I visited him there every day—I knew Jan needed me. Because I felt very strongly that I needed to be with him too, I took the risk of a possible infection to sit with him daily. Fortunately I did not become ill.

When Jan was released, we needed to hire two home health aides since he could not yet look after himself. But almost immediately after arriving at our apartment, one came down with Covid. By this point, test kits for Covid were available, so everyone in our household began testing daily. Much to our relief, none of us had been infected. Two months later the Pfizer-BioNTech vaccine became available, and we were all vaccinated as soon as possible, thereby lessening our risks of serious illness or death from the virus.

When, ultimately, we did come down with Covid—Jan has now caught it three times, and I have had it twice—our cases were not severe. I suffered from a cough, runny nose, and many aches and pains, and I subsequently experienced a physical weakness that persisted for months after all the other symptoms subsided. Jan had a similar experience. Because he is older, he took longer to recover.

In December 2021, the antiviral medication Paxlovid became available, and a friend of Jan's who was an infectious disease specialist helped us by prescribing the drug for us when we became reinfected. The medication seems to have lessened our symptoms.

Unfortunately, my health troubles during the pandemic years were not limited to Covid. In June 2021—in fact, as I was starting this memoir—I saw my doctor about a persistent pain in my right wrist that was keeping me from writing or typing. He consulted with a neurologist, who recommended a brain MRI. My personal assistant, Sharmaine Cale, came with me to a clinic on East Forty-First Street, where the MRI revealed three metastatic tumors within my brain. When I called my doctor with this news, he advised me to go to the emergency room immediately. It was a quiet, rather warm Saturday afternoon, and the streets were eerily deserted due to the ongoing pandemic. One of the staffers at the clinic was kind enough to accompany Sharmaine and me as we walked the ten blocks to NYU/Langone. Sharmaine and I then spent the rest of the afternoon and evening waiting for the hospital administration to admit me and schedule the surgery. Doing so took until midnight. I remained in the hospital all day Sunday in preparation for gamma knife radiosurgery on early Monday morning.

Jan and I were alarmed at the idea of brain surgery, for my previous surgeries for Ménières disease had been painful ones, with the recovery taking months. But this new procedure was not an invasive surgery at all: rather, it was an operation in which precisely targeted gamma radiation destroyed the cancer cells via an entirely noninvasive procedure. The most difficult part of the surgery for me was in trying to lie perfectly still, for the slightest movement affected the precise work of the gamma "knife." But all three of the cancerous tumors in my brain were successfully destroyed over the course of the three-hour procedure. After just one night of observation, I was allowed to return home.

I remained well until three months later, when I fell unexpectedly, only to discover I had lost the use of my right hand and right leg. Tests revealed that I was suffering from cerebral edema—a swelling in the brain centered on the area where I had had the metastasis and gamma knife surgery. The swelling affected my brain function. But a steroid followed by an intravenous medication known as Avastin soon relieved most of the pressure, and I regained my mobility. After two weeks of rehabilitative therapy, I was able to function independently, albeit with reduced use of my right hand. Since then, I have had to return to the hospital only once, in 2023, for five more gamma knife procedures. My hand is still incapacitated, but with the help of physical therapy, it slowly improves.

During the Covid epidemic, Jan and I became ever more caught up in the life, work, and legacy of the painter Marsden Hartley. Living with his paintings led us to admire and love them more and more—particularly during lockdown, when leaving the house was basically impossible, I found myself returning to them again and again. Their variety, vitality, and exuberant use of color were, to my mind, balanced by a melancholy reserve. His still lifes in particular have always fascinated me; yet during the more difficult periods of my recent illnesses,

I have found myself drawn to his *Christ* (1941–1943), the very difficult painting that we acquired in 2018. As Hartley's lifelong restlessness, loneliness, and searching drew to its close, the artist returned several times to imagery from the Passion of Jesus: a bare-chested Jesus against a carmine background, his face contorted with anguish.

Our interest in Hartley was such that we started to take a deeper interest in Hartley scholarship, and in doing so we found that, alone among the most celebrated American modernists, Hartley has no catalogue raisonné. At the time of his death in 1943 he had no money, no longtime art dealer, and very few close friends or supporters. He had always lived a nomadic and impoverished life. An incomplete inventory of his known works was subsequently drawn up, but it was never published. More recently, other scholars had started such inventories, only to abandon them. Similarly, a biography project undertaken by the scholar Elizabeth McCauseland remains unfinished and unpublished.

Hartley's reputation declined after his death but revived again during the 1990s, thanks in large part to his inclusion in several significant exhibitions of American modernism. His brief 1933 memoir, *Somehow a Past,* was published by an academic press in 1997. A biography was published in 1998, and his lively, often desperate correspondence with Stieglitz during the years 1912–1915 was published with significant scholarly annotation in 2002. The Metropolitan Museum mounted a very beautiful exhibition of his Maine paintings in 2017, doing so at the Met Breuer, the building that had previously housed the Whitney Museum of American Art. But much more remained to be done—most important, the full cataloguing and documentation of his works. As a former curator in charge of the Catalogue Department at the Metropolitan, I felt very strongly that such a catalogue was needed—for the sake of scholars, curators, collectors, and the interested public.

After speaking the matter over with Jan, we decided in 2020 to fund a project based at Bates College led by the noted Hartley scholar Gail R. Scott. She is currently undertaking the research and writing of *The Marsden Hartley Legacy Project: The Complete Paintings and Works on Paper.* Rather than publish her work in book form, she has chosen to construct a comprehensive, annotated online catalogue listing all the known paintings and works on paper by Hartley, with each entry including basic information, provenances, and images. Because there are more than sixteen hundred known works, the project is labor-intensive. Scott intends to add exhibition histories, literature, and commentary for each work as her time and resources permit. In committing an initial $100,000 to the project, we have helped Professor Scott and Bates College to preserve and protect the life work of Marsden Hartley, hopefully enabling future scholars and curators to research and write about these works, as well as to write about Hartley himself.[24]

In late July 2020, just a few weeks before the metastasis was discovered in my lungs, Jan and I decided to visit Maine to do some research on Marsden Hartley. After many years of collecting and admiring his paintings, we were organizing a major traveling exhibition about Hartley's experiences in Europe, "Marsden Hartley: Adventurer in the Arts." We wanted to include several objects from the Marsden Hartley Memorial Collection at the Bates College Museum of Art, but the only way to select them was to visit the museum.

Bates is in Lewiston, the working-class mill town where Hartley grew up, and where he worked for a time as a child laborer in a shoe factory. Our plan was to visit the museum, meet its director, select the objects, and then briefly tour the city. We would then continue to

24 Jan and I continued to seek out good paintings by Hartley all through the Covid lockdown. We acquired *Still Life: Pink Begonia* (1928–1929) in 2020; purchased *Popocatépetl, Mexico* (c. 1933) in 2021; and a few months later bought *Waxenstein at Hamarsbach Garmisch, Bavaria* (1933–1934).

Down East Maine, to the tiny fishing village of Corea, where Hartley had spent his last years in poverty and obscurity.

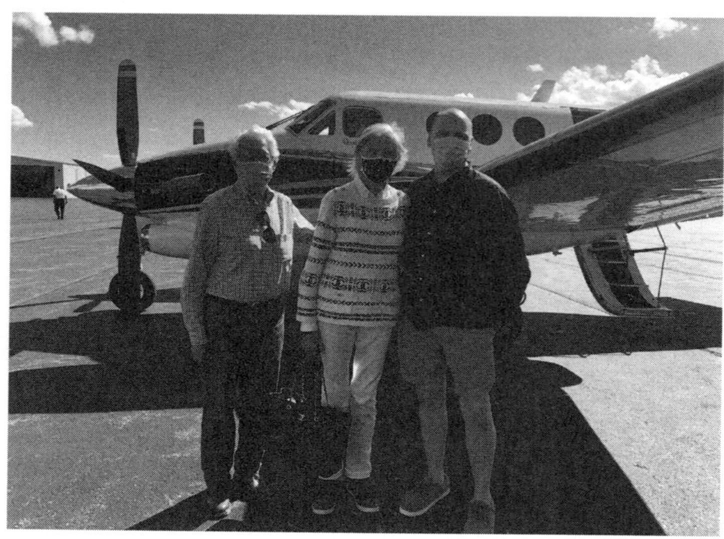

Our flight to Maine during the Covid epidemic, summer of 2020

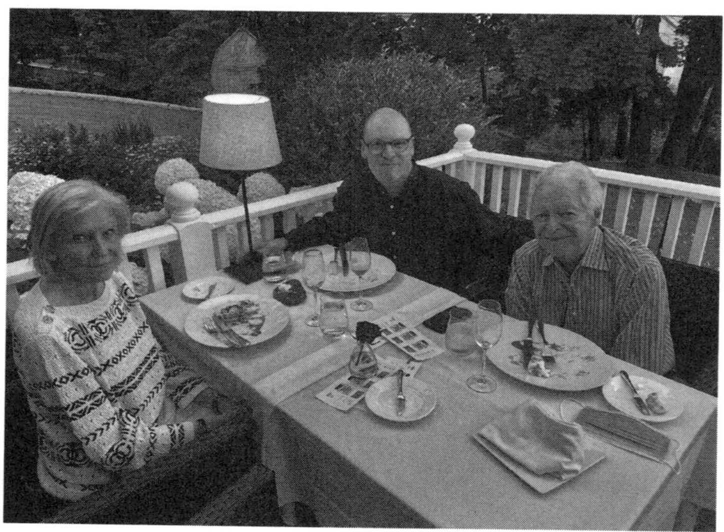

Dinner in Camden, Maine

Rick Kinsel organized the trip, which was complicated because of the Covid pandemic. Lewiston is a grim factory town with few comfortable hotels, so we decided to fly our chartered plane to an airstrip just south of Rockland, and to spend our first night in Camden, at a fine inn with views of Camden harbor and Penobscot Bay. The next morning we drove seventy miles west, to the Bates Museum, whose director, Dan Mills, patiently guided us through the collection of Hartley's personal effects, which includes textiles, ceramics, postcards, jewelry, travel souvenirs, and a few small pieces of ancient and pre-Columbian sculpture. We also saw Hartley's easel, several of his painting palettes, various personal photographs, drafts of his poetry, and a collection of his drawings. On our way back to Camden, we took a brief look at Lewiston, where we noticed many women wearing hijabs. We later learned that approximately 16 percent of the city's population consists of recent immigrants, primarily from Somalia, Afghanistan, and Iraq.

Our next destination was Corea, a hamlet in a cove on the far side of the Schoodic Peninsula. To get there from Camden—it was more than eighty-five miles away—we needed to fly from Rockland to Bar Harbor, and then drive east another thirty-five miles. At the Bates Museum we had already seen a number of photographs of Hartley's little studio in Corea, formerly a chicken coop, where he had finished out his days in the humblest of circumstances. That studio was long gone, and the town itself was just a lobster-fishing community of just over two hundred people, but we were delighted to come across the Corea Baptist Church because Hartley had sometimes painted there, and we recognized it immediately from his paintings of it.

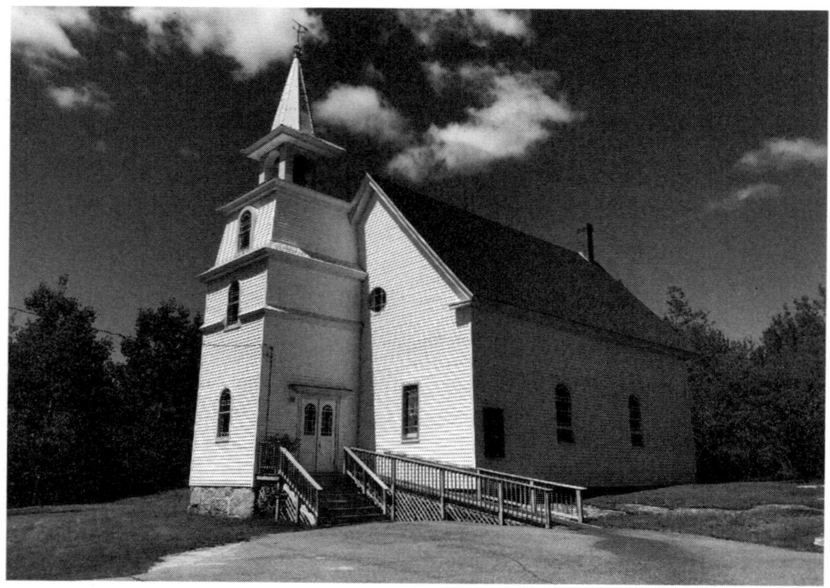

Corea Baptist Church as we found it

Corea's docks seemed equally familiar, thanks to *Lobster Fishermen* (1940–1941), a group portrait of lobstermen and their traps that Hartley had sold to the Metropolitan Museum in 1942. We had our lunch outside that day, overlooking those docks, enjoying the delicious lobster rolls for which Maine is so famous. The sunshine, sea breeze, and salt air were exhilarating. On the drive back to Bar Harbor, we took a short detour along Cranberry Point Road, with its dramatic sea view evocative of Hartley's *Off the Banks at Night* (1942).

I would have liked so much to stay in Maine. Jan and I found it indescribably beautiful. I would have liked to see Mt. Katahdin, which had been to Hartley what the Mont Sainte-Victoire had been to Cézanne. But our time was limited, and Covid a great risk to our health. Still, I am glad that Jan and I were able to get to Maine, and through that trip to have a better sense of Hartley's complicated relationship with that austere but ravishingly beautiful place.

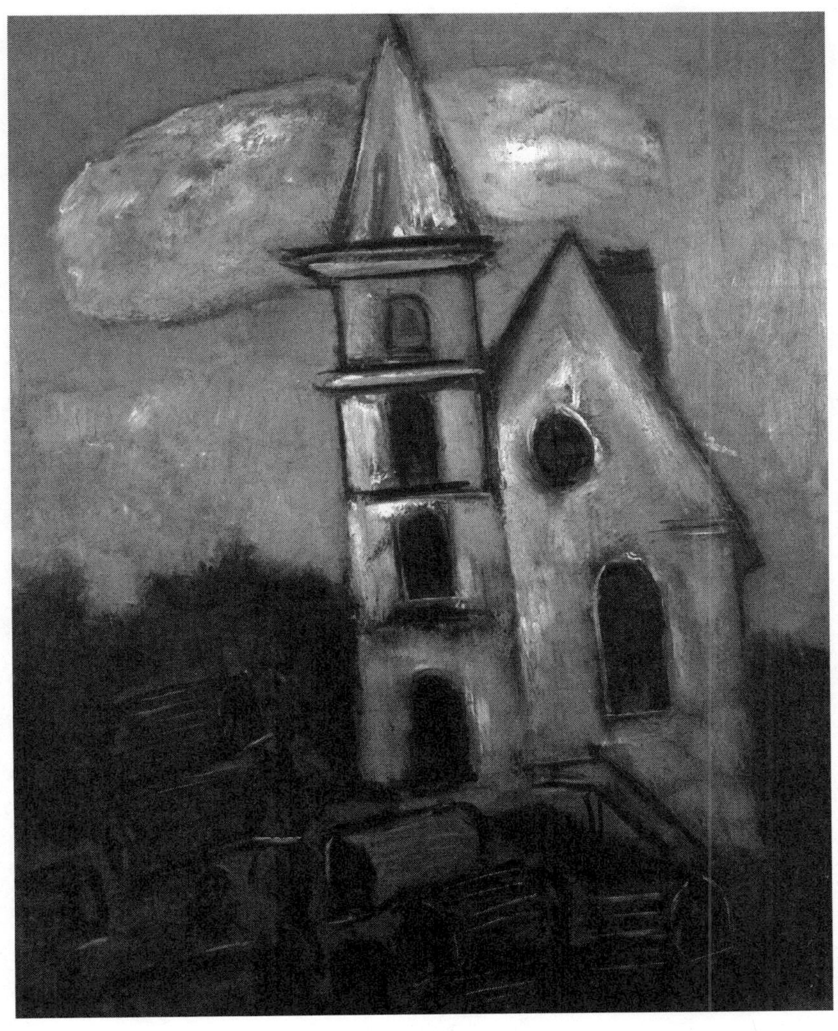

Marsden Hartley, White Church and Lobster Pots (c. 1942–1943)

AFTERWORD

When Rick Kinsel first urged me to write this memoir, I hesitated—mostly out of shyness, but also out of a sense of unworthiness. While I agreed with him that my life has been an eventful one, I pointed out that it had hardly been marked by great achievements—Jan, if anyone, is the celebrity in our household. But Rick gently pointed out that my experiences as a refugee turned curator might nonetheless inspire other immigrants, as well as other people in the arts from modest backgrounds. He also felt quite strongly that my account of our life would be a good counterpoint to Jan's 2016 memoir, which had focused primarily on his work as a research scientist.

Turning Rick's idea over in my mind, I came to see he had a point, for memoirs of lives such as mine, which are lived largely in service to others or in service to institutions, are somewhat rare. The American focus is always on celebrities, entrepreneurs, leaders, and visionaries who rise to positions of power and influence and wealth. Those who choose an opposite path—a life of public service, for example, or devotion to a worthy cause—are considered cultural anomalies. So even as I wondered that anyone should take an interest in my life story, I decided to write it.

In doing so, I have had some time to think about the many people who have shaped and influenced my life, and about the many personal choices I have made along the way. Sorting through these experiences and putting them into order—cataloguing them, in fact—has been good for me. For even as I was striving to compose a narrative that gave others a sense of my extraordinary journey from Bratislava to the Metropolitan Museum, I was coming to understand my life in a new way.

Consider, for example, my relationship with my parents. For much of my life I felt slighted by them, given that they were devoted to my charismatic older brother. But ultimately their influence over me (even, arguably, their relative indifference about my future) shaped me into the person I ultimately became—which is to say, a hardworking, high-achieving, and independent-minded professional in whom, I think, they might ultimately have taken great pride. I see now too all the ways in which my mother and I were alike: both of us excelled as students, maintained professional careers after marriage, and lived lives dedicated to the well-being of others—she, through her career as a teacher and headmistress; I, through my work in curating and, later, philanthropy.

I often remember how, after her memorial service, so many of my mother's former students came to me and my father and brother to express their gratitude toward her, for all the guidance and encouragement she had provided them. Much as my mother may have criticized and excoriated me, I ultimately followed a path similar to hers, and in retrospect, I see that she was, in her way, urging me on. I truly admire all she accomplished at her school, and am glad that she helped so many young people, myself included.

Similarly, as I look back on my thirty years at the Met, I realize that the deepest joy and satisfaction I experienced during my career came not from working among great works of art (though that was, indeed, a rare privilege), but instead from assisting and enabling others, particularly the young, to move forward in life. Helping when I could, advising when asked, proposing or suggesting whenever it seemed necessary and appropriate—whether I was helping curators track down a work of art, assisting scholars to locate some piece of lost information, or else simply showing a young student intern what it means to be a curator—all of these various actions taught me time and again that generosity is its own reward. It makes one feel good. Similarly, in my private life, I worked with Jan to assist newly arrived immigrants, either by giving them a few weeks on our living room sofa, guaranteeing their first lease, or providing them with a much needed job reference. Putting the needs of others before one's own often requires forbearance, and perhaps a degree of self-denial, but when you feel appreciated and connected to others through such efforts, it's hardly an inconvenience. In fact, it's the opposite—it's a joy.

I think the two greatest gifts my parents gave me, whether they intended to do so, were self-reliance and self-assurance. Growing up in terribly difficult circumstances, I saw no future for myself in Czechoslovakia, and so I resolved to leave. And after marrying Jan, I convinced him that we needed to leave—to flee communism and start a new life elsewhere. Even after arriving in the United States, a country about which I knew nothing and for which I was entirely unprepared, I never doubted that I would ultimately do all right for myself. Looking back, I am amazed at my self-assurance. But that self-assurance and self-reliance were both hard-won; I developed them in response to an early life filled with sorrow, rejection, isolation, and injustice.

These qualities continued to help me even after my arrival in New York. I wanted a career at the Metropolitan Museum, and so I simply found my way in—working my way up from library volunteer at the Brooklyn Museum to associate curator in charge of the Catalogue Department at the Met. It took me thirty years and many long hours of work, but it was the work that I loved and the career that I wanted. And even after being terminated by that institution under the most humiliating and unjust of pretexts, I believed enough in myself, and also in the museum, to ultimately reconcile with it and find my way back to it—first as a donor, then as a trustee. Starting in Czechoslovakia and continuing in America, I never gave up on my dreams and I held fast to my core beliefs. I never gave in to fear or self-doubt, to bitterness or self-pity. Whatever the setback, I simply collected myself, came up with a new strategy, and got on with my work.

So perhaps, as Rick suggested, my life story will be inspiring in that regard. I know that I am constantly telling young people that they need to be persistent and tenacious if they expect to realize their dreams. And if my experience has taught me anything, it is that immigrants in particular must hold fast to the vision of the life they hope someday to achieve—otherwise, they are lost. Immigration is so enormously difficult, and presents so many trials and challenges to the person moving from one culture to another (challenges that are not only personal and professional, but psychological and emotional), that negotiating it successfully takes the better part of a lifetime.

Ultimately, though, it was America, this extraordinarily open society, that enabled us to work and to achieve. Neither Jan nor I could ever have achieved so much nor risen so far in Bratislava or Prague.

America (and New York in particular) is truly a place in which anyone is free to *become*. I started out here with very limited prospects: I was a curator and art historian specializing in the medieval metallurgy of Central Europe, and I was unable to speak proper English. Yet no one ever stopped me; no one said I was unwelcome or told me to leave. And as I slowly became the person I had always wanted to be, working in the place I most wanted to work, I met and befriended so many similarly hardworking people—often finding, to my amazement, that they too were immigrants. Perhaps that is why I ultimately felt more at home in New York than I ever had back in Czechoslovakia.

Finally, for those who are not immigrants, I hope this memoir will give at least a small sense of the challenges an immigrant must face. And I hope also that it suggests to all Americans, immigrant or not, that each of us can, if we like, add to this great nation's energy, vitality, and variety through a combination of dedication, generosity, and altruism. Through our achievements, commitments, and labors, Jan and I have tried to express how grateful we are to be American citizens. America took us in when we were stateless and gave us a home; in return, and in thanks, we have worked to be worthy of that honor.

ACKNOWLEDGMENTS

Because memory alone is not always sufficient to the task of re-creating experience, I would like to thank several people for sharing their recollections with me in the writing of this memoir.

First and most important to this project was my husband, Jan Vilcek. Rick Kinsel, president of the Vilcek Foundation, participated in this project from start to finish and often supplied his own recollections of our many years together. For recollections and assistance at the Metropolitan Museum, I would like to thank: Katharine Baetjer, Carmen Bambach, Daniel Brodsky, Estrellita Brodsky, John Buchanan, Johanna Hecht, Morrison Heckscher, Harold Koda, Christine Lilyquist, Marilyn Jenkins-Madina, Joan Mertens, James Moske, Lisa Pilosi, Stuart W. Pyhrr, Andrew Solomon, Pari Stave, Penelope Hunter-Stiebel, Gary Tinterow, Thayer Tolles, Daniel H. Weiss, and Edelgard Winands. I would also like to thank the staff of the Watson Library for their gracious hospitality.

At the Vilcek Foundation, I would like to thank Elizabeth Boylan, Brian Cavanaugh, Christina Strassfield, Emily Schuchardt Navratil, Seamus McKillop, Victoria Melendez, Andrew Jonas Sanders, and Mark Toepfer.

At the NYU Institute of Fine Arts, I would like to thank Anne Ehrenkranz, Sarah Higby, and Joan Kee.

I would also like to thank my friends Dominika Andraskova, Alvin Friedman-Kien, Ryo Toyonaga, Christopher Vazan, Terezka Vazan, Jadranka Vazanova, and my brother Pavol Gerhath. My personal assistants Mary Sharmaine Cale and Peter Libron were also very helpful.

At Rodin Books I offer my thanks to Arthur Klebanoff, Jeremy Townsend, Barbara Aronica, and David Wilk. Pentagram did a beautiful job with our cover design; thanks especially to J. Abbott Miller and Zachary Newton. Many thanks also to our copyeditor, Trent Duffy.

For help with photography research, organization, and permissions, I would like to thank Melissa Totten of M + Co. For photography research in Slovakia, I would like to thank Lucia Almášiová, kurátorka Zbierky fotomédií at the Slovak National Gallery (Slovenská národná galéria) for her help, as well as for granting us access both to the gallery's institutional archives and collections. I would also like to thank Peter Mikle, director of the Nation's Memory Institute Archives (Archív Ústavu pamäti národa). Milena Kalinovska, Anna Pravdova, Adrien Rajter, and Alena Šefčákova were also very generous with their time and assistance.

For legal and contractual advice, I would like to thank Alia Hanna Habib of The Gernert Company and Carolyn Schurr Levin, of Miller Korzenik Sommers Rayman LLP.

Finally I am deeply grateful to my co-author, Justin Spring, who worked for five years on the researching and writing of this book.

Marica Vilcek

TEXT PHOTO CREDITS

Page 5: Photo courtesy of the author
Page 7: Photo courtesy of the author
Page 8: Photo courtesy of the author
Page 11: Štátny archív v Bratislave
Page 12: Map © Vilcek Foundation
Page 13: [top] Sueddeutsche Zeitung Photo/Alamy Stock Photo
Page 13: [bottom] ČTK/ullstein bild/ullstein bild
Page 15: UtCon Collection/Alamy Stock Photo
Page 17: Photo courtesy of the author
Page 18: "Požiar po bombardovaní" by Pavol Poljak/Slovak National Gallery
Page 19: Photo courtesy of the author
Page 20: ČTK
Page 21: Tribečské múzeum v Topoľčanoch
Page 23: "Mysľava" by Ladislav Rozman/Slovak National Gallery
Page 26: [top] Photo courtesy of the author
Page 26: [bottom] "Rafinéria Apollo a prístav po bombardovaní VII" by Pavol Poljak/Slovak National Gallery
Page 27: [top] TASR
Page 27: [bottom] Azoor Photo/Alamy Stock Photo

Page 28: Photo courtesy of Lýdia Titlová
Page 29: Photo courtesy of the author
Page 35: Photo courtesy of the author
Page 37: [top]Map © Vilcek Foundation
Page 37: "Predavačky kapusty" by Pavol Poljak/Slovak National Gallery
Page 40: Photo courtesy of the author
Page 41: Photo courtesy of the author
Page 42: Shawshots/Alamy Stock Photo
Page 43: Photo courtesy of the author
Page 45: ČTK
Page 50: Photo courtesy of the author
Page 66: Photo courtesy of the author
Page 69: Azoor Travel Photo/Alamy Stock Photo
Page 75: Collection J. Šedivý at PamMap.sk
Page 81: *ARS: Journal of the Institute of Art History of the Slovak Academy of Sciences* (4.1970)/Slovak Academic Press
Page 82: Andrey Shevchenko/Alamy Stock Photo
Page 85: Photo courtesy of the Rajter Family Archive
Page 88: Photo courtesy of the Vilcek Foundation
Page 90: Photo courtesy of the Vilcek Foundation
Page 91: Photo courtesy of the Vilcek Foundation
Page 93: AVU SNG (Rudolf Kedro/Photostudio SNG)
Page 95: AVU SNG (Rudolf Kedro/Photostudio SNG)
Page 96: Photo courtesy of the Vilcek Foundation
Page 99: Photo by Viktor Lomoz/FotoCTK, courtesy of the Vilcek Foundation
Page 104: Photo courtesy of the author
Page 105: Photo courtesy of the author
Page 107: Photo courtesy of the author
Page 115: [top, center, and bottom] Archív Ústavu pamäti národa, Bratislava/Nation's Memory Institute – Archive
Page 119: ullstein bild/Getty Images
Page 122: [top and bottom] Photos courtesy of the Vilcek Foundation
Page 123: Photo courtesy of the Vilcek Foundation
Page 129: Photo courtesy of the author
Page 132: Photo courtesy of Ivan Gerháth/Vilcek Foundation
Page 133: Photo courtesy of Ivan Gerháth/Vilcek Foundation
Page 136: Photo courtesy of the author
Page 148: Photo courtesy of the author

Page 150: © The Metropolitan Museum of Art
Page 151: Photo courtesy of the author
Page 153: © The Metropolitan Museum of Art
Page 159: Photo courtesy of the author
Page 170: © The Metropolitan Museum of Art
Page 171: Photo courtesy of Nick Machalaba/WWD/Penske Media/Getty Images
Page 173: © The Estate of Garry Winogrand, courtesy of Fraenkel Gallery, San Francisco
Page 178: © The Metropolitan Museum of Art
Page 183: [top and bottom] © The Metropolitan Museum of Art
Page 188: [top] Photo courtesy of Ivan Gerhath/Vilcek Foundation
Page 188: [bottom] Photo courtesy of the author
Page 189: Smith Archive/Alamy Stock Photo
Page 195: © Eva Šefčáková /Archive of Alena Šefčáková
Page 196: [top] Photo courtesy of the Rajter Family Archive
Page 196: [bottom] Archive of the Slovak Philharmonic
Page 197: *ARS: Journal of the Institute of Art History of the Slovak Academy of Sciences* (4.1970)/Slovak Academic Press
Page 203: Photo courtesy of the author
Page 205: Photo courtesy of the author
Page 224: Photo by Allan Tannenbaum/Getty Images
Page 229: © The Metropolitan Museum of Art
Page 232: [top and bottom] © The Metropolitan Museum of Art
Page 238: Tecnoxarxa/Wikimedia Commons
Page 240: Photo by Jacques M. Chenet/courtesy of The Lillian & Clarence de la Chapelle Medical Archives at NYU Langone Health
Page 244: Photo courtesy of the author
Page 247: Photo courtesy of the author
Page 249: Photo courtesy of the author
Page 253: Photo courtesy of the author
Page 267: [top] Photo courtesy of Jadranka Važan
Page 267: [bottom left] Photo by Steve Korn of Jadranka Važan
Page 267: [bottom right] Photo by Christina Iberl of Jadranka Važan
Page 281: Jay Brady/NYU Langone Health
Page 286: © Liz Ligon
Page 289: [top] Photo courtesy of the Vilcek Foundation/Juliana Thomas.
Page 289: [bottom] Don Pollard/The Metropolitan Museum of Art
Page 294: Photo courtesy of The Institute of Fine Arts, NYU/Sarah Higby

Page 295: Photo courtesy of The Institute of Fine Arts, NYU/Sarah Higby
Page 296: Photo by N. L. Roberts
Page 303: Photo courtesy of the author
Page 305: The History Collection/Alamy Stock Photo
Page 306: Photo by Paula Lobo
Page 314: Photo courtesy of the author
Page 325: Photo by Billy Farrell/Patrick McMullan of Getty Images
Page 328: Photo courtesy Barack Obama Presidential Library
Page 344: [top and bottom] Photo courtesy of Rick Kinsel/Vilcek Foundation
Page 346: Photo courtesy of Rick Kinsel/Vilcek Foundation
Page 347: Photo courtesy of Figge Art Museum, Davenport, Iowa. Gift of Linda and J. Randolph Lewis (2024.19.2).

PHOTO INSERT CREDITS

Vilcek residence, view from the entry hall to Marica's study. *Photo courtesy of Brian Cavanaugh/Vilcek Foundation*

Vilcek residence, view from the living room to the entry hall. *Photo courtesy of Brian Cavanaugh/Vilcek Foundation*

Isamu Noguchi, *Trinity* (1945/1988). *Photo courtesy of Brian Cavanaugh/Vilcek Foundation*

Vilcek residence, Marica's study. *Photo courtesy of Brian Cavanaugh/Vilcek Foundation*

Vilcek residence, the living room (northwest view). *Photo courtesy of Brian Cavanaugh/Vilcek Foundation*

Arthur Dove, *Centerport XIV* (1942). © *Vilcek Foundation*

Vilcek residence, the living room (southwest view). *Photo courtesy of Brian Cavanaugh/Vilcek Foundation*

George Ault, *View from Brooklyn* (1927). © *Vilcek Foundation*

Marsden Hartley, *Berlin Series No. 1* (1913). © *Vilcek Foundation*

Vilcek residence, view from the entry hall to the living room. *Photo courtesy of Brian Cavanaugh/Vilcek Foundation*

Marsden Hartley, *White Sea Horse* (1942). © *Vilcek Foundation*

Vilcek residence, the dining room (northeast view). *Photo courtesy of Brian Cavanaugh/Vilcek Foundation*

Morgan Russell, *Synchromist Still Life* (c. 1910). © *The Joyce Family Estate*

Stuart Davis, *Tree* (1921). © *2025 Estate of Stuart Davis/Licensed by VAGA at Artists Rights Society (ARS), NY*

Oscar Bluemner, *Red Night, Thoughts* (1929). © *Vilcek Foundation*

Stuart Davis, *Coffee Pot* (1931). © *2025 Estate of Stuart Davis/Licensed by VAGA at Artists Rights Society (ARS), NY*

Marsden Hartley, *Symbol IV* and *Symbol V* (1913–14). © *Vilcek Foundation*

Ralston Crawford, *Bomber* (1944). © *2025 Estate of Ralston Crawford/Licensed by VAGA at Artists Rights Society (ARS), NY*

Rick Kinsel, Marica Vilcek, and Jan Vilcek at the Vilcek Foundation's inaugural exhibition "Il Lee and Pouran Jinchi" at the Vilcek Foundation Gallery, 167 East Seventy-Third Street, New York City, June 2008. *Photo courtesy of the Vilcek Foundation*

The original Vilcek Foundation building, a renovated garage at 167 East Seventy-Third Street, New York City. © *Jürgen Frank*

Installation view of the exhibition "O Zhang: I Am Your Mirror," held at the Vilcek Foundation Gallery at 167 East Seventy-Third Street, New York City, September 15–November 10, 2012. © *Liz Ligon*

Installation view of "Ralston Crawford: Torn Signs," the inaugural exhibition held at the Vilcek Foundation Gallery, 21 East Seventieth Street, New York, City. The exhibition ran from May 15–November 13, 2019. *Photo courtesy Will Ragozzino of Scott Rudd Events*

Street view, the current Vilcek Foundation building, 21 East Seventieth Street, New York City. © *Elizabeth Felicella*

Garden view, the current Vilcek Foundation building, 21 East Seventieth Street, New York City. © *Elizabeth Felicella*

Installation view of "Marsden Hartley: Adventurer in the Arts" (Bates College Museum of Art, September–November 2021) showing a collection of Hartley's ephemera, including his palette, pen collection, and valise. *Bates College Museum of Art/Photo by Luc Demers*

A curator installing a photographic portrait of Marsden Hartley for Marsden Hartley, Adventurer in the Arts (Bates College Museum of Art, September–November 2021). *Bates College Museum of Art/Photo by Phyllis Graber Jensen*

Dancer and choreographer Jessica Emmanuel stages a performance piece activating Nari Ward's sculpture *Tumblehood* (2015) as part of the Vilcek

Foundation's exhibition "Nari Ward: Home of the Brave," February 16, 2023, (Vilcek Foundation Gallery May 31, 2022–March 24, 2023.) © *Liz Ligon*

Installation view (first floor, north wall) of "Grounded in Clay: The Spirit of Pueblo Pottery," curated by the Pueblo Pottery Collective and featuring works from the Vilcek Collection and the Indian Arts Research Center at the School for Advanced Research, Santa Fe, NM. (joint presentation at the Vilcek Foundation Gallery and the Metropolitan Museum of Art, July 13, 2023–June 4, 2024) . *Photo courtesy of the Vilcek Foundation*

Installation view (second floor, east wall) of "Grounded in Clay: The Spirit of Pueblo Pottery," curated by the Pueblo Pottery Collective and featuring works from the Vilcek Collection and from the Indian Arts Research Center at the School for Advanced Research, Santa Fe, NM. *Photo courtesy of the Vilcek Foundation*

INDEX

Note: Page numbers in *italics* indicate photographs. Page numbers beginning with "*P*–" (e.g., *P*–*5*) indicate photo insert section.

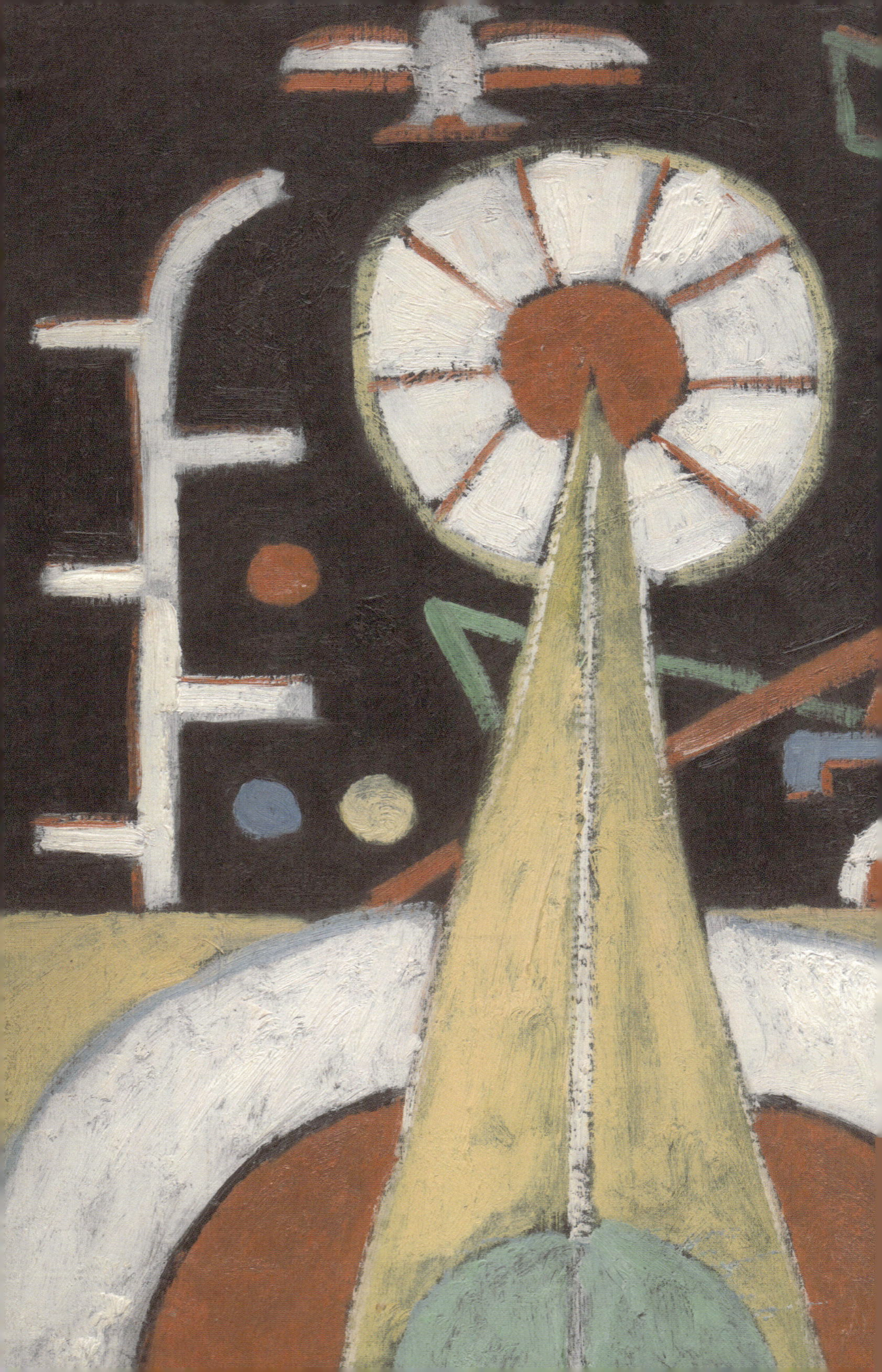